Palace of the People

Palace of the People

The Crystal Palace at Sydenham
1854–1936

J. R. PIGGOTT

HURST & COMPANY

LONDON

First published in 2004 by
C. Hurst & Co. (Publishers) Ltd,
38 King Street, London WC2E 8JZ

A Cataloguing-in-Publication data record for this book is available
from the British Library.

ISBN 1-85065-727-0

Designed and produced by David McLean in Bulmer type
Picture reproduction by David McLean and Cantate Battleys,
London

Printed for Cantate by Grafos SA, Barcelona, Spain

Frontispiece Philip Delamotte, 'Colossi of Aboo-Simbel', 1854

PICTURE CREDITS
Images listed by page number

PREFACE and ACKNOWLEDGEMENTS

The second Crystal Palace, Joseph Paxton's unquestioned masterpiece, stood for eighty-two years, a glittering diadem crowning bosky Sydenham Hill and dominating the southern sky-line of London. The Palace was conceived on a colossal scale, unimaginable today, but belonging quintessentially to the time of its creation. The speed with which it was planned, designed and built, considering the many problems and setbacks of the site and unlucky circumstances, was an even more phenomenal achievement than the first Palace in Hyde Park that housed the emblematic 1851 Great Exhibition.

In the Nave and three Transepts of this glass 'cathedral' a winter garden was created with tropical plants and heated basins for the *Victoria regia* lily from the Amazon that Paxton had coaxed to flower in England. The largest collection of plaster casts of statuary ever assembled was installed alongside the plants, forming a gallery of historical and contemporary works. In the 'Fine Arts Courts' magnificent academic 'reproductions', in painted plaster over brick, of historic architectural styles illustrated the development of architecture, and educated contemporary taste by showing how new buildings and their interior decoration could benefit from understanding the science of colour and the grammar of ornament.

The presiding genius of the Courts was Owen Jones – the 'colour king' – who had proposed to the Society of Arts after the Great Exhibition a scheme, part museum and part studio for architectural history and 'the education of the eye', to be housed in a new Palace for the people; he was supported in this ambition by his colleague Matthew Digby Wyatt and the other architects employed for the interior of the Palace.

The Fine Arts Courts, drawing on recent archaeology and on the sketch-books of the young architects who had studied the antiquities of Egypt, Greece, Italy, Sicily and Spain, had a theatrical as well as an educational character. One of the greatest calamities to befall the Palace was the early destruction of the astounding Assyrian Court and the colossal twin Aboo-Simbel figures in the fire of 1866 that permanently destroyed one-fifth of the original structure. Luckily the rapid development of the arts of wood-engraving in journals, chromolithography and photography coincided with the early decades of the Palace, giving us many views of the original interior (especially those of Philip Delamotte).

In its first prosperous decades the Palace was a monument to contemporary ideals of education and recreation for all, following the axioms of Prince Albert practised in the Great Exhibition: teaching the people, and the unity of nations. The intention was a three-dimensional encyclopaedia of both nature and art, with a much wider syllabus than at Hyde Park, that would help visitors to understand evolution and civilisation in relation to their own times; examples of the grandeur of the palaces, temples and villas of proud or decadent civilisations; ethnographic tableaux of the varied family of mankind; the botanical collection; and examples of the taxidermist's art.

The directors' ambition to outdo the Great Exhibition and the new museum at South Kensington determined even the landscaping of the vast sloping Park with its illustrations of primordial life on earth in the form of life-size reproductions of 'extinct animals' in appropriate settings. Paxton also deliberately exemplified the history of landscape gardening through various formal and informal modes in the Park. The waterworks – intended to surpass Versailles and Chatsworth in magnificence and extravagance – were surely the most elaborate ever created, although the *ensemble* of the astonishingly high fountains, the cascades and water-temples, in total comprising 11,000 jets, were used for relatively few displays before they were found impossible to maintain; and the expense of their construction, which Paxton insisted upon to improve the fortunes of the Crystal Palace Company, helped to bring about its ruin.

The Palace, although raised by private enterprise, became an arena for royal and national events, helping to forge the tribal identity of Londoners and of the nation itself in a succession of receptions for celebrated visitors and in the patriotic thanksgiving in the presence of the Queen at the end of the Crimean War. In later years, during the Festival of Empire of 1911 and its period as a naval training base in the 1914–18 War, and again during the four years after 1920 when it was home to the

Imperial War Museum immediately after its foundation, the Palace became a national and imperial symbol.

The Crystal Palace made a great and lasting impact on the British consciousness. In practical terms it was also enormously influential. The interior, popularising the use of colour and ornament, influenced architecture and interior decoration; and the Handel Festivals and Saturday concerts determined the style of large-scale musical performance in England and added considerably to the concert repertoire.

The history of the Crystal Palace and the many accounts of visitors refute the standard view that it declined rapidly into vulgarity. As well as its awesome structure and brilliant displays, the imaginative entertainments for mass audiences – especially the appearances of Blondin on the high rope and Brock's complex orchestration of firework displays and tableaux (undervalued as an art form) – won the affection, and often the affectionate mockery, of Londoners. The fire on the night of 30 November 1936 is itself now legendary.

Acknowledgements

In the summer of 1951, during the Festival of Britain, I was given a copy of Charles Gibbs-Smith's centenary book about the Great Exhibition. To an eleven-year-old boy its many reproductions of engravings of the Crystal Palace and its exhibits were totally engrossing. My school library contained bound volumes of *Punch* and the *Illustrated London News* from the reign of Victoria. Therefore my first debt is to Gibbs-Smith and the writers to whose work I have continually referred: Patrick Beaver, Anthony Bird, George Chadwick, Michael Darby, Christopher Hobhouse and Alan Warwick. To these must be added the work of many anonymous Victorian journalists, artists and engravers.

Many specialists and friends have been extraordinarily generous with expert advice or in opening up their own archives or collections: Kathryn Ferry, Mick Gilbert of the Crystal Palace Foundation, John Kenworthy-Browne, Jonathan King, Ken Kiss of the Crystal Palace Museum, Allan Ronald, and Robert Thorne. I owe special thanks also to Carol Flores, Jonathan Gestetner, Shelley Hales and Michael Musgrave.

Reading at the British Library, the London Library and the National Art Library is always a privilege. In the many other institutions which I have visited I have met with particularly kind help from Julie Anne Lambert, John Johnson Collection, Bodleian Library; Simon Finch and Elizabeth Silverthorne, Bromley Local Studies Library; Alan Tyler, Bromley Museum; Peter Day, Charles Noble and Andrew Peppitt, Chatsworth; Desmond Shawe-Taylor, Ian Dejardin, James Hall, Eloise Stewart and Victoria Norton, Dulwich Picture Gallery; John Fisher and Jeremy Smith, Guildhall Library; Guy Baker, London Metropolitan Archive; Dr Brent Elliott, Lindley Library; Richard Mangan, Mander and Mitchenson Theatre Collection; Graham Gower, Minet Library; Julie Cochrane, Museum of London; Peter Austin and Keith Holdaway, Norwood Society; Valerie Phillips, Royal Commission for the Exhibition of 1851; Oliver Everett and the Hon. Lady Roberts, Royal Library and Print Room, Windsor Castle; Lisa Heighway, Royal Photographic Collection; Susan Palmer, Sir John Soane's Museum; Jerry Savage, Upper Norwood Library; Anthony Burton, Charles Newton and Diane Bilbey, Victoria and Albert Museum.

For many favours and encouragement I thank most warmly Megan Aldrich, Leslie Lewis Allen, Michael Archer, Anthony Burton, Antony Bailey, John Ball, David Beevers, Mike Bott, Marianne Bradnock, Ian Bristow, Mary Butcher, Kate Colquhoun, Shirley Cooke, John Coulter, Gareth Davies, Chris Denvir, William Drummond, John and Yvonne Everitt, Christopher Field, Negley Harte, Alison Hill, Rosemary Hill, Ralph Hyde, the late Peter Jackson, Eric Korn, Godfrey Omer-Parsons, Michael Paterson, John Physick, Eric Price, Peter Rees, Nick Ritchie, Keith Rooksby, Anne Shelford, Harry Smee, Gavin Stamp.

The support of the Marc Fitch Fund and of the Paul Mellon Centre for Studies in British Art is gratefully acknowledged. The publisher Christopher Hurst has long been committed to this project and throughout has supported me editorially with skill and imagination. David McLean, the designer, has likewise contributed his great professional skill, determinedly ensuring that tight production deadlines were met. I thank them both.

A great debt is to my wife, to whom I offer this essay.

Sydenham, December 2003   J. R. P.

CONTENTS

ILLUSTRATIONS

Note the numbers refer to page numbers in the book.

THE 'PARENT BUILDING'

THE CRYSTAL PALACE IN HYDE PARK AND THE GREAT EXHIBITION, 1851

The Great Exhibition as an encyclopaedia

In August 1798 in Paris the Directory staged a 'Fête of Liberty' for the people. Chariots bearing Napoleonic loot – the gilt bronze horses from San Marco in Venice, the Laocoön, the Dying Gladiator, the Apollo Belvedere, a bust of Homer on a tripod, Raphael's *Transfiguration* and other masterpieces – were paraded through the streets of Paris with Swiss bears, African lions and a pair of dromedaries to be exhibited in a courtyard of the Louvre. More chariots carried huge stalks of bananas and other 'foreign vegetation'. Slogans were carried on banners praising Knowledge and Art – one proclaimed 'The arts seek those lands where the laurel flourishes.' This display was said to have had the direct result of genuine emulation of excellence in design among French manufacturers.

One of the first historians of the Great Exhibition, writing in 1852, saw this French triumphal gesture, which raised public awareness and inspired art and design, as its prototype. Nine exhibitions followed in Paris after 1798, up to and including the notable Exposi-

tion of 1849. This was housed in a temporary palace erected in the Champs Elysées covering more than 5 acres; 4,494 exhibitors showed raw materials, machinery and manufactures, and a cattle-shed was attached at one end. In London, also during the early nineteenth century, the Society of Arts, Manufactures and Commerce held a number of exhibitions at which prizes were awarded for manufactures such as carpets and porcelain. Its president from 1843 was Prince Albert, and by 1849, as is well known, he and the Society's Council were planning a 'Great Exhibition of the Works of Industry of All Nations' to be held in London; they sent Matthew Digby Wyatt to Paris to write a report on the Exposition. The Parisian gallery, 90 feet wide with two avenues, court-yards and a fountain in the middle, undoubtedly influenced the layout of the Hyde Park exhibition.[1] In Paris juries, reports and medals had become integral to such exhibitions. On a lesser scale the Society of Arts in London had put on a twelve-day Great Free Trade Bazaar of manufactures at Covent Garden Theatre in 1845. Contemporary historians looked further back in

After James Duffield Harding, *Panorama of the Exterior of the Great Exhibition Building in Hyde Park*, 1851, with enlarged detail opposite.

Prince Albert, 1862.

time for antecedents to the Great Exhibition, pointing to the great 'international' fairs in Frankfurt in the sixteenth century with Russian furs, Spanish wines and fruits, and what the early Victorians called 'art manufactures': for example Venetian glass and silks, Genoese fabrics, Belgian lace, and ceramics.[2]

The Great Exhibition of 1851 was to be the first truly international Exposition, and to emphasise that inescapable fact it was organised by a nation that in 1851 produced more coal and iron than France, Germany and the United States together, and owned half the world's shipping.[3] The history of the Crystal Palace at Sydenham, opened in 1854 and destroyed by fire in 1936, is inseparable from that of its 'parent building', the Crystal Palace at Hyde Park, and the Great Exhibition which it housed. This connection involves most obviously the building and its architects and designers – Joseph Paxton (1803–65), Owen Jones (1809–74) and Matthew Digby Wyatt (1820–77) – but also the contents. The earlier enterprise was a public one, but the second was organised by a company with shareholders. However, by its Charter and early practice the Crystal Palace

Company was committed to similar ideals and educational aims, and its organisers liked to think of the new Palace as a national enterprise. Both enterprises made a great contribution to the visual education of the people in architecture, sculpture, decoration and colour, as well as to the appreciation of raw materials and manufactures. At Sydenham the Park was part of an educational scheme as well as a recreational one, and visitors to both Park and Palace could learn rudiments of botany, geology and anthropology.

The Victorians were impressed by prodigious statistics, and the Great Exhibition gave birth to many. Even a century and a half later it is difficult not to be impressed by the facts and figures of the colossal undertaking. In the five and a half months when it was open it received 6,063,986 visitors, and even allowing for multiple visits and visitors from abroad it is estimated that one-fifth of the British population saw it, in what has been referred to as the greatest single movement of the population in the country's history.[4] Exhibitors from all over the world numbered 13,937, and they showed 100,000 objects; 536,617 bottles of soft drink were sold.[5] It was estimated that if all the copies of the first edition of the catalogues were to be piled one on top of another they would make a vertical column 6,000 feet high, and the second edition, topping 18,000 feet, 'would form a lonely peak rising to the height of Chimborazo or Cotopaxi'.[6]

In his speech to mayors at the Mansion House on 21 March 1850, Prince Albert, with his 'truly noble mind',[7] resonantly dedicated 'the Great Exhibition of the Works of Industry of all Nations' to 'a great and sacred mission': the advancement of humanity, both academic and practical, resulting from a display of productions of all nations in friendly rivalry, to move in peace and love towards the 'unity of mankind'. Britain's industry and its retarded sense of design (falling short of the attainments of its rivals on the continent) were to be stimulated by competition and comparison; it was man's duty to 'watch and study the time in which he lives'.[8] Lady Eastlake (Elizabeth Rigby, 1809–1893), the traveller and writer who was married to Sir Charles Lock Eastlake (P.R.A. and Director of the National Gallery), wrote of the occasion that the presence of provincial mayors gathered together to hear the Prince was 'no pledge of cordial concurrence, or even of comprehension of his views', but that Albert 'had so blown the magic horn as to disenchant the gross and torpid spirits around'.[9] The arts, Queen Victoria declared at the Exhibition, 'are fostered by peace', and 'in turn contribute to maintain the peace of the world'.[10]

Henry Cole (1808–82), to whose energy and practical imagination much of the credit for the Exhibition was due, wrote that it would show 'the choicest productions of commercial industry'.[11] International and pacific goodwill arising from an exhibition of artefacts was a noble motive. As well as encouraging commerce and industry, the Exhibition was intended to be an educational festival for all ages and all classes, and to teach reverence for the world's resources. 'From the first the Exhibition has been set forth as a great school.'[12] Albert at the Inauguration quoted from Psalm 24: 'The Earth is the Lord's, and all that therein is.' This watchword was stamped in turn on the engraved title-pages of the official catalogues. Man's skills in industrial processes, transforming raw materials into products, were to be taught. Henry Mayhew wrote that the Exhibition was 'more of a school than a show',[13] and it was referred to as 'a living encyclopaedia'.[14] Albert frequently deprecated the narrow academic classical bias of English education, and the Exhibition was part of his agenda for an England that could compete with the continent. This call was repeated in lectures on the results of the Exhibition given at the Society of Arts from November 1851 to April 1852, chiefly by the distinguished chairmen and reporters of its various sections. The chemist, Lyon Playfair, demanded: 'How is it possible that dead literature can be the parent of living science and of active

L.C. Wyon, *Joseph Paxton*, 1854.

industry?'[15] Since the thirteenth and fourteenth centuries the aim of education had been to fabricate literati, he said, producing a culture 'wholly antithetic' to exact science: 'Until our schools accept as a living faith that a study of God's works is more fitted to increase the resources of the nation than a study of the amours of Jupiter or Venus, our Industrial Colleges will make no headway against those of the Continent.'[16] Writing in the *Art Journal Illustrated Catalogue* on 'The Vegetable World as contributing to the Great Exhibition', Edward Forbes, Professor of Botany at King's College London, regarded *flora* as a text for the visitors: 'There is a deep lesson and politic meaning contained in the scientific idea of a plant – a lesson and a meaning not dissimilar from those that constitute the true moral of the Great Exhibition.'[17] The University of Oxford set up lectures on mining, minerals and manufactures to prepare undergraduates visiting the Exhibition.[18] The Master of Trinity College, Cambridge, William Whewell, reviewing his chosen topic of 'the general bearing of the exhibition on the progress of art and science', closed his lecture to the Society of Arts by expressing satisfaction that such an increase of 'intercourse, sympathy and regard among producers, manufacturers, artisans and artists' had been brought about: 'We were students together at the Great University of 1851.'[19]

The awakening of the populace to the possibilities of knowledge and the sudden access to so many branches of inquiry and understanding of technologies had an impact on the age for which parallels can only be found in our own day, although at Hyde Park they saw actual objects. The displays were excellently classified, and even the ground-plan of the building was a kind of index: the Transept was conceived as representing the Equator, with the tropical countries nearest to it and the colder zones at each end of the Nave. Whewell said that the individual visitor 'found that image of the world and its arts, which he had vainly tried to build up in his mind, exhibited before his bodily eye in one vast crystal frame'.[20] The Exhibition's greatest achievement was 'enlargement of mind', a writer declared in Tallis's three-volume *History and Description of the Crystal Palace and the Exhibition of the World's Industry* (1852).[21] Albert himself devised the main classifications and divisions of knowledge at the Exhibition, the 'Generic Division' as it was known: raw materials, machinery and mechanical inventions; manufactures; sculptures and plastic art. This was to have a strong influence on the divisions of the institutions, colleges and museums later founded at 'Albertopolis' in South Kensington from the profits of the Exhibition.[22] On the west side of Exhibition Road the Natural History Museum and the Science Museum continue to show Categories I and II of the Great Exhibition: Raw Materials and Machinery. On the east side at the Victoria and Albert Museum are Categories III and IV: Manufactures (including crafts) and Fine Arts (including Sculpture).

Whewell drew a lesson from anthropology to stress the primal significance of industry: 'From Otaheite, so long in the eyes of Englishmen the type of gentle but uncultured life, Queen Pornare sends mats and cloths, head-dresses and female gear, which the native art of her women fabricates from the indigenous plants.'[23] The bee-hive was a common metaphor for industry applied to the Exhibition at the time, 'to present the world more in its true aspect of industry, all its work being for the common good, and all its labourers interested in the growth of intelligence and the permanence of peace'.[24] Cruikshank made an etching for Mayhew's *Adventures of Mr. Sandboys* (1851) which he called 'The Opening of the Great Hive of the World, May 1, 1851, or the Industrial Exhibition of All Nations', transforming the outside view of the transept with the barrel vault into an enormous hive. Actual beehives, 'exceedingly curious little palaces of industry', were among the most popular exhibits.[25]

Knowledge of the natural world also taught responsibility. The great zoologist Richard Owen (1804–1892) gave one of the lectures at the Society of Arts, with Prince Albert in the chair. His theme was 'On the Raw Materials from the Animal Kingdom':

Whatever the animal kingdom can afford for our food or clothing, for our tools, weapons or ornaments – whatever the lower creation can contribute to our wants, our comforts, our passions or our pride, that we sternly exact and take at all cost to the producers. No creature is too bulky or too formidable for man's destructive energies – none too minute and insignificant for his keen detection and skill of capture. It was ordained from the beginning that we should be the masters and subduers of all inferior animals. Let us remember, however, that we ourselves, like the creatures that we slay, subjugate and modify, are the results of the same Almighty creative will – temporary

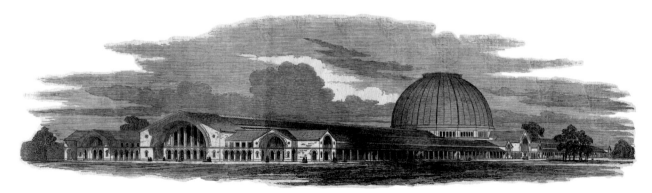

Committee design, 'The Building for the Great Industrial Exhibition', 1850.

sojourners here, and co-tenants with the worm and the whale of one small planet. In the exercise, therefore, of those superior powers that have been intrusted to us, let us ever bear in mind that our responsibilities are heightened in proportion.[26]

Owen later played an important role in the installation of the life-size models of Antediluvian Animals in the Park at Sydenham, and wrote for the Crystal Palace Company the Handbook to go with them, *Geology and Inhabitants of the Ancient World*. He also had an influence on the Fine Arts Courts inside the Palace: as Paxton said at a meeting in 1852, it was Owen who had first suggested to him that only in such a building could the history of sculpture be 'properly exemplified by a collection embracing the sculpture of every age'.[27]

For Joseph Paxton's second Crystal Palace at Sydenham, double the size of the original building in Hyde Park, the aims again were idealistic and educational as they had been at the Great Exhibition, and this was written into its Charter. In her speech at the inauguration on 10 June 1854 the Queen said:

'It is my earnest wish and hope that the bright anticipations, which have been formed as to its future destiny, may under the blessing of Divine Providence, be completely realised; and that this wonderful structure, and the treasures of art and knowledge which it contains, may long continue to elevate and instruct, as well as to delight and amuse, the minds of all classes of our people.'[28]

Latent in her words was the conflict between 'elevate and instruct' and 'delight and amuse' that over a period of sixty years was to be intricately associated with the decline of the new Crystal Palace.

The Crystal Palace: iron and glass

Described in its own day as the Tenth Wonder of the World, the 'Exhibition Building', as it was first known, a great mansion dedicated to light and air, was given its famous name by Douglas Jerrold of *Punch*.[29] The phrase connoted fairyland, and the 'fairy enchantments' of the Palace were to become a common sneer of Ruskin in later years. The phrase itself was apparently coined by Shelley in *Prometheus Unbound* (1820) where in Act IV the Chorus of Spirits sing of a submarine palace; it was used again in the translation from the German by Caroline Norton of De La Motte Fouqué's popular romance *Undine*, published in 1843, describing the submarine palace of the water-nymph in the Mediterranean; Queen Victoria had seen a ballet version of it in the same year.[30]

An affectionate nickname could hardly have been used of the building designed in committee, called 'the Building for the Great Industrial Exhibition, to be erected in Hyde Park'. Paxton knew his own building first by its official title as 'the Great Industrial Building'.[31]

The Commissioners had earlier rejected all 245 competition designs, including two iron and glass structures. There were also entries in Egyptian and Saracenic styles,[32] anticipating two of the historical reproductions to be seen inside the new Palace at Sydenham in the Architectural Courts. The Building Committee was made up of two peers, three architects (Charles Barry, Charles Cockerell and Thomas Donaldson) and three engineers (Robert Stephenson, Isambard Kingdom Brunel and William Cubitt). The building they designed after the failure of the competition was heavy and far from palatial – a cavernous warehouse or railway shed with an immense rotunda and a sheet-iron dome.

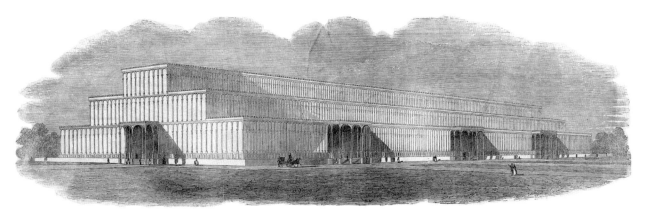

Paxton's design, 'A Building for the Great Exhibition of 1851'.

This 'child of many fathers' was condemned at the time for its 'extraordinary ugliness'; it was 'too large, costly and cumbrous' for its purpose.[33] As in Paxton's actual building in Hyde Park the rainwater from the roof was designed to be taken off down hollow columns. The most interesting feature – the dome 200 feet in diameter with a cupola 150 feet high, larger than that of St Peter's in Rome[34] – was designed by Brunel. Two of the architects involved in the design, Matthew Digby Wyatt and Owen Jones, were to become the designers of the interior features in the Sydenham project. Both 'made extensive working drawings' for the Committee building.[35] For Paxton's first building Digby Wyatt was subsequently appointed as superintendent for the construction and Jones was to be 'decorator' of the interior, to whom all questions of design and display would be submitted. Working drawings for the new building were to be made by Wyatt, Jones and Charles Heard Wild.

The building designed by the Committee called for 17 million bricks,[36] leaving aside doubts as to whether it could be erected in time for the deadline – the walls would certainly not have dried. The romantic story of Paxton's impulsive design for an exhibition building in iron and glass made during a Midland Railway board meeting on a piece of blotting-paper, his publication of the design in the *Illustrated London News*, and his submission of it to the Committee after its own design was published, is well known, as is the dubious story of his direct adoption of the structural principle of the ridge and furrow roofing from the 'natural engineering' of the *Victoria regia* lily (now known as *Victoria amazonica*). Paxton had made this enormous water-plant to flower for the first time outside its native South American rivers at Chatsworth on 9 November 1848, and with its 'radiating cantilevers and cross girders' it had a similar structural principle, he told the Society of Arts, to the 'longitudinal and transverse girders and supporters' of the building.[37]

In the words of Paxton's obituary in *The Times*, 'Prospero's wand waved' and the Exhibition 'was saved from deadlock and national fiasco'.[38] James Fergusson (1808–86), architect and architectural historian, who was to work for the Crystal Palace Company at Sydenham first as architect of the Assyrian Court with the archaeologist Austen Henry Layard and then as general manager from early 1856 to mid-1858, greatly admired the Palace

as architecture, but declared that its lack of decoration meant it could not be Fine Art. He wrote that 'while men puzzled over domes to rival the Pantheon and halls to surpass the Baths of Caracalla', Paxton inaugurated a new style of architecture 'which promises to have a still greater influence on the future'. The construction was 'absolutely truthful throughout. Nothing is concealed and nothing added for effect. In this it surpasses any Classical or Gothic building ever erected.'[39] Other critics admired its perfect symmetry and the long vistas, and the building was felt to be eminently practical for the exhibition, with no partitions and with 'large open avenues for the passage of visitors'.[40] However, among architects and in the press praise for Paxton's building was not universal: the agglomeration of prefabricated units was compared to a banal table with side-rails, or to a gigantic packing-case.[41] Its novelty was peculiar: Thackeray's comic Mr Molony in *Punch* called it 'the Palace made o' windows'.[42] It inspired some bizarre images, one comparing its effect to paper in a glass bottle.[43]

In 1851 some said that Paxton had invented a new 'order' in the historical evolution of architecture.[44] Under the First Column placed at Sydenham was a bottle with a text that included the not strictly true boast that here was 'a building of purely English architecture'.[45] The barrel vault, strictly speaking, was Roman, and the prefabricated units were in Charles Barry's Italianate style. To the boast that a magnificent new architectural style of iron and glass had been invented, Ruskin's sarcastic response, in his pamphlet *The Opening of the Crystal Palace* (1854), was that the styles of the past were doubtless all now eclipsed: 'Doric and Palladian pride [was to be] reduced, dazzled by the lustre of a few rows of panes of glass.'[46] When A.W.N. Pugin (1812–52) first met Paxton, he told him to stick to conservatories while he, Pugin, stuck to his churches; he was naturally against the new style, pointing out in *The True Principles of Pointed or Christian Architecture* (1853) a stultifying monotony in the design with its mass-produced units: 'Cast-iron is a source of continual repetition, subversive of the variety and imagination exhibited in pointed design.'[47] Ruskin in the *Two Paths* (1859) took this criticism further, describing with the febrile urgency of his hyperaesthesia 'the endless perspective of black skeleton and blinding square' at Sydenham.[48] Unexpectedly perhaps, the style was praised by an article in the *Ecclesiologist*; the writer spoke severely of the classical and Italianate schools, but was 'lost in admiration at the unprecedented inner effects' of Paxton's design, while still insisting that the Palace could not be called 'architecture'.[49]

Paxton told the Society of Arts in November 1850 that his building was now to have 'a semicircular roof, like that of the great conservatory at Chatsworth'. The barrel vault of the Great Stove, the conservatory that covered an entire acre at Chatsworth, had the same span and construction.[50] (Paxton's conservatory work was perhaps not quite so original as is generally assumed: in the autumn of 1824 an iron and glass conservatory designed by Cockerell with three barrel-vaulted aisles separated from each other by ridge and furrow roofs was made in Birmingham and transported to Grange Park in Hampshire.[51]) Paxton's admirers believed that light, 'the prime work of God', would disperse the dark and gloom of previous architectural eras, and looked forward to a future of 'lofty halls' where sculptures would be flooded with light.[52] Light could also be a disadvantage, and a *velum* or canvas that could be cooled with water was hung over the roof to protect exhibits and visitors, as had been done for plants in Paxton's greenhouses; the seams of the canvas were arranged to align with the gutters to drain the rain-water. The transept made the body of Paxton's Hyde Park building cruciform; the ground-plan was actually 1,848 feet long (3 feet short of measuring its own year, as was originally intended – Paxton's measurements were all in multiples of 24 feet) by 480 feet broad, with an extension of 48 feet along 936 feet of the north side. Because of their shapes, both the Hyde Park and Sydenham Palaces were often compared to cathedrals – hence the terms 'nave' and 'transept' used to describe the main compartments – and this fuelled Ruskin's rages against the Palace.

Cast iron was used for the famous mass-produced prefabricated units, for the columns, the beams and the girders, but the tie-rods were of wrought iron. The floor was of wooden boards, which allowed a half-inch gap for accumulated dust and the water used in washing the floors to be swept down on to the earth below. Paxton designed an ingenious form of sweeper with mechanical sprinkler and rotating brushes. When the Palace was finally dismantled, the contractors Messrs Fox and Henderson granted 'treasure trove' to their workmen: coins, fine purses and gold-topped canes were found fallen on to the dried turf below.[53] Wood (including some

unseasoned deal) was used for the main 'Paxton' gutters, sashes and troughs on the roof, and even for some girders and trusses;[54] this fact was used after the Exhibition to argue that it would be imprudent to retain or extend the building on the Hyde Park site. The ventilation by galvanised iron louvres in a wooden frame was again a highly ingenious system devised by Paxton – having first considered and rejected a contrivance like an enormous *punkah* fan.[55]

Glass, an almost supernaturally wonderful building material, had only recently been freed from a crippling tax, thanks to Sir Robert Peel, and was now a cheap and popular commodity.[56] Jacob Bell, M.P., speaking in the series of Society of Arts lectures after the Exhibition, said that a worse evil than the tax had been the 'inquisitorial restrictions' placed on manufacturers by the espionage of the Excise, which stopped their experiments to develop the manufacture of glass. The 'incubus' removed, the Crystal Palace 'was called into existence as a monument to commemorate the event'.[57] 'A man must have had much more of criticism than poetry in his composition', wrote James Fergusson, 'who could stand under its arch and among its trees by the side of the crystal fountain, and dare to suggest that it was not the most fairy-like production of Architectural Art that had yet been produced.'[58] The glass, hand-blown, was laid on the roof by a nimble 8-feet square 'glazing-wagon', with a canvas awning over hoops against rain; it was hoisted and placed on four small wheels that ran in the 'Paxton gutters' of the roof, glazed on the 'ridge and furrow' system. Eighty men installed 18,000 panes in one week.[59]

After John Leech, seal to commemorate Paxton as gardener and architect, commissioned by the Duke of Devonshire, 1851.

The barrel vault

Paxton's original plans and drawings were modified by the committee, by Brunel and Charles Barry in particular. Barry and his allies claimed that the idea of the barrel vault over the great Transept in Hyde Park was actually Barry's. In one of the after-dinner speeches at the Assembly Rooms in Derby on 5 August 1851 the Duke of Devonshire praised Paxton's character, and Paxton paid tribute to the way the Duke had fostered and moulded him; he referred to their travels on the continent, and joked that the Duke was a 'nobler work of nature' than the great *Victoria regia* lily they had famously made to flower. Then Paxton made a deliberately public counterclaim, reported in the press, against Barry: 'At length I hit upon the plan of covering the transept with a circular roof similar to that on the great conservatory at Chatsworth and made a sketch of it', with which he said Brunel was pleased. 'I have been led into these minute details – first to show that the circular roof of the transept was designed by myself, and not by Mr Barry, as currently reported.' Henderson, Paxton's contractor, also spoke, endorsing Paxton's claim that he and not Barry had 'originated' the circular roof for the transept, and 'carried it out according to his intention'.[60] The barrel vault, set over the transept at right angles to the long nave, was first designed to preserve the trees in the Park from destruction; because of the position of the trees on the site, the transept over their heads was not placed at the exact centre of the building but 48 feet off-centre. The great elms became in turn a happy feature of the interior. Barry had originally proposed barrel vaults over both the transept and the nave, as was to be done for the new Palace at Sydenham in 1854.

In the course of a discussion at the Institute of British Architects in January 1851 about the aesthetics of the building and about iron and glass structures, seen partly as a dialogue between utility and beauty, and polarised uncomfortably between the roles of engineers and architects, William Tite, architect of the Royal Exchange as rebuilt in 1848, said that 'the only feature which in his opinion redeemed the Exhibition Building in Hyde Park from downright ugliness, namely the arched roof of the transept, was the suggestion of Mr Barry, and they might therefore claim it on behalf of the architects.'[61] Barry's son, Edward Middleton Barry, in a professorial lecture at the Royal Academy, insisted that Paxton's Crystal Palace was not architecture, but was 'constructive ingenuity,

and thus only the assistant or handmaid of architecture'.[62] The painter J.M.W. Turner, after a lifetime's study of buildings, wrote in one of his last letters that the Palace 'looks very well in front because the transept takes a centre like a dome, but [looked at] sideways ribs of Glass framework only Towering over the Galleries like a Giant.'[63]

Charles Barry possibly made the design for the lunette, the fan-shaped semi-circle at the ends of the great barrel vaults of the Transept, which in the late twentieth century became a cliché of post-modern Paxtonesque shopping malls and city atria, a debased descendant of what was described in 1851 as Mr Barry's 'noble effect'.[64] Conservatories were built before the Crystal Palace with fan-lights above the main doors, and this motif, the 'giant fanlight' (as E. M. Barry described it) with its 'twelve radial segments' and eleven 'sticks' to the fan,[65] may have been taken by Barry from just such a familiar feature above the front doors of houses in London streets and squares, but the design closely resembles the shell lunettes of his much admired windows, with the same number of segments, on the *piano nobile* of the garden elevation of the Traveller's Club in Pall Mall (1829–32).[66] Fox, the contractor for the Crystal Palace, declared during the same speeches in Derby that Barry made 'valuable improvements to the beauty of the building'.[67] When Barry died, Digby Wyatt said in a review of his career at the RIBA:

> The section of the columns, with its ingenious provisions for attachments of girders, and superposition of other columns, and the general proportions and arrangement of many of the leading parts, and the form of the transept roof, which I saw him sketch on the suggestion of Brunel, that rather than cut down or exclude the large trees, it would be better to roof them in, were all his; and but for his having been beaten on the score of time and expense on the view he took of the desirability of covering the nave, as well as the transept, with a semi-cylindrical roof, as has been done at Sydenham, he would no doubt have continued to render greater practical assistance than he did till the opening of the Exhibition.[68]

The Commissioners formally thanked Barry for 'much of the grace and proportion of beauty of form', and in particular for his alteration of Paxton's original ratios for the 'form and distribution of the arches and filling in frames, as well as of the columns'.[69] As well as his improvement to the shape of the prefabricated cast-iron units, he gave the mouldings of the columns their Italianate look. His change to the proportions of the prefabricated units can be appreciated by comparing the *Illustrated London News* engraving of Paxton's original proposal with the more familiar prints of the actual building. Barry apparently designed the 'scalloped enrichment' on the parapet, a Gothic trefoil;[70] Paxton's blotting-paper design merely shows a squiggle all along it.

Even at the time, the *Art Journal* could write in its *Illustrated Catalogue* that the accounts given by Paxton and Barry of their 'respective shares in the plans' were 'not strictly reconcilable with each other';[71] however, the architectural establishment seems to have accepted that Barry deserved the credit for the barrel-vault. At the same time they rather unfairly thought Paxton too ready to submit to modifications to his designs by others, and therefore lacking the integrity to be counted among them as a professional architect. E. M. Barry was to adopt his father's giant iron and glass fanlights in his design for the Floral Hall (1858) built next to the Covent Garden Opera House. (The Floral Hall has lost its original glass dome and a short south transept, but is today the best place to feel something of the effect of the Crystal Palace).[72]

Joseph Paxton and Charles Barry, the prefabricated eight-foot bay.

Essential differences between the Crystal Palace of 1851 and that of 1854 arose from their locations. At Hyde Park among formal avenues of trees and by the Serpentine it was as if the Palace was set in the Tuileries, with fashionable 'loungers'; at Sydenham the Park and Palace were to be Paxton's version of Versailles for the people to take an excursion to the suburbs of London. He had visited Versailles with the Duke of Devonshire in the course of their continental tour of 1838–9, and been disappointed with the *grands eaux*.[73] The press was not slow to recognise that his ambition at Sydenham was 'to vanquish not only Chatsworth but Versailles, and everything else'.[74]

The influence of Paxton's Crystal Palace

Paxton's triumph in Hyde Park was soon emulated by a number of cities, such as Madrid (1873), that put up their own Crystal Palaces. Among the most important was the much smaller one built in New York in 1853. For this there was first a scheme to buy the Hyde Park structure and ship it across the Atlantic,[75] and Paxton drew up a brilliant competition design, based on his 1851 building,[76] but it was rejected in favour of an iron and glass structure on a Greek cross plan; the successful architects were a Dane, Georg Carstensen, and a German working in New York, Charles Gildemeister. This so-called 'Palace for the People' featured a central rotunda with a dome and a glazed lantern, and gas lighting; the contents included Marochetti's colossal equestrian statue of George Washington, the two most popular statues from Hyde Park (Hiram Powers's *Greek Slave* and Kiss's *Amazon*), an Otis elevator and other ingenious ideas. Walt Whitman and Mark Twain liked it, but as a commercial venture it failed, even when P.T. Barnum was brought in at the last moment to save it. It burnt to the ground in half an hour on 5 October 1858.[77] The Munich *Glaspalast* of 1853–4 by Voit and Cramer-Klett was very similar to Paxton's first entirely rectangular design for Hyde Park with a 'ridge and furrow' roof, but was a quarter of the size; again the columns were hollow to drain the roof. Its glass was painted and protected with mesh. It survived as an exhibition hall until it caught fire in 1931.[78] The Paris Universal Exposition of 1855 had a 150-foot barrel vault of iron and glass, but external walls of masonry. At Dublin in 1853 a Crystal Palace, designed by John Benson, had three glass domes and closely followed Owen Jones's colour scheme. In 1859 Jones

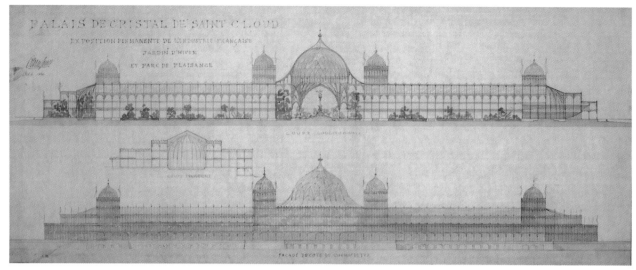

Owen Jones, design for *Palais de Cristal*, 1860. © Victoria and Albert Museum.

designed an ugly but fascinatingly elaborate Crystal Palace for Muswell Hill (later the Alexandra Palace) in north London and the next year he designed for St Cloud a more elegant *Palais de Cristal* with a Saracenic dome.[79] Neither was built.

Fergusson summarised the potential of the Crystal Palace for 'railway stations, places of assembly and floricultural purposes'.[80] The buildings for the great Manchester 'Art Treasures of the United Kingdom' exhibition of 1857 and the 1862 International Exhibition at South Kensington were obvious descendants of Paxton's buildings.[81] At the same time that Digby Wyatt was working on the Crystal Palace at Sydenham, he and Brunel designed Paddington railway station, which was constructed by Fox and Henderson with a 'Paxton roof' 1,000 feet long by 300 feet wide.[82] Owen Jones assisted over some decorative details.[83] Paxton declared in 1850: 'I am now in fact engaged in making the design for a gentleman's house to be covered wholly with glass' – he believed that his prefabricated modular units of iron and glass could be used together with stained or painted glass for domestic buildings and even for churches.[84] David Watkin has noted that for the three *châteaux* he designed for the Rothschilds after the Crystal Palace Paxton actually used neo-Elizabethan or neo-Renaissance styles.[85] Paxton's unbuilt scheme for the *Great Metropolitan Way* (1855), a 'Grand Girdle Railway and Boulevard under glass', was almost on a megalomaniac scale: extending for eleven and a half miles

(almost on the route the Circle Line was to follow in the 1880s) it was to be constructed of Crystal Palace units, 'an extended Crystal Palace', with shops and houses lining its sides, and 'a monster arcade' to connect the railway stations with the Palace of Westminster. The Way was to be 72 feet wide, the width of the Transept at the Crystal Palace, and 180 feet high, capable of taking two railway tracks, with a roadway above. It also featured a double wall with an air current to make an acoustic barrier between the thoroughfares and the houses and shops.[86] When Paxton died, Digby Wyatt paid tribute at the RIBA to a dear personal friend whom he had known for many years 'under the most trying circumstances of success and depression':

'He was a man of warm affections and ardent imagination, and his artistic capabilities were the property of the world. Though not a practical architect, the way in which he proved the capabilities of iron and glass structures, rendered [architects] so much indebted to him, that they ought never to be forgetful of his memory.'[87]

Followers of the Modern movement in the twentieth century admired the functional undecorated simplicity of Paxton's original Crystal Palace of 1851,[88] claiming it as the first truly modern building in the world. A few preferred the more elaborate and ambitious second Crystal Palace at Sydenham of 1854 with its enormous transept and two lesser ones at each end; when it burnt down in 1936 John Betjeman declared it to be 'a far nobler memorial to the great and misunderstood Prince Albert' than the earlier Palace, which by comparison was 'a top-heavy tabernacle'.[89] The Modern Movement's claims for Paxton's two Crystal Palaces as signifying a new style of architecture were voiced by Le Corbusier, Henry-Russell Hitchcock and others. After the loss of the second Palace, Corbusier wrote an elegy in the *Architectural Review* with a resounding tribute to Paxton: 'This architecture was the fruit of discovery, of the joy of creation, and of enthusiasm.' The 'magnificent vaults of iron and glass' where 'all was grandeur and simplicity' were 'the heralds of a new age'. It led him to conclude that 'architecture is not a manifestation of the styles of schools. It is a way of thinking, of achieving order, and of expressing contemporary problems in terms of materials. [...] When two years ago, I saw the Crystal Palace for the last time, I could not tear my eyes from the spectacle of its triumphant harmony. The lesson was so tremendous that it made me feel how puny our own attempts still are.' Morton Shand wrote in the same issue of the magazine that Paxton's structure was 'a precept as inspiring as the Parthenon, an exemplar as vital as the Pont du Gard' and 'as important a representation of its own age as Stonehenge, Ely Cathedral and the Senate House at Cambridge were of theirs'.[90] J.M. Richards in 1940 claimed that the Crystal Palace 'embodied a more genuine return to pure and lively structure after the Gothic spirit than anything Pugin or the Gothic Revival produced'.[91] For Hitchcock the Crystal Palace was the 'direct ancestor of modern architecture'.[92] (A very respectable replica of the Sydenham Crystal Palace, shorter but featuring the three transepts, was built in 1985 on the Stemmons Freeway in Dallas, Texas, to house the Infomart, an 'information processing market centre'.)

The interior

It was said in 1851 that the Palace itself, rather than the Great Exhibition, was what struck visitors most.[93] It was a plain box in which highly ornate and colourful objects were set in a conservatory or a winter garden with large plants and flowers in pots. Even before it was built, Paxton regarded it 'with a view to its permanence as a winter garden, or vast horticultural structure'; the interior was to have shrubs and climbers, and be a thoroughfare for 'carriage drives and equestrian promenades'.[94] This was to be a 'national winter garden', he said – an idea he had 'long cherished'.[95] Paxton probably remembered a high-point of his early career, Victoria and Albert driving in a carriage through the Great Conservatory at Chatsworth in December 1843 in a 'forest of tropical vegetation, naturalistic rockwork, pools of water, fountains, rock crystals and exotic birds flying in the air'.[96]

An essential difference between the displays at Hyde Park and at Sydenham was the range of reference in their time-scale. The Great Exhibition showed a contemporary 'Museum of all Nations',[97] but the Crystal Palace Company aimed to show a comprehensive historical museum of evolution and of civilisations. Nevertheless, the setting in the nave and transepts of the two Palaces had many similarities, and print-sellers still today easily confuse the two interiors. In the main avenue of both palaces there were plants and large working fountains, white marble or plaster statuary (the larger subjects included stags and historical figures on horseback), great medieval or Celtic crosses, and *eau-de-cologne* fountains. The central avenues brought the larger and more 'artistic' objects to the fore; most of the manufactures and raw products and machinery were to the sides of the main thoroughfare. In the courts were the displays of natural materials, such as hardwoods, kelp, spices, gutta percha, rattan, and vanilla.[98] There one would find Birmingham and Sheffield goods, such as Wilkinson scissors, steel, silver, silver plate, and cotton, woollen and mixed fabrics from the Northern mills. The botany of the Palaces differed, being much more ambitious at Sydenham. Accounts of its counterpart at Hyde Park are vague: 'shrubs and flowering trees', and 'eastern exotic trees, palms and palmettos'. The palms and other tropical plants were supplied by Messrs Loddiges, the most famous horticultural specialist in London, and Dr John Lindley was in charge of 'floral decorations'.[99] 'Machinery in motion' was one of the most popular features of the great Exhibition. Paxton accordingly allowed considerable space at Sydenham for this, hoping to raise considerable income, but it was not a success; the exhibiting manufacturers preferred to show at international exhibitions rather than in a London suburb. In 1851 there were small ethnographic models of Indians, including a snake-charmer uneasily juxtaposed with a government tax-collector, and Mexicans.[100] Living tribesmen were to be seen in the courts: American Indians – Iowas 'two poor red-skins' who 'displayed profound sorrow'[101] – and some Tunisians. This was not a novelty: in 1822 at the Egyptian Hall in Piccadilly, 'the most fashionable place of amusement in London', living Laplanders had

After Joseph Nash, 'Turkey, No 1', 1851, with the Nave, elm tree and Osler's fountain.

been exhibited along with a panorama of the North Cape, sledges, reindeer and domestic implements. At Sydenham there were no living 'examples' of native peoples; they were presented woodenly by life-size models.

Two of the most popular exhibits in 1851 were later transferred to Sydenham, and both remained there until consumed in the fire of 1936. One was Osler's Crystal Fountain, which for its 'purity and crystalline effect' was 'perhaps the most striking object in the Exhibition'; it stood 27 feet high and its skeleton of iron bars was cunningly hidden. The glass weighed 4 tons, not including its dish that weighed nearly one ton more. Charles Barry took a great interest in it, and gave advice and assistance.[102] Richard Redgrave (1804–88), in his official 'Report on Design' added to the government *Reports of the Juries*, criticised it for imitating architectural stone forms;[103] he thought glass unsuitable as a foil to sparkling water. Digby Wyatt's chromolithographic plate in *The Industrial Arts of the Nineteenth Century at the Great*

Exhibition, 1851, and Tallis's description convey the charm that held most visitors:

> In the centre arose like some fantastic spectacle or splinter from an iceberg, a transparent crystal fountain, glittering with all the colours of the rainbow, which, towering from a solid base up to a point, poured down upon an overflowing crystal basin an unceasing stream, with a delicious bubbling sound.[104]

The other exhibit transported from Hyde Park to Sydenham – a favourite of the Queen and people alike – consisted of the grotesque tableaux of taxidermist's figures sent from Stuttgart, Herrmann Ploucquet's 'Comical Creatures': anthropomorphised frogs, cats, foxes, stoats and weasels. 'It would seem to have been the most popular group of objects in the Glass Palace', wrote Tallis, noting 'the predominance of family parties in the collection', such as the kittens at the tea-table, 'with their 'most whimsical air of sentimental gentility'.[105]

There were 'Fine Art Courts', a title ridiculed by connoisseurs. This was a category applied later with

'The Tea Party' from the Wurtemberg 'Comical Creatures'.

more justification to the Architectural Courts and the sculpture at Sydenham. At neither Palace did painting and contemporary architectural drawings form part of the exhibition (although there were architectural models and casts); in effect there was no 'high art' except sculpture. This led to resentment and some bending of the rules. As Tallis said at the time, although high art was 'rigorously excluded' at Hyde Park, there was plenty of 'little art'. He went on to suggest a very different kind of exhibition, such as was actually to be mounted at the Manchester 'Art Treasures Exhibition of the United Kingdom' of 1857 – on an ambitious and magnificent scale:

> The vast avenues of the Crystal Palace, which might, without much trouble, have been prepared for the purpose, would have afforded an admirable opportunity for forming an exhibition of bygone art, arranged in order of schools; an exhibition of the highest interest and utility, which, from the nature of circumstances, has never yet been carried into effect, and for which the spacious resources of the world's Fair in Hyde Park afforded the first, we hope not the latest opportunity… Noblemen and private gentlemen would have rather shown a Raffaelle or a Rembrandt than a "jewelled hawk"[such as the Duke of Devonshire sent].[106]

The Commissioners' ruling in 1851 had excluded 'oil paintings, water-colour paintings, frescoes, drawings and engravings unless they were illustrations or examples of materials and processes'.[107] Some 'works of art' crept in because this clause admitted items that could be shown to result from new inventions or techniques; chromolithographs were admitted but not steel engravings. Some ivory paintings found their way in for the given reason that 'the artist joined panels together by a

process of his own invention.'[108] Thus one could also find 'art' in the form of wax flowers and novelties. Tallis attacked the Commissioners, saying that the rule had turned the so-called 'Fine Art Court' into a toyshop, 'an object of ridicule to all observers of a mature age'. Works of the chisel were admitted but not works of the palette; feeble 'artistic delinquencies' were admitted classified under ivories and 'patent silica colours'.[109]

The term 'court' at Sydenham and at South Kensington to describe divisions and compartments of the exhibition or museum was used with conscious derivation from courtyard and cloister, and was chosen in 1851 presumably for its connotations of (now long vanished) palatial grandeur. Certain sections of the Exhibition were separated from others by partitions, 'an arrangement which the construction particularly lends itself to'; bridges from the galleries at intervals divided the avenues, suggesting divisions into courts.[110] The Zollverein Department was set in a compartment with partitions in the Strawberry Hill Gothick style, a ceiling with beams and an octagonal aperture. The display from Turkey was set in an elegant room designed by Gottfried Semper in the form of a tent. The Refreshment Rooms had 'open courts'. At Sydenham the term 'court' became standard, as in the 'Nineveh Court' and in the 1930s a 'Holiday Court' for travel agents' promotions.

Owen Jones and the decorative scheme

The most controversial aspect of the Palace was Owen Jones's decorative scheme, which seems initially not to have had the support of either the Prince or the press. Once it was completed (at great speed, with an army of 500 painters) the world seemed to acknowledge it as a success. Jones believed in the use of primary colours and adhered like a disciple to the principles of the famous colour chemist George Field (?1777–1854), who discussed in *Chromatography* (1835) the effects of a triad of red, yellow and blue, and their proper ratios; especially important to Jones (as to J.M.W. Turner) was Field's theory of how the effect of blue on the eye was to make the object recede and of yellow to make it advance towards the viewer.[111] Jones held practical demonstrations for the Commissioners when they first met inside the Palace on 4 November 1850, with Albert presiding. At this meeting he hung 'a series of carpets at a distance of 24 feet from the columns' to make his point about their colouring.[112] It was decided to paint the ironwork on the

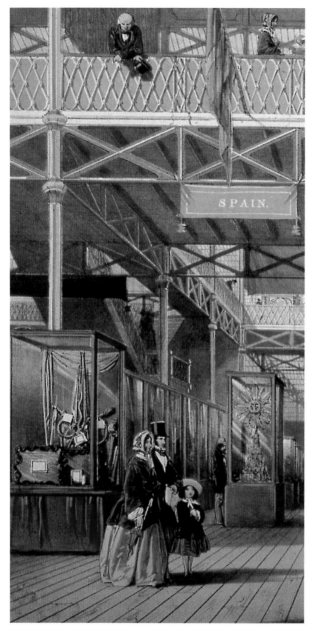

After Joseph Nash, 'Spain and Portugal', 1851, showing Owen Jones's colour scheme.

outside 'a uniform stone colour'- later changed to what *The Expositor* called a 'sickly fading blue'.[113] The same magazine described Jones's demonstration:

> Mr Owen Jones, who illustrated his proposal by coloured drawings finished, as everything about the Palace is, in six days, proposed to paint the columns blue, white, yellow; girders, blue and white, red; roof, red, white, yellow. It was determined the roof should be in blue and white; the columns

and girders, blue and white with just sufficient yellow to soften the effect. We are satisfied it would have been best to have omitted the yellow; and indeed in a building where so many articles of every shade and colour are to be displayed, plain for every part of the building would have been most suitable.[114]

A coloured drawing, surely made for this meeting,[115] shows Jones's blue, red, yellow and white scheme for the columns and girders with a sequence of red, yellow and blue textile hangings in spandrels. Jones intended his colours to bring out the construction, he said, making the building appear loftier, longer and more solid.[116] The familiar coloured lithographs in Dickinson's magnificent series after Joseph Nash's designs, *Comprehensive Pictures of the Great Exhibition of 1851, from the originals painted for H.R.H. Prince Albert*, published in 1854, show the columns blue, white, and yellow and the under-sides of the girders red; the ribs of the transept are in the sequence blue, yellow, yellow, blue. The term used at the time for work of this kind was 'parti-colouring'; the practised eye was said to be able to 'tune yellows, reds, and blues like a musician'.[117] As for the columns, Jones said, to paint them in only one colour rather than in blue, white and yellow stripes would destroy the 'beautiful shape' of Barry's design.[118] Jones decreed red for horizontals, blue for concave surfaces, yellow for convex surfaces, and white vertical lines between the blue and yellow; this carried the eye into the distance, and increased the height and magnitude of the building. There was 'very severe censure' of his scheme, as Jones wrote,[119] and the majority 'favoured bronze' for the paint on the columns.[120] Gottfried Semper admired the combination of yellow and blue, but contradicted Jones's axiom that red 'must always be wedded with them'.[121]

According to Jones's obituary in *The Times*, 'the Prince Consort was at first aghast at the daring originality of the scheme of colour, and opposed it eagerly, arguing it almost day by day with the designer', but on the opening day 'with the best grace, [he] acknowledged his success.'[122] In the manuscript version of his lecture to the R.I.B.A. in December 1850, 'On the Decorations Proposed for the Exhibition Building', Jones says that he painted one column red 'for one of his critics'; in the printed version he altered this phrase to read 'in obedience to the wishes of some critics'. From this it seems correct to deduce that he did this for the Prince. He went on to say that red columns would not be acceptable, being 'in direct violation of the principles which I had laid down as the basis of my operations'.[123] Ironically in the colour scheme he carried out at Sydenham the columns were painted red. J.G. Crace in a letter to *The Builder* in January 1851 wrote that while Jones's yellow, white and blue might suit wooden columns, they were quite unsuitable for iron; he attacked the 'heavy' marginal lines of red on the roof. Crace disliked Jones's primary colours, and suggested instead a scheme of pale bronze green columns with the circular parts in maroon red; the two colours were to be separated by a subdued gold line.[124] Crace's scheme was actually adopted for the International Exhibition at South Kensington in 1862, but not generally liked.

A persistent campaign against Jones from a Great Exhibition periodical, *The Expositor*, spitefully mocked his scheme but abruptly ceased when the Palace opened. The painting of the Palace, it reported, began with the inside of the roof, and was 'in Mr Owen Jones's gewgaw yellow, blue, and red, there being most of blue, but most of all, an exhibition on the part of the Commissioners of a total want of taste, and an utter ignorance of the science of colour'.[125] The attacks took on a sharper tone, complaining of 'lunatics let loose'; 'our evil genius breaks out on the decoration of the building, and set to work with wonderful diligence to daub it out in blue, yellow, and red…It is to be decked out in motley, as if it were intended for a display of morris dancers, or an exhibition of Ojibbeway Indians.' When criticised for the colour scheme, according to the writer, Palace officials merely replied with ill humour, 'I don't think so.' Jones's enemies perfectly understood his credentials: 'Mr Owen Jones has studied these colours on stained glass windows, Egyptian mummy cases, and the walls of the Alhambra, and so the iron columns and transept take on the colours of stained glass and coffins, and Moorish tapestries.' It was also suggested that Owen Jones should be locked up until the end of the exhibition. The scheme was 'garish', resulting in a 'harlequinaded Palace'; the magazine thought it should be painted black or brown or a 'rich stone'.[126] The Commissioners had been taken in, they said, by 'learned nonsense of the professor about neutral tints to be obtained by streaks of yellow, red and blue'. Why not just mix the three colours together?[127] The effect of the form of the structures was spoiled, so that the ironwork looked like broken parts; there was a heavy mass of thickening colour in the distance. Owen Jones should design 'a set of motley' for the

Commissioners, himself, and attendants with gloves in different colours, yellow hat, red handkerchief, blue waistcoat; mocking Jones's imitations of the decorations of medieval manuscripts in his chromolithographic books on view in the Exhibition such as *The Preacher* (1849), they suggested that 'the fingers might be pleasantly illuminated'.[128] The criticisms became less specific in later weeks, and it is obvious that Jones 'in blue and yellow ecstasy' had become an easy butt of their wit. Yet facetiously they described exactly what was to be realised at Sydenham with the building of the Alhambra Court: 'During all the progress of the Crystal Palace he has dreamed of the Alhambra, and longed by the magic of illumination to transform the common show-room of the world's workshops into the Great Moorish Hall of the Lions.' Jones had 'raised up from the ruins of the past such exquisite theory of stripes and patches, that it is rank presumption in anyone to say a word about colours while he lives.'[129]

When his work was done at Sydenham, Jones was to bring about, from the 'stripes and patches' of the past, a new awareness of design and found a school of designers with his book *The Grammar of Ornament* (1856) with its rich chromolithographic plates. The book had a considerable influence on the continent. The fastidious *Art Journal* gave its opinion after the Exhibition that his scheme of blue, red and yellow was first feared to be too glaring, but with the long perspective it won 'very general approbation'. The colouring of the exterior, the 'delicate blue upon a white and stone ground', was thought less successful.[130]

A strict order signed by Matthew Digby Wyatt on behalf of the executive committee – of which Jones was not a member – spelled out Jones's other major responsibility: 'All arrangements which affect the general decorative effect of the building must be referred to Mr Owen Jones, and sanctioned in writing by him.'[131] He also held a general brief for all 'architectural matters', designing the railings for the galleries,[132] and was superintendent for sections of the exhibition, principally the sculpture. This is perhaps not a fine art that one readily associates with Jones, but he was chosen to tour the continent with Digby Wyatt for the Crystal Palace Company before it opened in 1854 at Sydenham to commission many hundreds of plaster casts for the new Palace. Jones was regarded as a comic figure, though doubtless affectionately, as is shown by John Leech's cartoon

CLOSING OF THE EXHIBITION.
The Amazon Putting on her Bonnet and Shawl.

Amazon (to Greek Slave). " WELL, MY DEAR ! I'M VERY GLAD IT'S OVER. IT'S VERY HARD WORK KEEPING IN ONE ATTITUDE FOR FIVE MONTHS TOGETHER, ISN'T IT ? "

John Leech, 'The Amazon putting on her bonnet and shawl'. (Owen Jones on the Amazon's Horse.)

nudity – to go home and resume their normal lives, like actresses leaving the theatre.[133] Jones uneasily bestrides the Amazon's horse.

Other classes for which Jones was responsible were models and plastic art, mosaics, enamels, paper, printing and bookbinding. In mosaics and printing he had practical experience and was an authority.[134] Especially remarkable were his early experiments in chromolithography, in which he and Pugin shared an interest, and which won him prize medals from the Council at the Exhibition.[135] Over the royal party at the Inauguration is to be seen a canopy of crimson velvet and gold plumes of ostrich feathers, set up by Messrs Jackson and Graham the day before and designed by Owen Jones (he was the principal designer for the furnishers).[136] He is also given credit for Keith's 'silk trophy' with its large looking-glass and sides hung with furniture silks with a 'richly emblazoned banner',[137] but another source names George Wallis, superintendent of the textile fabrics, as the designer, and Jones may have only sanctioned or modified it.[138]

published in *Punch* at the close of the Exhibition, picturing him among the sculptures. 'The Amazon putting on her Bonnet and Shawl', shows the Amazon and the Greek Slave, the two most popular works, as living persons ready – their outdoor clothes covering their

Jones added even more colour to the interior of the Palace with carpets and textiles he had hung from the roof, and liberal use of rich red cloths draped on tables and stands or hung and gathered behind statuary, and with his red signs indicating the categories or the names of the exhibiting countries, with gold lettering and tassels. Outside, at Charles Barry's suggestion, flew the flags of the nations. These touches were only part of Owen Jones's mission, which was to educate a puritanical public in the gospel of primary colours and the 'Grammar of Ornament' and bring to an end an era of drabness in decoration, casting aside the 'trammels of the last age of universal whitewashing'.[139] Like Pugin he spoke of 'true principles', and envisaged a 'paternal and wise' government which, for our children's sake, would punish those who produce 'abortions in art' as well as 'those who lower the moral tone of society'.[140] Jones's vision for the interior was more luxurious and colourful than he was allowed to carry out: *The Expositor* recorded in January 1851 that he had 'called for the lofty windows and high roof to be glazed with rich mosaics of stained glass, and the sides hung from the top with tapestries of Gobelin and Aubusson, and leathers of gold'.[141] These decorative schemes resemble the plates from *The Grammar of Ornament*.

For the fanlight lunette of the South Transept Jones designed an enormous semi-circular clock-face. The hands, of gilded copper, were double the conventional proportions, and extended across their axis like partial diameters. The length of the minute-hand was 48 feet and of the hour-hand 32 feet. These hands functioned by alternating with their own opposite end to tell the hours and minutes the moment they crossed the horizontal base line to enter the semi-circle. This semi-circle served as a novel twelve-hour clock-face: it was numbered 'XII' at its apex, as in a normal clock, but the hours were marked in a sequence from 'VII' on the left of the horizontal base of the semi-circle (where a normal face shows 'IX'), to 'VI' on the right. The numbers were blue on a white ground. The driving mechanism, devised by William Shepherd, used electro-magnets[142] and was housed 50 feet below in the Gallery.[143] Two smaller clocks were driven by one battery from the same mechanism, sharing one pendulum to synchronise them.[144]

The Medieval Court

Pugin's Medieval Court at Hyde Park was a significant influence on the interior at Sydenham, in that it must have suggested to Owen Jones and Matthew Digby Wyatt the architectural Fine Arts Courts. Pugin's designs and the skills of Hardman, Crace and Minton, his manufacturers in metalwork, stained glass,

furnishings and ceramics, made the Court a genuinely original as well as popular section of the Great Exhibition, and encouraged public interest in Cole's movement to inspire British manufacturers to design 'art manufactures' – in other words, everyday articles in good taste. Pugin's pupil J.H. Powell wrote that Pugin induced his three manufacturers to fit up the Court, 'he supplying designs and trying to find buyers for them. They emulated each other in their efforts.'[145] Looking back on the Exhibition, Tallis commented that although the Court was 'perhaps a little too theatric in effect [it was] still harmonious and suggestive', and on the whole 'excited the most general interest'. He was perhaps worried by the monstrances and orphreys on show, since he quoted an 'acute and learned' contemporary as saying that the Court represented 'sentiments which exist no longer' and were absurd in 'an enlightened age'.[146] Pugin's Court obviously differed from the Courts at Sydenham in that it showed newly-designed manufactures in a 'revived' style and not archaeological 'reconstructions' or 'illustrations' of historical styles.

However, the Medieval Court at Hyde Park and the Fine Arts Courts at Sydenham helped to educate public taste. They declared war both on colour-shy Evangelical puritanism and – despite Jones's Greek and Roman Courts – on the Neo-Classicism that had inhibited contemporary taste and was seen as a hang-over from the Regency. Also, as contemporary engravings make clear, the Medieval Court was to influence nineteenth-century Gothic Revival church architecture, furnishings and domestic interior decoration; there was a prie-dieu, a lectern and vestments (though jardinières and an enormous domestic stove were present). The *Art Journal* pronounced it 'quaint and beautiful'.[147] The *Illustrated Exhibitor* wrote that the Court 'will at least have the merit of suggesting to many, who would not otherwise have heard of such facts, the fullness of beauty and character, and the homogeneousness of medieval design, however applied, to domestic as to ecclesiastical purposes.'[148] Pugin's court was defended from the criticism that it was a 'galvanic' resuscitation of a dead style as many called it – 'galvanised corpse' was Owen Jones's term for the Gothic revival[149] – on technological rather than aesthetic grounds: the manufacturers had used new techniques such as mechanical wood-carving or chromolithography. Minton showed encaustic tiles printed by the Collins and Reynolds patent process;

After Joseph Nash, Pugin's
'Mediaeval Court', 1851.

these used transfers printed by the same chromolitho-graphic techniques that Jones was using for his architec-tural and decorated books and that were also used for Pugin's plates in *Floriated Ornament* (1849).[150]

In his lecture to the Society of Arts on 'Form in the Decorative Arts' shortly after Pugin's early death, Digby Wyatt said that 'in the treatment of furniture, much was to be learnt from the sensible construction of poor Pugin's medieval woodwork.'[151] Ralph Wornum (1812–77), an associate of Ruskin who became an impor-tant figure in the London art world, wrote a prize-winning 'Essay on Ornamental Art as Displayed in the Industrial Exhibition in Hyde Park, in which the Different Styles are Compared with a View to the Improvement of Taste in Home Manufactures' (origi-nally a lecture to the Central School of Design in 1851, and published by the *Art Journal*). Wornum objected to the title of Pugin's Medieval Court, since it omitted the Romanesque, Byzantine, Saracenic and several Italian varieties that were 'more extensively influential in the middle ages'.[152] Wornum mistook Pugin's purposes, as if the Court was a type of history lesson about the past rather than a show of what could be done in the present

in revival and adaptation. Like many people, Wornum attributed the popularity of the Court to latent Catholi-cism, to 'sentiments distinct from ornament', and con-sidered the Court not only 'fatiguing and palling to the mind' but even 'a 'warning to us against making this style familiar in our dwelling-houses'.[153] On the other hand Richard Redgrave, in his 'Report on Design' included in the official *Reports by the Juries*, gave a measured, intelli-gent and informed summary of the contents, and praised the Medieval Court as the best section for ornament: he admired the flat and 'conventionalised' decorations and the 'few simple diapers'. While it adhered strictly to 'true principles', it was 'too purely ecclesiastical and tradi-tional, even in domestic works'. However, 'for just prin-ciples of decoration, for beautiful details, for correct use of materials, and for excellent workmanship, the general collection is unique.'[154] Mrs Merrifield, writing for the *Art Journal* on 'The Harmony of Colours as exemplified in the Exhibition', praised the 'gorgeous' exhibits, but thought that the Court as a whole lacked 'general har-mony of effect.'[155] It was undoubtedly a popular success: the 'blaze of gold and colour' contrasted with the 'rough and colourless specimens of colonial industry' in the adjacent Canadian Court.[156]

Ornamental design

Certain key factors that were common to the theories of design of both Jones and Pugin influenced practice later in the century – for example, 'conventionalising', the term used by Jones for stylised ornament. In 1851 he wrote in the *Journal of Design* praising the surface decoration of the Oriental work shown in the Exhibition:

> Their general guiding forms were first considered and these forms decorated. Their flowers are not natural flowers, but conventionalized by the material in which they worked. We do not see, as in the European world, a highly-wrought imitation of a natural flower, with its light and shade struggling to stand out from the background on which it is worked, but a conven-tional representation sufficiently near to suggest an image to the mind, without destroying the unity of the objects it is intended to decorate…. There is a total absence of shadow…. In their conventional foliage in all cases, we find the forms flowing out from a parent stem.[157]

W.H. Rogers, from *The Art Journal*, 1851.

Digby Wyatt quoted and endorsed this passage, and in his lecture 'Form in the Decorative Arts' given at the Society of Arts aligned himself with its principles: 'All decoration, the forms of which are borrowed from nature, to be pleasing, must undergo a process of conventionalizing.'[158]

The stylised floral principle became gospel for Jones's pupil and disciple, Christopher Dresser. Redgrave too attacked popular fabrics such as muslin curtains with three-dimensional designs of palm trees and landscapes; he thought Renaissance design and its influence meretricious. It was 'essentially pagan in all its details' and conveyed 'no symbolic truths to the hearts of men'.[159] Not all would have agreed with him; Tallis tacitly acknowledged that the Renaissance style of workmanship, despite being more fit than 'the classical slough', was now 'under a complete ban'.[160] The Roman church at the Renaissance was to blame. Pugin not only avoided the 'present mere sensualism of ornament' and 'puerilities', but the reason why the works in the Court were so often alluded to, according to Redgrave, was that they were 'examples of careful and strict adhesion to true *principles* of construction and ornamentation'. The subject of Pugin made him eloquent: '[his works] deserve commendation for their illustration of truth, and as showing what one man, by earnest and well-directed attention, can achieve in the reformation of taste, and in the training and forming of other minds to assist in his truthful labours.'[161] The public associated the Medieval Court so closely with Pugin that it appeared on the map of the layout of the exhibition given to his customers by the caterer Mr Schweppe as 'Pugin's Court'.

The Examiner published a satirical sketch of an unenlightened county family being shown the Court by a precious young relation from the fashionable St James's parish in London:

> If, as is possible, he be affected with the moral and mental tinge which was once young-Englandism, he discourses with tolerable learning of ecclesiology, of vestments and stoles, screens and fonts, and becomes in his discourse highly picturesque and medieval, to the great bewilderment of the county family, who don't in the least understand the difference between the early English and the flamboyant styles, and wonder whether the Renaissance is anything to eat.[162]

Pugin's attitude to the Great Exhibition was ambiguous. He was very sharp about Paxton's 'crystal humbug', the '*monstre verre*'; the Crystal Palace was 'as friendly and intimate as Salisbury Plain'.[163] Pugin showed great courage in setting up the Medieval Court; a mere glance at contemporary numbers of *Punch* makes clear how violent opposition to Catholicism was at the time. Pugin

also managed to persuade the Commissioners to break their strict methods of classifying manufactures to allow him to show all his works together and not in the separate classes of furniture, ceramics and stained glass. He wrote to his wife: 'There were such crowds of people, we have 4 police & 2 soldiers to clear the way. I assure you we were grand men & no mistake you should have been there to see the girls run to see us.'[164]

The exhibits

The Exhibition was said to offer 'the education of the eye',[165] and this phrase was taken up almost unanimously as the slogan for the Sydenham project by Owen Jones and its other promoters and organisers. At both Palaces the eye learnt from a comic mixture of objects: (in 1851) railway locomotives, pins, taxidermy, nude statues and Gothic stoves. Some of the more outlandish ones are familiar from the countless descriptions and engravings of the Palace's contents; these include 'Fletcher's Gladiatorial Table' from Ireland, the circular top of which was supported like a shield by the crouching gladiator beneath; vases 'most ingeniously made of human hair' or of mutton fat;[166] the penknife with 500 blades;[167] bellows that played 'God Save the Queen';[168] fountains like

elaborate cakes;[169] over-embellished pianos; and beds said to look like 'young cathedrals'.[170] Such items could easily distract attention from the beauty and remarkable designs to be seen elsewhere in the Exhibition, which one journalist imagined being visited by Voltaire; he pointed to the 'costly fooleries', and said that the citizens of Bruges or Florence were no worse off in the fifteenth or sixteenth century than those of the 'monster metropolis' of London.[171] Jones, Digby Wyatt and Pugin became official arbiters of taste or educators of the eye in the Exhibition, and at its close were commissioned by the Board of Trade, along with Redgrave and Cole, to make a report on the exhibits and select objects to be bought out of the profits for the Government School of Design as a national collection to serve as 'models of taste'.[172] Their choice determined in part the original composition of the collections in the South Kensington Museum. As early as 1850 John Field Gibson, a member of the Commission, was quoted as hoping for 'a vast school of design' from the Exhibition.[173]

British exhibits were compared with continental and American ones, inevitably to the detriment of the latter. The United States Pavilion was generally felt to be unequal to the large space secured for it in the Exhibition (40,000 square feet, the second largest after France's 65,000). It showed mostly raw materials; Colt's revolver, McCormick's reaper and Newell's patent lock aroused admiration, but the cynosure was the statue by Hiram Powers, the *Greek Slave*. National prejudices were freely expressed: a Frenchman was reported as saying that by comparison with the elegance of French goods all others seemed 'common and provincial'.[174] The British saw German goods as cheap, nasty and derivative, although its sculptures were admired. Germany did not become unified till 1870, and the tensions between its component states were mentioned in many press accounts of the Exhibition.[175] In Doyle's panorama *Visitors and Extra Articles to the Exhibition* an exhibit of a gigantic Meerschaum pipe[176] was to be seen being carried by some self-satisfied Germans.

The best of the English critics realised that, compared to the continent, England badly needed education in design – although the official government School of Design had been in existence since 1835. They also saw the French manufactures as mostly meretricious luxury items. The Exhibition marked a new direction in taste from the Neo-Classical to the Renaissance. This

'François I' style was taken up architecturally by Digby Wyatt in the Renaissance Court at Sydenham, but interest in it barely outlasted that period. The taste of the producers was mostly 'uneducated', wrote Wornum, and the French exhibits (with a quarter of the exhibition space) were 'paramount'. He was surprised to find so little of the then outmoded Neo-Classical styles, and contrasted Wedgwood and Flaxman designs favourably with 'such endless specimens of the gorgeous taste of the present day, which gives the eye no resting-place, and presents no idea to the mind, from the want of individuality in its gorged designs'.[177] He feared that the Exhibition might 'do nothing for the age if it only induced a vast outlay of time and treasure, for the enjoyment of the extreme few who command vast wealth'.[178]

It was the colours and design of 'native' cultures and craftsmen that impressed Jones and Pugin; they chose 200 items of Indian cotton for the School of Design. Jones praised the oriental designs, and attacked the luxurious character of the three-dimensional designs of Parisian carpets and fabrics. He wrote penetratingly that the 'Mohammedan' entries – from India, Egypt, Turkey and Tunis – showed the greatest unity and truth of design, skill and judgment, combined with elegance and refinement, in the entire exhibition, compared with the 'fruitless struggle after novelty' of Europe.[179] Professor Royle in his Society of Arts lecture of 18 February 1852 on 'The Arts and Manufactures of India' said that Owen Jones particularly admired the Rajah of Kotah's saddlecloths and matchlock accoutrements and 'the goldheaded nails fixed into green velvet'.[180] The sharp-eyed Wornum in his essay on the Exhibition as a lesson in design praised the 'harmonious combination of colours' in the Indian textile fabrics.[181] The Society of Arts lectures seem to share a common attitude to the more 'primitive' works of art, as when Lyon Playfair spoke on 7 January 1852 on 'the Chemical Principles involved in the Manufactures of the Exhibition':

So far as regards beauty or design and harmony of colours, European nations had little to teach, but much to learn. The rude pottery of Tunis was more elegant in form than the common pottery of modern Europe. The shawls and carpets of India, both as to design and harmony of colouring, were unequalled. So long as the influences involved human labour and a perception of beauty as their principal elements, the less civilized states equalled, and often excelled, the productions of Europe.[182]

From Tallis's commentaries on the Exhibition one sees what was admired: 'gorgeous variety' of bright colours – in Courts deliberately darkened for contrast the eye was educated by colour and form in productions from Venice and the Levant. The fabrics called to mind the oriental literary works of Byron, Goethe and Thomas Moore. It so happened that the designs praised, such as gold patterns on light blue ground, suggest the work of Owen Jones.[183]

The range of stylistic reference to past cultures in the contemporary designs seen at Hyde Park in 1851 was wide, but the derivative (or debased) objects obviously could not be presented methodically, as at Sydenham, to teach the development of styles. Wornum in his essay traced the history of design in a sequence leading from the Byzantine to the 'Saracenic' and the Gothic, and thence to the Renaissance; this was the same historical development of architectural and decorative styles as was to be taught by the 'illustrations' of the Fine Arts Courts at Sydenham.[184] When the writers in the *Art Journal* commented on the many engravings they published of select exhibits in 1851, they revealed strong design principles – often revealed implicitly rather than by contemptuous dismissals. A sideboard was in a style 'freed from the affectation with which designers are apt to deform it';[185] Derbyshire artefacts were praised for 'simplicity and taste',[186] and a butter-cooler was 'of very chaste design'.[187] New styles in 1851 derived from travel or archaeology: 'Alhambra' wallpapers and 'Alhambraic' chandeliers in coloured glass,[188] a 'massive fish-carver of Moorish design',[189] bracelets and ear-rings suggested by the 'Nineveh monuments',[190] an 'Arabesque' tea and coffee service,[191] Etruscan bookbindings,[192] and 'Arabesque' painted ceilings in the Courts.[193] There were Irish brooches with ancient Celtic motifs.[194]

Digby Wyatt in his Society of Arts lecture of 21 April 1852 spoke of 'the debilitating effects of nearly a century's incessant copying without discrimination'. The Great Exhibition, he said, had been 'an extraordinary stimulant to design', and at the same time a humbling experience: 'Those we had been too apt to regard as almost savages were infinitely our superiors.'[195] The jury's comments on furniture anticipated twentieth-century doctrines: 'unnecessary embellishment' had spoiled function, and there was a lack in the Exhibition of 'simple well-constructed ordinary furniture for general use'.[196] For Wornum an important reason why so many of the exhibits were ridiculous was that ornament distorted or perverted function – due to 'the very general mistake that quantity of ornament implies beauty, many objects being so overloaded with details as to utterly deny the general individuality of expression of the object, and even to render it at first doubtful what the object can be'.[197] In Redgrave's view, machines with their 'noble simplicity' could be said to have more integrity than many of the exhibits. His terms for the exhibits were like Ruskin's in a somewhat diluted form: 'florid', 'gorgeous tinsel', 'strained invention', 'veneers'. The dessert service – which he ridiculed – with dishes supported by drooping ceramic fuchsias was clearly 'florid'. His strongest image of the decadence and the perversion of function in contemporary design was conjured up by gas-jets that 'rush forth from opal arums'.[198]

In the Middle Ages the hand and mind of the craftsman wrought together, mostly from piety. For Redgrave the Medieval Court was the best section in the Exhibition because of the Minton tiles designed by Pugin, Gruner and Wyatt that it contained. He encouraged designers and craftsmen to 'lead to the rejection of what is meretricious and false, and to a more simple, grave, and earnest style in modern ornament'.[199] Meditating on the exhibits at Hyde Park, Wornum concluded that, while the use of nature for decoration was legitimate, it was a false principle to take the form of artefacts from nature. Form should be geometrical: he attributed this to psychological reasons, noting 'the laws in the mind to regulate principles of symmetry and contrast'.[200]

On the continent, as the *Art Journal* pointed out, serious sculptors worked for and advised manufacturers; 'the absence of this union of powers as supplied by the artist and artisan, so to speak, has long been felt in England, and has doubtless operated injuriously upon British manufacturing art: it will not long continue.'[201] Implicit in most of the literature of the Exhibition is an assumption that the artist and designer have quite separate functions from the artisan and manufacturer. The engraved title-page to the *Art Journal Illustrated Catalogue* to the Exhibition (1851), designed by 'Luke Limner' (John Leighton [1822–1912]), shows this divorce: a precious-looking artist with palette is handing his design for a chalice to an honest workman like Joe Gargery with his anvil. Ruskin insisted many times on the integrity of the craftsman as his own designer, most eloquently perhaps in his discussion of the modern carvings of the capitals and other works at the new University Museum in Parks Road, Oxford.

Among the manufactures displayed at Hyde Park were casts of works of art and architecture, shown separately from contemporary sculptures. For example, in the British Department, alongside Minton tiles and white Doulton terra cotta columns and revived-Tudor chimneypots, there were casts of a contemporary spandrel in Hereford Cathedral and some Gothic ornaments.[202] In the French section there were small bronze copies cast by Barbedienne of Ghiberti's Baptistery Doors in Florence.[203] Sydenham was to have a vast gallery of casts and statuary, intended to teach the historical development of cultures and styles.

Clearly not all the objects shown were interesting as design. Products that would have profound significance for a later age were on show as novelties: animal and vegetable food in 'hermetically sealed tin canisters' from an Arctic expedition of 1824, found by Sir John Ross in 1849 and brought home;[204] 'the electric light' from Paris;[205] Goodyear rubber; and photographs.[206] On the other hand, the much-promoted latex substance *gutta percha* used in the manufacture of a comic range of articles – sailor's hats, buckets, dentures, ear trumpets, speaking trumpets, communion plates, picture frames – was exhibited, but has faded from history just as the material itself disintegrated physically.[207] The machines (strictly 'Machinery in Motion') fascinated visitors well aware of the source of the nation's prosperity; these were powered from a miniature Crystal Palace structure outside the main building, containing five boilers, a large tank and steam-driven engines of 150 horse-power. The machines included cotton-spinners and Jacquard looms from Manchester, Leeds and Glasgow, and the Mule Jenny, with silk skeins winding on to bobbins. The Rev. Robert Willis, Jacksonian Professor of Applied Mathematics at Cambridge, pointed out in his lecture of 1852 to the Society of Arts that the selection of machines at the Exhibition had been 'edited' since many others not on show were 'noisy, offensive, and dirty', and maintained that the public were sufficiently interested to be able to cope with machines for printing newspapers, weaving, spinning and envelope-folding.[208] In the display from the Zollverein states, at the foot of the monumental sculpture of August Kiss's *Amazon*, was a Krupp six-pounder canon in an elegant little canvas pavilion on poles with a canopy, more suited to a regatta. This

aroused some complaints because of the obvious irony of its presence in an Exhibition dedicated to Peace: the lecturer on Naval Architecture at the Society of Arts complained that weapons of war should have been excluded.[209] The *Art Journal* likewise thought that a French shield showing 'the Massacre of the Innocents' failed to 'elevate the moral and social condition of humanity'.[210]

At both Hyde Park and Sydenham commerce as well as instruction was in evidence, although at Hyde Park price tickets could not be displayed – prices could be obtained on request. The Commissioners provided deal counters, and fancy cases, shelves and more solid counters could be supplied at an agreed price. Queen Victoria was at the Exhibition 'almost every other day'; her visits involved a fair amount of shopping – a tiara and a brooch from Paris were among her purchases.[211] Karl Marx made the characteristic point that the Great Exhibition was a pantheon for the British bourgeoisie to worship gods in its own image.[212] Materialism was unconcealed and vanity given full play: the press noted the rapture of the 'dazzled multitude' at 'the huge bazaar' and 'colossal Babel'; modish women were drawn to the 40-foot looking-glass, 'the largest in the world', commemorated in a *Punch* cartoon,[213] and to the fabrics, and gazed with delight at the 50-foot Spitalfields Silk Trophy and the Lace Trophy.[214] A degree of national arrogance was displayed in the description of the Koh-i-Noor diamond as a 'forfeit of Oriental faithlessness and the prize of Saxon valour'.[215]

Rival attractions

Both in 1851 and 1854 there were other attractions in London to compete with the Crystal Palaces. Contemporary guide-books and other sources reveal what the people of the day liked to visit. Vauxhall and Cremorne gardens were rather déclassé by this date, but the Zoological Gardens in Regent's Park were popular. Ambitious painted panoramas and dioramas (even a Cyclorama and a Cosmorama) were to be seen.

The enterprising Egyptian Hall in Piccadilly, built in 1811 and long since demolished, came nearest to being a model for the Crystal Palace at Sydenham, with its displays of fine art, antiquities, stuffed animals, history and ethnography. It had a 'grand moving Panorama of Fremont's Overland Route to Oregon, Texas and California', and one could visit a Swiss cottage, a stalactite cavern or a Gothic aviary. Anticipating Owen Jones's works at Sydenham, there was a 'Roman Hall' inside for displays, and models of the Tomb of Beni Hassan and the Temple of Karnac with 'gigantic sitting statues'.

Wyld's 'monster' *Globe* – a sphere 56 feet in diameter painted inside with the world turned inside out, which the visitors could view from a platform at the top of a spiral stair – had been intended for the Great Exhibition but being too large was shown instead in Leicester Square. The highest number of visitors to the Great Exhibition in one day (7 October) was 109,915; by comparison, on Easter Monday in 1851 there were 21,005 visitors to the British Museum, 21,000 to Vauxhall and 150,000 to Greenwich Fair.[216]

Sculpture

The fashion at the time was for statuary in a conservatory setting. The popularity of the sculpture – intermingled with plaster casts – in a glass house was a surprise: 'The statuary is remarked to have attracted much more attention from the general public than was expected'; although 'the higher classes' were familiar with the fine arts, it was 'new, rare and surprising' to the multitude.[217]

Thackeray's Mr Molony in *Punch* was dazed:

> *There's statues bright*
> *Of marble white*
> *Of silver, and of copper;*
> *And some in zinc,*
> *And some, I think,*
> *That isn't over proper.*[218]

After photograph by J.J.E. Mayall, 'Great Exhibition. Main Avenue, Group One'.

Outside the Palace stood Baron Carlo Marochetti's *Richard Coeur de Lion* in plaster, destined to be cast for the Palace of Westminster in 1860. Inside the building in the central aisle was another colossal equestrian sculpture, Eugene Simonis' *Godfrey de Bouillon* from Brussels.

Although the predominant styles in decorative art at the Exhibition were Renaissance and Gothic, the statuary was mostly Neo-Classical. The most popular pieces, August Kiss's *Amazon* and Hiram Powers' *Greek Slave*, derived respectively from 'an antique gem'[219] and from the Aphrodite of Knidos. Monti's *Veiled Vestal* was another favourite with the public; his *Veiled Slave in the Market Place* was bought by the Duke of Devonshire and is now at Chatsworth. The version of Hiram Powers' *Greek Slave* actually shown in the Exhibition – he made six full-size marble versions of it – is at Raby Castle in County Durham.

In 1853 the *Art Journal* wrote of the planned 'Museum of Sculpture' at Sydenham: 'We hope for the day when every gentleman who builds a drawing-room (intended to contain pictures) will add to it such a conservatory leading from it, to be adorned with sculptures.'[220] In the opinion of the *Art Journal*, the best sculpture represented, for realism and idealism, was in the English Sculpture Court, especially John Bell's *Una and the Lion*, 'a highly poetical work'.[221] In general, however, the foreign pieces were the most admired.[222] The French sculpture was suspect, some of it being 'perverted and degraded by low sensuality';[223] significantly the *Bacchante* by J. Clesinger, showing a woman rolling drunk on a bed of vine leaves and grapes, was not among the countless engravings published from the Exhibition. From the front of the New Museum in Berlin came a copy in bronzed zinc (costing one-eighth of the price of bronze) of Professor Kiss' *Amazon* on horseback, defending herself from a tiger with a javelin.[224] By 'universal consent', according to *The Athenæum*, this was given 'the palm of superiority';[225] according to Tallis, its 'tremendous energy' and the 'terror and determination' expressed

George Baxter, August Kiss's *Amazon. Gems of the Great Exhibition*, no. 6

made it 'the single most praised object in the whole exhibition'.[226] At the inauguration of the Great Exhibition the bogus Mandarin, Hee Sing, kissed its foot.[227]

The *Greek Slave*, by the American Hiram Powers (1805–73) who had lived in Florence since 1837, caused a sensation. It showed a captive Christian girl in a Turkish bazaar 'deprived of her clothing, standing before the licentious gaze of a wealthy eastern barbarian'.[228] Some disliked the piece and its popularity; when the young Millais heard that the Judges had given a bronze medal to 'the most sickening horror ever produced, "The Greek Slave"', he wrote that he despaired of ever gaining his rightful position.[229] Cathartic 'sorrow and indignation' seemed to affect its admirers. It moved Elizabeth Barrett Browning, who first saw it in Powers's studio in 1847, to write this sonnet:

HIRAM POWERS' GREEK SLAVE
They say Ideal beauty cannot enter
The house of anguish. On the threshold stands
An alien Image with enshackled hands,
Called the Greek Slave! As if the artist meant her
(That passionless perfection which he lent her,
Shadowed, not darkened where the sill expands)
To, so, confront man's crimes in different lands
With man's ideal sense. Pierce to the centre,

Art's fiery finger! – and break up ere long
The serfdom of this world! Appeal, fair stone,
From God's pure heights of beauty against man's wrong!
Catch up in thy divine face, not alone
East griefs but west, – and strike and shame the strong,
By thunders of white silence overthrown.

As may be seen from the *Punch* cartoons for 1851, the Exhibition and the resulting prospect of foreign visitors excited some xenophobia and insular mockery. The British were well aware of the dependence on black slaves of the 'Slave States' of America.[230] Richard Doyle in his Great Exhibition panorama, *Pictures of Extra Articles and Visitors to the Exhibition*, drew a series of items conspicuously absent from the commercial displays, and his mordant frieze of Americans shows slavery as a barbaric aspect of American industry carefully kept out of sight. Doyle presents the figure of Liberty herself, wearing a Greek shift and sandals; her eyes, feet and hair are clearly those of Powers' *Slave*. However, she has a strong Slaver's chin and holds her head high. Over her shoulder she has jauntily slung fasces weighted down with a bag of dollars, and she leads her slaves in manacles, followed by happy entrepreneurs smoking cheroots and carrying an enormous scourge. 'We have the Greek Slave in dead stone – why not the Virginian slave in living

George Baxter, Hiram Powers' *Greek Slave* flanked by *Rinaldi and Armida* and *Alfred the Great receiving from his mother the book of Saxon poetry*. *Gems of the Great Exhibition*, no. 3.

ebony?', *Punch* demanded; the following week it published Tenniel's cartoon 'The Virginian Slave. Intended as a Companion to Powers's "Greek Slave"'.[231] After the Exhibition Thomas Bazley lectured to the Society of Arts on cotton, then the most important branch of British industry, and referred to the 'dark spot' of slavery which sustained its imports of cheap cotton;[232] 85 per cent of the cotton for the Lancashire and Glasgow mills in 1851 came from the American South,[233] and Bazley hoped that sources would be developed within the Empire.

T.S.R. Boase in the *Oxford History of English Art* noted in 1959 the high incidence of damsels in distress among the subjects of the most popular sculpture at the Exhibition.[234] There was a ready response to this mode of catharsis, not only through the *Greek Slave*, but also through Raffaelle Monti's *Veiled Slave*, Kiss's *Amazon*, an *Andromeda*, a *Procris* and a piece commended by Tallis, 'Macdowell's beautiful portraiture of "The First Sorrow" of a Lovely Girl weeping over her dead bird'.[235]

Visitors

The merging of social distinctions at the Exhibition was frequently noted. There were the fashionable loungers in the Nave, as seen in Leech's *Punch* cartoon of the 'Idlers of the Crystal Palace',[236] but also the 'shilling visitors' whose orderly conduct was a pleasant surprise. Rural clergymen brought their parishioners: the Rector of Godstone in Sussex came with 800, the men all wearing new smocks.[237] A ragged school attended, with only six of the twenty boys wearing shoes.[238] Other parties included 900 Blue Coat boys (from Christ's Hospital,

" DOOCED GRATIFYING, AIN'T IT, CHARLES, TO SEE SA MUCH IN-DASTRY ? "

John Leech, Kensington swells and idlers at the Great Exhibition.

the ancient school in the City of London) and the crews of Lord Dundonald's private yacht and of the Royal Yacht, the *Victoria and Albert* – '130 jolly tars in great glee'. The immensely wealthy philanthropist Angela Burdett-Coutts brought the boys of St Stephen's church school in Westminster.[239] At a banquet in York in November 1850, Richard Cobden rose to toast the working classes: 'The Exhibition would make all the classes better known to each other – would bring the working millions of the Nation to London, where their courteous demeanour would prove how wrongly those estimated

Richard Doyle, 'America'. *Extra Articles and Visitors to the Exhibition.*

them who set these workers down as a rude ferocious mob.'[240] The rightness of this judgment seems to have been universally admitted: *The Expositor* commented that when the royal couple attended, the shilling visitors behaved much better then the five-shilling ladies.[241] However, some thought that although a vast number entered the Palace on the cheap 'shilling days', this had not really brought in 'the people'. In September 1851 *The Expositor* wrote: 'It is a matter beyond dispute that the labouring population, in the strict sense of the word, have not visited the interior in any fair proportion', because they could not afford it. A modern estimate puts the figure of working-class visitors, out of the total of 6 million, at one million.[242] However, eating inside the Palace polarised the classes. *The Examiner* satirised the Londoner Lady Blanche from St James's parish turning up her nose, after her strawberry ices and wafers, at the 'hearty, wholesome' rustic dame from St Giles's who smacks her lips vigorously after stout from a stone bottle and her husband's Brobdignag sandwich from his untied handkerchief.[243]

Finis

The Great Exhibition closed at 5 p.m. on 11 October 1851, after being open for five months and eleven days. Mr Belshaw, the Recorder of British Goods, waved a red flag, and just before this signal the feathery jet of water from Osler's Crystal Fountain ceased. A 'dense mass of black hats' were removed and a discordant National Anthem was sung. Thousands of feet stamped, and from the gallery of the Transept someone lowered a banner inscribed with Prospero's elegiac speech in *The Tempest*: 'Our revels now are ended'. Paxton's Palace, like Shakespeare's 'gorgeous palaces' and visionary 'baseless fabric', was now to dissolve like the clouds, and 'leave not a wrack behind'. Bells and tom-toms were sounded; many filled bottles with water from the Crystal Fountain, and the Executive Committee met 'jubilantly' in the Transept.[244]

At the brief closing ceremony Prince Albert presented medals, among which were a number for beauty of design, as 'a testimony to the genius which can clothe the articles required for the use of daily life with beauty that can please the eye and elevate the mind.' He said that he expected an improvement in taste and an impulse to the arts of design.[245] The *Halleluiah Chorus* was sung, as it had been at the opening and would be again at Sydenham on 10 June 1854.

The clearest thinking about the ideals for a new Crystal Palace, and the form it should take, and at the same time the clearest expression of all that would be good about the Palace at Sydenham in its early years, came from Owen Jones's lecture at the Society of Arts on 28 April 1852:

> This civilising influence, I say, would result from the empty building; but when we imagine, in addition, its vast nave, adorned with a complete history of civilisation recorded in sculpture from the earliest times to the present, with casts of the statues of our great men which now adorn our squares and public places, invisible from London smoke; – when we imagine the plants of every region, however distant, climbing each column, spanning each girder; – the sides of the building set apart for the formation of collections, recording man's conquests over nature, where hundreds daily may be taught to see with the mind as well as the eye, an education as necessary to the governors as to the governed; were such a scheme carried out nobly and lovingly, the success of the Great Exhibition would be, in comparison, failure itself.
>
> To effect this, and in further developing the movement in favour of bringing art-knowledge within the reach of all, the Government may do much, but the public must do more; it must depend for success on the co-operation of all.
>
> It is a movement that may not be delayed; we must be up and stirring; if we would not that England, in the midst of her material greatness, become a byword and a reproach amongst nations.[246]

This stirring prediction was partly fulfilled.

' WHAT IS TO BE DONE WITH THE CRYSTAL PALACE?'

Instruction and recreation

Owen Jones had proposed a second Crystal Palace where the People would learn and enjoy themselves. Samuel Laing made a speech to the same body, the Society of Arts, in July 1854, and claimed that the Crystal Palace Company, of which he was the first chairman, had achieved just that: the new Palace, he declared, was both *utile* and *dulce*, (just as Horace said a good poem should be).[1] What form and purpose it might take had been hotly discussed in Parliament, a government committee, public meetings, private cabals, the press, and a war of pamphlets. The debate polarised the issues of utility and pleasure, and over the years at Sydenham the lofty ideals to improve knowledge and taste at the new Palace were to be largely undermined by lower cultures of pleasure. The conflict was present in discussion at the start.

Even before the Great Exhibition opened people wondered what would become of the building they admired and what institution might take its place. The original Act of Parliament that gave authority for it to be built in Hyde Park contained a condition that it should be removed when the show was over. In March 1851 there was a plan to dismantle and sell the Palace, which belonged to the contractors, and to ship its units to New York for the Exhibition there the following year.[2] However, there was strong public feeling against the idea of losing it. In July 1851 Paxton petitioned the House of Commons for the Palace to remain at Hyde Park until 1 May 1852; a triennial international exhibition was proposed. The Crystal Palace meanwhile stood in Hyde Park, stripped and desolate, used for occasional meetings, concerts and promenades, and raising hopes through the winter after the Exhibition that it might be permanently sited there. However, on 29 April 1852 the House of Commons voted that the government must honour the promise made to the inhabitants of Knightsbridge and return the site to turf.

The fashionable world had to some extent regarded the Palace in Hyde Park all along as an entertainment rather than a school, and used it as a promenade or 'lounge'. A satirical letter was written to a newspaper in July 1851 from a fictitious worldling, Adelicia Belgrave, suggesting that the Palace be converted to a ballroom. She has a fantasy about a finale for the Great Exhibition, a 'Ball of all Nations' in the Palace. Among her partners would be Colonel Sibthorp, M.P., unrelenting manic enemy of the Exhibition, famous from *Punch* cartoons of the time for his denunciations and prophecies of disaster. 'Only think! What a sweet place for a ball – the Crystal Palace! I quite long for a polka with a Turk in the nave, a quadrille with a hindoo, or even a gallop with the gallant Colonel Sibthorp in the transept. Then, the compartments – what delicious snuggeries for a tête-à-tête with your partner.'[3]

Paxton, as we have seen, always intended the Palace to remain as a winter garden, and insisted that he did not want its interior to be 'a great trading bazaar'.[4] His vision of the Crystal Palace in Hyde Park as a permanent winter garden for the two-and-a-half million Londoners was appropriate for its setting in aristocratic Kensington, and a combination of two features at Chatsworth: the famous conservatory he had designed – 'the Great Stove' – through which carriages could drive, and the Sculpture Gallery. Paxton published an engraving of his proposed improvements to the building in the *Illustrated London News*, and wrote a pamphlet, *What is to become of the Crystal Palace?* He exhibited a picture of the proposed interior at Grieve and Telbin's gallery in Regent Street. He wrote: 'Here would be supplied the climate of Southern Italy, where multitudes might ride, walk, or recline amidst groves of fragrant trees, and here they might leisurely examine the works of Nature and Art with snow and the biting east winds outside.'[5] Meanwhile Owen Jones and his colleagues, who intended the new Palace as an extension of the lessons learned in design at the Great Exhibition, to raise awareness of art and architecture among the people, were putting a case for mostly historical artefacts and reproductions to fill the Palace. At a meeting just before the sale of the building to the Crystal Palace Company, Paxton said that 'a very extended school of design would be a mockery without the assembly of natural objects in it... Nature is the great artist after all, a studio with real objects of beauty to copy.'[6] It was freely acknowledged at the time that the Great Exhibition had taught the British that their industrial arts were inferior to those produced on the continent, particularly in France.[7] The *Art Journal* argued that since the state had neglected to attend to this task, it should now be taken up by private enterprise.[8] Paxton's insistence on studying botany for the principles of design is consistent with the ideas of the major designers associated with both Crystal Palaces – Pugin, Jones and Christopher Dresser – although these men all agreed (as has been seen in chapter 1) that ornament required stylisation of the forms found in botany rather than literal representation. Paxton's excitement suggests that he was impatient for the ponderous Great Exhibition to be removed from his Crystal Palace, to be replaced by the delights of his own realm, Chatsworth, to give pleasure to millions and to improve their taste. Statues and fountains would represent Art, while visitors' 'intellectual enjoyment' could be derived from displays of geology. Exotic birds would fly about inside. And he would make 'enchanting and gorgeous' effects with 'creeping and clustering' plants winding up the columns and

'festooning in every diversity of form'. There would be bright indoor parterres, tropical and temperate trees, an interior canal with ornamental bridges, and large basins with water at 80–85 degrees Fahrenheit – warm enough for the *Victoria regia* to flower. Oxygen transformed by the plants overnight from the 'carbonic supply' would invigorate the visitor's body and spirit. Gas chandeliers would light the interior. The project would be financed by an annual national grant, or it could be self-supporting; he estimated the annual cost of upkeep at £8,000.[9] Paxton's bird's-eye view of the building showed the addition of dramatic semi-circular wings, in form like Bernini's colonnade in front of St Peter's, Rome, through which carriages could pass into the Palace, and towers for the heating system. At the same time there was an apparently serious architect's proposal by Charles Burton, published in a wood-engraving in *The Builder* and as a lithograph, to take the prefabricated units and make them into a skyscraper, a 'Prospect Tower' 1,000 feet high. The Tower, Burton proposed, as well as serving as a belvedere, should contain galleries with displays of art and industry, and winter garden features of plants and statuary.[10]

Paxton was supported by *The Times*, the *Morning Post*, the *Illustrated London News* and his friends at

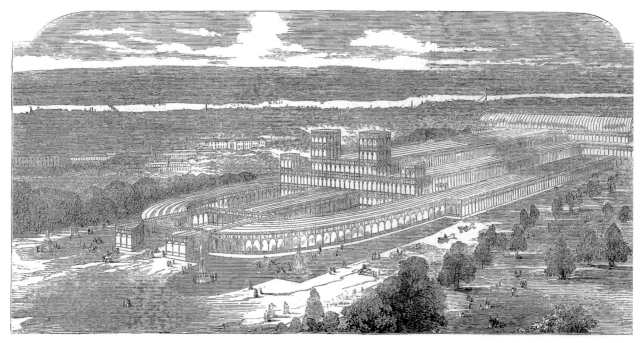

After Joseph Paxton, 'The Crystal Palace in Hyde Park – proposed new entrances, and additions', October 1851.

Charles Burton, 'Design for converting the Crystal Palace into a Tower 1000ft high', May 1852. © Victoria and Albert Museum.

Punch, and by Henry Cole who wrote an encouraging pamphlet entitled *Shall we keep the Crystal Palace and have Riding and Walking in all Weathers among Flowers, Fountains and Sculpture?* Under the pseudonym 'Denarius' (a penny), he argued that the promise to remove the exhibition building from Hyde Park referred to the brick building originally proposed and not to Paxton's prefabricated iron and glass structure; he rightly claimed that public opinion was strongly in favour. On one day in April 1852 at a 'Grand Promenade' at the Palace 100,000 people signed a petition to keep it on its existing site.[11]

Among the proposals for rebuilding the Crystal Palace elsewhere were one, from Lord Seymour, to put up thirty-three bays and the Transept at Kew Gardens,[12] and another to adopt an attractive riverside location in Battersea Fields (now Battersea Park), promoted by William Cubitt;[13] this was to have a landing-stage, and a prospect of the 'suspension Bridge [the Albert Bridge], now being erected'.[14] Seymour and Cubitt, together with Dr John Lindley of the Royal Horticultural Society, formed in December 1851 the official Commission to hear evidence and discuss the future of the Palace.[15] Battersea had originally been proposed as a site for the Great Exhibition,[16] although the Fields were associated with low entertainments – pigeon shoots, gambling booths, rat killing and dog fights. Lord Granville had written in July 1851 to Prince Albert's Secretary, Colonel Charles Grey, recommending that the Palace be turned over to the Horticultural Society.[17] A plan for a sanatorium was put forward by Francis Seymour Haden (1818–1910), a surgeon and later a distinguished etcher, that instead of Paxton's 'Arcadia of his own imagining' with riders on horseback, consideration should be given to the health of Londoners, particularly those with tubercular and respiratory complaints: 'We would sink wells in the Crystal Palace and establish a system of Baths which should combine all that is desirable in the Spas of Germany with all that is decent in the Roman Thermae.'[18] Meanwhile the riders and carriage-owners who frequented Hyde Park hoped that it would provide a pleasing extension to their rides. Lord Campbell in the House of Lords quoted from the *Quarterly*, ridiculing Paxton's proposal for an artificial climate on medical grounds. Paxton then wrote to the press to deny that he intended to reproduce the summer climate of southern Italy in the winter; what he meant to do was imitate the winter climate, 'which will be about ten degrees colder than the ordinary heat of our dwelling houses'.[19] Those who favoured the Palace as a museum or an illustrated encyclopaedia suggested an extension of the British Museum, which was now seriously overcrowded with recent acquisitions: the Nineveh antiquities were 'literally underground' once again, and the marbles from the Acropolis had been 'cramped down in a dark hole'.[20] Other proposals were a permanent residence for invalids, a vast and permanent picture gallery, an international library, a polytechnic institution, a theatre, and a riding-school.[21]

A weighty opponent of the winter garden scheme was Prince Albert, who did not wish to see the noble ideals or the profits of the Exhibition squandered on mere leisure:

'The purchase of the Crystal Palace for the purpose of establishing a Winter Garden, or museum of Antiquities, or a public promenade, ride, lounging place &c &c, has in my opinion, no connexion whatever with the objects of the Exhibition.'[22] Queen Victoria wrote in her journal that Albert wanted 'no part of profit towards Palace of entertainment'.[23] Once the threat to the Exhibition profits was removed by plans for the purchase and development of the site in South Kensington familiarly known as 'Albertopolis', another document shows that later he was more sympathetic to Paxton's idea. He wrote to Lord Derby that 'a winter garden strikes me as the best use it can be put to'; likewise he endorsed the commercial plan eventually adopted by the formation of the Crystal Palace Company: 'Mr Fuller's proposal', he said, 'appears to me in every way a proper one.'[24]

It is certain that the government seriously considered taking over the Palace: the Treasury Commission set up a committee to discover the cost of maintaining and removing it, and to painting it inside and out every four years. Paxton told them that the Palace would last for fifty to a 100 years.[25] At a public meeting at Exeter Hall the Dukes of Devonshire and Argyll, the Earls of Shaftesbury, Carlisle and Harrowby, Lord Palmerston, the banker Meyer de Rothschild and the railway magnate Samuel Morton Peto agreed to be Trustees.

A dramatic development followed within two weeks of the decision by the House of Commons of 29 April 1852 to dismantle the Palace: this was the formation of the Crystal Palace Company. Paxton had been saying in public – speaking, he said, as a man of the people – that a national Palace 'should be entirely free to the people' and that 'more than any other since the world began, [it] had been dedicated to themselves.'[26] However, he was now deeply committed to the commercial venture, having already secured capital of £500,000 by 7 April.[27] A later pamphlet by Paxton ('for private circulation') shows how he had compromised with his architect associates: he still described his winter garden as a setting for 'the advancement of Arts, Science and Manufactures', but with a Gallery and Museum of Design to improve taste among the manufacturers and the public, together with new inventions and trade collections, equipped with lecture rooms.[28]

It was suddenly announced that the Palace had been sold for £70,000 in cash to the nominal purchaser Francis Fuller (1807–87), acting on behalf of a consortium of railway proprietors and others, their stated aims being 'floriculture and the fine arts'. The railways presumably viewed the Palace as a speculation, since large profits had been made in excursion tickets from the rest of England during the Great Exhibition. There was now 'a scramble', as it was described, between the rival lines of the South West which favoured Kew, Chiswick and Battersea as a site, and the London, Brighton and South Coast line, whose small Anerley station in the south-east suburbs stood a mile below Sydenham Hill. A director of the Brighton line, Leo Schuster, had a large estate on the hill, Penge Place, which was bought by the Crystal Palace Company for the Palace's new site. Schuster was reported as saying: 'I had made up my mind to spend the remainder of my days on the estate. I would rather give it up than you should be without a suitable site; and you shall have the park.'[29]

The Times supported the Company's plans, saying that the claims of the new institutions of South Kensington as a rival to the new Crystal Palace to educate the people in science and the arts were 'delusive hopes'; by comparison with the 'healthy commercial enterprise' at Sydenham, they were already showing 'symptoms of somnolency'. 'The Prince himself has not been slow to manifest the interest which he feels in an undertaking, the direct work, indeed, of a private company, but which can trace its origin by no dubious pedigree to the industrial gathering of 1851.'[30] However, Albert's true loyalties were naturally with Cole and South Kensington, and he might have disliked Samuel Laing's use of his name in claiming that the new Palace was 'emphatically and peculiarly a child of the illustrious Prince'.[31] Charles Phipps wrote to Cole on behalf of Prince Albert that the Crystal Palace group was largely motivated by 'love of gain…and public notoriety'.[32]

A penny pamphlet by John Small, *Caution to the Brighton Shareholders and the public at large against the Crystal Palace Removal to Sydenham*, warned that naturally the public could not be so safe in the hands of the guarantors – Francis Fuller, 'a thriving man in money speculations', and Leo Schuster, rich and Jewish – as in the hands of the public-spirited Trustees agreed at the Exeter Hall meeting. Small was suspicious of the motives for siting the Palace in the suburbs 'near an obscure railway station', and for Laing's claim that Schuster's Penge Place was the best of the twenty-one sites considered by the Company. He would have preferred Kew, Chiswick or Battersea, and believed that the project was just a 'make-weight, a piece of by-play' for a railway company. He predicted that as a 'great house of public entertainment' it was a most unsafe investment for shareholders.[33] This proved absolutely right.

Sydenham

Samuel Laing (1812–97), the chairman of the new Crystal Palace Company, was a man of wide intellectual interests who pursued a career in railways, politics and finance. Initially a Fellow in Mathematics of St John's College, Cambridge, and a barrister, he joined the government Railway Commission in 1845, wrote reports on current railway schemes, and resigned when parliament (unwisely) rejected the Commission's recommendations. In 1848 he became chairman and managing director of the London, Brighton and South Coast Railway, but in 1855 resigned from both the Railway and the Crystal Palace; during these years of expansion the Brighton Railway's passengers nearly doubled, and the dividend rose from 3.5 to 5 per cent. From 1852 he was also a Liberal Member of Parliament, and built railways in Canada and on the continent.[34] From 1867 till 1894 he was again chairman of the Brighton Railway.

Six of the promoters of the scheme for the new Palace, including of course Paxton, had been closely connected with the Great Exhibition. Francis Fuller, the building's nominal buyer, had been the surveyor; John Scott Russell said that without his work with Grey, the Prince's private secretary, the Exhibition would never have been possible. It was Fuller who had suggested to Albert the Mansion House dinner with the provincial mayors.[35] He was said to have refused a knighthood at the close of the exhibition when Paxton accepted one. For twenty-five years Fuller was the surveyor and land agent for the London, Brighton and South Coast Railway. The most active members of the Society of Arts in setting up the Great Exhibition with Prince Albert had been Fuller and Scott Russell along with Cole and Cubitt, Digby Wyatt and Owen Jones. Scott Russell (1808–82) was an associate of Brunel, and built at his Millwall shipyard the immense screw and paddle steamer the *Great Eastern*; he was himself an inventor and a 'naval architect'. Paxton teased him that the new Palace was his 'monster ship'.[36] Scott Russell was in financial difficulties in 1856;[37] his entry in the *Dictionary of National Biography* refers to 'a certain lack of stability'

in his character. George Grove (1820–1900) was the secretary of the Society in 1849–52. Two partners in a firm of solicitors, T.N. Farquhar and Joseph Leech, first suggested to Schuster a private company to buy and manage the Palace, and 'Mr Laing heartily concurred.'[38] Sir Joseph Paxton was appointed 'director of Winter Garden, Park and Conservatory'; Matthew Digby Wyatt 'director of the Works'; Owen Jones 'director of Decorations'; and Grove secretary.

The Company was registered provisionally on 17 May 1852, and an eloquent prospectus was issued. Two 'great facts' about the Great Exhibition must be taken into account, prospective shareholders were told: first, it had been 'highly remunerative', and, secondly, it had been the poorer classes, the 'shillings', who accounted for the greater part of the receipts from admission.

> Refined recreation, calculated to elevate the intellect, to instruct the mind, and to improve the heart, will welcome the millions who have now no other incentives to pleasure but those which the gin palace, dancing saloon, and the ale house afford them… The triumphs of industry and art, and the natural beauty of flowers and plants from every climate will meet at the Crystal Palace… [in] the genial atmosphere of a winter garden, eighteen acres in extent.

A challenge was issued with a promise to outdo the fountains at Versailles; special trains would carry an enormous quantity of visitors, just as on the popular lines between Paris and Versailles. As at the Great Exhibition, 'machinery at work', geology, and botany would be illustrated, but 'on a far greater scale than has ever before been attempted'. Sculpture, architectural remains and casts would occupy 'every salient part' of the building. Prospective shareholders were reminded that the Company would have greater powers to reject inferior manufactures sent for display than the Commissioners had in 1851. They would use a method of 'classification' for exhibits, just as these had been divided into groups and catalogued at Hyde Park, but they would make it more complete and instructive. Horticultural shows were an important part of the promised attractions. While the Palace's contents were to be 'a miniature of the world', the Park – remarkably in view of Paxton's later more ambitious gardening schemes – was to be 'thoroughly English'. Intoxicating drinks would not be permitted, and the general amusements of the tea garden and the dancing saloon 'will be strictly excluded'.

The announcement made a virtue of the project not

George Baxter, 'The Exterior', 10 June 1854. *Gems of the Crystal Palace, Sydenham*, No 1.

being backed by the government, congratulating the Company itself and its future shareholders on their public spirit in making up for the government's deficiencies:

> They know full well the Governments of other countries deem it their duty to provide for, and carefully to watch over, the national character of the masses given to their charge, by affording the means of recreation and instruction during their holiday and leisure hours. But here the wise and good among us must do these things for themselves, for British governments revolve in fixed political orbits, and the people shrink from official interference in their personal, social and domestic movements.[39]

Within two or three weeks of this announcement, and after two advertisements in *The Times*, on 18 and 22 May 1852, half a million pounds had been subscribed in £5 shares; in November the flotation was increased to £1

million. The London, Brighton and South Coast Railway was the majority shareholder,[40] and Samuel Laing told a meeting in June that the Duke of Devonshire was 'a large subscriber'.[41] The value of the shares rose to £9 but receded below par.[42] 'No profligate sovereigns or corrupt ministers and subservient legislatures' but capitalism and 'mere private enterprise', they boasted, would build a Palace.[43] By its new charter the Crystal Palace Company was enjoined 'to preserve the high moral and educational tone' of the Great Exhibition; and it was at this point that the sale of liquor and Sunday opening were ruled out by law. On the very eve of the Inauguration the Company was asserting that it would outdo the Great Exhibition; the new Palace would be more educational than commercial, showing not just 'the world as it is' – contemporary manufactures and natural resources – but also 'the world as it has been', the history of civilisation.[44] *The Times* reported in May 1852 that it expected

After Philip Delamotte, 'From the Rosery', 1854.

the new Palace to open on 1 May 1853.[45] The site chosen for it by the Company was what at that date could still be referred to as the 'English Tyrol',[46] next to Norwood and close to the resort of Beulah Hill. The ample park consisted of the still wooded brow of the hill with its magnificent panoramas, 'exceeded by only few in the world':[47] overlooking the park towards Surrey and Kent, and on the other side towards the tall buildings of London and the masts of ships; below the brow lay Schuster's redbrick Penge Place, rebuilt in Elizabethan style by Edward Blore,[48] and used by the Company for workshops before it was demolished.[49] In the park Paxton, sitting under a cherry tree, sketched his 'vast idea' of the Crystal Palace Park. He was to retain many original trees.[50]

In this setting on the brow of the hill the Palace would be its own advertisement to foreigners coming from the continent by way of Brighton and the South Coast to London Bridge Station, and was the colossal first feature of the metropolis to meet their eyes. The Company bought the 349 acres of the park for £80,661 12s. 6d and an additional estate across the main road to Anerley for £81,000, but it almost immediately sold 149 acres of the estate to a friend and associate of Paxton's, George Wythes of Reigate, 'a very well known and eminent contractor', for the development of 'first-class villas', between what is now Westwood Hill and Anerley Road;[51] on this it made a profit of £50,000. Sydenham was then a quiet hamlet with villas, cottages and alehouses; now a new town was to spring up (one suggestion was that it be called 'Paxtonia'). The building of the Palace, as if by natural cause and effect, made the price of an acre of land in the vicinity rise in twelve months from £300 to £1,600.[52] A lease of 67 acres of the ancient Dulwich Wood across the hill from Penge Place was taken from Dulwich College for £2,000 per annum, and Wythes was intending to spend £40,000 over five years on building there.[53] On the south-west side of the hill £17,825 was spent on roads and approaches, including the magnificent 'serpentine road' up the hill from Dulwich, completed in June 1855.[54] Paxton lived on the estate in a Regency house called Rockhills to the north of the Palace on the summit of West Hill. The year 1854 was a difficult one for him personally: on the very day the Palace opened, the Duke of Devonshire had a stroke and

After Philip Delamotte, 'North Transept from the Tower', 1854.

was paralysed on his right side; Paxton's father was dying, and his ne'er-do-weel son George was behaving worse than ever.[55]

In January 1856 Paxton was reported to be buying Rockhills, but Fuller recommended that he live there rent-free for life and be retained by the Company in an advisory capacity with a 'salary' of £100 a month.[56] At this time he was accused in a shareholders' meeting by Alderman Wilson of drawing £1,000 a week from the Company, which he angrily denied, asking Wilson to prove it; he was given a vote of confidence. Paxton also told the shareholders that he could have speculated in land around the Palace, but had not done so, saving the Company £50,000.[57] The Duke of Devonshire stayed with Paxton at Rockhills for weeks on end, and even suggested living there permanently;[58] he bought a house a few hundred yards away on Sydenham Hill for his friend Lady Hunloke.[59] The Duke presented many plants to

the Palace and was often present at functions; a piece of plate that he presented to Paxton on the opening day was displayed in the centre transept.[60] Paxton died at Rockhills in 1865. The house was advertised (as 'the favourite abode of the late Sir Joseph Paxton') for rent or sale with its 2.75 acres of land in 1879.[61]

A report of a soirée at the Literary Society of Sydenham, organised by George Grove on 10 November 1853 with Paxton in the chair, gives an idea of the intellectual milieu of the Crystal Palace protagonists: books, portfolios and models of temples were on display, with some of the life-size ethnographic models intended for the Palace and splendid photographs taken by Philip Delamotte of its construction. There were fireworks, and English and German glees were sung.[62]

The new Palace

When Owen Jones was twenty-six he gave a lecture on

the influence of religion on art, and described ancient temples as having mountain-tops as platforms or pedestals. To him the Palace on Sydenham Hill doubtless suggested a sacred Acropolis of art, its terraces and statuary resembling one of those temples he described which one approached through sacred groves and 'avenues of exquisitely-wrought sphinxes'.[63]

The new Palace was nearly 50 per cent larger in cubic content than the one at Hyde Park, and had almost twice the surface of glass. The work of construction was much heavier; it took twenty-three months to build compared with Hyde Park's eight months. *The Times* said that it 'so far transcended the original' as to make one rather ashamed of having admired the first Palace.[64] In 'majesty and grace' it was 'more vast, more beautiful, more permanent, and devoted to more comprehensive purposes', said *Chambers's Edinburgh Journal*.[65]

Comparing the two buildings they cited words of Horace, '*O mater pulchra, filia pulchrior*'.[66] In a leaflet published by the Company in March 1853 it was said that Paxton's plans were 'something on a very much larger scale, and something much more magnificent than any of us originally contemplated'.[67] Paxton had designed the first Palace with the simplicity that has always seemed its most admirable characteristic; he said that this was the result of economy, 'to make it as cheap as possible… I left out almost everything in the shape of ornament.'[68] The second Palace rose 44 feet higher – high enough, as they boasted, to accommodate Wren's Monument to the Fire of London under the barrel-vault of the central Transept with six feet to spare.[69]

The nave was 1,608 feet long, 312 feet wide and 104 feet high at the crown of its vault; it was crossed by three transepts. The great centre transept was 384 feet long, 120 feet wide, and 168 feet to its crown; the two side transepts were 336 feet long, their width and height corresponding closely to the nave. On the south or garden side the three transepts were extended 24 feet into the open air to make arched recesses. Digby Wyatt said that these 'noble recesses', which threw impressive shadows, were the 'happy suggestion' of Owen Jones.[70] *The Times* thought it a pity that (for economy's sake) there were none on the west side facing the Parade.[71] The two smaller side transepts were referred to as the North or Sydenham Transept and the South or Norwood Transept.[72]

Sir Charles Barry had suggested for the Hyde Park building that the Nave as well as the Transept should be

'Upper Gallery of the Crystal Palace', 1854.

vaulted, and although the idea won approval it was finally rejected as too costly. The press in 1851 had remarked on the 'shed-like character' of the flat roof of the long nave at Hyde Park, disproportionate in length to its width and height.[73] At Sydenham the nave was magnificently vaulted with a translucent barrel-roof; many visitors remarked on the sublime effect of the sky seen through it, and the same 'arches of cobweb-like tenuity' that had been admired at Hyde Park.[74] The ribs of the barrel-vaults were glazed by Paxton's ridge and furrow method. The central transept was raised by two more tiers, and accordingly was twice the width of the transept at Hyde Park; at its tallest the building was six storeys high. A brilliant innovation was the narrow 'Telescope Gallery' on the third storey, 'close under the springing of the arched vaults'.[75] This was formed of 'ring' or 'bull's-eye' cast iron girders,[76] 'circular hoops', set about 20 feet apart, giving a fine diminishing perspective.[77] Another novel feature was the use of panels made of plastered canvas, formed into patterns of lozenges and triangles in blue and white and placed on the spandrels, high above the semi-circular vault at the intersection of the barrel-vaults of the nave and the main transept – these are to be seen in Joseph Nash's water-colour of the Inauguration. In 1858 Owen Jones designed 'The London Crystal Palace', an elegant bazaar at Regent Circus in Oxford

Philip Delamotte, 'South End of the Nave, Interior'.

Street: the *Illustrated London News* described such geometric panels, made of plaster over coarse canvas by M. Desachy of Great Marlborough Street and enriched in triangles painted blue and white, which were simply affixed by nails in the bays at the end of the semi-circular iron and glass roof; it said that these were also used for the roof at the Crystal Palace at Sydenham. Desachy, whose men also constructed Owen Jones's colossal Egyptian figures, used very light plaster: a Venus de Milo cast by him weighed only 20–25 lbs compared with the usual 320 lbs.[78]

There was a particular feature of the new Palace which made the structure more stable – the galleries at Hyde Park, though safe, were called 'tremulous' – and added aesthetic interest to the interior. This was the series of pairs of columns advanced 8 feet into the Transept at intervals of 72 feet, supporting the arched girders of the vault. Pairs of columns 24 feet apart also advanced 8 feet into the Nave. Lining the main avenue, they formed as it were an open arcade resembling an aisle in a great cathedral; they emphasised the perspective more clearly and, in contrast with the uniformity of the Hyde Park interior, gave grander masses of varied light

and shade.[79] It was indeed said, in an official Crystal Palace Company pamphlet written by George Grove, that this feature of the design derived from the columns and aisles of Gothic cathedrals, and was therefore likely to have been a conscious historical reference originating with the architects themselves.[80] Ornamental spandrels or brackets were placed beneath each junction of girder and column. There were eight flights of stairs 23 feet wide and eight spiral staircases, dramatically placed to show in silhouette against the glass curtain walls.

By August 1853 the personnel listed in the original Prospectus had changed: Digby Wyatt and Owen Jones were now responsible for the 'Restorations' (the Architectural Courts), and Charles Wild was described as the engineer, as he had been for the building of the first Palace. The ailing Wild proved unsatisfactory, and left the Company soon after the collapse of the first water-towers.[81] As at Hyde Park the contractors were Fox and Henderson. The chairman, in his speech of 17 March 1853, said that assistance was given in the drawings for the Palace by Paxton's nephew and son-in-law George Stokes (1827–74), who was also responsible for 'the architectural features of the external terraces and fountains, and the Sheffield Court [an Industrial Court]'.[82] His obituary in *Building News* noted that in spite of his youth he was the 'chef' of Paxton's large staff at Sydenham.[83]

Construction

At the ceremonial Placing of the First Pillar (one of those brought from Hyde Park) on 5 August 1852, six workmen in patriotic 'Sunday clothes' – red ties, white trousers, and blue jackets and caps – carried a banner bearing the legend 'Success to the Palace of the People'. Eminent architects and luminaries attended, and the names of supporters were read out, including Faraday, Carlyle, Tennyson, Thackeray and George Cruikshank.[84] Samuel Laing declared this to be the first palace built without slaves. The elegantly dressed ladies in crinolines described in Samuel Laing's speech (and pictured in the engraving of the event in the *Illustrated London News*) were said to be seated in a 'circle of beauty' in an 'indistinct image of the central transept', as if a central dome was originally to be a feature of the Palace of the People. This would appear to be the case, as a report printed in the *Athenaeum* in July 1852, supplied by the Directors, says that in addition to the barrel vault along the Nave, 'over all will tower a dome of

'Placing the First Pillar', 5 August 1852.

immense proportions.'[85] Sir Charles Barry evidently thought the original Crystal Palace, though simple and efficient, 'ineffective and ugly', and prepared a design for the improvement of the Palace at Sydenham with a great central iron and glass dome and lantern, cupolas and turrets that would have cost an insignificant sum compared with what was lavished on the waterworks and other less important objects, but (as his son Alfred records)[86] it was 'rejected with thanks' by the directors.

James Fergusson, who admired the building passionately, wrote of it in terms which can only astonish today:

As re-erected at Sydenham, the building has far greater claims to rank among the important architectural objects of the world. It was colossal; four times the space of St. Peter's at Rome, and ten times the space of St Paul's... Its construction is absolutely truthful throughout, nothing is concealed, and nothing added for effect. In this respect it surpasses any Classical or Gothic building ever erected.

He admired the form of the great transept and of the two minor ones and the vaulted roof of the nave. Nonetheless he added that the building as a whole lacked solidity or an appearance of permanence and durability, and would have benefited from some coloured brickwork and terra cotta;[87] he thought that the builders had been hampered by having to use the materials from Hyde Park. Indeed, the major exhibition buildings that followed the Crystal Palace mostly used brick: the buildings for the French Exposition of 1856, the International Exhibition at South Kensington of 1862 and the Palais d'Industrie of 1864 all consisted of a solid box with a crystal palace lid.

The foundations for the new Palace, which included brick walls

After Sir Charles Barry, 'Crystal Palace (as proposed)', 1852–3.

Philip Delamotte, 'Delivery of materials from Hyde Park'.

and arches to carry the earth for the plants, were to be set on sloping ground, formed of loose soil. The great terraces were suggested to Paxton by the line of the ridge of the hill, and made from the foundation earthworks there. Wood from Hyde Park was used for some of the foundations, and by 1874 the Company had to spend 'an immense sum' replacing this with brick.[88] At Hyde Park easy drainage, gas and water supply presented no problems, but at Sydenham Paxton found it impossible to bring enough water by the conventional means of commercial supply for the fountains and waterworks he was conceiving. By November 1852 work had begun on a very deep Artesian well at the bottom of the Park to provide water that would then be pumped up to enormous tanks at the top of the site.[89] Francis Fuller was a partner in a quixotic unrealised proposal to raise £75,000 to bring sea-water by a canal from Brighton to 'a large marine reservoir' at Sydenham, and turn the village into a medical sea-bathing establishment. The scheme was to be extended to supply fountains at Charing Cross and sea-water baths for private houses and hotels.[90]

The *Illustrated London News* reported that the London clay was 'as tough and smooth as a bad imitation of stilton'.[91] Masses of concrete and brick went under each column.[92] At Hyde Park the wooden floor had been too close to damp earth for a permanent building. Paxton added a basement rather than levelling the slope, a reminder of the 'Great Stove' at Chatsworth with its

underground tunnels with rails for transporting coal; in this case 'the Paxton Tunnel' was 26 feet below the road level, with 7 miles of piping from twenty-two underground furnaces for the heating system.[93] In Hyde Park there had been no need for heating. Paxton spent three hours a day for three months designing this system for Sydenham.[94] It expanded to 50 miles of hot water piping: 11,000 gallons of water travelled one and three-quarter miles between the boilers with hot water and the basins for the *Victoria regia*; the hot water pipes, as well as heating the water for the basins, also heated the Tropical Department, maintaining 'the climate and luxuriant vegetation of sunnier regions'.[95] Together with the system for the indoor fountains, this was the most ambitious system of water pipes ever attempted. Ventilation was provided by regulated louvres in the upper galleries; the theory was that, since dry heat mounts, 'pure invigorating air' for plants and people would come in from louvres at ground level, and hot summer days would be cool.[96] From Hyde Park the iron and glass – 550 tons of wrought iron, 3,500 tons of cast iron and 400 tons of glass [97]– were brought by drays, since there was not yet a railway to the Palace. Two-horse teams pulled 2-ton loads with great strain up Sydenham Hill;[98] 150 tons arrived daily during August 1852. The road, now Fountain Drive, was re-engineered to ease the one-in-eight gradient. Phillips's *Guide* says (unconvincingly) that all the materials from the Hyde Park building were used again except for the glass on the roof and the framing of the transept-roof, which was now made from ribs of wrought iron rather than of wood. The glass from Hyde Park, weighing 16 ounces per square foot, was used for the walls, but new 21-ounce glass was used for the roof; any glass that was broken could be remade cheaply. The makers of the glass, as for Hyde Park, were Messrs Chance of Birmingham.[99] George Myers was responsible for the roads and masonry.

The wooden gutters and ventilators used at Hyde Park were unsuitable for a permanent building, and those who worked in the Palace were well aware of the damage to the wooden flooring and the substructure

Philip Delamotte, 'The Open Colonnade, Garden Front'.

caused by watering the plants. George Purchase, Jones's head of staff, thought the 'unrivalled conservatory' unsuitable as a 'repository for works of art or industry'.[100] A letter to *The Builder* in 1861 noted alarmingly uneven flooring and feared for the joists and girders, 'most manifest near the large masses of vegetable earth in which plants are grown, and which are kept constantly wet'.[101] Wood was used in the gutters; some of it unseasoned, and over the years neglected paintwork, cracked putty and slipping panes let in the rain.[102] Only a year after the Palace opened, Paxton was told at a meeting that rain poured 'in torrents' through the roof among the exhibitors, and replied that it was 'as good as any railway station roof'.[103] The roof of the Centre Transept needed complete reglazing in 1899.

Wild designed towers to the north and south, combining chimneys and water-tanks, made of Paxton's prefabricated units – they are to be seen in early views of the Palace. According to Paxton's obituary they were thought to spoil the effect of the grouping and the outline of the Palace. Brunel's towers were to replace these, and prompted Ruskin's famous metaphor in *Praeterita* for the 'stupidity' of the Palace's hollow bulk between its towers, possessing 'no more sublimity than a cucumber frame between two chimneys'.[104] These earlier towers, too weak to support the enormous tanks of water to supply the proposed waterworks, were an expensive failure.

A great gale in 1861 caused the North Wing to collapse.[105] This was not the first storm to damage the building: *The Builder* reported and illustrated with two wood-engravings the calamitous result of an extremely forceful wind in January 1853 that tore up the scaffolding for the circular rib; 150 tons of iron were destroyed and broken columns and girders were 'smashed into tiny pieces'.[106] There were also serious accidents, the worst being on 15 August 1853 when three trusses in the central nave fell from the scaffolding and thirteen men died. Accidents on sites were more frequent at that time: a painter at Hyde Park had been killed when a girder gave way, and a carpenter died in another accident.[107] John Wolfe Barry, the architect of Tower Bridge, wrote in a chapter he contributed to a history of its construction: 'It is gratifying to record that the loss of human life during the construction of the bridge has not, considering the

magnitude and nature of the work, been great. In all, eight men have met with fatal accidents, and at least one of these accidents was the result of a fit.'[108] The scaffolding for the ribs of the central transept at Sydenham had not been built from ground level but from the fifth tier of the galleries. There were three structural collapses in 1853: the gale in January, a fall in July, and the calamity in August. Another fall in September was hushed up.[109] It was said that the men on the scaffolding had panicked a few times before the major disaster, both because of the damage caused by the January gale and because of the height. Paxton reported to the Company that the storm damage had caused two or three weeks' delay and that the struts had subsequently been strengthened.[110]

Philip Delamotte, 'Breakfast time at the Crystal Palace'.

The reason the workmen gave for the major disaster of 15 August was that the wooden scaffold had contracted with the heat. 'The general belief is that [the accident] arose from the enormous span of the arch, and the timber and ironwork being too heavy for the span.' On being pushed forward to receive the third rib, the 'key' shifted due to the strain on the scaffold. Six trusses had been fixed, and of these three, each weighing five to five and a half tons, fell 102 feet carrying with them seventeen of the twenty men on the scaffold fitting bolts. There was a suggestion that the men had been cutting corners by walking on a platform and not on the scaffolding. Fox and Henderson claimed that the trussing and staging were undisturbed, and that there was a defect in the materials or in the work of making the structure secure; 'an unusual amount of supervision and oversight' was carried out.[111] During the inquest, reported in *The Times* for 19 August 1853, John Cochrane, Henderson's assistant, who narrowly escaped death, said that the top gallery was well supported by a method used in bridge building, and that the timber or the struts gave way. The jury was told that this could not happen again, since a scaffold would be raised from the ground. After this accident scaffolds for such roofs were always built from the ground.

Fox and Henderson said that the work on the trusses was considered the biggest job, and that the workmen sought it. These men, as at Hyde Park, earned up to 5 shillings more a day than the ordinary navvies. The jury, who visited the site, gave a verdict of 'accidental death', and no criminal negligence was assigned to Fox and

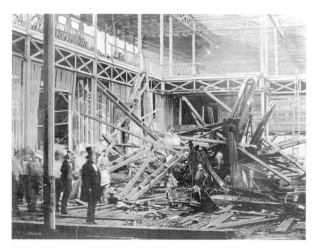

Philip Delamotte, 'Fall of scaffold from first pair of Great Transept ribs'.

Henderson. A photograph taken by Delamotte at the site of the accident shows Owen Jones in his top-hat standing in the foreground. 'Every workman was at his post at the usual hour on the following morning.' At the funeral of ten of the thirteen victims in Sydenham churchyard a procession of thousands, the entire work force[112] set out from the central nave of the Palace led by Cochrane. Fox and Henderson provided pensions for the widows.[113] Paxton's obituary said that some of the blame for the accident went to him, but that he had no connection with the scaffolding.[114] That working relations were not invariably harmonious is shown by a strike of a considerable number of painters, plasterers and masons working on the Fine Art Courts, reported in April 1854.[115]

By July 1853 Paxton was able to report that his tunnel was nearly finished, and that the Fine Art Courts were 'rapidly advancing'. The towers were to receive the colossal water tank in August. By November many casts had arrived: the copy of the equestrian statue of King Charles I at Charing Cross, Schwanthaler's colossal Bavarian head, the Nineveh bulls and lions, and plaster arabesques. Outside, the terraces and steps were formed, but finding a large quantity of stone for the cascades and basins was a problem.[116] Monti's *Italy* and Bell's *Australia* statues and the sphinxes were in place.[117]

By March 1854 the scaffolding was coming down from the Centre Transept and the exterior walls of the Alhambra Court had been built.[118] *The Times* wrote on May 8, just before the Palace was due to open, that since so much was still rough and unfinished the ceremony ought to be postponed; however, the Company wanted to catch the full tide of the London season that summer for a brilliant inauguration. Owen Jones's Courts were nearly finished, Digby Wyatt's were 'still very incomplete', and the 'illustrations of the different families of mankind' were also incomplete. The writer was particularly fascinated by the moment in the evening, often described, when the Crystal Palace, 'struck by the rays of the summer sun, warms up into a real "mountain of light"' – a reference to the Koh-i-Noor diamond shown at Hyde Park – turning at sunset into a ruddy glow.[119] By day the best view of the Palace, 'one vast arch of rainbow light', was said to be that from St Martin's Hill in Bromley. [120]

The following account of costs was presented to the shareholders in February 1854:

Land: 105,728, less resale of 55,488, = £50,240

Materials of original building: £95,000

Construction of main building: £135,050

Tunnel, heating apparatus: £24,536

Wings of Crystal Palace, Water Towers: £34,090

Hydraulic works, fountains, cascades, lakes, basins, artesian well, reservoirs &c.: £93,670

Park, terraces, gardens, walls, balustrades, decorations &c.: £98,214

Natural history illustrations, including geological islands, preparation of extinct animals, zoological and ethnological collections, raw produce, agriculture: £11,176

Fine Art Courts –Pompeian, Alhambra, Assyrian, Greek, Roman, Egyptian, Medieval, Renaissance, Italian; and Byzantine £52,500

Collection of sculpture, foreign and national, portrait gallery of busts, pedestals &c.: £32,000

Sundry fittings, boardings, gas fittings &c throughout the building: £7,000

General expenses, including engineering staff, superintendence, officers' salaries; law and parliamentary expenses, surveying, rent and taxes and misc…: £35,384.[121]

The main expenditure – for Paxton's waterworks – was still to come, and the additional sums they consumed were so colossal that before they were finished it was commonplace in the press to say that (including Brunel's monumental Water Towers built to replace the inadequate original pair) they cost as much as the whole Palace and its contents. Fuller reckoned that Paxton wasted an additional £250,000 on the hydraulic systems, against Scott Russell's advice.[122]

The workmen

The largest number of labourers ever employed at any one time in Sydenham was 6,400;[123] at Hyde Park the maximum, in December 1850, had been 2,260.[124] At noon between 2,000 to 3,000 hungry men, many of whom had arrived by the down train at 5 a.m., would pour out in search of a meal; Philip Delamotte photographed them eating outdoors both at 'Breakfast Time' and at dinner. Queen Victoria was startled on one of her visits to see at the sounding of the dinner bell 1,000 men descending ropes and sliding down the columns like firemen.[125] The skilled craftsmen for the Fine Arts Courts were mostly foreign, recognisable from their 'moustached lips and jaunty caps'; one smoked a meerschaum pipe while painting a Cupid, amid tubs of paint, great lumps of putty and crates of glass;[126] the Germans sang choruses and songs in four-part harmony. Several Delamotte photographs show bearded French and Italian workers plastering the Egyptian figures. When the Queen came to visit, the foreign workmen sang 'God Save the Queen', 'in first-rate style'.[127]

Another journalist's sketch describes them taking their dinners from paper and handkerchiefs inside the Palace with the English workmen, or from pots over braziers and grates.[128] Owen Jones and Digby Wyatt gave a dinner for their 200 French, Italian and English workmen at the Beulah Spa Hotel in December 1853, with banners of the nations, 'cordial greetings and hearty shaking of hands'.[129] For five shillings visitors could tour the works.[130]

The presence of so many labourers in the district led to some rough scenes, especially scuffles with recruiting officers for the Crimean War in the neighbourhood.[131] Paxton announced at a public dinner in his new constituency, Coventry, that he was

Philip Delamotte, 'Setting up the Colossi of Rameses the Great'.

organising 1,000 men who had worked at the Palace to join up as an 'Army Work Corps'.[132] In the Crimea they made roads from Balaclava to the camp, dug trenches and laid down a railway. (The venture was not judged a success; the navvies were unpopular with the military because they received higher pay, and were supposedly lazy and drunken. General Simpson wrote in a letter of resignation that they were a constant vexation to him and were 'by far the worst lot of men ever sent here'.[133])

The spiritual needs of the men at work on the Palace were attended to by the kind anonymous author (Catherine Marsh) of *English Hearts and English Hands, or the Railway and the Trenches*, of 1858. From this chronicle of the lady and her tea-parties, at which 'not an expression was used which we could have wished was otherwise', and of the little Testaments she gave the men which they carried to the Crimea, we have a vivid picture of their life: for some near-starvation before their pay day, the temptations of liquor, drunken fights with the police at Penge, and knifings among themselves. She feared for how they would spend the Sabbath evenings at Croydon.[134] The men came from the north of England, Cornwall, Scotland and Ireland; Catherine Marsh mentions 'some warm-hearted Irish Roman Catholics'.[135] She put the numbers of Paxton's Army Work Corps at 4,000, between the first ship on July 1855 and the last in December. Her open-air evangelising was done in the Palace grounds and her Bible readings were given in cottages. She admired the strength and skill of the men, many of whom showed 'high and delicate feeling'.[136]

Chambers's' Edinburgh Journal in November 1853 described the men at work in the Transept dwarfed by the vastness of the place; they can be seen in a contemporary wood-cut (presumably engraved from a Delamotte photograph), which shows preparations for the laying of pipes and foundations for the basins [p. 49].[137]

The interior

The imaginative vision of Paxton, Owen Jones and others ensured that the interior of the Sydenham Palace would appear altogether more wonderful than that at Hyde Park. The early planning, according to *The Times* of 26 June 1852, was for 'quadrangles', similar to the Fine Art and Medieval Courts at the Great Exhibition. The manners and costumes of different countries, such as India, were to be displayed, and a feature proposed at an early stage was 'a reproduction of one of the twelve courts of the Alhambra by Mr Jones'. Tropical plants were to be at one end of the building, and temperate ones at the other. In the Park a 'Victoria Fountain' was to throw up a jet 150 feet high. The scheme of the exhibits inside the Palace was educational, and would show a 'connexion and progression of all the different parts'; the details of the illustrated encyclopaedia were being planned. An early lithographed ground-plan, with annotations by the directors, now in the Guildhall Library,[138] shows basins with bridges, fountains and 'handsome circular cages filled with singing-birds',[139] split into quarters and arranged around the projecting columns of the Nave; these would house nightingales, paroquets and blackbirds.[140] This idea was abandoned, but there was to be a well-stocked aviary in the tropical department where the weaver-birds nested.[141]

Refreshment rooms are marked on the plan at this point to be in both the Alhambra and Pompeian courts, and there were booths for ices. 'We can eat Bath buns and study decorative architecture at the same time', said *Chambers's Edinburgh Journal*; at this date the Byzantine Court too was intended for refreshments.[142] Printed Fabrics, Flax and Hemp, Woollen Goods, Silks and Shawls and Lace are assigned Courts on the ground floor; in the galleries were the less glamorous categories of goods familiar from the Great Exhibition catalogues. The Fine Arts Courts are named as 'Flemish Renaissance'; Italian and 'Revived Classical'; Medieval, Byzantine, Romanesque and Norman. On the plan for the Nave are marked two features that were never carried out: two genuine antiquities in the form of 'Greek column' and 'Egyptian Obelisk'. The latter was 'Cleopatra's Needle', which Jones proposed to the directors to take from the desert and ship at Luxor; the Company at one time was negotiating this transaction with Lord Derby. George Grove wrote in his pamphlet *The Crystal Palace and Park in 1853: what has been done – what will be done* that the obelisk will be 'the gem of the collection'.[143] Samuel Leigh Sotheby (1806–61), an influential major Crystal Palace shareholder and pamphleteer, as well as being a book auctioneer and writer on the fine arts, did not think much of this idea: the obelisk was 'broken and ill used'.[144] It eventually arrived in London in 1878 to find a permanent home on the Thames Embankment. In 1856 the Company paid for the carriage of an Assyrian sculptural slab to be sent by Colonel Henry Rawlinson from Baghdad. However, James Fergusson, as general manager,

'Present state of the Interior of the Crystal Palace', November 1853.

The Nave, *c.* 1860.

later wrote to Rawlinson that there were no funds to put up these marbles, and they were sold by the Company to the government of Prussia.[145] A large painting by Henry Phillips showing Paxton explaining his plan for the Crystal Palace to Prince Albert was hung in the north wing, near to the Royal Apartments at the north-west corner of the Palace.[146] Paxton put on view drawings and models of elaborate fountains for the Palace by Owen Jones, Digby Wyatt, John Bell, Marochetti and John Thomas,[147] but lack of funds prevented them from being executed.[148] Only Osler's Crystal Fountain and Monti's 'very beautiful and artistic' bronze fountain at the tropical end[149] were installed. Raffaelle Monti went bankrupt before he could fulfil his commissions for the outdoor fountains, Paxton reported, losing the Company much money.[150] A Crystal Palace programme from 1855 says that the interior fountains would play at 2.30 p.m.

The ill consequences of combining museum displays with the atmosphere of a winter garden had not been given sufficient consideration, as became apparent by the end of the year. John Edward Gray, Keeper of Zoology at the British Museum (1840–74), wrote to Samuel Leigh Sotheby of the ludicrously 'incongruous mixture' of plants, stuffed animals and plaster casts in the same building. It was obvious, he said, that plants need moisture and plaster casts need dry conditions. Moths would attack the stuffed animals and green insects would live on the plaster casts. Grey ridiculed the stuffed lion amid potted plants a few inches high that pretended to show a natural habitat. He liked the Alhambra Court, but detested Waterhouse Hawkins's models of the Extinct Animals.[151] The Assyrian Court was seldom visited, he said, except as a quiet place for the visitors to eat their provisions. He was not alone in thinking it a mistake to place the hot-house plants so near to the Architectural Courts,[152] however wonderful they looked in the photographs. In 1859 a glass screen was placed between the tropical and temperate zones, running across the Nave from the Roman to the Medieval Courts.[153] At one point they thought of a painting to replace 'the ugly bed-tick' curtain that enclosed the Tropical End. In 1859 David Roberts sketched out for the Company an enormous allegorical painting for the Tropical Department, to be painted by Mr Dawson.[154]

Colour

Owen Jones produced a colour scheme for the interior quite contrary to the assertions he made against his critics at Hyde Park – most probably the Prince himself, as has been seen in Chapter 1 – who urged him to paint the iron columns a uniform red rather than his striated blue and yellow scheme. Jones had had one column at Hyde Park painted red to prove his point, and to show that it was 'in direct violation of the principles which I had laid down as the basis of my operations'.[155] This change is puzzling: since the columns were again of octagonal section they could have had Jones's striped parti-coloured scheme applied to them. To apply red now was to use the strongest of his 'primaries of prismatic intensity'.[156] This use of a richer and warmer colour than the preponderant blue at Hyde Park was liked by *The Times* and by *Chambers's Edinburgh Journal*.[157] *The Builder* found the red pillars combined with the foliage, 'very agreeable; the eye wanders on refreshed and invigorated.'[158] The *Crystal Palace Herald* said that at Hyde Park the use of red on the upper lines of the building was thought 'too terrible'

Osler's Crystal Fountain and the Nave, *c.* 1854. Stereopticon photo.

until the whole effect was seen. At Sydenham Jones was said to have now abandoned timidity and moderation, and the red columns to 'obstruct the eye' interestingly.[159] The effect of the paler columns at Hyde Park had been to improve the long perspective while the richer red was said to suggest the idea of enclosures within the vast space.[160] The framework of the roof was once again painted blue and white, as were the girders.

The nude statuary

Owen Jones and Digby Wyatt had been sent to the continent by the Crystal Palace Company in August 1852, shortly after the first column was erected, with a budget of £20,000 to commission plaster casts for the comprehensive gallery of sculpture. Before the opening the statuary caused a serio-comic hitch. On 8 May 1854, a month before the opening of the Palace by the Queen, the following letter appeared in *The Times*, signed by the Archbishop of Canterbury, the Bishops of London, St Asaph, Winchester, Lichfield, Salisbury, and a group of peers including the philanthropist Lord Shaftesbury. They claimed that they could add signatures 'almost to any extent':

> We, the undersigned, desire the directors to accept our assurance that we address them in no unfriendly spirit regarding the present condition of the nude male statues of the human form prepared for exhibition in the palace.
>
> We are persuaded that the exhibition, to promiscuous crowds of men and women, of nude statues of men in the state there represented must, if generally submitted to, prove very destructive to that natural modesty which is one of the outworks of virtue, and which a great French writer has called 'one of the barriers which Nature herself has placed in the way of crime'.
>
> We firmly believe, however, that large numbers of the men and women of England need only to be put upon their guard by a public raising of the question to keep aloof from the Palace rather than witness and sanction this innovation. It did not prevail in the Hyde Park Crystal Palace, nor will it, it is hoped, hold its ground long in any public institution. But the scale on which the whole Sydenham preparations are carried out, though not theoretically affecting the question, will in reality do much to concentrate public opinion upon it. Once awakened to the subject and its importance, will not tens of thousands assert their disapproval by the absence of themselves and their families?
>
> We, the undersigned, have grounds for declaring that a strong feeling is rising on the subject, and that, unless this slight concession is made, the matter will be so resolutely brought before the public in London, and in other parts of the kingdom that every one will be driven to form a decided judgment on the point; and it is our fixed expectation that such an agitation will prove very damaging to the interests of the company.
>
> We would also press the question upon the directors on other grounds also. It seems to us not surprising that this custom prevailed in the heathen cities of Greece and Rome, knowing what we know of the habits of life which resulted from their religion; but we protest against the adoption of this usage in Christian and Protestant England, where the pure Apostolic faith ought, we conceive, to be free from such a reproach.
>
> We, the undersigned, only add that we should deeply regret to see the fire of public remonstrance opened in full force against the magnificent undertaking of the committee, which we are fain to regard as a national glory. We demand but a small thing, not at all a sacrifice in point of artistic beauty – viz. the removal of the parts which in 'the life' ought to be concealed, although we are also desirous that the usual leaf may be adopted.

The Times specifically reported Owen Jones's 'horror' when the Directors agreed to the proposal; according to the *Illustrated Crystal Palace Gazette*, they had already decided to do this before the petition.[161] There was not enough 'plaster foliage' to be found in time: 'So extensive an order for the earliest fashions of Paradise was never before issued, and was therefore not so easy of execution.'[162] A letter to *The Atlas* complained about the humbug of the letter in *The Times* and the 'cant of superior modesty'.[163] This was the second occasion when Owen Jones had provoked philistine Evangelical Puritanism. It seems that he managed to prevaricate, for by December there were still nude statues without fig-leaves, and they were in Jones's Greek and Roman Courts. A solemn count was made of fifty adult nudes still without 'the usual leaf' and twenty more of the 'near-adult'.[164] *Punch* published a spoof letter from George Grove suggesting that second-hand underwear should be sent to the Palace.[165]

The inauguration

Before the royal inauguration of the Palace, the Queen and Prince Albert visited the site several times. In June 1853 they made a tour with Paxton and Jones,[166] and in November stayed for three hours. Albert 'conducted the Princess of Brabant to the highest point, above the fifth gallery'; they saw the drawings and models for fountains, and Mr Fergusson 'explained' his plans for the Assyrian Court. In the Park they saw the shed where Waterhouse Hawkins was modelling the Extinct Animals, taking a specially laid path of faggots and gravel among the mire.[167]

The Times was careful to rationalise the difference between the commercial venture and the grand State Occasion which the inaugural ceremony had become: 'Though a private enterprise in one sense, in another it aspires to be, and is recognised as, national.'[168] The presence of the Archbishop of Canterbury saying prayers for a commercial enterprise was thought to be humbug; Charles Dickens wrote in a private letter about these 'monstrous pretences' of the Palace, and was tickled by a clever article sent to him to publish in *Household Words* pointing out that Madame Tussaud's in Baker Street never had the Archbishop to say prayers for it.[169]

The opening of the Palace on 10 June 1854 by the Queen, accompanied by Prince Albert, the royal children and the King of Portugal, closely followed the formula from 1851, although there were attempts to outdo it. Given that the Queen had written in her diary that the 1851 inauguration was 'a thousand times superior' to her Coronation,[170] this was a considerable challenge. According to the *Illustrated London News*, the character of the opening signalled that after all the doubts and fears Paxton's second Palace was a greater success than the first. Surrounding the royal party there were fair faces and pretty bonnets, 'the élite of the aristocracy', ambassadors, clergy and government ministers; Paxton himself undertook the placing of the most important visitors. The galleries glowed with crimson cloth, and a chorus of 1,800 singers sang the Hundredth Psalm and the *Halleluiah Chorus*. The soprano Clara Novello rendered 'God Save the Queen'. Palmerston wrote afterwards to the Directors that the Queen had taken special pleasure in the music; it was 'the finest effect that her Majesty had ever heard'.[171] Richard Redgrave, R.A., wrote in his diary that when Miss Novello sang her solo with her 'sweet, clear, full voice' he had to make a strong effort to control his sobs.[172] Albert wore his Field Marshal's uniform and Victoria a blue glacé silk dress and a white lace bonnet trimmed with roses. Samuel Laing in a long speech declared himself proud of the Palace as 'the fitting ornament of the greatest metropolis of the civilized world, an unrivalled school of art and instrument of education'; it was already a monument. He placed particular emphasis on 'the complete historical illustration of the arts of sculpture and architecture from the earliest works of Egypt and Assyria down to the modern times'; he

thanked the museums abroad for their help in providing casts. The past, particularly the Courts showing the 'buried empires', would lead us to 'the portals of the temple of knowledge'.[173]

Henry Cole was also present, the main mover at the South Kensington Museum, which had been directly endowed from the profits of the Exhibition and professed to improve public taste and knowledge of art. He disapproved of the commercial foundations of the Palace and, no doubt, of its showmanship. He described the occasion in his diary as 'a fair second Edition of 51 but no equal to it except the music wh: was heard better: much unfinished and no fountains'. Cole had reason to disparage Sydenham; he wrote in his Diary for 2 June 1852: 'O. Jones called & said the CP wd beat us in the end.'[174]

At the ceremony the directors of the Courts and the other authors presented their handbooks to the Queen. Digby Wyatt behaved with 'true courtly bearing and self-possessed demeanour', but Owen Jones's clumsiness provoked mirth: 'learned and distinguished authors and artists turned their backs upon her Majesty, or awkwardly descended the steps of the dais in bodily fear of swords which dangled inconveniently, and threatened to invert the polychromatic heels of at least one distinguished artist.'[175] The *Evening Standard* said that Mr Owen Jones 'was as cool and ferocious looking, in his solemn black beard, as one of the Nineveh bulls', and that when he took his eight or ten steps backwards the Queen tried to frown to stop laughing.[176]

Dickens was one of the many famous people who attended; he thought that the Palace was 'very remarkable in itself', but that the scheme was 'the most gigantic Humbug ever mounted on a long-suffering people's shoulders'.[177]

The 'illustrated encyclopaedia'

The statements of both the Company and the press about the concept of the new Palace and its visitors make frequent use of didactic terms: not just 'instruct' but 'aspire', 'raise', 'elevate', 'expand'. An 'illustrated encyclopaedia' that would 'combine scientific accuracy with popular effect' was the intention;[178] the Palace and Park would create 'a perfect Cosmos – a brilliant illustration of all that is noble and elevating in the world'. Jones's theories had become the official policy. We are told that visitors 'will be taught through the medium of the eye to receive impressions kindling a desire for knowledge, and

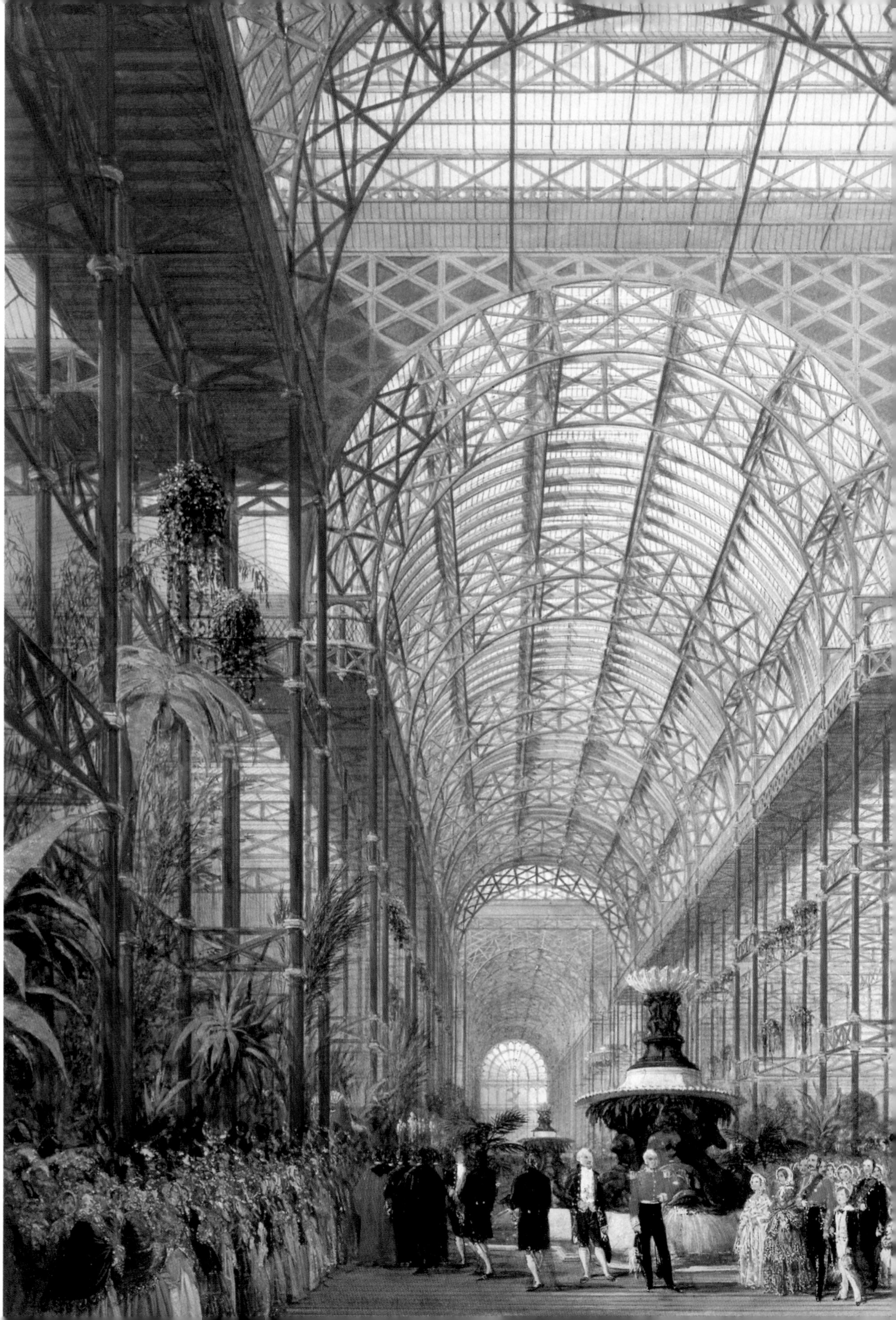

Joseph Nash, *Opening of the Crystal Palace, Sydenham, by Queen Victoria, June 10th., 1854*. Private Collection.

awakening instincts of the beautiful'.[179] These displays would teach much better than 'ponderous tomes'.[180] Waterhouse Hawkins, in a lecture given in May 1854 at the Society of Arts, named the educational theorist who encouraged intellectual awakening 'through the eye' as the Swissteacher, J. H. Pestalozzi (1746–1827).[181] A liberal spirit of modern science would prevail, free from the commercial jealousies and international prejudices of the great Exhibition.[182] The opinion of *The Builder* was that the Palace 'may be made the most powerful educational institution in the world'.[183] The layout was intended to resemble 'a well arranged book', in which one might 'proceed from subject to subject at one's discretion', unlike a labyrinth.[184] William Michael Rossetti wrote that while the British Museum was a better mistress in Egyptian and Greek art, 'she takes a longer time in giving her curriculum' than Sydenham; he praised the 'linked chain of sequence and divergence whose significance it is difficult to miss altogether'.[185]

The Palace displays and personnel were to play a part in the wider history of London museums and the display of architecture, sculpture and natural history. After the 1914–18 War the Crystal Palace became the original home of the Imperial War Museum: it was inaugurated in 1920 and remained there, housed on a large scale, for four years. The Palace had a National Portrait Gallery (being so called at the time),[186] consisting of 130 casts of busts of British worthies, which formed a section of the Portrait Gallery along the aisle on the garden side of the south Nave. The latter contained 499 heads including notable classical and continental figures and some living people, with a biographical handbook. George Scharf (1820–95), a talented artist and writer who was to become the first Secretary of the actual National Portrait

A VISIT TO THE ANTEDILUVIAN REPTILES AT SYDENHAM—MASTER TOM STRONGLY OBJECTS TO HAVING HIS MIND IMPROVED.

John Leech, from *Punch's Amanack for 1855*.

Gallery in 1857, wrote the handbooks for the Greek, Roman and Pompeian Courts at Sydenham and painted frescoes for them. Joseph Bonomi (1796–1878), who carved and moulded sculpture and casts for the Egyptian Court at Sydenham and advised on Egyptian culture, became the second curator of Sir John Soane's Museum in Lincoln's Inn Fields (1861–78).

Ruskin – although full of melancholy and despondency at the time of the opening of the Crystal Palace – wrote a pamphlet for the occasion recognising that there was real 'hope of knowledge, contemplation, instruction, and enjoyment', and that 'it is impossible to estimate the influence of such an institution on the minds of the working-classes' pursuits, health, intellects roused into activity within the crystal walls.'[187] The *Art Journal* said that visitors in August with guidebooks in hand gave the impression that 'a great work of education is indeed going on.'[188]

At Hyde Park there had been two lecture halls inside the building, and for Sydenham Paxton had promised lecture rooms as well as a museum.[189] Occasional lectures were given at the Palace, several of them by Digby Wyatt. From 1859 instruction by lectures and in classes with a wide syllabus was offered at 'the Crystal Palace School of Art, Music, Science and Literature'; dancing and deportment were also on the syllabus. The School of Art had commodious studios in the South Wing, and many of the Palace's collection of plaster casts of statuary were taken there to assist drawing classes. Up to 400 students took advantage of the cultural advantages of the collections.

In October 1854 the *Art Journal* said that 'a narrow spirit of gain' was 'degrading' the educational work[190] – within a week of the Palace opening seven hundred muslin dresses had been sold[191] – but by 1908 the high cultural aims of the founders would seem definitely to have been eclipsed. *The Times* wrote that the value of the art and the architecture collection had been 'overshadowed by the reputation of the Palace as a resort for fireworks, football and other avocations'.[192] It was recognised as inevitable that many visitors would altogether fail to respond to the educational stimulus on offer, like the crying schoolboy hand in hand with his portly father, pictured walking among the Extinct Animals in Leech's cartoon, 'A Visit to the Antediluvian Reptiles at Sydenham. Master Tom strongly objects to having his Mind Improved'.[193] The *Crystal Palace Herald* observed that 'on every side you will hear the popular voices exclaim, "It's all very pretty, and must have cost a sight of money, and we should like it very well if we could understand it."'[194] The Fine Art Courts were passed by the great mass of people in the Nave 'without exciting any particular interest'.[195]

Observers resented the commercial enterprises and made fun of the absurd contrasts in the Palace resulting from the combination of a shop with a museum on such a large scale: at Christmas in 1855 'the most trumpery exhibitors' pitched their stands for ten shillings in the Nave 'as a sort of counterpoise to the high art lessons taught by everything around'.[196] At this 'disgraceful' bazaar, *The Times* complained, one could buy quack medicines and fancy corsetry, such as 'resilient bodices' and 'corsatelloes de Medici'.[197] Ribbons and gloves on circular counters were close up against the Fine Arts Courts.[198] There was a studio for portrait photographs[199] and a Tourists' Court selling 'tickets to all parts of the World'.[200] By 1902 the 'Crystal Palace Arcade', containing shops with fancy articles including 'New Hairdressing Salons' and an American Toilet Club, filled one-eighth of a mile.[201]

The proper 'commercial departments', as distinct from the stalls and shops, had become a bitter failure at an early stage. The Company stated that newly-married couples would wish to furnish their houses from the commercial courts,[202] and that everyone would want to come out to Sydenham to choose a piano from the displays of the leading manufacturers, where a Collard and a Broadwood piano could be tried side by side, thus making visits to several London showrooms unnecessary. However, this opportunity to display merchandise was not taken up significantly.[203] A note of desperation is apparent in the Company's advertisements, with free space being offered to those bringing back goods 'of higher class' from the great Exposition in Paris in 1855.[204] The salesmen in the galleries were either perishing with cold or scorchingly hot; rain falling on the roof leaked on to their displays.[205] By the time that Arundel Society prints were advertised for sale in the New Court in April 1856, the Palace was so notorious for cold that the advertisement included a note that the Court was 'warmed with stoves'.[206] In July 1855 the small shops in the Bazaar were fully rented out, but the major Industrial Courts in the Nave were almost entirely untenanted. Paxton had resigned as manager of the Industrial Department, and the directors conceded to a shareholders' resolution that 'as an exhibition of British industrial productions the Crystal Palace has entirely failed.'[207] The forecast of annual revenue had been £60,000 to £135,000, but as Sotheby reported to shareholders in his pamphlet of August 1855, only £5,000 had been received.[208] However, in 1862 the receipts from rentals had risen to £14,000.[209]

Sunday admission and the sale of alcohol

While Owen Jones was the object of puritanical attacks on his colouring and on the naked male statues, the Company was assailed on two points by fierce public campaigns – against Sunday opening and against the sale of alcohol, both of which would considerably affect its revenue. Saturday was the favoured day for the aristocracy to visit the Palace, but large numbers of working-class visitors with cheaper tickets on a Sunday would help the Company, already in difficulties. On Saturdays admission cost five shillings, and on Fridays half-a-crown; the shilling days were Monday to Thursday. A year's season ticket cost two guineas.[210]

Both the issues – Sunday opening and the sale of alcohol – set off a war of pamphlets and public meetings. The Rev. Barton Bouchier, in a penny pamphlet titled *The*

Poor Man's Palace and the Poor Man's Day, 1854, argued rather too plausibly that it was money the Company had in mind, and that it had influential friends. The working classes were kept away on Saturdays by the high price of tickets, and of the four million supposed to constitute that class, two million were compelled to work on the Sabbath, while they could attend on a Saturday. The Palace contained in its own Architectural Courts warnings of pagan civilisations punished for sin: Egypt, Assyria and Pompeii had polluted their holy days.[211] Laing had told the shareholders that initially Saturdays were to be only five-shilling and season-ticket days, but that they might be changed in time to shilling days.

Meanwhile very few working-class visitors were to be seen in the first month.[212] Although a government select committee in 1852 reported in favour of the proposal to open the Palace and grounds to the people on Sunday afternoons, the government lawyers then discovered a Bill of George III that prohibited paid entry to places of amusement on Sundays. The shareholders resolved at a meeting on 2 July 1858 to ask the directors to open the Palace to themselves,[213] but the Attorney-General and the Solicitor-General warned against it. On Sundays the parks and interiors at Hampton Court Palace and Windsor Castle were open, as Kew Gardens had been since 1841, while the British Museum and National Gallery remained closed. Some British people took pride in the fact that the Great Exhibition was never open on a Sunday. Francis Fuller observed at a meeting in August 1855 that on one Sunday at that time '250,000 took excursion tickets on the railway, but most went to pubs or places not quite so innocent.'[214] Fuller wrote to Sotheby on 22 November 1853 that clergy could not subscribe to licensing public houses to do business on Sundays, and yet oppose Sunday opening at Sydenham.[215] *The Times* and *Punch* supported the Company's plans to open on Sunday.[216] A satirical lithograph, *Sunday Afternoon in the Gardens of the Palace of the People in 1853 – as objected to,* shows contented working people, looking remarkably middle-class and well-conducted, strolling on the terraces in front of the Palace.[217] The *Morning Herald* in a leading article tried to terrify its readers with the possible consequences: here was 'an introduction to that continental view of the Sabbath... The mischief began with

'Sunday Afternoon in the Gardens of the Palace of the People in 1853 – as objected to'.

Popery'. With 'park, ball or theatre after Mass on Sunday morning', it was no wonder there were revolutions in Paris, Munich and Berlin in 1848.[218] *The Times* reported in February 1856 that between 100 and 150 gentlemen, including W.E. Gladstone, called on Lord Palmerston, the Prime Minister, to protest against plans to open the Palace on Sundays. The Archbishop of Canterbury 'spoke with evident emotion'. A plumber and a coal-heaver were introduced who spoke against the idea.[219] On the other side Lord Derby said in the House of Lords that the proposal to open the Palace in the afternoons was reasonable; far from being a desecration of the Sabbath, 'it would promote morality.' He understood from the Company that only the Park, garden and conservatory would be involved – this was perhaps disingenuous, since the Company could then presumably say that 'conservatory' referred to a winter garden, which was the Palace itself. Lord Derby had support from Lord Campbell and others. Henry Mayhew, author of *London Labour and the London Poor*, made a speech in favour of Sunday opening on 30 February 1853.[220] *The Times* wrote that it would be stupid and inhuman to suggest that the people should spend Sunday 'in their own dark and dismal hole, breathing the reeking atmosphere of close courts and yards'.[221] A letter, placed as an advertisement, warned of the dangers to 'giddy and unguarded youth' of self-display and finery on show on the Sabbath. The *London Journal* warned of the 'scamps in garb of gentlemen' and the 'unseemly pursuit of young women by idlers' that would result.[222] Certainly not much later in its career the Park was thought to be a place where unaccompanied ladies should not attend 'without the risk of insult'. Meanwhile *The Times* considered that such bigotry should not overrule the health and moral welfare of the people.[223] The idea of the nude statuary, which *The Times* admitted was 'on the whole of a sadly Pagan character', being visible on a holy day fanned the protests.[224] By a legal subterfuge the Palace and Park were eventually opened on Sundays, but not till 1860.[225] On one Sunday in May 1861 there were 40,000 visitors.

The most celebrated opponent of the sale of alcohol at the Palace was the illustrator and cartoonist George Cruikshank. In *The Glass and the New Crystal Palace* (1853) he wrote that he received strong assurances from George Grove that the Palace would never allow the sale of alcohol 'at any time or in any circumstances', and reminded the Archbishop of Canterbury that on a

Sunday within a few paces of his own garden he may see 'drunken, youthful and mature debauchery' fuelled by liquor.[226] The Crystal Palace Company applied for a licence to sell liquor without asking the shareholders, petitioning the Queen in Council in February 1855. The licence was granted, reneging on the original Charter.[227] *Cassell's Illustrated Family Paper* regarded this as a shocking breach of faith and asserted that, combined with Sunday opening, it would degrade the Palace to the level of the Vauxhall and Cremorne gardens in the previous century.[228]

Food

Leech drew a cartoon for Punch, 'Some Varieties of the Human Race', in which civilised ladies at slate-topped tables nonchalantly eat ice-creams next to the wooden anthropological figures brandishing assegais.[229] This was no less than the truth, since 'Refreshment Tables' were indeed placed 'among the surrounding inhabitants of Africa and America'.[230] When visitors arrived from the lower railway station and entered the Palace by way of the Refreshment Department, their first impressions

CRYSTAL PALACE—SOME VARIETIES OF THE HUMAN RACE.

John Leech, from *Punch's Amanack for 1855*.

were 'a roast fowl; then a beautiful screen of the kings and queens of England; then a white-cravatted waiter; then a brown-skinned bare-legged Sandwich islander; then a lobster-salad; then a palm-tree from the tropics; then a small bottle of pale ale; then a tiger climbing up a tree, then a plate of ham.'[231] In the Dining Room in the South Wing one could eat lobster salad, cold fowl, *roulade de veau* or *carbonnade de mouton* for two shillings; in addition there were jellies, ginger beer and lemonade.[232] In the second-class refreshment room beef with bread was available for sixpence.[233] A third-class refreshment room under the stairs had a filthy floor[234] and dirty plates; refuse and half-empty pots of porter met the eye.[235] Eating and drinking inside the Palace annoyed serious visitors; for the *Art Journal* it was 'repulsive' – 'the merely animal propensities of the English' should be kept in the wings.[236]

Sotheby was offended on arrival by the 'perfumes' in the Tropical Department 'as if from the adjacent closets', and by the 'obtrusive clatter of pots and plates'.[237] He maintained that the Company had at first wanted no more space for catering than at Hyde Park – small portions of the Pompeian and Alhambra Courts were thought sufficient, with a few corners for ices – but demand forced them to install tables in front of the Screen of British Kings and Queens, and £26,000 was spent fitting up the kitchens for their licensee, Walter Staples.[238]

The enormous profits expected by the Company never materialised,[239] and further losses were suffered as the result of litigation and contracts with licensees. Getting rid of the refreshment directors cost £16,000, as reported in 1874.[240] In 1910 the Company's losses from this litigation were estimated to have been as high as £24,000.

Transport

The rich visited the Palace by horse and carriage, and their needs were catered for by stabling for 300 horses on Westow Hill. Many years later a local man recalled the heyday of the Palace and Park in the late 1860s, when they were kept in beautiful order and the concerts, flower-shows and fireworks were at the height of their popularity: the road would be full of carriages, with their postilions wearing white beaver hats, on their way to a Handel Festival.[241] The journey from Paddington in a horse-drawn omnibus took an hour and a quarter. Other

services left from Fleet Street, Oxford Street and Gracechurch Street in the City; south of the river special omnibuses left Clapham and Rye Lane, Peckham, every ten minutes. However, most visitors came by train. An additional railway line had been built from London Bridge station (return tickets cost 1s. 6d); another purpose-built line (closed in 1915) brought working-class visitors from Greenwich. Until the High Level Station connecting the Palace with Ludgate Hill and Farringdon Road (and thence King's Cross) was opened in 1865, travel to the Palace by rail was much criticised for long waits, extreme slowness and too many stops. The poor arrived in cattle-trucks, while the first-class passengers were made as comfortable as possible.[242] The fatiguing ascent by so many steps up through the 700 feet long iron and glass colonnade to the Palace from the Lower Level Station to the South Wing caused constant complaint. Reaching the Centre Transept on foot from the railway took ten to fifteen minutes.

The Horticultural Fêtes

Paxton's Horticultural Fêtes, organised by Paxton himself and by George Eyles, were the main events held in the Palace in the early years. In June 1855 Prince Albert arrived on horseback and, according to *The Observer*, the occasion was one of 'matchless magnificence', for life, light, motion, colour and sound.[243] Those that followed in May, June and September 1856, with 190 exhibitors competing for £800 worth of prizes, were said to be 'a perfect success', with the 'brilliant company' of the beau monde[244] and bands playing. An engraving of the Fête of June 1855 published in the *Illustrated London News* clearly shows the interior of the Palace in its fashionable heyday.[245] A pamphlet announcing the 1856 event promises a display of pitcher plants, and invites the 'artistic' arrangement of fruits.[246] From July 1860 there was an annual Rose Show.

Visit of Napoleon III

The visit of the popular French Emperor Napoleon III and Empress Eugénie, accompanied by Victoria and Albert, on 20 April 1855, the Emperor's birthday, set a pattern for the use of the Palace for state and national occasions. Paxton's first and least ambitious series of fountains on the upper terraces, the 'Upper Fountains', played for the first time, and when the Emperor saw the Park, with 20,000 well-dressed people on the Terrace cheering, he exclaimed 'What a place for a fête!' An elegant saloon, decorated by J.G. Crace 'in the Italian style' with panels of green silk and arabesques, was used for luncheon[247] – it was one in a suite of three rooms called the Queen's Apartments, at the entrance to the Palace from the North Wing. Retiring rooms and a drawing-room for the Queen and Prince had been provided at Hyde Park, and this new suite at Sydenham was presumably a signal that the Crystal Palace Company hoped the Royal Family would frequently be seen there. The whole length of the Nave inside the Palace was garnished with red cloth and floral flourishes; gold and silver fish swam in the marble basins of the Pompeian Court. Mr Jones 'explained' his Courts to the royal party; the Alhambra Court, where the Spanish-born Empress Eugénie spent longer than elsewhere, was almost completed.[248] The Emperor, 'much occupied with preparations for the great Paris Exposition', was fascinated by the Palace,[249] which Paxton and Samuel Laing had already described to him in Paris the previous year.[250] On that famous day the Company made a profit of around £10,000 from the sale of guinea admission tickets to those who were not shareholders or season-ticket holders.[251]

The Society of Arts

The Society of Arts, Manufactures and Commerce, the 'parent society' of the Crystal Palace, held its anniversary dinner at Sydenham with 750 guests on 1 July 1854. The speeches consisted of mutual congratulation and hopes and plans for education. Among the diners at the 'Art' table were Henry Cole, Charles Barry, David Roberts, Charles Eastlake, Owen Jones, Digby Wyatt and Roger Fenton. John Rennie, Charles Fox and Robert Stephenson were among the engineers and Matthew Arnold sat among the elite of the educational establishment.[252]

The Crimean War

The Crimean War and the opening of the Palace coincided. Laing said defiantly to the shareholders in February 1854 that although the public mind was on the contest by the Black Sea, he expected the venture of the Crystal Palace to be a great success,[253] but in July the same year he mentioned public preoccupation with the war to them again, and ruefully conceded that this had been a setback.[254] However, the directors created a focus for popular feelings about the War by special displays and ceremonies. In December 1854 a gun and mortar

taken by Captain Giffard, R.N., from the Russian fort of Bomarsund in the Gulf of Bothnia, where the war ended, were put on display,[255] and by September 1855 the Stationery Court had become the Crimean Court, with a model of Sebastopol showing James Fergusson's impregnable artillery defence system of ramparts that was compared to the works of Vauban.[256] Arms, clothing and many captured articles were shown. On 9 May 1856, after the declaration of victory, the Scutari Monument, a facsimile in imitation granite of the actual memorial at Scutari designed by Baron Marochetti, was unveiled in the South Nave by the Queen. The *Art Journal* grumbled that he had been paid too much, and that the memorial was 'a slur upon the Crimean War, and an insult to Art', which 'wants a British sculptor'.[257] The Peace Trophy erected at the same time to the north side from a design by G. Stacy, the storekeeper at the Tower of London, was thought inadequate: its 'female figure with arms outstretched', clad in gold and silver tissues and proffering a real olive branch, was standing 'on the ugliest pedestal'. *The Builder* wrote: 'It would do discredit to a third-rate confectioner.'[258] The Queen was not impressed with the occasion, complaining in her diary about the music, coarse decoration and the 'blundering' in the management and timing of the ceremony.[259] Five or six hundred men who had fought in the war paraded inside the Palace and were cheered; the bands played pieces from *Il Trovatore*, *Semiramide* and *The Magic Flute*, Verdi's *Miserere* and the slow movement of Beethoven's Eroica Symphony.[260] A pattern was being set for 'ceremonial of a national character'.[261]

Visitors

In its first year the Palace received 1,322,000 visitors, including 71,000 children.[262] The Tower of London, Hampton Court, Kew Gardens, the British Museum, the National Gallery, the Museum of Practical Geology and the art exhibitions at Marlborough House attracted no more than two million in the same period (five of these did not charged for admission).[263] From the opening of the Palace in June 1854 to the end of 1886 there were nearly 60 million visitors. At the Foresters' Fête in 1862 alone 84,955 were counted, and at a Patriotic Fund Fête for the benefit of widows and orphans of Crimean War dead, and wounded soldiers, 90,000 paid for their entry. Paxton and one or two directors were said to have stood beside the turnstiles taking half-crowns in their hats.[264]

The Crystal Palace Company

Laing claimed at the raising of the First Column: 'We are but acting as the instruments of that beneficent and over-ruling Providence which is guiding our great British race along the paths of peaceful progress.'[265] However, behind the theatricality of the ceremonies, the fashionable visitors, the groomed terraces with their statuary and tazzas, and the protested aims of social and educational improvement of the nation,[266] the difficulties of the Company and the shareholders were real and bitter. An early drawback, admitted by Laing, was the Paris Exposition of 1855, which distracted the attention of ambitious exhibitors and investors away from Sydenham's potential as successor to the Great Exhibition. Laing's speech of resignation on 8 February 1855, reported in the *Morning Post*, gives the impression of the captain leaving a sinking ship: having been defeated by the war, the high costs of provisions, the state of the money market, the depression of trade (which 'never entered into their ideas at the start'), and now outbreaks of cholera. The people were 'almost totally absorbed by war'.[267] Other sources gave the 'extortionate' railways as a reason for the disappointingly low number of visitors.[268]

The projections made before the opening of the Palace for annual income of £10,000 from refreshments and £145,000 from exhibitors[269] were now revealed to have been absurdly over-optimistic; from the sublime to the ridiculous, as Sotheby commented on the £5,000 received from exhibitors in the first year.[270] An editorial in the *Crystal Palace Herald* of April 1856 said that the Palace was now revealed in its true light as a commercial speculation, 'no more the people's than any of the London exhibitions', and that it should 'bid high for the people's shilling'.[271] Thomas Hughes (1822–96), the author of *Tom Brown's Schooldays* and now an M.P., became Chairman after the disastrous fire in 1866. In 1874 a shareholder, Mr Eames, in the course of an acrimonious four-hour shareholders' meeting with Hughes in the chair discussing the Company's extravagance, said that 'high art' was the affair of the nation and not of the Company; another shareholder said that there was no point in duplicating the cultural displays at South Kensington, which had now overtaken Sydenham with 'immense advantages', and that the Palace should be sold.[272] Undoubtedly Paxton's schemes, brilliant but megalomaniac and irresponsible, over-reached the resources of the Company, even after the capital had

been increased by a further £250,000.[273] The major cause of the impending financial disaster was Paxton's waterworks, which he had assured the shareholders would surpass all the other attractions at the Palace.[274] At the meeting of the Company in September 1855 after Laing's resignation as chairman and Fuller's departure, Paxton was reported as saying that 'he felt he should wind up with the past, and no longer stand responsible for the outlay of large sums of money in the expenditure of which he was no longer concerned (hear, hear).'[275] Fuller, who held 12,000 shares in the Company,[276] resigned in May 1855. The reason given was a difference of opinion with the board over a scheme of his to reduce the Company's capital by converting shares into life-tickets, expressed in a pamphlet of August 1855,[277] but his real reason was Paxton's 'imprudent speculations'. Shareholders' meetings at this time were interrupted by 'violent clamour and vulgar abuse'.[278] Fuller and Scott Russell had 'strenuously resisted' the waterworks and Brunel's Towers.[279] Shares in the Company dropped in value from £130 to £50 shortly after Fuller's resignation.[280] The Palace, said *The Builder* in November 1856, was grossly mismanaged.[281] Damaging suggestions were made in the *Daily News* of loans to Johnston, Farquhar and Leach from the Company's funds, and of a 'false entry' in the accounts.[282] Relatively easy retrenchments were made: the Company's office in Paris was closed, and its London office moved from Adelaide Place near Charing Cross into the Palace itself.[283] In 1858, for the first time, the shares paid a dividend of 2.5 %, and in this year the Handel Festival was a great success, notably among the wealthier classes, and made a profit of almost £9,000.[284] In 1862, the Company's best year, preference shares paid 7% and ordinary shares 3%.[285]

In November 1874 Scott Russell wrote a report on the dilapidated condition of the Palace, and criticised the Company for its ruinous neglect since the fire of 1866. He said that by neglecting to spend £100 in repairs to the Cascades when they had first begun to deteriorate they had landed themselves with an expenditure of £11,000 now, and that the under part of the Palace was 'like the disgraceful cellar to a warehouse'.[286] The machinery for the upper fountains had been sold – yet the Company still boasted that the waterworks 'rivalled Versailles'.[287] Russell blamed the poor management of the last ten years for lowering the Palace's tone by attracting 'uneducated and unrefined' visitors with 'amusements'.[288]

Opposite: John Tenniel, *Inauguration of the Scutari Monument and the Peace Trophy at the Crystal Palace, Sydenham, 9 May 1856.* Watercolour. The Royal Collection © 2003, Her Majesty Queen Elizabeth II

Fuller accused the directors of letting building frontages worth £4,430 for £1,410 when a director and an official of the Company were two of the three lessees.[289]

There was a shares panic even in the first year of the Company, and throughout the years the poor returns became a standing joke.[290] The press noted that the world had assumed that the Crystal Palace would be the *ne plus ultra* of efficiency, but that Paxton himself for months past had been 'entrusted with the sole and entire management of the place'.[291] There were many ready to sneer at Paxton, 'Dominus Do-All', and his extravagance.[292] A correspondent of Sotheby wrote in January 1855 that he was 'in hopes we had got rid of Sir Joseph Paxton' – who had been elected a Liberal Member of Parliament in November 1852. The same writer remarked that he should not 'look through the glass' in attending to his parliamentary constituency.[293] The Ordinary General Meeting of the Company was told on 9 August 1855 that Paxton's engagement would end 'entirely with the completion of the few remaining works', but that he would be kept on in a position 'analogous to a consulting engineer'.[294] When Laing resigned as chairman, he announced an award of £4,000 to Fuller, who had given up his 'very lucrative business' out of zeal to carry through the new Palace scheme.[295] He was succeeded by Arthur Anderson, chairman of the Oriental Steam Navigation Company, and in consequence the Museum of Naval Architecture, 'the hobby of Mr Anderson', was set up at the Palace.[296] Richard Redgrave wrote in his journal that Anderson had visited the Paris Exposition in 1855 to solicit exhibitors for Sydenham and had meanwhile written asking Henry Cole to suggest other attractions. Cole replied suggesting that the Company should introduce a 'Chamber of Horrors', meaning a new version of the famous display of grotesquely ugly English manufactures that Cole and Redgrave had selected for an exhibition at Marlborough House to shame manufacturers and educate the public in design. Anderson thereupon told Owen Jones in Paris that he thought Cole had gone out of his mind – he had understood Cole to mean 'that chamber of hanged cut-throats, ruffians and murderers at Madame Tussaud's'. Owen Jones was 'convulsed with laughter'[297] – the mirth of highbrow aesthete at the expense of the ignorant shipping magnate reflecting the chronic tension between high artistic ideals and no-nonsense commercialism.

The Company's accounts were not in order; they lacked detail, and some large frauds occurred. George Grove put out a handbill offering a £250 reward for the arrest of a clerk, William Robson, also described as a playwright, who was keeping 'a beautiful curricle and pair' with a liveried servant on his salary of £150, and managed to embezzle £20,000 in shares over two or three years. Robson paid the dividends, but falsely accounted for the shares; it was reported that the architect and architectural theorist James Fergusson, 'suffering from ill health', had trustingly 'left a great part of the management of the office to him'.[298] Robson was tried and convicted at the Central Criminal Court and sentenced to twenty years' transportation.[299] The amiable and learned George Grove, later a promoter of the great musical achievements of the Palace, was said to be a lazy administrator.

In January 1855 Paxton asked Henry Cole if he would accept the management of the Palace, on his own terms and conditions. Richard Redgrave noted in his diary: 'I can see he inclines to accept it', but the Prince Consort hinted to Cole that it would not be in his interest, and said to him: 'Do you think that that even your administrative ability would suffice to secure the Crystal Palace from failure & prove that it may be self supporting?'[300] There were calls in November 1855 for a proper manager,[301] who would provide 'amusements'.[302] James Fergusson, who had already been employed by the Company to design the Nineveh Court, was appointed general manager in March 1856, on a modest salary of £700 but with 'a 2.5 % share of the net profits set aside for division among the principal officers'. His activity and courtesy were noted,[303] and he was said to manage the concerts and flower shows 'admirably', but he left the post in mid-1858.[304]

It would have been hard by this time not to accept that Paxton's vision of Sydenham appealing to vast numbers of Londoners in the way that an excursion to Versailles did to Parisians was wide of the mark – an American observer, Horace Greeley, was quoted as saying, 'It ain't handy to the citizens of London.'[305]

Another hope that stayed alive was that the 'West End' railway line would improve attendance. When the Alexandra Palace at Muswell Hill was devised in 1859, some mistakes made at Sydenham and some weaknesses of its location were among the Great Northern Palace Company's considerations. A quarter of London lived south of the river; nine-tenths of England, including potential visitors from the 'manufacturing districts' lay in districts with easy railway access to the north of London rather than to the south. Owen Jones made an ambitious but strange and rather cumbrous design for the Alexandra Palace that was not adopted, although it was twice shown in engravings in the *Illustrated London News* as 'the most recent specimen of a novel style of architecture in glass and iron' set, like the Crystal Palace at Sydenham, on a platform above a sloping park. The design again drew on 'some of the characteristics of the cathedral style'; the ends of the transept again were to have Jones's recessed arches, and Jones added six saracenic domes with crescent-moon finials. The new Palace would have full gas lighting and be profitable day and night, and in what seems an oblique disparaging reference to Sydenham's poor railway access from the Lower Level Station, it was emphasised how the new Metropolitan Railway line would lead directly into it. The plans for the interior showed presumably what Jones and others thought would improve the amenities at Sydenham. There was to be a properly 'acoustic' concert hall for 10,000 people in the centre and a colossal dome 280 feet in diameter above it; a promenade, a winter garden, a Fine Arts nave, a gallery of English history, a picture gallery, and large displays of machinery and raw products. At the ends semi-circular colonnades, built on a ground-plan of the lunette from the Hyde Park building, would give a much more commodious area for refreshments than anything in Sydenham. 'Artificial' gardens were planned in Italian, French, Old English and Modern English styles.[306]

Early in the history of the Crystal Palace Company its financial problems prompted the suggestion that part of the Park should be sold for housing. In 1874 Paxton's carefully planted 'belt' along the north-east side, by all accounts a marvellous collection of 'nearly all that was beautiful in the trees and shrubs of northern and temperate regions', which 'so gracefully cut off the grounds from the chimney-pots around', was sold off to make way for red-brick villas.[307] Fuller continued to propose schemes to recoup revenue – none of them was accepted – such as a 'Tontine' for an 'association' of shares, for which he was given 'loud hisses and cheers' in 1874; a scheme of Art Union prizes in 1875; and finally a plan for international art exhibitions in 1879.[308]

The Palace suffered much bad luck and bad management in its early decades, but from 1920 it was to be pulled up again at the end of its career by an outstanding manager, Sir Henry Buckland, who proved through dedicated hard work that the Palace was not necessarily a 'white elephant' and a disaster. He remained in his post for sixteen years, and by 1936 had brought the annual tally of visitors once again to a million, and had repaired the Palace and restored the Architectural Courts. His work was only cut short by the Fire in that year that destroyed the Palace for ever.

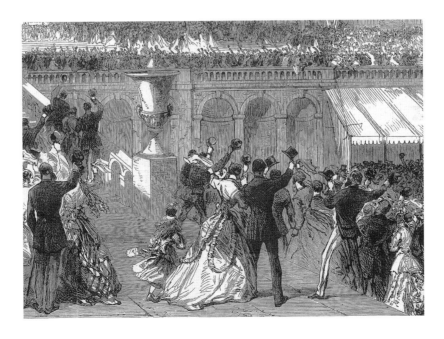

THE FINE ARTS COURTS, I

OWEN JONES

The Crystal Palace had a crucial influence on museums and the display of architecture, sculpture and natural history. The series of ten Architectural Courts illustrating historical styles – actually called the Fine Arts Courts – were the most ambitious and original feature of the new Palace at Sydenham. They were meticulous 'reconstructions' by architectural grand tourists and grand archaeologists: large model buildings, mostly a hundred feet square, built of brick, plastered and painted. There is plentiful contemporary evidence for the pleasure they gave and for the influence they exerted.

Prosper Mérimée visited and wrote about them in 1857, confident that they would inspire the young to practice architecture and design:

> Sans doute on a fait de grandes dépenses pour élever ces modèles en plâtre de monumens de tous les pays et de toutes les époques; mais plusieurs millions d'hommes ont vu la reproduction si exacte de l'Alhambra, d'un temple égyptien, d'une maison grecque. Je suis fort trompé si la vue des excellentes copies de M. Owen Jones n'a pas fait étudier le dessin et l'architecture à maint jeune garçon qui ne s'en serait jamais avisé avant d'aller à Sydenham.[1]

As for the directors of the Fine Arts Courts, Owen Jones had spent months drawing and measuring in Egypt and at the Alhambra, where he claimed to have made tracings or casts of every decorative detail, and Digby Wyatt had filled sketchbooks with details of buildings in Italy and Sicily. The 'restorations' of buried empires that took shape in the Courts were the result of recent discoveries and publications. In particular the Nineveh Court was designed with the co-operation of Henry Layard (1817–94), who had excavated the originals on the banks of the Tigris as recently as 1845. Digby Wyatt sketched out the plan for his Pompeian House at the site of the actual excavations, and the elaborate decorations for it were executed by Giuseppe Abbate, a Neapolitan who had been court painter to the King of Naples for nineteen years, and spent twenty-four years recording ancient Pompeii, where since 1819 major discoveries were still

being made. Whether or not they had a direct part in the design of the Courts, academic authority was given to the project directly, through advice and the writing of the Company's Handbooks, by Henry Layard, G.H. Lewes, the German architect Gottfried Semper, and Anna Jameson. Taken together the assemblage of sculpture and architecture, though reproduced in plaster and paint, could be called 'treasures of art never yet seen before by the English people', and 'a collection not even a Roman emperor could put together'.[2]

The architects' aims were to produce historical reproductions of the styles of building and decoration they admired and with which they wished to instruct the visitors. They referred to these Courts variously as 'living reproductions', 'illustrations' and 'restorations'.[3] The Courts were to be a main feature of 'the education of the eye', to form a three-dimensional and full-colour encyclopaedia of the 'complete history of civilisation'. This, Jones had told the Society of Arts on 28 April 1852, was what the Crystal Palace should offer the people. It was also central to Jones's architectural mission to impart architectural education to the people by demonstrating the historical evolution of styles; the lecture to the Society of Arts was titled 'The Necessity of an Architectural Education on the Part of the Public'.

The Courts were to be interpreted, in sequence, in official handbooks published as guides to the Courts. The need for literary interpretation was expressed in the *Crystal Palace Expositor*: the handbooks would provide the thoughtful visitor with an overview of civilization.

> Every one feels that he ought to prepare himself by a course of historical and antiquarian study… He stands in the presence of a vast panorama of extinct life, of vanished institutions, of habits and usages long since passed away, of decayed forms of polytheism, and of superseded arts. It is from the reproduced memorials of the past that he desires to penetrate into the inner life of those by whom those monuments were constructed, to institute comparison, to pry into hidden secrets, and recall into existence the buried generations of distant countries.[4]

The Courts formed a curious and fascinating three-dimensional *musée imaginaire*, reproducing the architecture and sculptures among which one would most like to walk and study. They offered an experience that was at once true and false. The Rev. Charles Boutell, in a series of articles on the Courts in the *Art Journal*, said of the 'Sydenham Museum' that that what it taught was 'clear, expressive and easy to understand'.[5]

The Handbooks, as we have seen, had a splendid ceremonial launching during the inauguration of the Palace, much mocked by *Punch*:[6] they were laid at the feet of the monarch by their authors wearing court dress and mounting the steps of the red-carpeted dais. The Company claimed that they were a 'great auxiliary to the work of education which it is the first aim of the Crystal Palace to effect'.[7] On sale at the opening of the Palace in June 1854 were a general guide, ten separate guides to the Courts, Jones's *Apology for the Colouring of the Greek Court*, guides to the sculpture, the Portrait Gallery, the ethnological and zoological departments, the extinct animals and the geological illustrations, and an industrial directory. In their paper wrappers, these cost between 3d. and 1s. 6d., and in July they were also offered collected into three volumes, 'handsomely bound' in dark blue cloth, at 13s. 6d. Bradbury and Evans, among whose clients were *Punch* and Charles Dickens, were the printers, and the firm opened a branch inside the Palace, later called the Crystal Palace Press, for the printing of programmes and posters.[8] Dickens found these Handbooks 'a sufficiently flatulent botheration in themselves', and refused to add to 'the great forge-bellows of puffery at work' by promoting them in his magazine *Household Words*. Possibly also he considered that the network of printer, publisher and his own friendship with Paxton might attract attention.[9] The excellent general *Guide to the Crystal Palace and its Park and Gardens* was written by the 'Director of the Literary Department' of the Company, Samuel Phillips, a clever and caustic Jewish journalist on *The Times* who died suddenly aged thirty-nine four months after the Palace opened.[10]

The cheap Handbooks were of uneven quality. The one describing the Roman Court referred to the haste of its composition, and indeed several categories of information printed in the text under each entry, such as dimensions, were left incomplete. The hurry was partly due to a change of policy. The architect J.B. Waring, who collaborated with Digby Wyatt in writing the Handbooks to the latter's Courts, says that Wyatt originally asked him to Sydenham to write a *catalogue raisonnée* of the contents of the entire Palace, but in 1854 told him that the directors had decided on a series of small books instead, presumably to bring in more famous names. Waring did not enjoy his part in Wyatt's Handbooks: his historical knowledge was evidently slight, and Wyatt gave him a reading list in four languages.[11] By March 1854 Phillips was general editor of the series. Sir John Gardner Wilkinson (1797–1875) was originally named as the writer of one of them, presumably that on the Egyptian Court.[12]

Jones, as might be deduced, already took a passionate interest in the Courts, and intended his Alhambra Court and the colossal reproductions of the two figures from the temple of Aboo-Simbel to be places of almost occult powers of transformation. Writing in his eloquent *Handbook to the Alhambra Court* – a polemic and didactic text as well as a guide – Jones sees the Palace and its promoters in almost Miltonic terms, regenerating the British public. He says that in 1851 the government, 'an unnatural parent', abandoned the Palace at Hyde Park, but that luckily it 'fell into the hands of men animated by the noble desire of rendering it subservient to the education of all classes, whilst providing for their innocent recreation. The defects [in knowledge and taste] which the Exhibition of 1851 proved to exist, may be remedied through the Exhibition of 1854.'[13]

Plainly the architects' intention in the Courts was historical and archaeological, but for Jones and Wyatt it was also a campaign to influence the public and architects to accept and to think about the use of colour and ornament. Both architects were intent on promoting the union of architecture, sculpture and decorative painting, and particularly the use of polychromatic enrichment. Jones mocked the ignorant incongruity of architecture with furniture and interior decoration in his day:

> How can Greek porticos, – nondescript pretty decorations, – Louis Quatorze furniture, – cinquecento ornament, – floral papers and floral carpets, be made to harmonise in a London mansion of the nineteenth century? The decorative arts are of one family, and must go hand in hand with their parent architecture: the effort to raise the one will help the other.[14]

Jones intended to correct false and ignorant historicism and bad public taste and design. Digby Wyatt's vision of the function of the Palace is clear from the introduction

Opposite: H.W. Phillips, *Owen Jones*, R.A., 1856. Oil painting, © RIBA Drawings Collection.

After Philip Delamotte, 'The Egyptian Court from the Nave', 1854.

After Philip Delamotte, 'Exterior of the Assyrian Palace', 1854.

After Philip Delamotte, 'The Greek Court', 1854.

After Philip Delamotte, 'View of the Exterior of the Byzantine Court', 1854.

After Philip Delamotte, 'The Alhambra', 1854.

'The Mediaeval Court', 1854.

After Philip Delamotte, 'The Pompeian Court', 1854.

After Philip Delamotte, 'The Italian Court from the Nave', 1854.

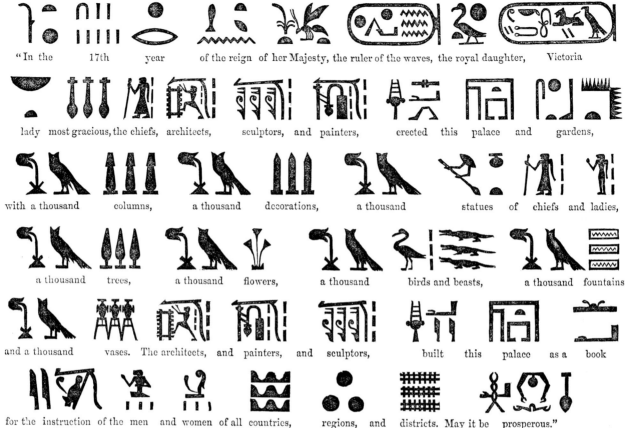

"In the   17th   year   of the reign of her Majesty, the ruler of the waves, the royal daughter,   Victoria

lady most gracious, the chiefs, architects,   sculptors, and painters,   erected this palace   and   gardens,

with a thousand   columns,   a thousand   decorations,   a thousand   statues   of chiefs and ladies,

a thousand   trees,   a thousand   flowers,   a thousand   birds and beasts,   a thousand fountains

and a thousand   vases. The architects, and painters, and sculptors,   built   this palace   as a   book

for the instruction of the men   and women of all countries,   regions, and   districts. May it be   prosperous."

Hieroglyphic inscription, Egyptian Court.

to his book *Views of the Crystal Palace and Park, Sydenham*, published for the first Christmas of the new Palace in 1854, with splendid chromolithographic plates: the Palace was to bring 'the higher cultivation of taste and design' in the Fine Arts, which had already spread from the aristocracy to the *bourgeoisie* and thence to the masses. His hope was that through study of the displays at the Palace – which was to serve, in Ralph Wornum's phrase, as an 'inexhaustible studio'[15] – artisans and manufacturers would learn good taste; shops that sold good designs would be patronised by consumers with newly-acquired good taste who would laugh their friends out of over-decorating their apartments, and teach them the pleasures of more 'simple' and beautiful decoration and ornaments. Like Jones he believed that improved taste would result in improved morals. In a passage which uncannily foreshadowed the actual Victoria and Albert Museum, he imagined the Crystal Palace as one day being filled with classified historical artefacts.[16]

Jones did not offer styles and ornaments as patterns to copy; nobody could have been more severe against reproduction or 'copyism' in contemporary architecture of 'dead' styles and motifs. New styles were rather to be stimulated by adaptation, in the way that Christopher Dresser was to modify Jones's own work in the second half of the century to produce original decorations. Jones's wallpapers and silk fabrics were original, and he would no doubt have disliked the derivative paper hangings displayed for sale in the Palace in 'Alhambra', 'Pompeian', 'Greek' and 'Gothic' designs.

An inscription in hieroglyphics was to be seen in the Egyptian Court, presumably the work of Jones's friend and associate Bonomi. Translated back into English in the Palace literature, it read:

In the 17th year of the reign of her Majesty, the ruler of the waves, the royal daughter, Victoria, lady most gracious, the chiefs, architects, sculptors and painters erected this palace and gardens with a thousand columns, a thousand decorations, a thousand statues of chiefs and ladies, a thousand trees, a thousand flowers, a thousand birds and beasts, a thousand fountains [tanks] and a thousand vases. The architects, and painters and sculptors built this palace as a book for the instruction of the men and women of all countries, regions, and districts. May it be prosperous.[17]

One press report imagines schools and colleges growing up around this encyclopaedic Palace, and offers a slightly comic fantasy of masters walking there with their disciples as in the groves of an Ancient Greek *academe*.[18]

However, the Courts aroused strong criticism among academics and in the art world: they were inconsistent in scale relative to each other, they were inaccurate and conjectural,[19] and they combined elements of different originals. Indian architecture was not included, and the eighteenth century was pointedly omitted, along with much of the seventeenth, especially the Louis XIV style. Particular ridicule was reserved for the polychromatic coats of paint the Courts had received according to Owen Jones's principles (not only his own Courts were subject to his influence), and for his 'improving' of the historical evidence for the colours of the originals.

The Courts were not limited in their significance to the history of architecture. They also suggested a certain politics of empire, a philosophy and even a morality: the fall of proud, wealthy and luxurious civilisations. Jones spoke with a certain triumphal pleasure about the fresco on the walls of the Egyptian Court of 'the greatest of the Pharaohs' in which 'the conqueror in his career crushes beneath the wheels of his chariot crowds of the enemy'.[20] The official *Guide to the Palace* by Samuel Phillips admonished the reader to trace the course of art to the present, and to gain 'an idea of the successive stages of civilization rising and falling', until 'overturned by the aggression of barbarians or the no less destructive agency of a sensual and degraded luxury'.[21] The Nineveh Court, for example, was a monument to imperial power and pride, the architecture of the conqueror, showing subject peoples slaughtered in battles won in dusty fields; it was surely with the hopes for the Crystal Palace itself in mind that the official *Guide* described the Nineveh Court as a place of 'great public ceremonies, national triumphs or religious worship'.[22] Nineveh for all its pride fell in a day in flames, and it took only an hour for the sybaritic Pompeii to be buried in ash.[23] The Temple of Karnac in Egypt, like Shelley's Ozymandias, was buried in sand. The Nineveh Court stood like a beckoning prototype for

the grandiose New Delhi of Edwin Lutyens and Herbert Baker, and at the same time as a prophetic *memento mori* of the possible demise of the British Empire. Visitors to the Pompeian House were expected to make the connection: 'He who only gazes with curiosity and admiration at its recovered treasures, can never appreciate the moral lesson which its catastrophe is so well calculated to teach.'[24] The exquisite Court of Lions in the Palace's Alhambra Court actually represented a scene of barbaric cruelty and treachery where heads cut off by the tyrant were thrown into the basin of the fountain among the vacuous lions – 'queer quaint dolls' copied here by Raffaelle Monti from the originals.[25]

In 1781, depressed by the dissolute and self-conceited times in which he lived, the poet William Cowper wrote in a letter: 'How stands it with our Nineveh now?'[26] Not only Evangelicals but cultivated and thoughtful early Victorians of other persuasions were accustomed to reminders of God's punishment of worldly cities such as John Martin's apocalyptic painting *The Fall of Nineveh* (1827–8), with its bolts of lightning, and J.M.W. Turner's Bible illustrations showing mounds over ruined cities (1834–6). London was frequently compared to doomed Babylon, and quotations from *Isaiah* and *Jeremiah* were applied to the excavated buried empires 'illustrated' at the Crystal Palace; the visitors were reminded that scenes of Assyrian pride and luxury were now the haunts of wild beasts of the desert, owls and doleful creatures.[27]

In promoting polychromy to puritan English visitors to the Palace, Owen Jones made the point that although English painters had long been regarded as colourists, England was far behind 'in employment and appreciation of colour' in interior and exterior decoration.[28] Although the colouring of the Courts in their heyday seemed garish to most people of refined taste, who needed reminding that Jones's bright colours were from Eastern countries of intense sunshine,[29] to most people it must have possessed a special theatrical excitement and presented new patterns and harmonies of colour. The vandalism of Protestant reformers had created 'universal eternal snows' by whitewashing the walls and columns of cathedrals, every inch of which had formerly been coloured.[30] The people were disinherited of the spectrum, and Jones now brought its sumptuous primary colours back to them. 'Men were reluctant to give up their long-cherished idea of the white marble of the Parthenon and the simplicity of its forms, and they refused to regard it as a building, coloured in every part, and covered with a most elaborate system of ornamentation.'[31]

A remarkable by-product of Jones's work designing and constructing his Courts at Sydenham was a work of genius on colour and design, *The Grammar of Ornament*, published in imperial folio in 1856. In this book he aimed to establish, in the form of dogmatic axioms, principles for colour combinations and the forms of ornament. He drew on Digby Wyatt and Joseph Bonomi for information, and on other colleagues and pupils at Sydenham for illustration: Albert Warren and Charles Aubert ('ornamental draughtsmen') and Christopher Dresser ('Professor of Ornamental Art and Botany in the Crystal Palace, Sydenham'). Of the book's chromolithographic plates the *Athenaeum* said they were 'bright enough to serve a London family in summer instead of flowers, and to warm a London room in winter as well as a fire'.[32] Boutell in the *Art Journal* recommended students to use the work in combination with the Courts themselves, which had probably been Jones's intention.[33] Thirty years later, in 1887, Lewis F. Day wrote that *The Grammar of Ornament* had marked 'a turning point in the history of English ornament', and that 'no man did more than [Jones] towards clearing the ground for us, and so making possible the new departures which we have made since his time.'[34]

It was thought at the time that with his polychromatic 'experiments' and his 'grammatical' ornaments Jones had stamped his ideas and taste too heavily on the Courts, and – according to Sotheby – Digby Wyatt had caught the 'colour fever' from him.[35] Certainly the use of strong colour at Sydenham was a deliberate programme. Jones habitually emphasised its use in Gothic architecture: in a lecture to the Royal Institute of British Architecture in 1851 he said that medieval geometrical forms 'depend entirely on colour for their full development'.[36] He also adduced the original colouring of buildings in Assyria, Egypt, Greece and Turkey. The word 'polychromatic' runs like a motif, or even like a party line, throughout the Company's Handbooks to the Courts. Colour and ornament were paramount, and a critic in the *Art Journal* wrote with some truth that although ornament was profusely illustrated at Sydenham, the 'higher order of beauty arising out of structure' was not.[37]

Even so, the south-north enfilade through the Courts, looking through the side-doors from the Egyptian to the Greek, to the Roman to the Alhambra, must have been like viewing a marvellous peep-show, or a contemporary toy theatre with 'wings', 'cut scene' and backdrop, suddenly life-size and 'actual'; or a sepia stereopticon held up to both eyes that turned full-coloured. The perceptions originally concentrated into one sense, sight, would expand to embrace all five senses, and one could walk around within the image, in a secondary reality. An imaginative child would have had the sense of stepping, like Lewis Carroll's Alice, through a looking-glass directly into the three-dimensional illustrations of a book. The closest we can come to the Fine Arts Courts of sculpture and architecture at Sydenham today is in the Cast Courts at the Victoria and Albert Museum (*c.*1870), which by a twist of fate have housed the Fontevrault casts since the Crystal Palace was burnt down around them in 1936.

Prints and photographs of the interior of the Sydenham Crystal Palace show the rich frontages and flanks of the Courts adjacent to iron columns, girders and tie-beams, together with floor-boards and benches such as one would see in a local railway-station. But incongruity was very evident on the ground: the Courts and other works of art were housed next to a shopping arcade and among people eating and drinking. The Pompeian Court was adjacent to perfumery and hairdressing shops, where 'Pompeian Hair Dye' was on sale.[38] The Monuments of Christian Art were set among ice-cream stalls and orange trees in the Nave.

Critics complained that the Fine Arts Courts, particularly the Egyptian and Assyrian, were 'theatric' and 'scenic'[39] rather than strict academic reproductions. In contrast to Hyde Park, where the sections of the Exhibition had temporary partitions constructed or hung between them, the Courts at Sydenham had walls of plaster over brick. Some compartments of the Courts were enclosed, with painted plaster ceilings, and others had mosaic or marble floors made by 'art-manufacturers' of the day such as Maw or Minton: these specialist ceramic firms collaborated with Jones and Wyatt in their other commissions making floors for churches, clubhouses and the private houses of the rich.

When Jones and Wyatt made what they called a 'court' for the Fine Arts, this was to enshrine it within a walled enclosure such as a quadrangle or cloister, with light falling from above into the centre of the structure, or even a temple area surrounding a sanctuary. The *Oxford English Dictionary* notes that the word 'court' meaning 'an area of Exhibition building or museum open above to a roof' appears 'to have originated in 1851' to describe the rectangular sections at Hyde Park that were divided in the central area and open to the lofty roof, with galleries at the sides supported by pillars; this term then became used for sections within buildings. The *Dictionary* cites the Tunis, Canadian and Building Courts at Hyde Park, and quotes the *Illustrated London News* on the natural subdivision of the original Crystal Palace into four large courts and two smaller ones, and the interesting features these create.[40] From its usage at Sydenham, according to the *Dictionary*, the term came to mean the central open space of a museum or an atrium, surrounded by arcades and galleries. The University Museum in Parks Road, Oxford, has a 'Great Court' with 'a glass roof, iron columns and arches… surrounded by an open arcade of two storeys'.[41]

By June 1852 the Sydenham 'courts' were already being mentioned in the press: 'Portions of the palace will be converted into quadrangles similar to the fine art or medieval courts of the Exhibition. These courts will be made to represent the manners, costumes, &c. of different countries.' Mr Jones was to reproduce one of the courts of the Alhambra, and an Egyptian Court, a Nineveh palace and a Pompeian Court are mentioned, the last assigned to Digby Wyatt; these are intended to show the 'architectural collections' in 'progressive series'. In July 1852 the *Athenaeum* reported that an Indian palace and a Chinese court were planned; these were never realised, although plans for them were still being mentioned in the *London Journal* the following year.[42]

In 1856, over the signature of George Grove, the Crystal Palace Company announced that an exhibition of Indian manufactures would be on view 'in a specially appropriated Court or compartment' with facsimiles of the Ajanta frescoes, all to be directed by James Fergusson.[43] With faint praise the *Athenaeum* noted the result in June, calling it 'small' and 'as yet rather incongruous and conglomerate… without unity and without effect' and with too many 'show goods'. James Fergusson's wooden models of temples, mosques, gateways and bungalows, among saddle-cloths, garments and musical instruments, were made to sound uninteresting.[44] The Indian and Chinese displays were situated in the Galleries over the Egyptian and Greek Courts; here were also shown some Persian and Japanese goods. The *Crystal Palace Herald* reported in November 1855 that

these minor courts were 'hardly known and seldom discovered'.[45] Digby Wyatt was architect to the East India Company (hence his court built in 1867 for the India Office in Whitehall, now part of the Foreign Office) and designed the Indian display at the Paris Exposition of 1855, 'a gay Eastern tent'.[46] An imaginative early proposal, never carried out, was for a representation in the basement of the Crystal Palace of an Egyptian archaeological site: 'In the basement below the present ground floor will be reproduced one of the largest Egyptian tombs'.[47]

Jones and Digby Wyatt were commissioned by the directors to go 'on an artistic tour through France, Italy and Germany for the purpose of collecting illustrations of Architecture and Sculpture, the histories of which arts are to be represented by ancient and modern specimens in the New Crystal Palace'. They returned in November 1852 to work on their Courts.[48] Although Jones and Wyatt had toured museums and sites on the continent in their youth, the few months they had to commission casts, even with the 'liberal purse' and letters from the Secretary of State Lord Malmesbury, were very short to see and order the complete history of sculpture in plaster that was planned. That they achieved so much testifies to their energy and conviction. George Godwin wrote in *The Builder* that the Courts would offer the people and 'those who stay at home' a grand tour of works of art, and that the Courts might have an advantage 'even for our professional brethren'.[49] However, some observers remained sceptical. Dr Vaughan, Head Master of Harrow, wrote in a pamphlet against Sunday admission at the Palace in 1852 that 'no gallery of painting or of sculpture will have any abiding attraction for the class thus described… no display of art will allure them to civilization.'[50]

Doubtless Jones and Digby Wyatt had to stand up to Paxton for adequate space for Art in dialogue with Nature in the Winter Garden at Sydenham. Jones referred to the Sydenham Crystal Palace simply as 'the Exhibition', and in the early years it was quite often called 'the museum'. Jones and Wyatt wrote a letter of fairly dignified anger to Paxton on 9 March 1854 over the position allotted to works of art in the Nave. They complained that in wanting to keep the Nave a wide thoroughfare placing the works of art to the side, he had referred the matter to the Board without properly discussing it with the Fine Arts Courts directors themselves; they had 'hitherto worked in harmony' and 'ever been willing to meet your wishes in all things'. They clearly realised that the Board would side with Paxton and bring pressure on them.[51] In its earliest years the Palace had no manager: Fergusson was only appointed in 1856, and till then Paxton in effect had autocratic powers.

The 'complete historical illustration of the arts of sculpture and architecture from the earliest works of Egypt and Assyria down to modern times'[52] was, as we have seen, designed to illustrate a chronological sequence and teach the evolution of styles. Assyrian architecture was thought to lead to Egyptian, and thence through Greek and Roman to Byzantine, and thence to both Gothic and the 'Saracenic' Alhambra.[53] Digby Wyatt in his Handbook to the Byzantine Court traces this same evolution. The *Crystal Palace Expositor* took up the theme of a programme: studying the Italian Court after the Renaissance Court would lead to the understanding of 'continuity' and to a 'comprehensive view…of the rise, the advancement, and the perfection of art'. George Godwin in *The Builder* thought it quite wrong to see the Saracenic style as 'evolving from the Roman'; in any case the Alhambra, being of the thirteenth or fourteenth century, was scarcely the best example of Saracenic art influenced by Byzantium.[54] The *Crystal Palace Expositor*, which often appeared to draw on ideas emanating from the Palace itself, hinted at the lessons to be drawn from contemplating the evolution of styles, and anticipated that the Palace would be recognised as a triumph of higher intelligence:

> Great epochs are the creations of great men, on which they stamp the impress of their genius. The Crystal Palace is a register of epochs, illustrating them by monuments of science and art, and then tracing the progress of intelligence from era to era in different countries. In this resides the utility of the instruction it affords; and it would be a trivial and almost barren task to describe the treasures of a temple as a mere catalogue, and omit all mention of those by whom the treasures were called into existence. The Crystal Palace itself forms an epoch in architecture, and posterity will read with interest whatever relates to its projector and his coadjutors.[55]

Conflict between the claims of those promoting the Palace's Courts on the one hand and the carpings of malice or of academic criticism on the other was perhaps predictable. The accounts of early visits that Lady Eastlake recorded in her diary and in a fifty-page article about the Courts in the *Quarterly Review* reveal an enthusiastic, unbiased and well-informed eye and mind as a guide and companion to the riches of the Palace. She was deeply interested in the architecture and sculpture, but lamented the lack of original paintings, saying that half the amount spent on casts would have bought 'a magnificent collection' of old masters.[56] Though full of admiration for the project, she was highly critical of the colouring of all the Courts except the Alhambra and Pompeian which, like other visitors of her kind, she thought had too much 'scenic effect' about them. She enjoyed being among people of all classes, guide books in their hands, and sensed 'no bad passions' among the visitors. The Palace was 'the highest compliment ever yet offered to a people'.[57] Like Ruskin in his pamphlet on the opening of the Palace, she subscribed to the view that the educational programme at Sydenham could have regenerated architecture and the British people themselves. Jones himself was of the opinion, expounded several times in lectures, that if art education, the 'cultivation of the eye', were taken seriously the prisons of England would be less full.[58] Lady Eastlake expressed sympathy for the

> hopes for civilization and the turning point of a new architecture and the nursery ground of new resources. It is a pleasure to see young people turned loose among these monuments. Many a one in future days will trace their first realisation of the mysterious affinity of the best Christian art to the soul to some sunny dream-like visit to this building, when impressions were received which time has strengthened and extended, but which have never been sweeter than then.[59]

She had attended the inauguration, sitting in the front row of the centre transept, and felt excitement, especially at the 'electrifying' *Halleluiah Chorus*, but regretted that the effects did not include the fountains (not yet working), the hangings and the 'gorgeous masses' of colour of the interior at Hyde Park.[60] Returning on 7 July, she wrote:

> Yesterday was quite a bright day in my annals, for the Crystal Palace is a place of enchantment. We were there about two o-clock and left just before six. It is now a paradise of flowers and works of art, and one big enough for every creature, high and low, to enjoy; and last, though not least, the air is so invigorating that you gain strength faster than you spend it.. We *flâné*'d at first a little, and then applied ourselves to a few particular courts – the Norman, the Nuremburg, and best of all, the Italian Renaissance court, with its exquisite doors, monuments, bas reliefs, &c., from Genoa, Pavia, Florence, and other

places: all in the zenith of high art, and giving one a delight equalled only by seeing a fine gallery of pictures. We then inspected the English sculpture, for here a school is seen and studied at once. Nothing has ever been devised like this palace; the comfort and pleasure of all have been provided for. If many make it only an amusement, it will be an innocent one; but judging from myself, it must be an improvement, and raise the whole standard of education. Then there are seats by the million, just where you want them, while from time to time the band, engaged at 7000l. a year, bursts forth like the service of Antwerp Cathedral. It is a thing both to rave about and think about. No reminiscences of the first Crystal Palace, charming as that was, can compare with this, which is of a far higher order.[61]

Londoners could already have seen 'illustrations' of all the architectural styles of the Fine Arts Courts except the Byzantine and Assyrian. The Pompeian style, a favourite of Victoria and Albert, was already in vogue; structures in the 'Alhambra' and Egyptian styles were also hardly a novelty. However, the Royal Panopticon of Science and Art in Leicester Square, described in 1855 in *London: what to see and how to see it*, was said to be 'a very fine specimen of the Saracenic architectural style, derived from the Alhambra'. This minor rival to the Crystal Palace was a 'school for the instruction of the community in matters scientific and artistic', offering 'excellent selections of modern sculpture' and manufactures. There too machinery was displayed within a circle formed by statuary, and an ornamental basin with eight converging jets and one in the centre; also a hall for lectures on literature and art, a colossal electric apparatus, and a grand organ. The Egyptian Hall of 1812 in Piccadilly was well known; the façade was 'completely Egyptian', and it had a pair of colossal Egyptian figures, like the Aboo-Simbel statues at Sydenham, fronting the street above an entablature.[62]

From 1851 to 1862 London boasted three Medieval Courts: the first, at the Great Exhibition, contained works made from designs by A.W.N. Pugin; the second was the historical Medieval Court at Sydenham with casts from Gothic originals; and the third was at the International Exhibition at South Kensington in 1862 where (along with various important architects and designers) the firm of Morris, Marshall and Faulkner exhibited modern revival 'art manufactures'. The adolescent William Morris had refused to accompany his parents into the Great Exhibition, and remained sulking on a bench outside,[63] but by 1862 he was adapting some

principles of the conventionalised heraldic designs promoted by Pugin and Owen Jones at the Exhibition. In the course of a lecture, 'Hints on Pattern Making', in 1882 he held up illustrations from Jones's *The Grammar of Ornament* as examples of the historical development of ornament.[64]

The press lamented the lack of guides or lecturers in the Courts to answer 'even the simplest' questions.[65] Owen Jones's head of staff George Purchase, who left because of a disagreement with 'the committee', thought that there should be more direct teaching of the principles of design, with diagrams set up in the Courts to teach 'the effect of combinations of vertical, horizontal, oblique and curved lines; the contrasts, harmony, and purpose of colour &c'.[66]

According to an early press report, Jones and Wyatt might have been disappointed at first with the response to their cultural mission, but interest in the Courts was not slow in developing. At first the public were more responsive to the Natural History, Ethnology and Industrial Courts and the life-size models of Extinct Animals in the grounds, and to the gardens, music and places for refreshment. Although the Courts and sculpture were 'undoubtedly more in advance of the public taste and intelligence', these were now 'influential' and 'explored with zest'. According to the same source the Pompeian, Alhambra and Renaissance Courts were the most frequented.[67]

Owen Jones

The life and theories of Owen Jones had a strong influence on the appearance of the Palace at Sydenham – he was responsible for half of the Fine Arts Courts, grouped together in a line along the north-west side of the Nave – and on the messages it was intended to convey. Admiration for the Alhambra Court and its colouring was almost universal although, as might have been predicted, Ruskin dismissed it tartly. Jones also had to endure a barrage of hostile articles in the press and sneers from academics and connoisseurs at his colouring of the casts of the Elgin Marbles (the Panathenaic frieze). It was even worse than the colour wars in 1851.

In the wooden box of his medals and papers, now at the Bodleian Library in Oxford, is his handwritten list of major works in architecture and in book design; he refers to the Courts as the 'Western' Fine Arts Courts.

Jones was born in 1809 in Thames Street, City of

London, to a prosperous furrier of the same name from Denbighshire in North Wales. The elder Owen Jones was a formidable antiquary and editor of Welsh manuscripts, and the son seems to have inherited his remarkable energy and zeal, expressed in designs for major and countless minor works. Admitted to the Royal Academy Antique School on 26 June 1830, he showed no talent for drawing the figure but was expert in mathematics, geometry and acoustics. He was apprenticed for six years to Lewis Vulliamy, the architect, whom he probably assisted in his work on St Bartholomew's church in Sydenham (1827–32), where his unmarried sisters settled, a short walk from the Palace. In 1831 he travelled to Paris, Milan, Venice, Rome, Sicily and Greece, and in 1832 left for Egypt and the Levant. In Greece he met a French architectural student Jules Goury and the two travelled together. Joseph Bonomi, who lived for eleven years in Egypt, described two boats full of Englishmen arriving at Thebes where Jones and Goury showed him their drawings. Bonomi said that the pair made measurements and drawings in Egypt of 'astounding accuracy and detail…never as it seemed to me did two men work together in better harmony and success.'[68] From his lecture to the Architectural Society of 1 December 1835, we see that Jones revered the Egypt of the Pharaohs, with its imperial grandeur and phenomenal energy, as the 'great parent of civilisation', the inventors of writing and of the sublime in architecture. He admired their solemn mysteries and their understanding of the stars and planets. He was to place two copies of the Rosetta Stone and a translation in the Egyptian Court at Sydenham.[69] The young artists travelled up the Nile to Nubia, ate rice and lived 'in Arab simplicity'; the Fellaheen built them a wall and carried the ladders they used for taking measurements.[70]

Jones and Goury next stayed in Constantinople for six months before moving on to Granada to study the Alhambra. Jones laboured obsessively tracing or casting every ornament at the Alhambra during a six-month cholera quarantine when nobody was allowed to leave Granada; they seem in part a tribute to Goury, who died there from the cholera in August 1834 aged thirty-one; Jones took his body home to France. He returned to the Alhambra to make more drawings in 1837. On the title-page of his *Plans, Elevations, Sections and Details of the Alhambra*, 1836–45, with the monumental chromolithographic plates he printed himself in an atelier at the Adelphi, and on which he was said to have 'thrown away a fortune', he named Jules Goury as co-author and dedicatee.[71] Jones was said to have been drawn to the Alhambra by Victor Hugo's poems; in his *Handbook to the Alhambra Court* he quoted Hugo's image of the moon shining through a thousand Arab arches making repeated white trefoils on the walls of the courts and halls, creating a grammar of ornament in moonlight:

> Ou l'on entend la nuit de magiques syllables
> Quand la lune, à travers les mille arceaux arabes,
> Sème les murs de trèfles blancs.[72]

For Jones the Courts were plainly a world away from an adolescent's post-card album of fine art; they were a sanctuary for his deepest feelings about what is sacred in architecture and colour. The Egyptian Court and the colossal Aboo-Simbel figures allude to the origins of the sublime; the Alhambra Court was intimately connected with his theories on the benefits of colour and patterns to the psyche. An obituary referred to the Alhambra Court as 'his masterpiece in every way', and tells us that probably the happiest days of his life were directing and watching its construction. The writer recalls the romantic origin of the court when Jones was young,

> the enthusiastic student who bivouacked for three long years in the silent and deserted courts of the magnificent Palace of the Arab conquerors of Spain until his whole genius became penetrated and imbued with the secrets of that mysterious symmetry, that marvellous unity in diversity pervading the symbolic ornamentation of the stately courts of the Alhambra… a voluntary exile and anchorite.[73]

His award in 1857 of the R.I.B.A.'s Royal Gold Medal was in recognition of what he had done at Sydenham; the Institute's portrait of him by Henry Phillips shows 'Alhambra' Jones standing in front of the gilded diaper patterns of the Court. The Crystal Palace was at the heart of his programme to regenerate English taste, extend education in architecture and decoration, and teach the history of civilisation. It was also the climax of his ambitions. Among the intricate diapers of the Alhambra Court and on the pediment of the Egyptian Court he incorporated slogans praising art education, like the ponderous legend inscribed on the Alhambra Court: 'Thou wilt reap benefit of a commentary on decoration.'[74] Asked by Paxton, at the laying of the First Column of the Palace, to address an audience among whom were all the investors and railway promoters, Jones made the somewhat unworldly statement that it was 'rare to find gentlemen willing to lay out such a vast sum on the art education of the people'.[75]

Jones shared some important tenets with Pugin, most notably the belief that the Reformation had been 'a death blow' to architecture and church decoration, since it had separated 'the tie which had ever existed between religion and art'. The styles of art he believed in, particularly the Islamic, proclaimed both God and virtue in magical Koranic inscriptions interwoven with geometrical ornaments and floral motifs.[76] He became 'the most potent apostle of colour' in a 'whitewash period', successful 'in his resolution to diffuse the love of colour in decorative art'. When speaking of the 'true principles of the Moors', Jones was as eloquent and fierce as Pugin laying down the 'true principles of Gothic'.[77] Like Pugin, he detested the decadence of modern European art, and in particular the luxurious vulgarity of the French furniture and fabrics on view at Hyde Park: 'the fruitless struggle to produce in art novelty without beauty – beauty without intelligence: all work without faith'. In ornament, as we saw in Chapter 1, he insisted on what we would call the *stylising* (then called *conventionalising*) of natural forms such as flowers. This quality he found and admired in Islamic, Chinese and early medieval work.[78] He could not abide 'realistic' three-dimensional representations, such as bouquets on fabrics or carpets and 'scenes' on wall-papers. In a letter of 2 July 1852 to George Godwin he wrote that Indian floral designs – a Paisley shawl is a Jonesian artefact – and Pugin's wall-papers shared a high common factor: flowers were treated as 'flat as a diagram', and both followed 'well-defined modes of conventionalising natural objects'.[79] Pugin published *Floriated Ornament*, a chromolithographic book with thirty-one plates, in 1849; Jones may have had some part in the publication, and in the adaptation of chromolithographic techniques to Pugin's Minton tiles. When Pugin wrote to *The Builder* in 1845 to criticise the School of Design for making its pupils copy the stale models of Pompeian arabesques and Greek capitals, which led to 'a miserable system of adaptation of obsolete symbols and designs, appropriate only to times and peoples from whom they originated', he declared that 'the real source of art is nature', and mentioned his current work on *Floriated Ornament* in which he would 'reveal the geometrical forms in vegetable and floral ornament'.[80]

Jones despised the Gothic Revival, which he called a 'galvanized corpse', and berated John Britton and Augustus Pugin (1762–1832), the father of A.W.N. Pugin, for their influence on it.[81] This animus becomes easier to understand when Jones proclaims, as he does several times (even quoting the very phrasing he used in his Society of Arts lecture in 1852), that Victorian architecture should be the result of 'intelligent and imaginative eclecticism' and not 'indolent and servile imitation'.[82]

Twenty years after the Sydenham Palace opened Owen Jones was dead, possibly from over-work – he had laboured eighteen hours a day for three months on the architecture and decorations of the Viceroy's Palace in Egypt. Jones's obituary in the *Athenaeum* invited the reader to 'look back upon the state of his favourite subject before his time', implying that he had played a significant part in changing puritan Victorian taste. Before Jones, *The Builder* said, colour 'was feared like the smallpox'. But not all would agree entirely with his dogma that there is no architecture without colour and that 'form without colour is like body without soul.'[83] *Building News* declared his work at Sydenham a genuinely transforming influence: 'To the genius of Owen Jones we owe that revival of polychromatic decoration in which England, for the last few centuries, was far behind all other nations. [...] The teachings of Ruskin may have done something, but the beautiful works of Owen Jones and the examples of the true principles of decorative Art he has left us at Sydenham, have largely educated the popular eye and taste in his direction.'[84] The doctrine of polychromy in architecture was spread to the United States by Jones's assistant John Mould (1825–86), who emigrated there in 1852. The Great Exhibition had helped to strengthen Jones's beliefs, defining himself by opposition to current English and European taste, and declaring that the cushions and a pair of colourful slippers in the Morocco section 'far outstripped' the artefacts from the United Kingdom on show.[85]

Jones's structures at the Crystal Palace, especially the Alhambra Court, were decorated again according to George Field's theory of the combinations of primaries: blue, red and yellow (or gold). There is almost a religious flavour in Jones's phrase 'primaries of prismatic intensity'. The two buildings named by him as having the 'most perfect modern decorative schemes', the Royal Chapel in Munich and the church of St Vincent de Paul in Paris, were coloured, he tells us, in schemes of blue, red and gold.[86] Much later, in 1882, Edward Poynter said in a

Owen Jones, drawing for *The Grammar of Ornament*, Plate XXXVIII: 'Turkish 3'. © Victoria and Albert Museum.

Owen Jones, Moresque ornament in primary colours for J.G Lockhart, *Ancient Spanish Ballads*, 1841.

lecture that Jones 'appears to have thought that in decoration one blue is as good as another, and one red as good as another', and unfairly attributed to him the Pompeian Court which he dismissed as 'coarse and offensive'.[87]

It is relevant to our theme that Jones's other passion was the decoration, illumination and printing of colour books, at which he worked in association with colleagues from the Crystal Palace – Henry Warren[88] and Henry Layard. The firm of Day and Son, who printed most of these books including *The Grammar of Ornament*, laid out more than £50,000 on their production.[89] Jones's book decorations involved a dialogue of blue, red and yellow in intricacies of 'Saracenic' convolution, intricacy and harmony.

Jones believed that early illuminated manuscripts and stained glass used strong primary colours; this was characteristic of earliest and purest architecture and decoration – he cited Nineveh, Central America, Pharaonic Egypt and Greece. Pompeii, on the other hand, employed secondary and tertiary colours. He believed that at the Alhambra the original blue and red of the Moors were painted over with green and purple by

'The Egyptian Court', showing enfilade through the Greek and Roman Courts to the Alhambra.

Charles V, and that when the Greeks conquered Egypt harmony was spoiled by the introduction of secondaries.[90] Jones used prismatic blue, red and yellow as his livery in decorating the exterior of the building he designed for an Oxford Street bazaar in 1858, called 'the London Crystal Palace'; the roof was decorated with stars in ruby, sapphire and topaz yellow in stained glass 'mosaic'. The same colour scheme predominated in St James's Music Hall, Piccadilly (demolished in 1905), 'by Owen Jones, the decorative and polychromatic artist', with its 'Alhambran enrichment in alto-rilievo'.[91]

In 1865 Jones published *Joseph and his Brethren*, one of his most successful chromolithographic 'illuminated' books; his wide polychromatic ornamental borders were in a free Egyptian style. His old associate and friend the landscape water-colourist Henry Warren (1794–1879, like Joseph Bonomi a pupil of the sculptor Nollekens)

made the illustrations. The story of Joseph was a natural choice for this work because of its homage to the polychromatic principle, and it is a surprise to find Warren's representation of Joseph's coat of many colours clearly striped red and blue with thin *green* lines in between. Potiphar, on the other hand, is clad in a splendid tunic of orthodox red, yellow and blue.

The Egyptian Court

It was by means of the Egyptian Court that Jones paid homage to the style that had been thought the parent and prototype of all architecture. It was also a memorial to his excited and assiduous early days of studying the antiquities of Egypt in company with Goury and Bonomi. He designed for it a composite temple rather than a model of one particular monument. While a visit to this Court was said to be of greater value than a year spent in Egypt itself,

Philip Delamotte, 'Avenue of Sphinxes', North Transept, looking across Nave to Alhambra.

it was criticised for its reduced scale, which was particularly misleading in a series that contained full-size 'reproductions' such as the domestic Pompeian House – and for offering the folio of Egypt in duodecimo.[92] Jones was also criticised for putting together this anthology of different temples and halls, some saying that a model of one entire single building might have been better, but Jones argued that since space was limited (to 100 square feet), he would show features of different styles and periods in the same way that the temples themselves showed accretions of different periods.[93] He gave as his sources the drawings that he and Goury made in 1833 and the familiar works by Sir Gardner Wilkinson and others. Delamotte's photographs of the construction show Jones's workshop boarded off and the plaster pieces for the court scattered around, with sphinxes and portions of columns, just as a news report describes them in May 1853.[94]

From the Nave an avenue of eight lions, cast from a pair brought from Egypt by the Duke of Northumberland, led up to the entrance portal. The 'Ptolemaic' façade was based on the portico at Edfu, with columns and capitals copied 'from examples of the best period', and on the panels of the pilasters Bonomi placed the names of the directors of the Crystal Palace Company in hieroglyphics. The visitor then passed under a winged globe with serpents, a protecting divinity of entrances, to a court reproducing the Hall of Columns in the temple of Karnac; the façade as formed of eight splendid Osirides

Nelson's *The Crystal Palace*, 1862.

from the Ramseion at Thebes – also called the tomb of Ozymandias – each holding a flail. Sotheby thought that these 'Lilliputian' Karnac columns, a 'mimic imitation', were 'most uninteresting'; one of his correspondents compared them to skittles.[95] Passing through an inner court the visitor could turn to the Egyptian Museum or to the representation of the tomb of Beni-Hassan painted with frescoes of everyday life in ancient Egypt and a small 'model' of the complete temple and figures at Aboo-Simbel in Nubia, which gave a context for the two colossal seated figures from it that were reproduced full-size by Jones in the Transept. Papyrus-capitals, which so fascinated Jones as a decorative motif, stood here. On the outer walls of the court were more frescoes, of Kings being crowned or initiated into sacred mysteries. Jones was of course familiar with contemporary knowledge about Egypt; the *Crystal Palace Expositor* in its commentary on the Egyptian Court mentioned Schlegel's writings on Egyptian culture and its penetration into deep mysteries, and Plato's most sublime speculations after his Egyptian studies, the source for his belief in *anima mundi*, the immortal universal soul.[96]

As for the colouring of the Court, the critic of the *Art Journal* was charmed by the 'extreme beauty' of the columns and capitals, but thought the blood-red faces, like Banquo's visage, had been painted 'with the colours of a clown in the circus'. Lady Eastlake compared the colouring of the Court (as in the Nineveh Court) with the 'gaudiest hues of Manchester cottons', and 'colours that even Mme. Tussaud would disdain'. Gottfried Semper wrote that turquoise blue was used as the symbolic holy colour of the priesthood and aristocracy in Egypt.[97]

The Egyptian Revival style had been in vogue with

English architects and designers in a small way from the 1790s onwards, and was taken up by the polymathic designer Thomas Hope (1769–1831). Later Napoleon's campaign in Egypt intensified excitement on the continent over Egyptian antiquities and in London over the new acquisitions made by the British Museum and by Sir John Soane from Giovanni Belzoni's excavations. Jones's Egyptian Court delivered much historical and architectural interest but had little influence, if any, on architectural practice. Its original glories may only be dimly recalled in London by intimations of the style in some palm-leaved bases to Assyrian-Egyptian columns of cast iron at London Bridge Station, or in a Masonic temple at the Great Eastern Hotel, Liverpool Street. Edward John Poynter in his large and theatrical canvas *Israel in Egypt* (RA, 1867; Guildhall Art Gallery) reproduced a prominent fresco from the Egyptian Court and a carved lion (as painted in plaster reproduction at Sydenham); these and other details appear to derive from Jones's Court rather than from coincidence.[98] Thus a line of descent leads from Jones's Egyptian Court to the elaborate 'archaeological' reconstructions of Hollywood epic films. Apart from its imaginative hold on the visitor as a stage-setting, the Court's lasting contribution was the support it gave to Jones's teaching of the theory and practice of design with examples of the abstraction of natural forms and brilliance of colour.

The colossal Aboo-Simbel figures

An early scheme for the interior was for one 'colossal' Egyptian figure, 70 feet high, to stand at the north end of the Nave, one of the two most dominant positions in the entire Palace. However, when James Fergusson complained that the figure would have 'extinguished' the Assyrian bulls of his Nineveh Court, Jones was invited instead to make a pair of identical figures aligned with his western sequence of courts at the back of the North transept adjoining the road-side, a temptation he could not resist. He proposed, probably at the same time, that he should create a Sphinx Avenue, formed of twenty cast from one original in the Louvre. The new positions of the figures and the Sphinx Avenue, marked 'lions', are inked in by some director's hand on the lithographic 1853 ground-plan of the Palace, now in the Guildhall Library. The avenue, in Egypt a mile long, was reduced to less than 300 feet crossing the Nave at right angles.

Sotheby wrote with a touch of malice that the move of

the colossal Aboo-Simbel figures to the less conspicuous site was 'fortunate for the credit of the Directors'. Jones's pair of figures – the Aboo-Simbel site had four – were 51 feet high; the originals were the largest in Egypt or Nubia, with the exception of the Sphinx beside the Pyramids at Gizeh.[99] The figures had been excavated from the sand by Belzoni in 1817, and Jones's own measurements made at the site were used for the design. Jones's figures were built up from sawn blocks of plaster by M. Desachy and French craftsmen from Paris over rectangular blocks of brick; the stages of their construction are shown in Delamotte's photographs. The general opinion was th;at the statues, whose heads were modelled by Bonomi from a cast at the British Museum,[100] looked well until they were painted. 'Hot and glowing', 'glowering and roasting', said the *Art Journal*. 'Monstrous', said William Michael Rossetti; 'covered in red, yellow and blue housepaint ordered by the hogshead', wrote Lady Eastlake.[101] Sotheby made a fool of himself over their colouring, writing: 'I happened to be at the Crystal Palace when the marbles [casts] were first being painted under the inspection of Mr Owen Jones. At the moment I was pleased with the novelty, and so expressed myself to Mr Bonomi. The next day, however, I called, telling him I had quite regretted having entertained such an opinion.' In 1855 he wrote a sour *Letter to the Directory*, saying: 'Now, Gentlemen, look at the two monster figures occupying a very important position of the building. In their present state, bedaubed with gorgeous colours, they are perfectly frightful, and devoid of all power to excite the smallest degree of awe or veneration for the marvellous remains of ancient Egypt.' Sotheby set himself at the same time against Jones on the notorious issue of his having coloured the casts of the Greek bas-reliefs, noting that he agreed with the late eighteenth-century architect 'Athenian' Stuart that traces of colour on Greek statuary were the work of barbarians in the Middle Ages. In a sarcastic footnote he suggested that Jones should persuade the Trustees at the British Museum to colour all the classical statuary there. He also attacked the 'glaring' colours of the Assyrian Court, pointing out that in Layard's description the original colours of the palaces were 'delicate' and occasional.[102] Lady Eastlake mocked the 'high-sounding, but now ever ridiculous name of polychromy'.[103]

In Sotheby's scrap-album (now at the Bromley Central Library) is preserved a riposte provoked by his attack in the form of a personal letter by Digby Wyatt in Jones's defence, written on 28 December 1854, the day that Sotheby's pamphlet was reprinted entire in the *Morning Post*. Wyatt had been placed in an awkward position by Sotheby's pamphlet having praised his own contributions to the Courts while violently attacking Jones's Courts and colours; after expressing his 'sincere regret' that Sotheby should have written the pamphlet and mentioning how kindly his own works and he himself were spoken of, he wrote:

> As sharing with Owen Jones the general responsibilities of the Fine Art Department, I feel much hurt by several personalities, which I am sorry to have met with in the 'letter'.
>
> Having known Jones intimately for many years, and during much of the last two having worked untiringly with him, I may almost say day and night, through infinite vexation and anxiety, I do feel acutely any attacks made upon him. If ever a man threw all his life and energy into his work – if ever a man had deeply at heart what he felt to be the profound importance of the task upon which he was engaged I am sure Owen Jones was that man. If the zeal and ability with which he has ever sought to promote what he considered to be the true interests of his employers, and the Public, should have at any time urged him too far forward, and led to his execution of works too daring or inadequate in design – surely the larger share of blame (if any should be due) should fall upon the shoulders of those whose duty it was to watch over, and if necessary, curb his ardour or stimulate his exertion.
>
> Pray do not misunderstand my protests, but forgive me for following your own example of speaking one's mind.
>
> I am, my dear Sir, Yours very faithfully,
>
> M. Digby Wyatt.[104]

While the letter is a defence of Jones, read between the lines it seems tacitly to admit that the quality of his work at Sydenham was uneven, owing to the great pressure to which he was subjected. It was often said that he had too much to do.

Both the Colossal Figures and the Nineveh Court were destroyed in the Fire of 1866, and the wreckage of the Figures is shown starkly in photographs and engravings. If they and the Nineveh Court were less brilliant than the Alhambra Court, they were together the boldest features of the Fine Arts Department.

The Alhambra Court

The finishing touches were only put to the Alhambra Court with the completion of work on the Hall of the Abencerrages, with some stained glass in red, blue and yellow, which finished in May 1855. *The Crystal Palace*

THE CRYSTAL PALACE AT SYDENHAM.—THE EGYPTIAN AVENUE: COLOSSAL FIGURES FROM ABOO SIMBEL.—(SEE PAGE 78.)

Illustrated London News, 1854.

A REVERIE AT THE CRYSTAL PALACE.

Punch, 1854.

Entrance to the Court of Lions.

Herald declared that even if it had been Jones's only work, his immortality would have been assured.[105] Here was the temple and manifesto of the primary colours, red predominating to recall the meaning of the name Alhambra in Arabic. The moulded surfaces in the Court of Lions were coloured a deep red, the portions in the shade were blue, and points exposed to the light were gold. Green tiles were used on the mosaic dado, but not on the stucco above it. This Jones explained as being licensed by his dictum (it became Proposition 17 in *The Grammar of Ornament*) that while primaries must be used above a dado, some secondary and tertiary colours might appear below it. *The Builder* referred to its 'radiant bloom'.[106]

Not surprisingly this court was the most talked about. When George Eliot and G.H. Lewes visited the Alham-bra itself in Granada, they thought it 'vastly inferior' to the work of their friend Owen Jones.[107] Even for Sotheby it was 'the perfection of decorative style'. In *The Ten Chief Courts of the Sydenham Palace* the difference between Jones's bright copy and the faded original was said to be that between 'a flower just ruffled open by the soft violence of the south wind, and the same blossom with its colours flown, its odour lost, hanging yellow and withering with decay'.[108] This is a strange doctrine for travellers sensitive to the softening patina of time's decay and to the numinous character of some old sites: 'Whenever and wherever man has built beautiful temples, churches, and palaces', Vernon Lee wrote in 1897, 'he has been impelled to bedizen them with primary colours, of which, in Venice and the Alhambra, time at last made something agreeable and time also, in Greece, has judged best to obliterate every odious trace.'[109] Boutell in the *Art Journal* suggested that models and photographs were needed at Sydenham to show the actual condition of the original buildings on which the Courts were modelled, that 'showed so fresh and perfect in the restorations'. In 1857 there were French photographs of Egyptian subjects, and by 1867 there were 400 French and Italian photographs of architecture and sculpture on show.[110]

The Alhambra Court was in three parts, the most ambitious being the Court of Lions with its arcaded cloister and fountain. This led into the Hall of the Abencerrages, through the centre of which a stream filled with 'brilliant fish' was intended to run, and the Hall of Justice. Both of these would already have been familiar to many visitors because of their particular literary associations: they were the subject of chapters in Washington Irving's romantic *Tales of the Alhambra* of 1832. A small museum housed some of Jones's original casts from 1837; chromolithographic plates from his masterwork on the Alhambra were displayed.[111] The moulding of the roof of the Hall of the Abencerrages, consisting of 5,000 separate 'stalactite' pieces, 'a hanging honeycomb of gold and richly blended colour', was made in gelatine, which Jones said was 'of essential service in aiding the rapid execution' of the Court, since the combinations could be made on the table rather than on the arch. The roof was of Blashfield terra cotta tiles, forming a kind of Moorish 'barge-boarding',[112] and the pavement and the mosaic dados were made by Minton. Digby Wyatt, in his Society of Arts lecture in 1858 on Minton's influence on ceramic manufacture, spoke of the tiles used by Owen Jones for the Alhambra Court being 'various modifications of azaleos…painted on white slip covering an earthenware body of the tile'. He added that some of these were perforated and others were 'modelled into foliage…at the suggestion of the late Welby Pugin'. Blashfield manufactured Alhambra, Byzantine, Pompeian, Roman and Greek tiles and Byzantine and 'Mauresque' ornaments, which he listed in his catalogues.[113] There were couches and cushions, 'somewhat improperly treated by the public', and plants; an inventory of 1909 counted 248 ferns. Camellias, fuchsias and myrtles were planted in the flower-beds.[114]

The Alhambra Court was a prodigy both in the research that went into it and in its construction. On 25 July 1842 an advertisement for Jones's monograph on the Alhambra stated that 'to insure perfect accuracy an impression of every ornament throughout the palace was taken, whether in plaster or onto unsized paper'. *The Times* said on Jones's death: 'He set himself down before the Alhambra, and made siege of it', and then 'revealed it to Europe at large and to the Spanish themselves'.[115] William Michael Rossetti noted that besides the passion for colour and pattern manifested in Jones's 'restoration', it was created 'in the spirit of genuine love'.[116] Four of Jones's Alhambra casts survive in the Victoria and Albert Museum, bought from his pupil the sculptor Henry Alonzo Smith; it also has to be recorded that in the twentieth century the Museum threw away more than 200 of Jones's paper impressions.[117]

Not everybody liked the Alhambra Court, and there were sneers, as an article in the *Athenaeum* that called it 'Othello in a Bond Street suit'.[118] Ruskin objected to the original on historical and aesthetic grounds and at the same time (1858) revealed his animus against Jones's decorative work, spitefully throwing back Jones's prolific activities against the Court:

> The Alhambra is no more characteristic of Arab work, than Milan Cathedral is of Gothic: it is a late building, a work of the Spanish dynasty in its last decline, and its ornamentation is fit for nothing but to be transferred to patterns of carpets or bindings of books, together with marbling, and mottling, and other mechanical recommendations. The Alhambra ornament has of late been largely used in shop fronts, to the no small detriment of Regent Street and Oxford Street.[119]

Francis Turner Palgrave despised the 'bastard and mechanical decoration of the Alhambra': it was bad luck that it had been brought to the public in the Court as the type of Oriental art, 'since it has little to recommend it except a certain ingenuity of linear arrangement and pleasantness of colour'.[120]

Jones's handbook *The Alhambra Court* reveals some of his theories concerning the deeper functions of the eye, meditating on patterns: 'It is as necessary for the happiness of man to develop the innate poetry of his nature by the cultivation of his eye, as to develop his intellect by acquiring the power of reading and writing.' He discusses, with diagrams, the effect on the eye and mind of contemplating the diapers on the Alhambra. He remarks on how the eye is carried towards a containing angle, and is immediately checked by lines with an opposite tendency, producing harmony and repose.[121] He would undoubtedly have been interested in Jung's theories of mandala symbolism and the healing harmonious reconciliation of opposites caused to the psyche by meditation on Hindu images. Jones in the handbook also repeats the doctrine that all good patterns emerge from a 'parent stem', like a hand or a chestnut leaf; this was Proposition 11 in *The Grammar of Ornament*. The theory was used by his disciple Christopher Dresser (as discussed above, pp. 20–21), who said that Jones first taught him to think.[122] W. M. Rossetti observed 'the endless intertexture and convolution' of the diapers on the walls, that exhaust the eye without wearying it', and understood Jones's theory that 'each minutest detail of a part of the whole, is an offshoot of a stem, a completion of some incompleteness.' Jones's handbook ended with a claim that Moorish decoration surpassed Greek, Egyptian, Byzantine and Roman work both in colour and in ornament by adding poetry in a satisfied combination of eye, intellect and the affections.[123]

At Sydenham Jones used his arabesque designs also in the Park with an enormous and complex arched ironwork structure for a 'Rosery' arcade. In 1863–6 he designed magnificent polychromatic 'Alhambra' recessed ceilings at the palatial town house of his patron and friend Alfred Morrison at 16 Carlton House Terrace.[124] A 'Moorish kiosk' by Jones in cast iron, measuring 80 by 40 feet, with double columns and 'open arabesque work' at the sides, was illustrated in *The Builder* in 1866. Described as 'intended for Bombay', it was temporarily erected in 1867 'on land at present in Exhibition Road adjoining the Horticultural Gardens' in South Kensington. *The Builder* called it 'perhaps the most remarkable specimen of ornamental ironwork yet erected'.[125]

Jones's masterpiece, the Alhambra Court, turned his faith into practice, educating the eye in ornamental grammar and oriental harmonies of primary colours, and popularising arabesque decoration.

The Greek and Roman Courts

Though designed with some original and imaginative features, the Greek and Roman Courts engaged Jones less deeply than the Alhambra, and the general view was that he was better at expressing 'barbaric splendour' than 'Greek refinement'.[126] An obvious model for the Greek Court was the Glyptothek of 1830 in Munich, designed by Leo von Klenze, which as well as a famous collection of antique statuary housed a number of plaster casts. Both Jones and Digby Wyatt knew it well, and Jones was obviously aware of competition from the British Museum and its real sculptures. *The Builder* said that both the Greek and Roman Courts showed little of architecture and a 'somewhat disorderly arrangement of works of art'.[127] The Greek Court was essentially a sculpture court, intended to resemble an Athenian agora; one side was formed of a two-ninths scale model of the Parthenon by Francis Penrose, and the many casts were rather crowded together. A few architectural models were on view, and architectural casts and bas-reliefs were fixed to walls, with candelabra, architectural scrollwork and palmettes, as in Sir John Soane's Museum. Jones decorated five painted trabeated ceilings with small stars in borders with light and dark backgrounds, and 'a diapering pattern in blue, red and gold, an object of very general admiration'.[128] The deeply coffered ceiling of the Entrance Hall of the British Museum (*c.* 1847) was a 'Grecian Doric' polychromatic forerunner of Jones's ceilings after antique precedents, 'enriched with Greek frets and other ornaments, painted in encaustic, in various colours, most harmoniously blended. The large gold star upon a blue ground, in the centre of each coffer has a superb effect.'[129]

Taken altogether there is not much evidence to support Christopher Dresser's assertion in his memorial eulogy that Jones's instincts were essentially Greek and only superficially inclined towards the Moorish. Jones can be shown to have venerated the Greek anthemion motif, as in his decorative embellishments to Millman's 1849 edition of Horace for John Murray, where it is used on page after page with variations of almost Art Nouveau elaboration, and on the plain *stele* of his tomb in Kensal Green cemetery, London, an anthemion crowns the inscription, curiously recalling the spokes of the semicircular lunette in the Crystal Palace transept. As Jones was well aware, this was a very ancient symbolic ornament, since the Greeks had adopted it from the Assyrian stylisation of honeysuckle.

The age of Pericles was chosen to be represented in the Greek Court, and Jones inscribed the famous Periclean phrases from the Funeral Oration – love of beauty with moderation and love of wisdom without effeminacy – on the frieze, along with monograms and the names of Greek cities inside wreaths. George Scharf painted frescoes of mythological scenes, Mount Olympus and the building of the Parthenon. At the centre of the hall were casts of the Venus de Milo and two other famous statues of the goddess, and to the side the Laocoön. The 217 casts (mostly statuary, but with some tombstones and architectural features) were white, but the bas-reliefs on the walls were coloured by Jones. The eyes and wounds in *The Battle of Amazons* were heightened with colour. Jones also coloured the horses and horsemen and the background in the Panathenaic Frieze, 214 feet long, which had been 'skilfully restored' in plaster by Raffaelle Monti.[130] This was a bold statement 'to show the various opinions that are entertained respecting the Polychromy of the ancients'. However, even as early as November 1853 *The Times*, which found the colouring excellent, forecast a row with the critics for his trespassing on 'classic propriety', and at his death his obituarist recalled that these decorations 'did not aid the author in gaining acceptance of his views'.[131]

The frieze was coloured in three sections: the first was 'like a picture', with the riders warm olive, their faces flesh-coloured with reddened lips, their hair gilded, and the drapery white; the section of the frieze that fronted the Egyptian Court was coloured white against a blue ground, just as the reproduction high on the facade of the Athenaeum in Pall Mall is today (in 1854 it was white). On the third section of the frieze, also against a white ground, the horses were painted dark brown and dun grey. The second and plainer of the two schemes was more popular.[132] An article in the *Morning Post* for 23 October 1854, summarising the row, said that Jones's most sturdy opponent was *Blackwood's*, which claimed that he had distorted his academic evidence. For example, the passage from Pliny that Jones adduced in his support for colouring statues actually referred not to painting in colours but to the varnishing and finishing of statuary. Jones expressed his genius in an impetuous way, the newspaper said: 'He would vermilionise the palest face of death.' Lady Eastlake liked Monti's restoration of the frieze but thought the colourings crude and heavy, creating a 'perverse hybrid'. The *Art Journal* said that painting casts destroyed 'delicacy and beauty', adding: 'If polychromy is to be resorted to in such terms, we think the tints should be very tenderly applied; anything like house-painting is repulsive.' The painted horses and horsemen were 'harsh and monotonous'.[133] When Sir John Gardner Wilkinson published in 1858 *On Colour, and on the Necessity for a General Diffusion of Taste among all Classes*, drawing on his experience of continental museums and their decoration, he praised the harmonies of Jones's Greek and Alhambra Courts. In the same book he complained that, while the working classes were prevented by their labours from visiting museums during six days of the week, the best means of instructing them, the Crystal Palace at Sydenham, was still closed on the seventh day. Henry Layard, writing in his autobiography about colour schemes in the Munich museums, appeared to agree with Jones:

> Nor do I like the Munich decoration. The horror which the Bavarian artists seem to have of pure colour gives all their external ornamentation a washed-out appearance, which takes away all strength and beauty from their works. Unfortunately, the taste established at Munich has spread to England, and Fergusson is one of its most ardent disciples. I longed to get a brushful of pure red or blue paint to dab a little over the frescoes in the Pinacothek and Glyptothek.[134]

W. M. Rossetti was unconvinced by Jones's scholarship – the so-called 'authorities' he adduced to support his case – and thought too much was conjectural, in addition to being too bright and new. The licence Jones took in putting into practice his theories of how the Greeks coloured their temples and statuary unsettled traditional academics and many well-educated people. The press also exercised their wit at his expense; the *Art Journal* said his efforts were like 'penny plain and twopence coloured' prints.[135] The critic in *Blackwood's* wrote that Jones's polychromatic colouring 'put your eyes out' and was an 'audacious insult', adding that the horses looked like fairground roundabout figures. No doubt, he predicted, Jones as 'Grand Polychromatic plenipotentiary' would soon take his paint pots to the British Museum to paint all the statues, and give the Venus de Milo a multicoloured wig.[136] Ruskin, repelled by Owen Jones's use of crimson, jeered at the attempt to 'restore' ancient buildings at the Crystal Palace, writing in 1856 in *Modern Painters* of their 'intense absurdity' and of 'ignorant colourists'.[137]

Jones wrote a rejoinder to his critics, *An Apology for the Colouring of the Greek Court*, published by the Crystal Palace Company in 1854 in the series of pocket Handbooks, but it makes uneasy reading. Where he seems to be aware of lack of sufficient evidence, he abruptly changes his tone and makes over-confident assertions. He printed as appendices to his essay learned supporting articles from G.H. Lewes and Gottfried Semper and an extract from the Elgin Marbles committee of 1836. He also drew on a R.I.B.A. report of 1842 on the issue, signed by Westmacott, Eastlake, Cockerell and Faraday, who had analysed paint samples from temples and concluded that there was a 'very strong probability' that excavated fragments showed traces of blue, red and yellow. The theory or fact of the Greeks having coloured their sculptures and buildings did not seem to distress Jones's contemporaries so much as the sheer indigestible effect of his strong colours used on familiar sculpture.

Jones insisted that he was 'alone responsible' for the decoration of the ceilings and the colouring of the Greek Court generally, and called his work an 'experiment': 'At a very early stage in arrangements for forming in the Crystal Palace a series of reproductions of architectural monuments, I felt that to colour a Greek monument would be one of the most interesting problems I could undertake.' Jules Goury and Semper had first interested him in the idea, and writers on the continent remained interested in the colouring of classical buildings and statues, in particular J.I. Hittorf of Paris (1792–1867), who wrote a study of the subject in the 1830s. According to Jones, 'white marble' had 'an artificial value in our eyes', and he believed that, like Egyptian columns, Greek temples had a thin coating of stucco which was painted – 'in a higher key', moreover, than his own attempts. Of his use of red and blue in this Court he wrote: 'I was led at once to adopt a blue ground' – as 'the Greek eye would have demanded it'.[138] In his colouring of the Choragic Monument of Lysicrates he admitted that he placed it before the public as an experiment, and had no authority for its colouring: a dark red ground, with a gilded fret, dead yellow leaves, and a row of green anthemia.[139] Semper said that the original monument bore slight traces of blue and red, with green for the acanthus leaves, and that on Trajan's Column green, blue and yellow were found with possibly some gilding.[140] The coloured Choragic Monument stands in the background of James Roberts's meticulous watercolour of 1855, *The Imperial and Royal Visit to the Crystal Palace at Sydenham*.[141]

Jones found that his plaster casts needed four coats of paint – plaster was an 'ungracious' medium because of its absorbent 'suction'. Another difficulty he mentioned was that, compared with the way the Greeks intended them to be seen, the bas-reliefs at Sydenham were too near the eye and too near the light. In 1857 the revised edition of Phillips's *General Guide Book* tactfully insisted that Jones's colouring of the frieze represented 'suggestions' rather than 'restorations'.[142] Jones gave the Roman Court walls of 'many-coloured marble', which was said to convey gorgeous magnificence in contrast to the reposeful Greek Court. The Court's external arches were copied from the bottom storey of the Colosseum. The largest compartment was the hall of a palace with statuary; three small courts represented baths, with frescoes by Signor Abbate, the authority on Pompeian decoration, and were graced by casts of the 'Venus Victorious', the Apollo Belvedere and a Diana. Large models, intended for the Court, of the Colosseum and the Pantheon were reported to be leaving Rome in December 1854.[143]

The multi-coloured false marbles of the Roman Court played a less striking role in Jones's scheme of education in colour than the major Courts, but all were designed to engage and excite the eye of the beholder. George Eliot, in her review of Jones's *Grammar of Ornament* in the *Fortnightly Review*, appeared to be aware of the pain caused to him by his critics, whom she reminded of her friend's noble aims to banish ugliness from our streets and homes, 'to make both the outside and the inside of our dwellings worthy of a world where there are forests, and flower-tressed meadows and the plumage of birds… Those who are most disposed to dispute with the architect about his colouring, must at least recognise the high artistic principle which has directed his attention to coloured ornamentation as a proper branch of architecture.'[144]

William Maskell, the antiquarian priest (1814?–90), wrote in 1876 of the colouring of statuary that 'modern taste is rather against decoration of this kind, and denies that sculpture gains an improved effect by means of colour. But we must remember that colour was used at the best period of the Greek school, and the most famous statues which the world ever knew were ornamented in this way.'[145] In 1862 the sculptor John Gibson exhibited at the International Exhibition in South Kensington one of the most controversial Victorian works of art, his *Tinted Venus*. This marble statue was mildly coloured – in the eyes, the flaxen hair and flesh tones and on the drapery – and waxed. Gibson believed in sculptural polychromy, and the *Venus* was shown along with two of his other coloured statues. For its display at South Kensington Jones designed a Greek temple, coloured black, red, buff and blue,[146] an amorous shrine to immortal polychromy.* Jones's inscription on the shrine reads

'*Nec vita, nec sanitas, nec pulchritudo, nec sine colore juventus*' [Without colour no life, nor health, nor beauty, nor youth].

Maskell wrote elsewhere, also in 1876, that people's appreciation of design, and 'judgement as to what is really good', had greatly improved in the last fifty years.[147] Rejection of the coarse and ugly was certainly helped by the education of the eye in refinement at both the South Kensington Museum (from 1857) and at the Crystal Palace, whatever their shortcomings, and by the teachings of the arbiters of taste associated with both institutions. Jones's 'Principles of Decorative Art' – both as theories and in their practical expression at Sydenham – were carried forward most by his distinguished disciple, the fertile 'ornamentist' Christopher Dresser (1834–1904). On the title-page of his *Art of Decorative Design* (1862) Dresser styled himself 'Professor of Ornamental Art and Botany at the Crystal Palace' – in clear acknowledgement of Jones's influence on this book published with its chromolithographic plates by Day and Son. In his many books and articles Dresser often referred the public to Jones's Courts at Sydenham and to their Handbooks. Paxton would have been pleased that Dresser also directed his students to his 'illustrated encyclopaedia', suggesting that they should study the water-lilies in the indoor basins at the Palace to understand the geometric arrangement of form.[148]

Dresser, who collected Owen Jones's drawings, thought that his master's best works were the Alhambra and Greek Courts and St James's Hall. When Jones died in 1874 Dresser gave the lecture in his honour at South Kensington, where a large memorial display of Jones's work was put on at the International Exhibition, and declared him to be 'truly a great man, the greatest ornamentist of modern times'. Dresser claimed in a lecture to the Society of Arts that ornamentation should have higher recognition: it was 'not fine art merely' but 'high art'.[149] Both Jones and Dresser were deeply interested in botany, and when lecturing on the subject at the Schools of Design at Somerset House from 1854 he made weekly visits to Kew Gardens for specimens to show his students. As a young draughtsman he designed for Jones Plate 8 ('Plans and Elevations of Flowers') for Chapter XX of *The Grammar of Ornament*, showing plants as it

were architectonically. Jones wrote of this illustration: 'It will be seen that the basis of all form is geometry, the impulse which forms the surface, starting from the centre with equal force, necessarily stops at equal distances; the result is symmetry and regularity.'[150] Dresser admired the force in spring buds, and the vitality of patterns influenced by them, and continued to teach the doctrine of the stylisation of plant forms. In this he was by no means alone, for many contemporary teachers and practitioners of design connected with the School of Design (of Marlborough House and formerly of Somerset House), such as Redgrave and Wornum, had learned from the stylised linear outline botanical engravings in Dyce's *Drawing Book of the Government Schools of Design* of the 1840s, or the plates in Pugin's *Floriated Ornament* (1849), or had read John Lindley's lectures to the School of Design, *On the Symmetry of Vegetation* (1854). The doctrine of 'conventionalising' plant forms is well illustrated in Richard Redgrave's *Manual of Design* where a realistic woodcut of a sow-thistle is printed opposite another showing the same plant rendered as a 'conventionalised' symmetrical pattern. Ruskin in 1858 vehemently attacked this school and its admiration for Indian designs: 'It will not draw a flower, but only a spiral or a zig-zag.'[151]

Dresser shared Jones's love of Islamic and oriental art, and later extended the understanding and influence of oriental arts by travelling to Japan. He also endorsed colour harmonies and Field's theories of prismatic reds, yellows and blues. He actually designed variations of the Architectural Courts for the Alexandra Palace, 'illustrations' of Moorish and Egyptian villas.[152] His loyalty to Jones can be felt even in the way he expressed his hostility to the 'coarse' Assyrian and 'cold' Renaissance Courts at Sydenham designed by the other architects. Jones, Dresser and Gottfried Semper were among the first to take the designs and patterns in tribal art seriously; the first plates in Jones' *Grammar of Ornament* showed designs derived from 'Savage Tribes', and Semper drew attention to the colour harmonies in the patterns of straw and rush carpets of Oriental, American and African native peoples.[153] This was a reminder that the most 'primitive' of the 'nations of man' shown in the anthropological displays of the Palace's Natural History Department were also the original grammarians of ornament.

---

* A significant example of Jones's theory put into practice is a decorative scheme of 1847 in the church of St Bartholomew's, Sutton Waldron, between Blandford Forum and Shaftesbury in Dorset. The Gothic columns are rendered in blue, red and gold stripes, and the walls carry illuminated inscriptions and grammatical ornaments from the master's hand. The church, now carefully restored, is still eloquent with the 'prismatic intensity of the primaries'.

THE FINE ARTS COURTS, II
MATTHEW DIGBY WYATT AND JAMES FERGUSSON;
SCULPTURE

Matthew Digby Wyatt

Digby Wyatt and Owen Jones were known for their 'brotherhood in art' and close friendship, which the obituaries of both men mention. Wyatt was described by his contemporaries as affable, energetic, systematic, gentlemanly and nervously excitable (especially at committees).[1] Among the artists he counted as friends were Frederick, Lord Leighton and Edward Lear. Wyatt first worked in the office of his brother Thomas Henry Wyatt, the architect of the Byzantine church of SS. Mary and Nicholas at Wilton (1840–6), and during two years of continental study in France, Germany, Italy and Sicily he made many sketches. Later he published illustrated works on patterned mosaic floors and pictorial walls. Like Jones he was interested in medieval manuscript illumination, and applied his skills outside architecture – for example, designing the first Crystal Palace Company share certificate. Wyatt's preference was for what his *Memoir* called 'Renaissance rococo', a 'decided predilection for some of the less pure forms of Renaissance ornament'. He was said to have more architectural knowledge and more 'artistical intellectuality' than Jones.[2] There is a distinct difference between Jones's and Wyatt's Courts (except perhaps for the Pompeian). Phillips's *General Guide* says that while Jones's Courts were 'architectural restorations' in 'forms or characteristics', generally of one building, Wyatt's were more like an anthology, 'collections of ornamental details stamped with unmistakeable individuality'.[3]

Wyatt's own architecture, consistent with his own theories and Jones's, was more an adaptation than an imitation of former styles. His Society of Arts lecture of 1852 is strongly worded: 'The debilitating effects of nearly a century's copying without discrimination, appropriating without compunction, and falsifying without blushing still binds our powers in a vicious circle, from which we have hardly yet strength to break the spell.'[4] *The Builder* called Wyatt not so much a practitioner in architecture as an influence, with his studies and 'illustrations'.[5] After his appointment as the first Slade Professor of Fine Art at Cambridge (balanced with Ruskin as the first Slade Professor at Oxford), he continued to preach the gospel of the Sydenham Palace. He had already impressed his doctrine on Cambridge with the polychromatic west front of the former Addenbrooks Hospital (1864–5) on the opposite side of Trumpington Street from the Fitzwilliam Museum,

Prosper Lafaye, *Matthew Digby Wyatt*, 1851. Pencil. © Victoria and Albert Museum.

which Pevsner judged 'highly insensitive'.[6] His lectures revived the original Sydenham programme, insisting on 'the education of the eye', and quoting from his colleague James Fergusson's *An Historical Inquiry into the True Principles of Beauty in Art, more especially with reference to Architecture* (1849), an eccentric book on aesthetics, which included a classified and tabulated conspectus of all the arts – he had already referred to this book in his Society of Arts lecture in 1852, twenty years earlier. In the Cambridge lectures he quoted from the Handbooks to the Sydenham Courts, and frequently illustrated his points by referring to the Courts and the Aboo-Simbel figures. He praised the Alhambra Court and its creator's 'almost intuitive affinity' with the arts of the Saracens, and once again referred approvingly, as he had done at the Society of Arts in 1852, to Jones's theories of conventionalising natural forms and floral decorations, the idea of the 'parent stem' in ornaments, from root to flower.(see above, pp. 20–21) [7] The lecture series discussed sculpture and painting as well as architecture, and (in the spirit of 1851) closed with two on Fine Art applied to Industry.

At Sydenham Wyatt designed the Pompeian, Byzantine, Medieval, Renaissance, Italian and Elizabethan Courts. Sotheby, who – as we have seen – embarrassed Wyatt with his praise when he was so sharp about Jones, spoke of the 'perfectly wonderful' combination of art in his Courts, and praised the Renaissance Court as 'marvellous'.[8] Indeed the Court was the most admired at the time of all his work at Sydenham.

The Pompeian Court

Digby Wyatt made his first sketch for the building of the Pompeian Court at Pompeii itself,[9] and indicated the proportions of the rooms. The decorations were by the most notable Pompeian authority of the day, the Neapolitan draughtsman Giuseppe Abbate whom Jones and Wyatt had met at Pompeii where he directed the excavations 'for many years', and about whose writings on Pompeian decorations Wyatt had addressed the R.I.B.A. in 1853.[10] Abbate made tracings and cartoons and brought them to Sydenham to supervise their execution – and before returning to Naples in January 1854 with the sculptor Raffaelle Monti, was presented with a silver cigar-case by his artists at a dinner in the new Royal Crystal Palace Hotel on Norwood Hill west of the Palace.

In the earliest plans this Court, as well as the Alhambra Court, were to serve as cafés or restaurants, and were placed strategically at the end or beginning of the row of Courts; luckily these two came to be thought too small for catering. The bright colourings of the Pompeian Court can be appreciated in contemporary prints – the chromolithograph in Digby Wyatt's *Views of the Crystal Palace and Park* and the patent oil-colour print by George Baxter (1804–67). Convincing and charming as it may appear, the *Crystal Palace Expositor* could still write that it was the 'least attractive' of the courts; Sotheby found it exquisite but 'sombre and melancholy – it chills the feelings'. The promoters instead thought that the design and colouring would be of great value to English art manufacturers.[11]

There were two obvious sources. The first was archaeological: Wyatt's House is closely based on the 'House of the Tragic Poet', excavated in 1824, and described and illustrated in the second series of Sir William Gell's *Pompeiana* of 1832.[12] The other source was Bulwer Lytton's *Last Days of Pompeii* (1834), a favourite of the circulating libraries, set in the same house, which Lytton minutely described and called 'the House of Glaucus'.[13] By the time the Court came to be built, the Pompeian style was fully in vogue, with rooms and garden houses at Buckingham Palace (1843–5) and at Osborne, the new royal residence in the Isle of Wight inspired by Prince Albert; these derived from Abbate's published drawings in Guillaume Zahn's spectacular folio on Pompeii, published in Berlin in 1828,[14] and a new Royal Box at the Haymarket Theatre (1850) in London with its 'light Pompeian pilasters'. Alfred Stevens, who painted a ceiling for Wyatt in the Italian Court, is said to have been involved in a Pompeian Room at a house called Deysbrook in 1847.[15] The handbook to the Pompeian Court claims that the sole similar undertaking before the Court at Sydenham was a villa, Pompeianum, built for King Ludwig I of Bavaria at Aschaffenburg in 1841–6.[16] However, the style was well established on the continent: Karl Friedrich Schinkel had designed a Pompeian saloon at Charlottenburg, Berlin, in 1825–6, and Ingres devised a Pompeian interior dominated by a brilliant red with pale yellow, pale olive green and black for his oil-painting *Antiochus and Stratonice* (1840; Musée Condé, Chantilly). The sources given by George Scharf in his Handbook to the Court are Cockerell, Donaldson, Gell and Wyatt himself. Among books Scharf decorated using Pompeian motifs were the edition of Horace for

THE FINE ARTS COURTS, II 99

Owen Jones, published by John Murray in 1849, and one of Keats for Moxon with a Pompeian 'Lamia' in 1854.

Wyatt found that the Palace's girders and columns obtruded on the construction of the Pompeian House.[17] It was white on the outside, which was said to give a dreary effect – surprisingly Jones had not colonised it for colouring.[18] The main room, an Atrium with its pool, or *impluvium*, which was to be imagined as open to the sky through the rectangular roof opening, or *compluvium*, was decorated with a Minton floor designed by Wyatt. Here Victoria and Albert were served lunch on one of their first visits to the Palace. Raffaelle Monti modelled the ornamental portions; the red terra cotta roof tiles, set in red cement, were made by Blashfield. A *tablinum* led to a miniature columnar cloister or peristyle, painted with a fresco of a garden. In the *tablinum* were placed bronze groups electrotyped and given to the Palace by Elkington and Co. Gold and silver fish swam in the mosaic pools. One critic found the interiors elegant but the colours crude – the strongest or darkest colours were at the bottom of the rooms, on the dado.[19] At the back was a library with scroll books of papyrus on shelves, and

Entrance to the Pompeian Court', 1854.

then *cubicula* with designs of Cupid, Psyche and peacocks on a black ground. Abbate's wall paintings featured Bacchus, Endymion, Ceres, Andromeda, hippocamps (giant sea-horses), white swans with purple ribands, and Cupid leading an ibex. Owen Jones in *The Grammar of Ornament* gave faint praise to Wyatt and Abbate's House, which he plainly disliked; he struggled to see a grammar in the ornament, but found it discordant, capricious and vulgar. Jones was known to dislike the decadent taste of the late Roman period.[20] The teachers at the School of Design at Somerset House in the 1840s had mostly disapproved of Ludwig Grüner's promotion of the Pompeian style and decoration, which they too thought decadent. Christopher Dresser put the matter succinctly in a lecture to the Society of Arts: 'Pompeian art was false, and Pompeii was destroyed.'[21]

The visitors were told that Pompeii was the fashionable resort of a hedonistic class; it would be helpful to think of it as the 'Worthing of Italy'.[22] Festoons of garlands – decorative flourishes added from Bulwer Lytton's novel – hung between the rafters. The press wrote over-ripe fantasies about Roman voluptuaries peopling the Pompeian Court, and their transient pleasures, such as this version of Lytton:

> Look into the *triclinium*, and you may see, with the mind's eye, the magnificent Glaucus at a repast with his friends. He has just thrown his costly ring into a crystal cup, to enhance the value of the gift, and presented it to the profligate Clodius, who has risen from his elbow to drink 'the beautiful solitary'. Pansa, the dandy Lepidus, and the caustic Sallust, are present, and if you listen, you may hear Nydia in the *atrium*, singing:
> 'Buy my flowers, – O buy, I pray.'[23]

The author of the *Guide to the Ten Chief Courts* adopted an even more extravagant style:

> In such a room as this, clad in the festive robes of purple, and crowned with flowers, Horace might have quaffed the juice of the Falernian grape in a cup of onyx, incrusted with gems, or a jasper goblet filled to the brim by a Moorish Ganymede, with the Setine wine that Augustus most affected. Here Cicero may have sat, and boasted of Catiline's ignominious flight, when he rushed from the senate-house, pierced by the lightnings of his eloquence; or the perfumed, bald Caesar with his wounds still fresh from the last campaign against the Qallobrogews, may have laughed when he talked of Britain, the little island that produced the best oysters and the dullest slaves. Here revelled the men who conquered the world that they might live at peace on snails and thrushes, flamingoes' tongues, Numidian pheasants, and the udders of sows.[24]

The Handbook offered a discourse on Roman dinners and cuisine. The Court, not surprisingly, stimulated thoughts of food and the pampered body, and the Crystal Palace Hairdressers and Atkinson's perfumery were close by.[25]

Goethe said that the calamity of Pompeii was 'replete with instruction and delight for remote generations'; certainly the idea of a sybaritic culture punished by the wrath of a volcano fed the visitor's imagination. Lytton's House of Glaucus was set with symbolic theatrical properties such as shattered wine-cups and withered garlands; in the Epilogue his avaricious and licentious characters turn to skeletons found among the volcanic dust.[26] A well-known erotic fable by Théophile Gautier was *Arria Marcella* (1852): a young man obsessed with the imprint of a woman's breasts in ash found in a Pompeian villa asleep and dreams of love in the restored city. This was referred to, surprisingly, in the text accompanying the plate 'Waiting for the Queen' in Dickinson's set of lithographs of the Great Exhibition.

There was an early proposal for an enormous Pompeian theatre in the Central Transept, serving as an Odeon or Musical Hall. The surviving design for it by Gottfried Semper shows a magnificent structure with an amphitheatre and colonnades, incorporating sculptures of a triumphal chariot and of standing and seated monumental figures, decorated in bright polychromy. The design, which once belonged to Richard Wagner,[27] shows the great ribs of the Central Transept and galleries of the Crystal Palace pencilled in above the theatre. One might suspect that this was an earlier design with its setting added to persuade the directors to build it, but the presence in the drawing of the Choragic Monument of Lysicrates next to it, positioned just where Jones placed it in the intersection of the Nave and Transept, suggests that the design was indeed made for the Palace. Semper as a young man worked and studied in Paris, at the time of the polychromatic restorations of medieval buildings. He left in 1830 on an architectural tour and with Jules Goury visited sites in Italy such as Pompeii and Paestum, and in Greece and Sicily.[28] He was one of a group of young architects fascinated by the colouring of ancient buildings, who made direct examinations of buildings for traces of colour and drew coloured reconstructions of them. In 1834 he wrote a pamphlet on Greek polychromy, which would have supported Jones's beliefs about the use of red, yellow and blue in classical temples, and touched on the colourings of Etruscan, Roman and medieval buildings; early efforts of historicist colourings were 'pale and timid' with elegant celadon green and rose-colours on temples rather than a robust blood-red. Jones reprinted in his own *Apology for the Colouring of the Greek Court* a short section of Semper's book *The Four Elements of Architecture* of 1852, with its overview of ancient polychromy, in which Semper declared that Greek architectural polychromy was of deep and bright colours. When Semper arrived in London as a fugitive from the disturbances of 1849, having defended the barricades at Dresden with the revolutionaries, he was already renowned as the architect of the Hoftheater (1838–41) in that city. He collaborated on the designs for the Duke of Wellington's Funeral Car in 1852, and once Henry Cole persuaded the Board of Trade that he was not a revolutionary, he was given a post lecturing at the School of Design. At Chatsworth in

1851 Paxton offered him a post as his 'personal design assistant', and he was said to have regretted not taking it.[29] At the Great Exhibition he designed the Turkish, Egyptian, Canadian, Swedish and Danish courts. He had a sense of theatre: his Turkish Court was in the form of a great tent full of colour, and in the Canadian Court he slung in the air a white birch canoe that had been paddled for 3,000 miles by twenty men for part of its journey to Hyde Park. As will be seen in Chapter 5, Jones was not happy with commissions being given to other architects inside the Palace at Sydenham. While Semper's *Odeon* would have been a wonderful visual feature in the centre of the Palace, it was doubtless too expensive a project at the time of Paxton's colossal outlay on waterworks – and it might well have upstaged Jones's Courts.

Wyatt's Pompeian Court, together with the classical and Egyptian Courts, might be thought of as stage-settings: they were to influence the popular paintings by the

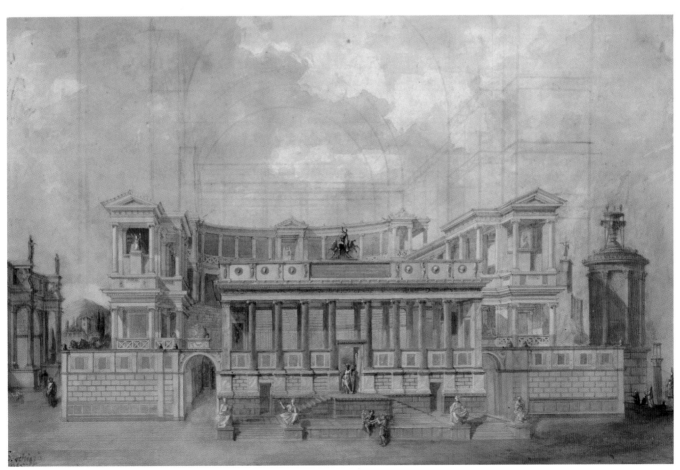

Gottfried Semper, *Theatre, Crystal Palace, Sydenham*, *c.* 1854. Watercolour. © Deutsches Architektur Museum, Frankfurt.

historicists Holman Hunt, Poynter, Alma-Tadema and Leighton of classical or Biblical architectural 'restorations', where ladies of infinite leisure, dressed or undressed, stand on mosaic pavements beside pools in Courts of polychromatic splendour, answering to some collective *anima* of the artistically-inclined public of the second half of the nineteenth century. They led in turn to Hollywood epics set amid architecture on a colossal scale.

The Byzantine Court

In Wyatt's view of the progress of architectural history the term 'Byzantine' was intended to explain the transition from Classical to Gothic. What was known as the Byzantine Court had as its formal title 'the Byzantine and Romanesque Court', by which Wyatt intended to demonstrate how the Romanesque and Byzantine architectural styles were part of a continuum from Roman to Rhenish, Venetian, Saxon and Norman, thus embracing the varied features of the Byzantine Court that might have seemed a generous muddle. The handbook, *The Byzantine and Romanesque Court*, written by Digby Wyatt with the help of J. B. Waring, is one of the best of the Crystal Palace guides, with an outstanding account of Byzantine art, architecture and symbolism based on Wyatt's studies in Sicily and Italy and his reading, and with many more woodcuts of the Court and its details than others in the series. Boutell said (wrongly) that nothing was Byzantine about it except the examples from San Marco in Venice, and that it should really have been called, more mundanely, the Romanesque Court.

The Byzantine Court was intended not as an architectural reconstruction but as an affectionate polychromatic anthology of ornamental details from Wyatt's tours

Exterior of the Byzantine Court, North-east Nave.

and sketchbooks. However, as can be seen from engravings and photographs, the principal structure facing the Nave gave the Court integrity. This consisted of a fine copy of the eighth-century cloister of St Mary in Capitolo at Cologne, massively arched with bold floriated capitals. Above the arches were painted copies of the famous mosaics of Justinian and Theodora at Ravenna (among others), made by a Mr Beenson of London from Wyatt's own 'studies'.[30] Pevsner admired Wyatt's watercolour of the Court, 'painted in hot colours under a smiling blue sky, with fat dark green and *sang-de-bœuf* columns and a general rotundity characteristic of the nineteenth century'.[31] Real mosaics were used for the arcade in *opus grecianum*, 'very carefully executed in real porphyry, serpentine and glass mosaic'. Inside the Court were painted casts of six recumbent figures from the Plantagenet royal tombs at Fontevrault; in front of the Court were the effigies of Crusader knights from the Temple Church in London 'restored' in colouring from fragments found on them. A fountain in the Abbey of Heisterbach near Drachenfels was copied in sculptured marble from the Duke of Devonshire's quarries.[32] An original altar frontal 'from the collection of the late Mr Cottingham' was another exhibit.

The Company's policy at the beginning had been to show original historical artefacts among the 'restorations'. On the other hand, they would only spend money on casts, as Grove wrote to Sotheby when the auctioneer offered to sell the Company some Etruscan vases in December 1852;[33] loans were plainly hoped for. In a Ceramic Court was exhibited a grand loan collection of original pieces, for example Greek vases, Meissen, Turquoise Celadon, old Wedgwood and modern Sèvres, lent by the Duke of Devonshire, James Fergusson, Sir John Gardner Wilkinson, Arthur Anderson (chairman of the Company) and other collectors. This was featured in the periodical *The Crystal Palace Expositor*.[34]

The famous Norman sculptured doorway of Kilpeck church in Herefordshire, set alongside the doorways from Mainz Cathedral

and bronze doors in plaster from Hildesheim, was 'restored' with colours and gilding. The polychromatic colouring was applied with the apparent authority of G.R. Lewis, who had published a learned lithographically illustrated book on Kilpeck in 1842, but without local evidence. Wyatt claimed that the colouring was applied from studies of continental examples of the same period. The door was surmounted with a bas-relief from Chichester and corbelling from Romsey.[35] An inner courtyard led though four paired columns from the cloister of St John Lateran in Rome, and to the side there was an Irish vestibule with three large Celtic crosses.

Wyatt made use of his knowledge of mosaic flooring, on which he had published a chromolithographic monograph in 1848, *Specimens of Geometrical Mosaics of the Middle Ages*. He made 'art-manufacture' designs for Maw, the ceramic firm, such as a polychrome chimneypiece of majolica tiles in stone, illustrated in *The Builder* in 1862.[36] Maw's presented to the Palace for the cloister an *opus alexandrinum* pavement in encaustic tiles to Wyatt's design.[37] Wyatt's chief superintendent for the Court, Charles Fowler, Junior, had written a series of clear and detailed articles on the engineering and construction of the Palace in Hyde Park for *The Expositor*.

William Michael Rossetti was the most appreciative of the informed critics of this 'imposing' Court, saying that it hinted at the New Jerusalem, 'grandiose, gorgeous and ceremonial in its decorations'. Wyatt had managed to realise the love of colour of the period,[38] and his own

Byzantine Court, showing Fontevrault casts.

account of the colouring in the Handbook endorses his and Jones's policy: 'Modern research leads us to believe that many an interior, now all bare and grey, originally glowed with colour and gilding; and that their walls and roofs were gaudily, if not tastefully, decorated with numerous subjects from the Holy Scriptures.' Since there was not much criticism of harshness of the colourings, it might be assumed that Jones did not attempt to superimpose his bright primaries on his friend's work. However, Routledge's *Guide to the Ten Chief Courts* said the imitation marble in the court looked bogus.[39] *The Builder* commented that all the reproduction of the mosaics from the Capella Palatina in Palermo should have been made in real mosaic, and that this would have been an economy since visitors had already damaged the painted surfaces; from an early stage a slip inserted in each Crystal Palace handbook stated: 'The Directors trust the People to respect and protect the beautiful objects of Art and Nature which have been collected for their pleasure and improvement.'[40] The Court was damaged in the fire of 1866, but restored.

The Medieval Court

A *Times* article on the Palace offered the opinion that visitors would know little of their national Gothic architecture, but because of their schooling would know something of Greek and Roman architecture, more remote in time and place. Wyatt was said by *The Builder* on his death never to have had much sympathy with 'the pure medieval architecture'.[41] This seems unlikely, given the knowledge and enthusiasm he displayed in the handbook, also written in collaboration with Waring. Certainly, since a Crystal Palace Court could not show on any satisfactory scale the larger and more powerful effects of the Gothic, which obviously rely on nave, aisle, clerestory, vault and spires, this presented the greatest difficulty of all the courts. Digby Wyatt called it an 'extreme difficulty', but he was judged to have risen to the challenge.[42] Casts were put together in an attempt at balance and symmetry, as the woodcuts in the handbook make clear, by recreating walls and parapets and fitting in the archways

and doorways, as well as housing painted plaster *disjecta membra* all in the confined space of a lady chapel; *The Builder* jeered at the 'carpenter's Gothic' of some of the niches made for statuary.[43] Delamotte's photographs show that it was more than an awkward architectural museum of casts. Wyatt, in his chromolithographic book of *Views*, chose his 'Cloister' to represent the Medieval Court: this had not been assembled from casts of fragments, and has the appearance of a successful example of Gothic Revival. Wyatt's Cloister was 'taken principally' from Guisborough Abbey in Yorkshire, and of course had polychromatic colouring; the encaustic pavement in it was again the gift of Messrs Maw.

The handbook chronicled architectural development in relation to the evolution of European Christianity. This was a European Gothic display, with a 'French and Italian Medieval Vestibule', for which Viollet-le-Duc made twenty-three casts from Nôtre Dame. There were casts from Vézelay and Chartres and after Pisano and Orcagna.[44] Particular emphasis was given to German medieval masterpieces, with a separate court for casts from Nuremberg, Mainz and Frankfurt. On the outside of the Court, fronting the Nave, were English monuments and German statuettes. In the *Art Journal* Charles Boutell welcomed this, saying that 'until lately' English Gothic had not been understood by comparison with Gothic works from other countries, and that the Court should properly be called Gothic and not Medieval.[45]

It is notable that the casts in the English Medieval section at Sydenham were referred to as 'the national Art-

'Façades of North East Fine Art Courts'. 1862.

Collection'.[46] Wyatt put together an anthology of casts of details from English cathedrals such as Lincoln and Wells, minsters and small churches, and included monuments such as the Black Prince's effigy at Canterbury. The casts were assembled through agents at home, and particular scorn was poured on some 'village Dogberry' at Beverley Minster who had refused permission for a cast to be made of its Percy tomb. However, conservationists today would probably not allow casts to be made at all; Sir John Soane's Museum refused to allow the Palace to mould a cast from its Belzoni sarcophagus for the Egyptian Court because of the delicate finish on the alabaster.[47]

Mediaeval Court, 1862

Digby Wyatt devoted a section of the handbook *The Medieval Court* to 'The Polychromatic Decoration', just as he had done for the Byzantine Handbook, and advanced his theory that colour acts as a unifying principle bringing various materials into harmony.[48] The Medieval Courts made stronger assertions about polychromy than the Byzantine Court, and ran into criticism. Some of it was doubtless from observers used to the bare stone interiors of English churches after the Puritans removed the paint and gilding. The Company claimed that these were being restored to their pristine sharpness and brilliance.[49] Digby Wyatt, writing at the end of 1854 in his *Views of the Crystal Palace*, and no doubt aware of how unpopular the colouring of the Court was, said that the intensity of the white light in the Crystal Palace made the colours look wrong, whereas in a church they would have been 'tempered' by interior gloom and by light filtered through stained glass windows. He may also have hoped that the bright light would cause their paintwork to fade and so restore a more 'harmonious effect'; meanwhile, he seems to imply that they fulfilled their academic task of showing how the colours would have looked. The Rochester doorway was illuminated in blue, red, green and purple,[50] and judged to be 'utterly destroyed' by its petty enrichments. *The Builder* wrote: 'Nothing requires so much moral courage and self-control as polychromatic decoration'; the programme was 'the besetting sin' of the Crystal Palace architects, who were enticed and lured on until they were finally destroyed. W. M. Rossetti said that the Court, 'picked out in reds and blues with clustered shafts with conspicuous patterns, and niches filled with statues coloured in imitation of life', should 'prove a blow to the cause of Gothic polychromatism'. Moreover, the paint was glossy, and there was no authority for painting angels in spandrels. Norman arches, said Lady Eastlake, were reduced to 'modern ribbons' and 'red striped Guernsey shirts and trousers'.[51] Wyatt claimed in the Handbook that the Rochester doorway was restored in polychromy 'after a very careful study of numerous monuments of the same period throughout the country, and more especially in Norfolk…its richness is by no means overdone'. For Ruskin the angels in Lincoln's Angel Choir with their gilded wings looked like 'the [tinselled] gingerbread of olden times'.[52] Warm monochrome sepia tones in Delamotte's and Negretti's surviving photographs of the Court have mercifully removed the evidence in the forgotten controversy.

The stained glass window by Hardman and Co. at the back of the Court towards the garden made a doctrinal point, in the spirit of Jones and Wyatt, since it represented the union of Architecture, Painting and Sculpture. One of the details was a ground-plan of the new Palace of Westminster, with which Hardman and Pugin had been so successfully associated.[53]

The Renaissance Court

Altogether lighter and more graceful was Wyatt's Renaissance Court: a clear, well-lit, rather theatrical arcaded space with a vase fountain from a French château, well-heads from the Doge's Palace in Venice, and in the

Philip Delamotte, 'Entrance to Renaissance Court', 1854.

against such novel highly ornamented surfaces; it was 'a style of art essentially foreign', as Measom's *Railway Guide* put it in its account of the Palace, where 'we feel less at home'.[55]

The arcade around the Court was in the François I style, with ornamented pilasters copied from the Hôtel de Bourgtheroulde at Rouen (*c.* 1520). The original pilasters were said to be in poor condition, and the 'restored' casts in the Court were made by M. Desachy of Paris and his men who had shaped the Aboo-Simbel figures. According to Lady Eastlake, this arcade was painted white and gold, although the *Illustrated Crystal Palace Gazette* wrote in August 1854 of the Court's decoration as blue, red and yellow, an Owen Jones livery. Lady Eastlake admired this arcade.[56] Wyatt called this a 'sculpturesque' period[57] and seemed at pains to introduce the public to his enthusiasm for Pisano, Ghiberti and Donatello (whose work was illustrated by four casts). The reproduction of the Ghiberti's Baptistery doors at the Duomo in Florence was said to be worth a visit in itself,[58] and there were examples of the work of Jean Goujon and Luca della Robbia, artists loved by the Victorians. Wyatt gave a prominent position in the Court to a cast of the altar-tomb of Ilaria de Caretto at Lucca, of which Ruskin 'reproduced' the mouldings and base on his own parents' tomb in Shirley churchyard (*c.* 1867). The floors were of paved marble and the doorway was magnificently surmounted by Cellini's colossal *Nymph* at Fontainebleau. We are made aware again in the handbook of current manufacturing processes and of Wyatt's part in them: Blashfield made the fountains for the Court. When discussing the lost art of glazed terra cotta Wyatt referred to a new process of Minton's, the results

middle Donatello statues. It is hard not to feel that here Wyatt's own spirits must have expanded: he saw himself as involved in this Court in a chivalrous defence and illustration of a style he loved. The Renaissance artists worked, he said, in 'a spirit of free and genial independence', of 'life and sensation'. He needed to vindicate a style that had been much abused in his day, while admitting that some versions of it were 'capricious' and 'fanciful'.[54] Until the opening of the Crystal Palace, he said, the continental Renaissance style was known to only a few and attacked by classical purists as 'pestilent'; he admired it for its grace of design, delicacy of execution and a 'chastened fancy'. There was indeed prejudice of which were then to be seen at the Museum of Practical Geology in Jermyn Street and decorating the booking-office at Paddington Station.[59]

Although Wyatt again wrote in the handbook to this Court a section called 'Polychromatic decoration', as he had in all his other handbooks, it is clear that the colouring in this Court was subtler. He writes the history of art from the novel point of view of a polychromatist, saying that while the artists of the early Renaissance made frescoes, 'the art of combining coloured enrichment of an architectural nature, so as to produce general effects as grand as those which had been attained in Byzantine times, was sadly neglected'. An 'agreeable polychromy was restored at last after the exhumation of the wonderful remains of the monuments at Rome.'[60] W. M. Rossetti was unconvinced by the decorations, finding them 'pleasing but profitless', insisting that the style was 'frittered and frivolous', full of 'vain elegancies and cumbrous obtrusions', and meaning 'well-nigh nothing'. An extension of this court was a separate compartment forming the Elizabethan Court, or Vestibule, its arcade and façade cast from Holland House in Kensington. Its contents included the tombs of Elizabeth I and Mary Queen of Scots in Westminster Abbey, Donatello's 'St George', and a reproduction of the Shakespeare head in the parish church at Stratford-on-Avon. Hence the emphasis was as much political and literary as architectural. Rossetti found it 'ugly and distorted'. Lady Eastlake noted the absurdity of importing didactic English slogans on to the architrave of the adjacent Renaissance Court, such as 'Be just, and fear not', and 'Manners makyth the man'.[61]

The Italian Court

Homage to Raphael and Michelangelo was the purpose of the Italian Court, a coda to the Renaissance Court. The separate handbook has an unsuccessful – even absurd – engraved sculptural title-page that is obviously intended as a memorial tablet to Michelangelo, whose monument to Lorenzo de' Medici among other works was magnificently 'illustrated' in plaster in the Court. Raphael was represented by a cast of his sculpture of Jonah and the Whale, and by painted reproductions of the Vatican loggia arabesques and an ornamental ceiling. The omission of real oil paintings by these and other Italian masters indicated the somewhat limited scope of the Palace architects' manifesto of the union of architecture,

painting and sculpture; by 'painting' the two architects intended polychromy, and so painters were omitted from a temple to the Renaissance in a Fine Arts Court. The works of the Old Masters, from Cimabue to Watteau, were alluded to feebly in the form of 142 framed watercolour copies by 'Mr West of London' located in this Court. The Arundel Society prints of Giotto's Scrovegni Chapel at Padua engraved in outline by Dalziel were also displayed. The façade of the Court was copied from the Farnese Palace in Rome, and ornamented with the busts of great men of the period. Within were casts of standing sculptures, principally works by Michelangelo, and including Cellini's *Perseus*.

The handbook showed Wyatt's animus against the 'Rococo', and its decorations of cupids, shells and stalactites; architecture had never sunk so low, achieving nothing better than 'the flaunting façade of some Jesuits' church'. Polychromy was celebrated in the Italian Court on the walls, particularly in Raphael's arabesques, in contemplating which the eye, 'pleased with an universal richness and intricacy, wanders delighted, neither oppressed nor confused'.[62] The patterned diapers in the Alhambra Court served the same end.

The most successful feature of the Court was perhaps Alfred Stevens's copy of Raphael's vaulted ceiling in the Camera della Segnatura at the Vatican, which was placed nearest the central transept. This work was much admired, Lady Eastlake saying that 'it is one of the unique boons to the public – it leaves nothing to be desired.' The Handbook said: 'It would be difficult to imagine a more faithful reproduction of his beautiful ceiling than has been made in the present court by Mr Alfred Stevens, whose long residence in Italy, and profound study of Raffaelle, had eminently qualified him for the task.'[63] In 1900 Charles Ricketts and Charles Shannon offered the Company £100 for it, 'which had it not been on plaster very difficult to remove, they would have sold'; it was eventually destroyed in the Fire of 1936. Stevens probably had a hand in the general design of the interior hall of the Court; a drawing of 1852–3 at the Victoria and Albert Museum shows a possible scheme.[64] Stevens also painted for the Court a ceiling in grisaille from Sebastiano Serlio's library in Venice.[65] Stevens, although the most talented of the artists to work at Sydenham, was never commissioned to carry out more than copies or pastiche.

'Interior of the Italian Court'. Casts of the Medici tombs and the Arcade with arabesques after Raphael.

The Nineveh Court; Henry Layard and James Fergusson

For visitors the Nineveh Court (also called the Assyrian Court or Nineveh Palace) was probably the strangest structure. Henry Layard (1817–94), who excavated the buildings on which it was modelled, had said a few years previously that a packing case would contain all European knowledge of Assyria.[66] Measuring 120 by 50 feet and 40 feet high, it was about one-fifth larger than the other Courts. It stood on the same axis as Owen Jones's series of Courts on the north-west side, but was separated from them by the intersection of the North Transept with the Aboo-Simbel figures, and faced the Tropical Department with its great palms and outlandish botanical flourishes. The Court was designed by James Fergusson 'under the general direction of A.H. Layard, Esq., M.P'. Fergusson plainly admired the monumental glory of his subject, and in 1855 he tactlessly wrote in the preface to his *Illustrated Handbook of Architecture* that people were 'getting satiated with the plaster prettiness of the Alhambra'.[67]

Layard had published his best-selling book about the excavations, *Nineveh and its Remains*, in 1848. In 1851 Fergusson lectured on the site at the R.I.B.A., and published *The Palaces of Nineveh and Persepolis Restored*, an illustrated book describing 'a love of polychromatic decoration among this people' and working out how the palaces would have looked, 'gorgeously coloured' and 'perhaps not always in the best taste'.[68] Owen Jones had contributed four chromolithographic plates for Layard's *The Monuments of Nineveh*, a great folio published in 1849–52 with 100 engravings 'from drawings made on the spot'; Jones's plates included a title-page in red-brown, yellow and blue, showing the same motifs as he was to use for the cover of the

handbook he designed for Fergusson, and a 'restoration' of a Hall featuring a bas-relief with a pale blue background.[69] Obviously the romantic story of the despatch of the colossal bas-reliefs and sculptured winged bulls and human-headed lions to the Louvre and the British Museum had caught the public imagination. Once the Nineveh Court had been constructed at Sydenham, *Punch* began a long series of winged bull cartoons, featuring Layard and other politicians.

The Court, as the educated critics complained, was an amalgam of two palaces of different historical periods. The very dramatic lower outside wall and entrances of five bays in front, 17 feet high, had painted plaster reproductions of winged bulls on the façade, cast from the Louvre, and giants strangling lions; on the doorway in the west wall were human-headed lions. This lower storey was meant to represent the palace at Khorsabad. Layard claimed archaeological accuracy for the details and ornaments. The upper portion, columnar and roofed, adding a further twenty feet exclusive of the

Philip Delamotte, 'Exterior of the Nineveh Court'. The winged bulls and giants.

Philip Delamotte, 'Entrance to the Nineveh Court', across the Tropical Department. The Great Winged bulls from Khorsabad and the dwarf columns with bull-head capitals from Persepolis.

battlements, was modelled on Persepolis, in its day 'the richest of cities under the sun'. The arcade consisted of columns with double-bull capitals. The main hall was modelled on the palace at Nimroud, at about one-third of the actual size,[70] and had in it four great columns modelled on those at Susa and Persepolis. The press divided on this 'grand fiction' of columns in a palace called 'Nineveh' inside the Crystal Palace. *The Builder* complained vigorously about the unhistorical combination of Nineveh and Persepolis.[71] Layard had touched in his book on the colouring of the palaces, and Fergusson had written fulsomely of their coloured decorations.

Fergusson was a many-sided intellectual with an unusual background: he worked briefly for a commercial firm in India, then became an indigo planter for ten years, and then returned to England to devote himself to architecture. Theoretically he was aligned with Owen Jones: in his *True Principles of Beauty in Art*, to which he gave a chromolithographic frontispiece of a 'restoration' of the court of the temple of Philae, he lamented that the arts in England had borrowed from other nations 'but have as yet no real root in the soil', and urged architects to use harmonious colouring on the outside of buildings, just as on the interiors. When he described the colouring of Egyptian and Greek buildings and suggested the application of colour to the outside of contemporary buildings,[72] it was almost as if it came from Jones's pen. Ruskin admired Fergusson's books; he had learned from them and regarded their author as a 'noble ally', although remarking that Fergusson was in danger of strangling himself with his own theories. *The Queen of the Air* refers to Fergusson's *Tree and Serpent Worship* of 1868 as 'a work of very great value'.[73] Fergusson had a practical interest in the running of the Palace in his two years as general manager from 1856. He was also an expert designer of fortifications with earthworks, which were used at Sebastopol. As a practising architect he achieved little – an exception being the remarkable top-lit Marianne North Gallery in Kew Gardens of 1881, a red-brick Doric temple with pillars *in antis* set on a first storey with an ironwork Indian verandah. He also had grand projects which were not carried out, exhibiting in 1862 a design for a National Palace of Fine Arts,[74] but it was for his exhaustive publications on architectural history, oriental and European, that he received the R.I.B.A. Gold Medal in 1871. Heinrich Schliemann dedicated his *Tiryns* to him in 1886.[75] Given Fergusson's background and special knowledge, it is odd that, although he did eventually create an Indian display in the Gallery at the Palace with artefacts and models of houses and buildings, there was no architectural court in the Indian style – a Taj Mahal Court might have stolen some of Jones's thunder.

Like the Crystal Palace itself, Sennacherib's Palace was built on a platform and terraces. The frescoes of Fergusson's Nineveh Court showed scenes of imperial triumph. The normally solemn *Illustrated London News* recognised a familiar mixture of text and engraving, and said that the walls of the Court were covered 'with plaster copies of the *Illustrated London News* of Nineveh, and chronicles in the arrowheaded character'.[76]

The associations of the Nineveh Court in contemporary minds were historical, biblical, literary and mythological. Assyria was a country of romance, the most ancient of the cultures recalled by the Sydenham Courts, the setting for the origin of civilisation and the rise and fall of a powerful monarchy. Assyria was associated with the biblical books of *Kings* and *Chronicles*, and the prophecies of Isaiah and Jeremiah about desolation;[77] Byron fired his readers with the culture of Sardanapalus and the fall of Sennacherib, when polychromatic cohorts in purple and gold came down like wolves on the fold. Alexander reduced Persepolis, the wonder of the world, to ashes.

Layard's *Nineveh* described a world of mythology and symbolism, of emblematic trees and holy cups, all painted in brilliant colours,[78] and lent his authority in support of the project at Sydenham by writing the Court's handbook. There he illustrated and discussed the winged animals, the eagle-headed men and the tree of life reproduced in the Court. The *Art Journal's* critic thought that the advantage of Fergusson's court was that it created illustrations to our sacred records, not models for architecture and design. Layard described the common Assyrian motif of honeysuckle in a semi-circle, and illustrated it with a sketch (for which he thanked Fergusson); the motif is to be found again in Jones's *Grammar of Ornament*, prominent on Plate XII.[79] The fine woodcut printed on yellow cover of Layard's sixpenny *Handbook to the Nineveh Court*, surely designed by Jones, shows sacred trees with honeysuckle fleurons, standing as if on an altar decorated with winged bulls back to back, while the protective Assyrian deity hovers above with bow and arrow.

Dante Gabriel Rossetti wrote a poem, 'The Burden of Nineveh', about the arrival of the Assyrian antiquities, the 'wingèd beasts', at the British Museum, which shows a dislike for imperial culture, and compares the streets of London with Nineveh. W.M. Rossetti, his brother, hated the Nineveh Court, which he called an oppressive 'nightmare Life in Death'; the Assyrians were a people 'strange and unexplored'. He found Fergusson's colours 'hard, glaring and uncombined – an opaque heavy patchwork of blues, reds and yellows, with ghastly oases of white'. What was originally 'refinement and impassive vitality' was rendered into 'aggressive unrepose'. The predominant paint used for the Court, to be seen to the right in Joseph Nash's watercolour of the inauguration, was ultramarine blue enamel. The 'colouring and ornamentation' of the Court was 'very ably imitated' by Leonard William Collmann, the renowned interior decorator of Curzon Street. Routledge's anonymous *Guide to the Ten Chief Courts* found the decoration too theatrical. It described the colouring in detail: the sculptured animals were in chocolate on buff grounds, or blue on red, or red on blue. The bulls of the portal were deep dull red with black beards and hair, their mitres blue and yellow.[80] The handbook says of the colours that their choices and contrasts were carefully studied; 'when there has been no authority for their use in any particular instance, a comparison with other monuments and especially with Egyptian remains has, in some instances, furnished the means of deciding which to adopt.' This must mean that when in doubt they asked Owen Jones. Layard adduced support from Sir Gardner Wilkinson, who described the Egyptians' use of blues; when Layard says in *Nineveh* that the first colours used in Assyria were blue, red and yellow, black and white, this almost suggests collusion with Jones – he certainly knew Jones before the work at Sydenham began, and referred in later editions of *Nineveh* to his work for his large folio publication *Monuments of Nineveh*. Layard asserted that all the Assyrian palaces were painted in brilliant colours well before it was planned to paint the Nineveh Court in enamels; from his description it is almost as if Owen Jones had designed them: they had 'coloured borders of elaborate and elegant design'. The plaster and paint had 'freshness and brilliancy'.[81] Lady Eastlake – she and her husband were close friends of Layard – wrote that the paint had made old Nineveh 'absolutely ferocious', and Fergusson defended himself in a letter to the *Athenaeum* on 5 May 1855, quoting *Ezekiel* as a source for the brilliant original colouring of the palaces, and referring to the painted plaster slabs in Layard's folio volume; Eastern mosques were gorgeously coloured with glazed tiles 'of startling brilliancy'. Lady Eastlake had shown merely 'the expression of her personal feelings'.

> The question whether the colouring is in good or bad taste, is one the Directors of the Crystal Palace Company, or those employed by them, never, so far as I know, asked themselves. Their object was to reproduce the works of antiquity with the utmost fidelity, and leave the public to form their own judgment as to the merits of the style. I of course, can perfectly understand that a person accustomed to the grey atmosphere of our climate, or the smoky dinginess of London, finding such decorations too brilliant for their enfeebled nerves; but under the glowing sunshine of the East, the case, I take it, would be widely different.

The sculptures were bold and vigorous, 'not to say coarse and barbarous', and thus no subject for delicate patterns and genteel subdued colouring. 'If, however, any one likes to assert that the taste of the Assyrian was bad, and their Art barbarous, that is a matter of opinion which I do not propose to discuss at present.'[82]

W. M. Rossetti also reacted to the politics of the Nineveh Court. He disliked the imperial civilisation depicted, a world of male ego and will:

> Force is the essence of Assyrian art; the physical force which struggles, slays and conquers; the personal force whose will is law, a question of something despotic and barbaric, stern, self-exalting, fixed. It delights in conflict and in gorgeousness. Its kings stand erect or sit supreme; its subjects fight, and swim, and besiege and minister to their monarch, and build under rigid taskmasters; it has few (if any) women, and them mostly servile or captive; its eagles scent the slain; its lions gnash on triumphing hunters; and its gods trample the ground with puissant spread wings and fronting countenance.

On the other hand, Fergusson in his *True Principles* seemed to approve when he wrote that the palace at Persepolis showed the paramount importance to the eastern monarch of the obedience and love of his subjects.[83]

Layard stressed the magnificence and luxury of the Assyrians, their cities three times larger than London or Paris, but responded imaginatively and feelingly to the triumphal warriors, the exploits of the chase, and conquests. The sculptured bas-reliefs 'painted in gorgeous colours' recorded a great empire on the walls of palaces with portals guarded by colossal bulls or lions of white marble. Digby Wyatt in his Slade lectures also appeared to relish the miles of bas-reliefs displaying the 'extent and dominion of the wielders of the destinies of the Assyrian empire'.[84]

Both at the opening concert of the Festival of Empire at the Crystal Palace in 1911, with George V and Queen Mary in the royal box, and at the opening of the Imperial War Museum in the Palace on 9 June 1920 with the royal pair again present, the choir and everyone present sang Kipling's 'Recessional', with its reminder that those who rule empires must be guided by the injunction in the Book of Common Prayer for 'an humble and contrite heart':

> God of our fathers, known of old,
> Lord of our far-flung battle-line,
> Beneath whose awful hand we hold
> Dominion over palm and pine,
> Lord God of Hosts, be with us yet,
> Lest we forget, lest we forget.

The couplet in the poem 'All our pomp of yesterday is one with Nineveh and Tyre' could only reinforce the lesson. Just as Alexander burnt an Assyrian palace, so in 1936 fire consumed the Nineveh Court. The destruction of the Crystal Palace itself, when it happened, was seen as a portent.

Exterior of the Roman and Alhambra Courts. Moresque diapers and Roman statuary: *Antinous* and *Mercury of the Vatican*.

The Sculpture

The sculpture at Sydenham fell into four categories. Inside the Palace stood the museum of plaster casts of historical and contemporary sculpture, and the gallery of portrait busts, also in plaster. Below the Palace in the formal gardens stood the series of large allegorical figures of cities and states, specially commissioned for the Upper Terrace. And lastly there were many reproduction garden statues, some of marble but mostly in cement composition or other artificial materials.

The collection of plaster reproductions of sculpture, referred to as one of the Fine Arts Courts, was on a palatial scale, and the quality of the pieces mostly matched the quantity. The inventory of November 1853 lists 858 pieces, including some architectural casts and the portrait gallery of busts.[85] This museum was said at the time to be 'by far the greatest collection of casts of the greatest masterpieces ever brought together', and 'the richest and most comprehensive in the world', with 'all the great schools of art and all the great masters greatly and worthily represented'.[86] Paxton – as noted in Chapter 2 – responded to the early suggestion of the naturalist Richard Owen to form an ambitious museum of sculpture at Sydenham based on historical principles, and plainly saw the Palace as ideally suited to a popularised version, greatly multiplied, of Wyatville's Sculpture Gallery and Orangery at Chatsworth. It was announced in 1853 that the statues, like the architectural displays,

Max Widnmann (1812–95), *A Hunter defending his family*.

1852 the Crystal Palace Company issued a statement that because the English public did not know continental sculpture, this would be remedied; Rauch, Schwanthaler, Cornelius and Schorr were among the sculptors who would be represented. The *Athenaeum* took up the call the following month, reporting that the public 'will make the acquaintance for the first time with German, French and Italian schools of sculpture'. George Godwin wrote in *The Builder* that the sculpture at the Palace was 'of more value' to students than the architecture;[90] this could not have been said in disparagement of the architecture, since on the whole he wrote warmly of the Courts.

Statuary had figured prominently in Paxton's original plan to convert the Crystal Palace into a winter garden, and Henry Cole had proposed to show pieces from the overcrowded British Museum. Although Paxton was encouraged by Owen to form a didactic historical collection and had learned to appreciate sculpture in the company of the Duke of Devonshire, he was a less well-informed traveller than Digby Wyatt and Owen Jones, the directors of the Fine Arts Courts; Wyatt was also a great admirer of Michelangelo and Donatello, and Jones had supervised the modern sculpture at Hyde Park. They were also determined to promote the union of architecture and sculpture. Many nineteenth- and early twentieth-century buildings in London attempt a union of architecture and sculpture with little success, but one happy issue of the pair is the former University of London headquarters (1866–9) at the rear of Burlington House, designed by Sir James Pennethorne, with its pantheon of philosophers, scientists and writers, seated or standing in niches, on portico and parapet. Some were the work of sculptors represented at Sydenham.

The omission of paintings from the education of the eye and in an encyclopaedia of civilisation was absurd, and the attempted remedy of introducing watercolour copies of old masters and a commercial gallery of contemporary art was unworthy. Some conscious rationalisation seems evident in the statement in the official *Guide* by Samuel Phillips that Art in the Palace is 'worthily represented by Architecture and Sculpture'.[91]

The statues admired at Hyde Park and Sydenham were largely in the classical tradition, chosen with knowledge and insight to present to the people a fine art of which many of them previously knew virtually nothing. Connoisseurs who expressed contempt for the most

would show a 'progressive series' of the historical development of the fine art of sculpture.[87] The generous selection of classical, medieval and Renaissance pieces was to be seen in the context of the architectural courts of their period where they were placed. Ruskin was enthusiastic, being a patron of the Venetian sculptor A. Giordani who made a cast of Verrocchio's famous equestrian statue of Bartolommeo Colleoni for the Palace; he also mentioned a 'noble cast' for Sydenham of one of the angles of the Doge's Palace.[88]

The 'Bachelor Duke' of Devonshire wrote of his collection at Chatsworth: 'My Gallery was intended for modern sculpture.'[89] In Rome he became a friend of Canova and had bought works from him and his pupils John Gibson and Bertel Thorvaldsen. Although famous antique and historic sculptures were generously represented at Sydenham, there was a strong didactic impulse to introduce the 'modern' to the People, with the help of an excellent handbook. The modern sculpture in 1854 amounted to 327 pieces, excluding the Portrait Gallery, with a particular emphasis on German work. In June popular of the pieces were surprised that the untutored public took so much interest in sculpture. The continental notion that classical sculpture was inspiring and its appreciation part of an educated man's consciousness still persisted; it had been introduced into England in the early seventeenth century by the Earl of Arundel with his sculpture gallery of 'marbles' at Arundel House in the Strand, visible in Daniel Mytens' portrait of him. In the galleries at Chatsworth, Woburn, Petworth and other great aristocratic mansions such collections were fashionable, and some contained contemporary works. A grand tour of sculpture on home ground for visitors who could not afford one abroad was the plan of the two Fine Arts directors, who had commissioned the casts from the museums where the originals were to be seen. Not all thought this a success. *The Observer* said in August 1855: 'All love pictures, but the sculpture and architecture courts, admirable as they are, are still somewhat cold and unsuited to the tastes and acquirements of the great bulk of people.'[92]

The project was impressive for its ambitious range and quantity, but also for its organisation. The continental tour of Jones and Wyatt, lasting no more than two or three months, to seek permission to order casts was mostly successful, and they were especially proud that in Munich Baron von Klenze persuaded King Ludwig to allow them to make the first casts from the Glyptothek, but there were refusals in Rome, Padua and Vienna.[93] Their mission was thought to be extravagant, and in January 1856 Alderman Wilson accused them at a shareholders' meeting of buying statues that were not contracted for, and for filling the cellars with casts which they did not want after all. Wyatt replied that the prices had all been set by the governments through which they were purchased, and that some £200 worth of casts were still in store. We know that some pieces arrived too late to be included in the catalogue and handbook.[94] The *Inventory of Statuary with Insurance Valuations* for November 1853 gives a total valuation of £10,756 12s. 4d, presumably a complete list of the two men's continental commissions; this is in the form of printed lists with figures entered in Jones's careful hand. The suppliers are named in Paris, Brussels, Naples, Rome, Florence, Turin, Milan, Venice, Dresden, Berlin, Munich, Frankfurt, Cologne, Stuttgart, Nuremberg, Prague, Vienna and Copenhagen – presumably the cities they visited. The list also includes a Venetian gondola ornamented

with seahorses, and with a Venetian flag and a carpet, costing £59 13s 4d; the artist of a view engraved for the *Illustrated London News*, 'The Crystal Palace, at Sydenham, as it will appear when completed', placed this gondola at the very centre of the picture on the large basin below the cascades and terraces, its waters reflecting the new Palace.[95] It is to be seen again in a coloured image from Nelson's *Views of the Crystal Palace and Park* (*c.* 1862), for hire on the lower lake. The presence of a genuine gondola was perhaps intended to improve on Hyde Park, where an Ackermann chromolithograph of 1851 shows visitors to the Great Exhibition being rowed on the Serpentine in English craft adapted with curtained cabins in the gondola style. Venetian gondolas had also been a feature of Louis XIV's Grand Canal at Versailles.

The installation of the statues and architectural casts – the equestrian pieces weighed three tons – was itself an impressive feat (George Augustus Sala was amused at the Laocoön being delivered by Pickford's). There was a price to pay for the speed with which it was carried out: the *Illustrated Crystal Palace Gazette* noted that a statue of Lord Chatham had been labelled 'Greek Boy Praying'. Joseph Bonomi made new parts for casts found on arrival to be 'defective'. There was also the question of positioning: Ruskin complained that 'the lovely temple of Minerva at Aegina' formed 'a vestibule to the Ladies' Cloak-Room'.[96]

The statues of equestrian monarchs with raised swords, and of Peel and Chatham (seated at the heart of the Palace close to the Transept), could be seen as making political statements. There was also an enormous architectural Screen of Kings and Queens designed by Digby Wyatt as a setting for the casts made by John Thomas to provide models for his statues at the Palace of Westminster; now coloured and gilded, they were bought by the Crystal Palace Company. The directors drew attention to the fact that by placing Thomas's figure of Cromwell among the anointed monarchs they had reversed the decision of a parliamentary committee to exclude him.[97]

At Hyde Park the statuary in the Sculpture Court had been of both marble and plaster; it had not been a museum display as at Sydenham, but consisted of statues sent by the sculptors for competitive exhibition in the hope of winning prize medals. It was placed in a sequence in the Nave among tropical plants and palms from Loddiges', a plaster reproduction of the Apollo

Philip Delamotte, 'Court of Monuments of Christian Art'.

Belvedere ('to imitate marble') and a few architectural pieces. The latter included a single monumental Irish cross (currently in fashion: there were to be many at the Dublin Crystal Palace the following year and a quantity at Sydenham in the short-lived Court of Monuments of Christian Art), a 'restoration' of part of Eleanor of Hainault's tomb made by George Gilbert Scott, and a modern Gothic monument.

In planning the contents at Sydenham, Owen Jones and Digby Wyatt would have known of the great popularity of the modern sculpture at Hyde Park. The contemporary British sculptors represented in the Nave at both Palaces were E.H. Baily, John Bell, John Hancock and John Graham Lough. W.F. Woodington, who later sculpted the monumental head of Paxton still to be seen

today in the Park at Sydenham, showed *A Young Girl at the Spring*.[98] The modern sculptures at Sydenham were first placed in the Great Transept; at prominent places in the Nave were giant equestrian statues of various periods: the Montecavallo horses (or Dioscuri), Donatello's Erasmo da Narni, Verrocchio's Bartolommeo Colleoni, François I, Le Sueur's Charles I and Marochetti's Richard Coeur de Lion.

There was the usual prurient disapproval of French sculpture, Sotheby writing that a young bacchanal was 'most indelicate and disgusting'.[99] He also mocked the notion of the historical 'series' as showing the progress of sculpture, when a Greek Hercules could stand facing Sir Robert Peel by Marochetti. The works of John Gibson and the Anglo-Roman school were at first grouped around the west (road-side) end of the Great Transept, together with the German sculpture which culminated in the colossal *Franconia* of Johann Halbig and the grand head of Ludwig Schwanthaler's *Bavaria*. The Italian and the French schools were placed at the Transept's east (garden-side) end.

That the sculptures were all casts apparently was not the directors' original intentions. They had proposed a scheme which, not surprisingly, did not appeal to the English artists: that they should donate examples of their own work. William Bell Scott later recalled this. A few years after the Great Exhibition, which presented a good collection of contemporary English sculpture,

> …the Sydenham Crystal Palace approaching completion, the managing committee, after purchasing many of the most important productions of the school of Germany, France and Belgium, bethought themselves of our own sculptors, now respected throughout the world, but instead of doing the same to the more eminent men, professors of the art, invited them to send their works in gratis. Nor did the committee meet the artists even half way; that remarkable display of casts, ancient and modern, ornamented with the works most celebrated in the history of the world, or in the later art of other countries, opened with a systematic carelessness of the works of our own. [100]

The Cast Courts (1872) at the Victoria and Albert Museum show how convincing artistically plaster casts can be. However, most of the casts at Sydenham were whitewashed – to the distress of the *Art Journal,* which knew the harm done by 'clogging up' plaster; its critic observed a muscular workman sandpapering the neck of a female figure. Ruskin spoke of one particular cast as a 'brittle white spectre'. The *Illustrated London News* said the 'long regiment of plaster becomes wearingly monotonous and harsh'. [101] One may question why Jones, as director of the sculpture, did not bring polychromy into play on them, but he may have been dissuaded by the cries of 'meretricious' showmanship at Hyde Park in reaction to the coloured lighting of Monti's *Dream of Joy*,[102] and the mockery directed at the rotating turntable and red velvet shrine given to Powers's *Greek Slave*. The official *Handbook to the Courts of Modern Sculpture* reminded readers that gypsum is hard and opaque, and 'so different in effect from the delicate, semi-transparent marble, which under the master-hand seems actually to soften into life'. [103]

The second obvious objection to the sculpture collection in the Palace was the fact that the rest of the displays and all the hubbub around it distracted the attention of the viewer. Ruskin, lecturing at Oxford, jeered at the sculptures 'mixed up with Rimmel's perfumery' (there were three Rimmel fountains, all designed by John Thomas, dispensing *eau de Cologne, Sydenham Crystal Palace Bouquet,* and toilet vinegar). He ridiculed the application' to the Palace of the word 'sublime'. Clamouring for attention in the one vast hall were 'Niobe, chimpanzee, wooden Caffres and New Zealanders, Shakespeare House, Le Grand Blondin and Le Petit Blondin; and Handel and Mozart; and no end of shops and buns, and beer'. [104] *The Crystal Palace Expositor* complained with justification that the spectator could hardly do justice to Michelangelo's Moses adjacent to the Great Transept 'among the noise and crowd': 'It should be seen amid the silence of a cathedral, with all those accessories of holy influence which a cathedral presents to the mind of contemplative man.' The Court of Monuments of Christian Art, which looks dignified in Delamotte's photographs, shared its space with orange trees and ice creams. [105]

The collection of modern casts played an important part in debate about sculpture in the 1850s and '60s, and the handbook commissioned by the directors for the Sydenham collection from the art critic Anna Jameson (1794–1860) to 'serve as a guide in some respects to the public taste' was independent and outspoken. It was also highly regarded. The nineteen pieces after Canova on view provoked her contempt: she called his work sentimental, meretricious, mannered and without character. On the other hand, she praised the forty works by Thorvaldsen for their 'pure taste and 'elevated moral thoughts'.[106] The strongest statements about contemporary sculpture during this period were made by Francis Turner Palgrave, famous as the editor of *The Golden Treasury*. In his essay in the official catalogue of the Fine Art Department for the International Exhibition of 1862, at which over 140 contemporary British sculptures (many in plaster) were on show, he wrote that this art was 'the forlorn hope of the modern world' ever since it had fallen to its lowest point in 1750. Compared with the civilisations of Assyria, Egypt, Greece and Rome, where it ranked second after poetry among the arts, sculpture was now in a deathly decline, and 'awakens but a cold, feeble, artificial interest'; it had fallen into the hands of the philistine rich and had become subservient to the 'lust for luxury and ornamentation'. It appeared that Palgrave only admired Foley among British sculptors, in particular his portraits; of the German sculptors he liked Rauch and Rietschel. He was particularly severe about the 'operatic sentimentalism' of Canova and Flaxman's 'antiquarian revival', while Chantrey was a master but had 'left a school in which the picturesque soon faded into commonplace, and severity into slovenliness'.[107]

The heyday of the sculpture collection at the Sydenham Palace lasted some twenty years from 1854. In 1878 the classicist Walter Copland Perry proposed a government purchase of casts for a gallery, with support from writers and painters, including Poynter and Leighton. In his pamphlet *On the Formation of a Gallery of Casts from the Antique in London* he referred to the decline of the Sydenham collection:

> The Directors of the Crystal Palace, it is true, made a gallant attempt to supply the deficiency of which we complain. But their fine collection of casts, arranged with so much knowledge and taste, has been partly destroyed by fire and partly removed to make room for other, certainly not more interesting objects, and the beautiful statues which are left are used chiefly for the purpose of decoration.

The advantage of a gallery of casts as against museum collections of classical originals was that the latter were partial, and links in the 'golden chain' were lost. Perry reminded Londoners that at the Berlin museums there were now 1,400 casts of antique statues. His initiative was successful, and the casts he obtained on the continent are now in the Victoria and Albert Museum.[108]

Despite its losses in the fire of 1866, the collection at Sydenham did not decline rapidly. In 1874 the statuary was 'repainted'.[109] When the Navy left the building after the First World War there were still 2,000 casts left to be repositioned in the Palace from lumber-rooms and odd corners. The statuary had suffered damage from the sailors and others, but it was repaired in 1925 and intermittently up to 1928, when Joseph Cheek, who had been in charge of it since 1895, set up a 'surgery' for missing noses, fingers, ears and limbs. Cheek loved his work, and once rescued the plaster model of Thomas Thornycroft's Boadicea (from which the bronze at Westminster had been cast) from a rubbish-heap where the London County Council had left it in pieces, repaired it and installed it at the Palace.[110] However, there are sad photographs from the 1930s showing Canova's Three Graces in a Crystal Palace interior grown bleak; another picture of that period shows the 'Holiday Court' promoting

package tours for pleasure and health, flanked by a forlorn-looking angel and a Cupid.[111] The final exhibition of the Palace sculpture is seen in photographs of the 1950s that show the graveyard of broken and overgrown statues in the Park, bearing auctioneers' numbers, when the London County Council sold them off.

Some of the fountains at the Palace, made of metal, patent stone and glass, deserve to be considered as sculpture. The most remarkable were two by Raffaelle Monti showing the four quarters of the globe and their racial types; Anna Jameson described them as 'very large, noble and poetical'. The water in them was said to 'foam and curl in sparkling fantastic ebullitions',[112] while thousands of goldfish gleamed in the basin.

Raffaelle Monti (1818–81), already mentioned above, came to work for the Crystal Palace as a political exile, like Gottfried Semper. A Milanese, he had joined the National Guard in 1847 and after a disastrous campaign and defeat at Custozza by the Austrians, he settled in London, where he was patronised by the Duke of Devonshire and achieved great popular success with his *Veiled Vestal*, shown at the Great Exhibition together with his *Veiled Slave in the Market Place* and his *Eve after the Fall*. Monti produced some sculptural details in the Architectural Courts, and contributed the colossal symbolic figures of South America, Italy, Spain, Holland, and the Zollverein for the Upper Terrace of the Palace garden. Inside the Palace was his Veritas, 'coquettishly unveiling herself', which Anna Jameson found 'open to objections in point of taste'.

Monti's bankruptcy some time before January 1855 was a serious financial blow to the Company.[113] Among his other commissions he had been contracted to write a sixpenny guide in the Palace series, *How to See the Sculpture in the Crystal Palace*; it was listed in all the other handbooks in the series in 1854 as 'in the press', but never appeared.

The sources of information about the statues at Sydenham are photographs of individual figures, taken as parts of series, including stereopticon double prints, general photographs of the interior, and the lists and descriptions in the handbooks. The casts of classical statuary were read, if the handbooks are a clue, as 'mythological subjects', with an emphasis on narrative and feeling, even at times mildly prurient, as in George Scharf's description of *Ariadne* in the Greek Court: 'The daughter of Minos is sleeping on the rocks of Naxos at the moment when the perfidious Theseus has abandoned her. So she appeared when the god of wine approached and became enamoured of her… Her tunic falls loosely, and the veil is negligently thrown over her head – the whole figure is characterised by disorder.'[114] Anna Jameson records the new reaction against classicism, saying that contemporary male statues tend to be titled 'a Boy at a stile' rather than 'Apollo as a Shepherd'; she imagines a man uneducated in the classics asking why we are to be forever haunted by the symbols of a dead culture rather than turning to nature. Her classicist is made to reply that the statue of Venus represents beauty and love, and Bacchus joy and fertility; 'it is not Athena with the thoughtful brows beneath her helmet, and aegis-guarded bosom, but womanhood armed in chastity and wisdom which stands before us.' Jameson recognised that modern sculpture was at a turning point, as was shown by the arrival at the Palace of the modern *naturalismo* Milanese pieces represented[115] and the works of Monti. A new romanticism and picturesqueness, with a latent expressionism, had arrived.

British sculpture was dominated by John Gibson's works, of which there were eighteen. In 1838 Paxton had been taken to visit Gibson's studio in Rome by the Duke of Devonshire, an enthusiastic patron, and he owned some of Gibson's minor works himself. The other sculptors significantly represented were John Bacon, E.H. Baily (with eight statues), John Bell (who was commissioned to make four of the 'colossal' statues on the Terrace, *California* being the most admired), James Crawford (an American), John Hancock, T.E. Jones, John Lawlor, J.G. Lough (with eight statues; this Northumbrian sculptor was the dedicatee of James Fergusson's *Principles of Beauty in Art*, 1849), Laurence Macdonald, William Calder Marshall, E.G. Papworth Jr, J. Richardson, the Westmacotts father and son, and Richard Wyatt (kinsman of Digby Wyatt and close friend and associate in Rome of Gibson; ten statues). There were two busts by Joseph Bonomi, Owen Jones's friend from his days in Egypt and his assistant at the Palace, who had studied under Nollekens. Anna Jameson thought, like Palgrave, that the English school (with some exceptions) showed 'a want of largeness of style, a poverty of invention, a want of fire and vigour in conception, and of elegance in execution'. Of earlier British sculptors there was a Shakespeare, said to be after Roubilliac but actually after Scheemakers, and nothing

from the works of Nollekens or Rysbrack. Even Flaxman, Foley, Chantrey, Banks and others were noticeably absent, to Jameson's regret, since they represented a serious gap where teaching the people about British sculpture was concerned. [116] W.M. Rossetti, reviewing the sculpture at Sydenham, wrote that the British, an inartistic race, were indifferent to sculpture and monuments, and easily taken in by technique, such as by Monti's veiled faces; he lamented the divorce between architecture and sculpture and thought Classicism an incubus of British work. The collection at Sydenham proved again the current lack in the British School of a definite ideal of expression and character, 'united with beautiful form'.[117]

From studying Jameson's handbook it is striking how many sculptors from the continent, not only living but young, were represented at Sydenham. She seems to express the typical British view of French sculpture at that time – not well represented, compared with the German and Italian contributions – calling it capricious, sensual, meretricious and marked by an 'appetite for sensation'. A reminder of Pugin's Medieval Court was a

John Gibson, *Psyche borne by the Zephyrs.*

statue of *Charity* by one of Pugin's carvers, Theodore Phyffers, originally of Louvain. She admired contemporary German sculpture for its power and poetic feeling, even when she thought it exaggerated, and singled out the twenty-three casts after Christian Rauch of Berlin and the fourteen after Ludwig Schwanthaler of Munich, whose noble colossal head *Bavaria* (54 feet high), cast from the bronze at Ludwig I's Ruhmeshalle at Munich, creates a powerful impression in Delamotte's photographs. Ernest Hähnel, Gottfried Semper's sculptor for the Dresden Hoftheater, showed a *Bacchanal* from its north façade.[118]

Jameson made no mention of Marochetti's works at the Palace, such as the colossal statue of Sir Robert Peel in the angle of the South Transept; presumably they arrived soon after her handbook was written. Baron Carlo Marochetti (1805–67) was an important and controversial sculptor. His enemies thought that being, in all but name, the official royal sculptor, favoured by Prince Albert in particular, he took advantage of his position to gain commissions for his characteristic large-limbed memorials. 'Effectivism', or showing-off, was a term applied to him.[119] Undoubtedly there was prejudice against him as a foreigner; when his model for the Scutari monument with its matronly angels was shown at Sydenham (described in Chapter 2), it was universally derided. Palgrave wrote:

Philip Delamotte, 'Colossal Head of "Bavaria"'.

'Not less than £15,000 were handed over to the Franco-Italian sculptor in question, for what was called the Scutari Monument. Few people will remember this, for the display of the model at Sydenham called forth such unfavourable comments that it was rapidly withdrawn. It consisted of four sentimental-looking women with long wings placed at the corners of a large block of stone, and as these angels were exactly alike, we can perfectly well believe what we have been told on professional authority, that from £3,000 to £4,000 would have been considered an ample price by an English artist.'[120] Palgrave thought his *Coeur de Lion*, prominent both outside the Palace at Hyde Park and in the Transept at Sydenham, 'essentially vulgar and low-class', and that the sculptor's work was spurious, sensational and full of tricks; Ruskin on the other hand declared that Marochetti's work was 'thoroughly great'. Samuel Phillips's *Guide* referred to Marochetti's *Turkey*, *Greece*, *India* and *Egypt*, together with Monti's *China*, all of them commissioned for the series of colossal allegorical figures on the Upper Terrace, as being of 'the modern Roman school'.[121]

The Portrait Gallery, intended as an inspiring element or chapter in the visual encyclopaedia, comprised busts and statues of 499 people who contributed to the history of civilisation, and a biographical handbook was written for it by Samuel Phillips. The Classical and Italian busts were shown near to the appropriate Court; they included the Court of the Roman Ladies, which one journalist thought 'so like the women one sees every day'. The portrait collection was catholic, showing a wide range of artists and scientists, both English and continental, many of them living people. Phillips's handbook is an informative guide to the figures admired by educated people in London at the time. The busts were ranged on the garden side of the south nave, behind the Musical Instruments and Textile courts. Phillips makes moral judgments about his subjects: Byron's poetry, 'instead of being a well-trimmed garden of beauty, had its choicest flowers entangled and half hidden in unwholesome, gaudy weeds', and he tells his readers all he can against Rousseau.[122]

Directly outside the Palace on the Upper Terrace stood the twenty-six carved monumental statues commissioned by the Company from Monti and the other sculptors, standing about 9 feet high. John Bell made four figures, and Hiram Powers' *The United States*; other sculptors were James Legrew, William Calder Marshall,

B.E Spence, William Theed, Marochetti, the Parisian Antoine Etex, the Belgian Willem Geefs, and Schmidt von der Launitz (a pupil of Thorvaldsen). These were of marble or stone, but Bell's *Australia* was of terra cotta by Blashfield, fired 'at the heat at which glass melts' for three weeks, at that date probably the largest ceramic work ever fired in one piece. The group also stood as an emphatic index to the state of contemporary English and continental sculpture in 1854.[123]

This conspicuous parade of sixteen colossal statues represented nations and cities (both British and foreign). Industry and commerce mostly determined the European selection; Russia, India, China and the Americas were present. In the spirit of 1851 the group was made up of Britain's trading partners and states prolific with natural resources, such as California. Thus the new Crystal Palace could be interpreted as an Acropolis sacred to the idea of nations productively united, and of a technological and artistic civilisation sustained by natural resources, manufactures and commerce. Inside the Palace the displays hinted that this mid-century achievement was the result of racial and political evolution.

Round the central circular basin on the lower terrace were white marble copies after Canova (*Paris* and others) and after Thorvaldsen (*Mercury* and others), and copies of famous classical statues (the Farnese Hercules and Venus de Milo). Aquatic figures, as at Versailles, reclined on the verges of the two vast fountain basins at the side. These were by unnamed sculptors: *Ganges*, *Amazon*, *Thames* and *Nile*; and the *Arctic*, *Indian*, *Pacific* and *Atlantic* oceans.[124]

The later history of the casts is melancholy. In 1902–3 the Victoria and Albert Museum thought well enough of Giordani's cast of the Colleoni statue to apply to purchase or borrow it. When in 1909 the Palace was almost bankrupt again, the Museum considered acquiring casts, but space was a problem, and they were wary of breaking up the Crystal Palace collection. A letter to the *Daily Telegraph* in 1910 said that the Fontevrault casts, 'coloured in accordance with the originals', were 'poked away in a dark alley' near an exit to the frivolous North Tower Gardens; fearing that in the following year the Festival of Empire crowds would damage them, the writer suggested their removal to South Kensington. A number of fruitless attempts were made to house the casts away from Sydenham; in 1911 the Society of British Sculptors offered to buy the collection for £15,000, and in 1923 the Palace had similar inquiries from the Imperial Museum in New York. The Victoria and Albert Museum again considered the forlorn casts when the War Museum moved into the Palace and they had mostly been put into store. However, the contemplated mass movement of plaster casts north across the Thames might yet have been reversed: in 1928 there was a proposal to send casts from the British Museum and the Victoria and Albert Museum to join the collection at Sydenham.[125] After the fire in 1936, Sir Henry Buckland offered the Victoria and Albert Museum the Fontevrault casts, which had been saved, but exposed to the weather; the contractors were clearing the site, and the matter was urgent. They accordingly joined the collection at the Museum in July 1938, and are now in the Cast Court.[126]

Raffaelle Monti's bronzed anthropological fountain of the Syrens (Caucasian, Nubian, North American Indian, Australian), parrot-stand and the Tropical Department.

5

THE INTERIOR
BOTANY, NATURAL HISTORY, THE INDUSTRIAL COURTS,
THE PICTURE GALLERY, PHOTOGRAPHY

Botany

The planting of the Winter Garden in its heyday was extravagant and wonderful. The Tropical Department, fronting the Aboo-Simbel figures and the Nineveh Court, was its most ambitious flourish for which, as we have seen, Paxton went to almost megalomaniac lengths to provide heating with hot-water piping. The north end of the Palace, with those pipes under the floor-boards, reproduced the 'mild and genial climate of Madeira in winter', and became known as 'the Tropical End'. Charles Darwin wrote in praise of Paxton's art after visiting the Great Stove at Chatsworth in 1845 that he felt 'like a child, transported with delight… the great Hot house, and especially the water part, is more wonderfully like tropical nature, than I could have considered possible. – Art beats Nature altogether there.'[1]

Paxton introduced great quantities of a climbing plant, 'Chinese twiner' (*Glycine sionensis*), which could grow up to 120 feet, along tie-rods and columns and up to the second tier of girders. There were between 300 and 400 hanging baskets about 4 feet in diameter, with bright colours and hanging tendrils. George Eyles, who had been brought down from Derbyshire, was Paxton's 'head general' inside the Palace – 'a chip off the old block, which was squared at Chatsworth and then moulded for the Crystal Palace'[2] – and considering the problems with heat and glare for plants inside the Palace, he did an excellent job. Twenty-four date palms from the East – typically advertised as very rare, the largest specimens and the longest-lived, and intended to join the tree ferns lining the Avenue of Sphinxes – arrived late at Southampton docks on the *Himalaya*, having been delayed by the Crimean War and troop movements in Malta. *Latonia borbonica*, the bulkiest plant at the Palace, which had belonged to the Empress Joséphine at Fontainebleau, was a Mauritian palm 35 feet high, with a plume of fan-like leaves at its apex. The palm itself weighed a ton, and in July 1854 thirty-two horses pulled it, its box of earth and the carriage on which it rested, a total weight of 15 tons, through the streets from Hackney over London Bridge to Sydenham; the leaves swept against the third-storey windows of houses.[3] It formed part of a collection of palms started ninety years earlier by George Loddiges, the leading specialist firm, whose entire stock Paxton bought. Samuel Phillips in his *General Guide Book to the Palace* wrote lyrically of the beauty of palms, 'the stem often rising to the altitude of 100 feet, in a stately column, crowned with a capital of beautiful leaves, radiating from its summit, or gracefully drooping; sometimes of a feathery form, sometimes fan-shaped of broader growth; some of dark, shining verdure, and others of a delicate silvery aspect.'[4] Queen Victoria donated a *Dicksonia* fern 15 feet high.

Donald Beaton (1802–63), the head gardener of Shrubland Park in Suffolk, who wrote a series of detailed articles on the plants inside and outside the Palace for *The Cottage Gardener*, praised the extraordinary health of these plants at the hothouse end: they had been brought from Florida, Java, India, Tahiti, South America and Australia, and were better off than in any conservatory, glossy and without dust. In the Palace Josephine's palm grew 5 feet in as many years. Paxton also bought a set of seventy-two indoor-trained orange trees from royal Neuilly and twenty-four pomegranate trees, some said to be 400 years old. Inside the Palace he planted 8,000 camellias and 10,000 geraniums, with many fuchsias and calceolarias. The Alhambra Court had 600 roses, set among variegated balsams. We also read of azaleas, double tulips, Persian lilacs and hyacinths; myrtle, petunias, heliotropiums and verbenas; scarlet lychnis, fraxinela and Eastern poppy.[5] The *Illustrated Crystal Palace Gazette* expected that the plants when mature would rival the hanging gardens of Babylon or the Garden of the Hesperides. Two splendid Norfolk Island pines given by the Duke of Devonshire, one 40 feet high, were an early feature. The Queen gave another pair.[6] These

Philip Delamotte, 'Tropical Plants'.

trees grow to 100 feet, and were said by Beaton to be the 'handsomest trees in the Palace'. The Queen also gave an *Araucaria excelsa* and twelve other plants, and the Duke of Devonshire an aquatic collection. Numerous rare plants and shrubs appeared, such as the American aloe, *Ageratum mexicanum* and musk. There were eight conservatory beds along both sides of the Nave and eight flower garden beds. Edgings were usually of lobelia. The bedding of indoor plants in the Palace's heyday was admired; Beaton in March 1858, after inspecting the spring flowers in the vases and marble basins round the crystal fountains, said that species such as narcissus were never better arranged. Plants

Philip Delamotte, 'First Arrival of Plants', 1854.

formed a display with the 'Ethnological Specimens' in a bed or parterre surrounding the painted wooden models of Australian Aborigines and American Indians. The *Illustrated Crystal Palace Gazette* absurdly expected visitors to laugh at the brown skins, thick lips, squatting postures and nose-rings in these portrayals, but to be instructed at the same time by the botany.

Tiny oaks were grown from acorns brought from Nineveh. Opposite the Byzantine Court were planted 'four funereal Cypresses from the Vale of Tombs, in North China'. In May 1855 there were young leaves of Paxton's celebrated *Victoria regia* in the basins; a full and perfect flower was reported in July, and by August they had grown to 6 feet. In 1854 *The Times* reported that the plants at the south end of the nave suffered from the heaviest snow for years having fallen outside,[7] but they were said after a second winter to be in fine order, particularly in the 'luxuriance and splendour' of the Tropical Department at the north end, protected by Paxton's heating system. Fuller claimed in his *Letter* to the shareholders of 28 August 1874 that even before the fire of 1866 many plants, including whole collections, had 'perished from sheer neglect'. Gone also in that disaster was all but one-fifth of the tropical conservatory. After this fire the directors spent the £38,000 paid by the

insurers on repairs to the rest of the building rather than on restoring the Courts, the colossal Egyptian statues and the plants.[7]

Of the Winter Garden at Sydenham before the fire, the quality of which can still be appreciated from Delamotte's photographs, the *Art Journal* said that 'nothing can be more charming', with its vista of fountains, citrus trees, palms, statuary and hanging baskets. By 1867 a gigantic wistaria was flowering indoors. While the botany in the Palace was intended to teach the wonders of the natural world, it was also expected that the union of architectural features and works of art with plants would set the fashion for entertaining among the rich. A writer in *The Cottage Gardener* wrote in 1858: 'I would advise gardeners in the country, who have to do with furnishings for balls, routs, and evening parties, or with conservatories which open into crowded drawing-rooms, to visit the Avenue of Sphynxes this spring to learn more of this *effect*.'[8]

Natural history

In the sections of the Palace not devoted to Fine Art there were installations for the three-dimensional *Encyclopaedia Paxtoniana* to teach the wonders and mysteries of Nature. Paxton rose to the scale that the building imposed; the word 'colossal' is a common motif in the official Palace literature. Charles Dickens made a telling joke in a letter to Angela Burdett-Coutts written in Milan after an Alpine holiday in 1853; he said that he had reported to the guides on the Mer de Glace that Mont Blanc had recently become such a nuisance (because of Albert Smith's Alpinist lectures at the Egyptian Hall) that there was 'some idea of authorising Paxton to take it down and re-erect it at Sydenham'. The largest item of Natural History was the bark of a section of the 4,000-year-old 'Mammoth Tree', a sequoia from the Sierra Nevada in California; in height this was merely 95 feet of its actual 363 feet. Formerly in the New York Crystal Palace, it was placed facing the Aboo Simbel figures across the North Transept until it was consumed in the Fire of 1866. A Crystal Palace programme booklet suggested a helpful idea to the visitors: 'Could it be endowed with the gift of speech, might it not be able to tell us of the destruction of Sodom and Gomorrah?'[9] There were flourishes and charm to the natural history displays, such as the white doves given by the adventuress Lola Montez, decorative macaws and cockatoos in pretty cages, singing birds (nightingales, blackbirds, wrens, robins), and strange marine zoology, such as sponges, in water-tanks. Honey bees could be studied in glass cases in the Gallery. In the 1890s the Natural History Department compromised its objective academic status as an important section in a living encyclopaedia, when one display was presented for amusement in the Entertainment Court, and moreover as a ridiculous political amusement: a 'Royal Exhibition of Working Ants' featured 'ants keeping domestics'; 'red ants keeping black slaves'; 'yellow ants grazing cows,' and 'queen ants with attendants'.[10]

The groups of painted wooden ethnographical models showing 'primitive' peoples were the most significant educational element of the Natural History Department inside the Palace. They were divided into the New World and the Old World, set up in tableaux on the earthed 'borders' with vegetation and stuffed beasts and birds from the climate of their origin. 'The illusive effect is almost startling', wrote Measom in his Brighton Railway Company Guide. The display was sometimes referred to as the 'Geographical Garden'.[11] The groups, designed to illustrate 'the different varieties of the human race', were placed right by the entrance to the Palace from the Colonnade in the South Wing that led from the Lower Station where the guide books assumed the tour of the Palace would begin. The plan was to make an initial impact in the Palace's teaching about progress, as if it were the first page of the encyclopaedia. The New World was on the south-west side; the Old World on the south-east. The models were expected to unsettle visitors, as Phillips put it in his *Guide* with remarkable smugness:

> If the visitor should feel astonishment in the presence of some of the phases of human existence here presented to him, he may do well to bear in mind that these are representatives of human beings endowed with immortal souls. […] It is not yet two thousand years since the forefathers of the present European family tattooed their skins, and lived in so savage a state that late archaeological researches induce us to suspect that they were not wholly free from one of the worst charges that is laid to savage existence; viz. the practice of cannibalism.

The Company was at pains to emphasise that this was the first display of its kind, and Phillips wrote that the 'picturesque groupings' must be infinitely better than the monotony of the plants in glass cases at Kew and the stuffed birds and animals at the British Museum that gave no geographical context. *The Times* agreed that the displays at Sydenham were much better than the 'miserably prepared specimens' of animal life at the British Museum and the conceptions they presented.[12]

London had only become accustomed in recent years to the sight of living 'savages' (Maoris, Indians and Africans), who were exhibited to the public in Piccadilly. Also 150 small-scale models of Indians and Mexicans had been shown at the Great Exhibition, variously exciting repulsion or derision. The *Handbook to the Courts of Natural History* declared that at the Palace botany, zoology and the 'new science' of ethnology would 'illustrate each other'.[13] Its engraved title-page showed Africans (holding a shield bearing the Company's initials), indigenous South Americans and Egyptians. The new science was the theme of one of Monti's fountains, which showed four 'Syrens': Caucasian, Nubian, American Indian and Australian.

The author of the handbook and the director of the Ethnological Department who designed and supervised the models was a polymath, Dr Robert Latham (1812–88), who lectured at the Middlesex Hospital on forensic medicine and *materia medica* but retired in 1848 to study and write, particularly on race and philology. In the 1860s he opposed the theory of the Aryan races originating in China; Theodore Watts-Dunton in his obituary praised his brilliant and independent intellect, encyclopaedic knowledge and unequalled conversation. His handbook does not spare the reader accounts of decapitations, head-hunting, blow-pipes and cannibals; a cannibal meal is described in a ghoulish passage from Marsden's *Sumatra*. Bizarre marriage and death customs fascinated him. However, he also quoted a description by Stamford Raffles of a peaceable, orderly, honest, industrious and happy people in a rich and romantic part of Java. Latham says that he had a mountain display planned to show altitudinal zones, with belts of Alpine vegetation and animals, but that regrettably this and other scenes could not be realised at Sydenham: 'Let us picture in our minds long lines of hoary coasts, the dark rock occasionally breaking through its frosty covering, the deep green waves tossing masses of ice, and bearing up towering and fantastic icebergs whose cleft and cavernous sides are beautiful with intense blue shadows.' This would be the Arctic background for the 'whales, jelly-fish, sea-birds and the great white bear' that could not be shown in the Sydenham encyclopaedia.[14] However, the 1857 *Guide* pointed to a new display of natives of Arctic Russia with snow-shoes, a Greenlander in his skin-canoe, and – a reminder of the Arctic expeditions to find Franklin – 'a polar bear killed by Captain Inglefield with a single pistol shot, when he was closely and dangerously attacked by the monster'. Reindeer and Eskimo dogs and seals were part of the display (arranged and designed by A.D. Bartlett).[15]

Owen Jones, as mentioned in Chapter 3, was the earliest writer on design to take the patterns of 'primitive' peoples seriously, and the first three plates of *The Grammar of Ornament* reproduced patterns in plaited straw, tattoos and woodcarving, copied from objects in the United Services Museum and the British Museum. His chapter on their ornaments commented with considerable depth of knowledge on the use by native artists of geometrical patterns and stars from their observations of Nature.[16]

It is not known when Latham was appointed director of the department; in August 1852 the Crystal Palace Company had published three short pamphlets by William Thomson, curator of the Museum of Natural History and Anatomy at King's College, outlining plans for Ethnological, Zoological and Raw Produce collections at Sydenham – Thomson was named as superintendent of all three. The pamphlets show that the first plans were different, and that the Company was appealing for donations of artefacts. Casts of hands and faces, specimens of hair, weapons, dresses and drawings, indigenous art, manufactures and objects of worship were mentioned. A list of tribes across the world was given. Whales and elephants, lemurs, rodents and reptiles were among the donations asked for among stuffed mammals.[17]

In one of the tableaux as actually set up in 1854 in the 'New World' section a drama was represented, involving one native Mexican saving another. A jaguar that had killed a deer, ostriches, a tapir, an alpaca and other animals completed the scene. The visitor was informed that 'it was consolatory to think' that the South Americans, with their lank hair and 'savage expression', had

Philip Delamotte, 'The Old World Court': Africa.

responded to missionary efforts to make them industrious. A black jaguar and ocelot were poised above them on a rock. North American Indians, 'savage and cruel in war', followed in a war dance. The Old World presented a group of 'Zulu Kaffres, Bosjesmen, Earthmen, Hottentots', and a female hippopotamus – the scene is familiar from Delamotte's photograph; Madagascans, East Africans with a camel, Danikils, West African slaves, a leopard looking down on an antelope, a chimpanzee, and a battle between two leopards. A dramatic tableau of a tiger hunt from India was popular; there were also Hindus, Malays, Tibetans; Papuans, and the excessively projecting jaws of what were said to be the 'most degraded forms of man', Australian aborigines. Properties in these tableaux included a wigwam, a tomahawk, rhododendrons, great horned sheep of Chinese Tartary, serpents and an eagle in a tree. The Zulu group was 'taken from life', being modelled from men lately exhibited live at St George's Hall in London. Latham had arranged a narrative and scene, including 'a fetish man in a rabid excitement'.[18]

Mortalities from a recent severe frost enabled some of the animals for stuffing – the leopards and an antelope – to be obtained from the Zoological Gardens at Regent's Park. An elephant that 'had recently died in the north' came from Wombwell's menagerie. The birds were the responsibility of the eminent ornithologist John Gould (1804–81) of the Zoological Society's Museum. The taxidermist was the same A.D. Bartlett who had arranged some of the displays. Another elephant added much later to 'the Jungle Scene' was 'Charlie' from Sanger's Circus, shot after killing a man during a stay at the Crystal Palace one Christmas; its body was donated by George Sanger. Outside the official literature few compliments were paid to Dr Latham's remarkable work on the novel ethnological displays. Brickbats were more normal: a shareholder wrote to the *Daily News* that they were crudely made – 'detestable and unworthy wild Indian figures which a showman's booth would have rejected'.[19]

The only significant addition to the Natural History displays made later was the ambitious Aquarium, a commercial speculation with its own shareholders. The architect was Harry Driver, construction began in May 1870, and it was opened in January 1872. However, it failed and was wound up in 1886. The manager was William Alford Lord who had worked in Munich. The great Aquarium, 400 feet by 70, was built on the site of the part of the Palace lost in the fire of 1866, at the end of what had been the North Wing wall below the original balustrade. 120,000 gallons of sea-water were brought by rail from Brighton, and circulated from a reservoir by steam-power. Thirty-eight tanks were on view, and the plain Saloon, to be seen in engravings, resembled a lofty railway station booking hall or hotel foyer. On winter evenings there was gas lighting to study the nocturnal habits of the creatures. A *Handbook to the Marine Aquarium* with a catalogue and plan was issued. A monster alligator was fed daily at 2 p.m.[20]

The Industrial Courts

A total of seven Industrial Courts were constructed under the Galleries on either side of the main thoroughfare with its wooden floorboards and indoor flowerbeds. These Courts, which with the exception of the Pompeian House and the Natural History 'geographical gardens' occupied the entire South Nave, were intended for manufacturing displays that would generate revenue to maintain the Palace and provide a dividend for the shareholders. The Palace *Guide* of 1867 said that the Nave was like a combination of Regent Street, Bond Street, Oxford Street and the Strand – meaning to suggest both convenience and elegance. In that year 600 people were employed in the Courts and the Bazaar of smaller shops that ran behind it, a kind of Burlington Arcade offering such merchandise as furniture, carpets, hardware, pottery, porcelain, glass, real Alpine kid gloves, toys, cigars, perfumes, soap and candles. The annual rents paid for these premises amounted to £16,000. The Galleries above originally sold perfumery, chemicals, leather, fire-arms, India rubber, 'philosophical instruments' (scientific instruments), surgical instruments, china and glass, and clothing. A manager, the popular Mr Belshaw who had been in charge of the British Manufactures at Hyde Park, was said in the Company chairman's pamphlet of 17 March 1853 to have been appointed, but all mention of him ceased soon after the opening of the Palace, and there were soon many references to mismanagement and discontent among the exhibitors. The *Crystal Palace Expositor* wrote that industrial features, including technology and science, should have been more prominent, with a fuller Trade Museum, and recommended the Conservatoire des Arts et Métiers in Paris as a model. By 1867 something like this was achieved with an Industrial Museum and

Technological Collection in the Gallery.[21] Industry was also one of the didactic subjects in the encyclopaedia, developing Albert's vision of universal peace and plenty, backed by commerce, as expressed in his Mansion House speech of 21 March 1850:

'It must teach us, if viewed aright, that progress and prosperity depend as much on commerce as on internal riches, and that all the members of the great human family may promote each other's happiness and their Maker's glory, by spreading the blessings of civilisation, by exchanging the natural or manufactured products of their respective countries, and, when they come to know each other better, by exchanging their thoughts, their aspirations, their books – the less-informed submitting to be taught, the wise and good daring to teach, and to carry out the divine mission of the Gospel, "Peace on earth, goodwill towards men." If the rulers of the earth would allow their subjects to hold free intercourse with each other, civilisation and its accompanying blessings would move more quickly, war and discord more slowly.'[22]

The directors at the same time claimed that the Courts would be 'beautiful as Works of Art' and illustrate new architectural styles. Some of the architects commissioned to design these Courts were interesting in their own right, but the results were uneven. At worst they could be said to be essays in shop design, although the *Athenaeum* thought that in the world outside they should inspire an improvement. Views of three Courts – Musical Instruments, Printed Fabrics and the Sheffield Court – were engraved for *The Builder*. Originally, and mistakenly, Charles Cockerell was announced as one of the architects. There is evidence that Jones, not surprisingly, did not take kindly to losing control of the design of parts of the interior: Cole, after visiting the Palace with Paxton and Redgrave in January 1854, wrote in his diary: 'Saw O Jones & Wyatt. The first annoyed at the introduction of other Architects in building. Central Roof not yet done. Dined with Paxton.'[23] An early lithographed ground-plan of the Palace made in 1853 has 'Flax and Hemp' and 'Silk and Shawls' printed in the position of these Courts, corrected by a Company hand to 'Printed Fabrics' and 'French Courts'.

The Court for Musical Instruments was designed by John Thomas, sculptor of the Palace of Westminster and architect of Samuel Morton Peto's mansion, Somerleyton Hall in Suffolk. The *Athenaeum* noted in the Court 'the splendours of chromatic decoration', the arches and glazed recesses. Cupids played various instruments, and in roundels were sculptures of the great composers, as

well as images of David, Miriam, Pan and Apollo. *The Builder* noted the large amount of modelling done by Thomas for the court, describing his busts of composers, shells, figures of St Cecilia and Erato in *alto-rilievo*, interspersed with quotations from Dryden and William Collins.

The Court for Printed Fabrics was the work of the younger Charles Barry and Robert Richardson Banks (according to some press reports, Sir Charles Barry was to have been the designer). 'Scarcely more than an elegant shop', said the *Athenaeum*. The engraving shows attenuated Byzantine double columns and round arches, in Barry's typical eclectic or 'free' style, surmounted by a parapet with ceramic urn-like finials, like his father's work at Trentham and Cliveden.[24]

The Court for Woollen and Mixed Fabrics was by Gottfried Semper. The *Illustrated Crystal Place Gazette* praised it as 'different from the rest, with a covered ceiling and a sort of square tower, with stalls before the first entrance. We rather like this design, which is under the guidance of Mr Semper; its ornamental decorations are novel, and in good taste.' The *Athenaeum* gave some details, in the absence of an engraving or photograph: low semi-circular doorways and high arches with cases. It was decorated with golden fleeces, allegorical figures, festoons and panels showing plants and manufacturing processes. There were twenty free-standing columns inside the court, pilasters on the wall and a cornice. Two Parisian friends of Semper, Charles Séchan and Jules Dieterle, decorated a large ceiling. Semper received the commission only in February 1854, and it was completed six months after the Inauguration. Semper received letters of complaint from the Company over the delays and his non-attendance; Paxton at first refused to spend an extra £500 on the Court, but in the end authorised £800.[25]

The Stationery Court was by J.G. Crace. The design for the interior can be visualised from his own drawing now in the Victoria and Albert Museum and from an engraving in the *Crystal Palace Expositor*. The *Athenaeum* described tasteful fittings in oak-work. 'Cinquecento' was the epithet used by Phillips; stained glass windows showed allegorical figures of arts and sciences, with cupidons reading and writing or 'engaged in the various mechanical and scientific arts having reference to paper, printing, and engraving'. The colour scheme was a 'rather heavy' chocolate, with white and

The Stationery Court, 1854.

olive borders and pale-coloured panels with red and black 'vandykings' (deep indentations). Books, photographs, engravings and chromolithographs as well as stationery were on sale.[26]

The Birmingham Court, 'a sort of iron architecture', was by Sir William Tite, architect of the new Royal Exchange in the City of London. This had a framework of iron screens, a 'restoration' of 'English ornamental iron enclosures of the 17th century'[27] with dark marble columns, and was embellished with leaves, pillars and scrolls. Panels painted by Mr Sang depicted allegorical figures of Utility and Art, and cupids in medallions, quarrying and hammering with presses, boilers and forges. An engraving of the interior, published in the *Art Journal*, shows the ironwork screens, and behind a tall display case can be seen just the head and the hand brandishing a sword of the statue of Boadicea by John Thomas, cast in bronze by Elkington from the marble made for Samuel Morton Peto (formerly Birmingham City Art Gallery). The contents, according to the *Crystal*

Palace Expositor, were 'but a poor exponent of the trade of that busy town'; they included the brooches of Celtic design that had been popular at Hyde Park, guns, Gillott's steel pens, needles and nails, Chance's 'extensive glass-house', and a complex *Iliad Salver* by Elkington, as well as gilt toys and Chubb's 'curious' locks.[28]

The Sheffield Court – plainly the star attraction among these Courts, being the only one of marked originality – was designed by Paxton's former architectural assistant, George Stokes, now his partner and son-in-law, who had originally been apprenticed to George Gilbert Scott. Reviewing it, *The Builder* said that 'to [Stokes] we believe, all the architectural details of the main building and terraces were entrusted.' One periodical called it 'an admixture of styles', but Phillips's *Guide* deemed it to be in 'a composite Moresque-Gothic style and elaborately ornamental'. The construction was of iron and plate glass with gilt mouldings, an upper double arcade of iron columns, and an ornamental penthouse. Huge glass panels canted out from the latter gave a reflecting mirror-like

Exterior of the Sheffield Court.

effect. Owen Jones's favourite red cloth was hung in the large lower panels. The interior arches were coloured blue, red and gold. The interior is seen in the chromo-lithograph made of it from his own drawing, and the exterior in a Delamotte photograph. The *Athenaeum* thought it 'light and fairy-like', and reminiscent of a Damascus bazaar. The roof was blue with coloured ribs, crockets and latticing. Frescoed medallions showed 'cupids engaged in various styles of manufacture – filing, crushing, rasping, till the rough ore grows smooth as a mirror and keen as a blade of a yataghan (Turkish sword)'. Outside were foxgloves and ferns.[29]

A French Court was not a success, probably because of the lack of interest from France, which was concentrating on its own international Expositions. In 1854 some 'magnificent Sèvres, Goblin [*sic*] and Beauvais works [were] sent by Emperor Napoleon.' The legend on the ground plan of 1854 was 'Foreign Court'. An

engraving of the interior in the *Art Journal* showed pointed arches and thin Gothic ornamentation with a projecting penthouse. The accompanying article said that it was for 'minor Art-productions of the Continent', mentioning scent-bottles and ink-wells, and complained how 'very secondary' the wares were. The Court was said to be 'light and graceful', and its inward sloping roof carried the names of cities and countries of Europe, but the writer named no designer or architect as being responsible for it. However, an entry in a printed Company account of 30 June 1855, 'FRENCH COURT Sir J. Paxton', may give a clue. By the second edition of the *Guide* to the Palace, in 1856, the French Court had been replaced on a ground-plan by 'Fancy Goods'.[30] The *Art Journal* engraving showed ceramics in cases; the director was a Mr Holt, whose 'establishment' it was thought to be. Early photographs of the Industrial Courts are hard to find.

'Industrial Court, No. 1. Sheffield Manufactures', 1854.

On the basement floor was the Agricultural Implement Department with machines for drilling, reaping and threshing. It also contained some prefabricated 'portable houses' for emigrants to take with them, and on this floor were forty-eight coaches from an Ipswich firm, and dog-carts. Here was placed 'Machinery in Motion', consisting of steam engines, cotton-spinning and weaving, all of which had proved so popular at Hyde Park. A Raw Produce Collection was originally housed in the North Wing, showing Soil, Produce of the Soil, and 'the Economic and Technological uses to which produce is applicable'. A Court of Inventions was to exhibit a mixture of large and small ideas: the prevention of railway accidents, cotton-reels, patent umbrellas, dressing-cases and Mr Brewster's optical instrument for stereoscopic pictures.[31]

Even in August 1854 the Courts were said to be ailing. The Sheffield Court was not quite finished, and in the Birmingham Court were few articles. The French Court and Music Court were not even half filled. A month after the opening, the 'paucity' of art-manufactures was called 'a serious evil', and 'the great and leading manufacturers' seemed not to be subscribing to a 'bazaar' principle. Originally there was 'an enormous tax' on exhibiting art-manufactures, which was reduced in January 1857 to a nominal rent. In August 1855, as mentioned in the account of the Crystal Palace Company in Chapter 2, the *Crystal Palace Herald* reported a meeting at the Woodman Hotel in Norwood at which Mr Deane and the directors conceded to the exhibitors' assertion that 'as an exhibition of British industrial productions the Crystal Palace has entirely failed.'[32]

The contents of the Courts were changed, and over the years many temporary exhibitions were installed. In the 1920s there were Colonial exhibitions in temporary structures such as the New Zealand and West India Courts. In 1860 the *Crystal Palace News* named the courts on the east side as 'Bohemian Glass Court,

Barnicott and Banfield's China and Glass Court, Ceramic Court, French Court'. In 1857 the Munich firm of Steierwald occupied the Glass Court. The Ceramic Court was 'brilliantly inaugurated' in August 1856 under Thomas Battam, formerly manager of Copeland's Works. By all accounts this was a serious and important museum, with 'rare and significant pieces' on show lent by famous collectors and authorities; it was related to the Architectural Courts in that it gave solid instruction on the development from antiquity of pottery to porcelain ('a historical series'), as well as being a shop for the best contemporary manufactures.[33] Behind the Birmingham and Stationery Courts was the Hardware Court with household utensils: mincing machines, cameras, artificial eyes, books advocating Temperance, piano wire, baths, tropical outfits, military clothing, India-rubber clothing, parasols, gas-fittings, mangles, sausage-machines, refrigerators – and cigars. In the Galleries above one could buy not only clothing but pickles, mustard, isinglass and bride-cakes; Mr Horniman showed his teas in growing specimens. The *Illustrated London News* imagined a newly-wed couple setting up house shopping for coal-scuttles, curtains, mirrors and coaches. Two firms which actually produced their stock-in-trade on the site were Day and Company, who demonstrated the lithographic presses for their prints of the Palace, and Messrs Pinches, who struck high-quality medals in a press that had great spherical weights on the rotating handle. This took place in the Nave between the Birmingham and Stationery courts.[34] Mr Charles Goodyear, following the success of his display in 1851, put up a Court made entirely of India-rubber. He sold sofas, work-tables, fruit plates and paper-knives made of the material, and speaking-trumpets made of gutta percha. The 'American stitching machines' that the *Illustrated Crystal Palace Gazette* said in 1854 'now stand in bold array in the central avenue of the Crystal Palace and deservedly attract a host of admirers' were presumably the sewing-machines of Isaac Merritt Singer.[35] The listings in the *Industrial Directory* published uniform with the Company's Handbooks in 1854 included much horsehair furniture, more Pompeian decorations, and Betjemann's patent chairs (manufactured by the family of the future poet). Thus the Crystal Palace, the 'illustrated encyclopaedia' that would transform taste and society, where one could study plaster casts of the dwellers on Mount Olympus, was gestating the Ideal Home Exhibitions that would later take place at Olympia.

The Picture Gallery

Presumably established in response to criticism rather than to educational idealism, and always a commercial operation, the Picture Gallery was never a great success. At times it appears to have had some professional management and indeed some interesting pictures to show, but it remained a disappointment that 'in a building which in great measure appeals to the favour of the educated classes under the character of a temple of the fine arts' there were no original pictures as part of the permanent display. The Gallery – 'ample and well-lighted from the top' – was housed in the North Wing. This was not

South London Exhibition, 1936

part of the Palace itself, but in symmetrical balance to the wing on the south side leading down through the glazed corridor to the Lower Level Station; until the disastrous gale of 1861 it was an elegant two-storey structure made from the standard iron and glass units. At the time of the 1867 *Guide* to the Palace, the Gallery was 700 feet long, consisted of six saloons, and housed 900 pictures from the British, French, Dutch and Belgian schools as well as some sculpture, all by living artists and for sale, with the prices marked on them; 5% commission was charged on sales. Copies of Raphael and Rubens and photographs were for sale.[36] In 1856 there were English pictures, 'generally bad' but including works by Roberts and Creswick, Landseer's *Forester's Family* and Leslie's *Don Quixote*. The French and German works, on the other hand, were said to be 'fine'. Eighty-five pictures were sold, for over £3,000. The manager, Mr Mogford, visited the continent, where his agent was said to be a Belgian ironmonger. By September 1856 the 500 despised English pictures had been returned, and replaced by works by 'the first artists of the continent'; these included Judas by Ingres. Courbet was another admired exhibitor.[37] The *Athenaeum* said that the pictures that had gone were Extinct Animals, just like 'the Megatheria that surprise our country cousins' – 'great smothery battle-fields, vile scripture pieces, gigantic sea-fights', in effect 'a mass of horrors'. The critic hoped they would all catch fire, including the 'silly, large-eyed damsels, doing little and meaning less'. The *Illustrated London News* reviewed the early exhibitions and included wood-engravings of some of the exhibits; in one article it advised Millais to go to Sydenham and learn from a maudlin and ridiculous canvas (which it reproduced) by Haussouillier, a French 'Pre-Raphaelite', and to abandon his 'unpleasant types of humanity' such as *Autumn Leaves*. In 1864 there were pictures by Frith, Millais and another by Landseer for sale. Lectures on the Fine Arts were instituted in 1857.[38]

The Naval Museum, Technology Museum, Polar displays, the 'Reno' elevator

Here should be mentioned the Naval Museum on the Gallery behind the Mammoth Tree with models from canoes to high-pooped ships and, appropriately, the Great Eastern, the 'gigantic paddle and screw leviathan now building for the Eastern Seas at Millwall', and involving Brunel and Scott Russell together. Naval architecture was the personal hobby of the ship-owner Arthur Anderson, the Crystal Palace Company's second chairman.

Additions were later made to the 'illustrated encyclopaedia': in 1875 there were 'illustrations' of Arctic Expeditions and a map of North Polar regions in the Technology Museum, and by 1881 A.E. Nordenskiöld's North-East Passage Expedition had been added. The Technology Museum had been given contributions from the International Exhibition of 1862 and the Paris Exposition of 1867, and it retained the type and style of the original Great Exhibition displays of resources and products.

In 1900 the Company signed an agreement with an American company for the installation of the first escalator in England, the 'Reno Elevator', which led from the ground floor to the first gallery.[39] Photographs taken after the Fire of 1936 show it standing but contorted.

Photography

When the Crystal Palace opened at Sydenham, photography was developing rapidly. In the three years since the Hyde Park exhibition the quality and skills of photographers progressed so fast that, although a few beautiful photographs were taken of the Hyde Park building, many early studies exist of the interior at Sydenham. From the start photographs or 'sun pictures' such as 'coloured impressions of ferns' were sold inside the Palace. The Gallery above the Mediaeval Court showed architectural photographs of 'churches, palaces, doorways, cloisters and the great seats of England'. Many professional people at that time were amateur photographers, and early in 1854 George Grove gave a lecture on photography to the Sydenham Literary Society.[40]

Philip Henry Delamotte (1820–89), of the Huguenot family of landscape and water-colour painters, was the original official photographer at the Crystal Palace. A deliberate record was taken weekly of the 'Works in Progress', and according to a letter of Sotheby to Grove of 17 March 1855 a series of 'above 120 photographs', forming 30 *cahiers* titled 'The Progress of the Crystal Palace', was for sale. The directors received two large folios of the mounted photographs, including a printed list of all the directors and superintendents and a list of contents. These include dramatic skeletal views of the structure, the horses and carts bringing the iron and glass from Hyde Park, and the arrival of the First Plants. There are studies of the workmen eating their breakfast

Philip Delamotte, 'The Princess Royal, Princess Alice, Mr Digby Wyatt, Mme Rollande, Miss Hildyard, Sir Joseph Paxton in front of the colossal Egyptian figures. 8 July 1854'. Royal Collection © 2003, Her Majesty Queen Elizabeth II.

alfresco and the picture of the tragic Fall, with a top-hatted official with the beard and figure of Owen Jones standing dismayed in the foreground. The *cahiers*, advertised at a guinea each at the back of Delamotte's *The Practice of Photography* (1853), 'will be found of much service to Engineers and Architects, and all who are interested in the Crystal Palace'; some views 'may be had for the Stereoscope'.[41] Delamotte also made a series of atmospheric studies of the Palace in its first magnificent unspoiled bravery and imaginative arrangement, showing Paxton's Winter Garden and the Courts in their first state. He also engraved lithographically all the ground plans for the Handbooks, including one of

'The Geology and Inhabitants of the Ancient World, The Extinct Animals'.

However, as early as March 1855 the *Crystal Palace Herald* announced that Delamotte was leaving the Photographic Department to take up an appointment as Professor of Drawing at King's College London, and was being succeeded by Mr Negretti. He was to publish books on photography and drawing. Many artists at that period took photographs, which were shown together with paintings at exhibitions. When Delamotte arranged the Photographic Department at the Manchester Art Treasures Exhibition in 1857, he included among his own work six English views and two studies of the

Crystal Palace, one being of the Mediaeval Court. At the Polytechnic Institution Exhibition of the Society of British Artists in Pall Mall in April 1854 might be seen 'an immensely enlarged view of the Crystal Palace at Sydenham', produced 'from one of the collodion pictures taken by Mr De La Motte'; the magazine praised the 'artist-like view of the subject'. The *Illustrated London News* reviewing the same exhibition liked best Delamotte's Crystal Palace views, and praised the 'gradations of light and tints' in the picture of the 'Colossi of Abu Simbel'.[42] When Waterhouse Hawkins lectured on his models of the Extinct Animals later that year at the Society of Arts (referred to as the 'grandparent institution' of the Crystal Palace at Sydenham), sixty photographs from Delamotte's grand series *Progress of the Crystal Palace* were on the walls. In June 1854 Delamotte took a 'sun picture' of the Princess Royal, Princess Alice and their governesses together with Paxton and Digby Wyatt in front of the Egyptian colossi. Quick off the mark, Negretti presented Queen Victoria with a stereotypic photograph of her party taken a few minutes earlier from the upper galleries in May 1856. When Prince Albert visited the Floricultural Show on 9 June 1855 Negretti took a five-second photograph of him.[43] Delamotte published

in 1856 *The Oxymel Process in Photography*, beautifully printed at the Chiswick Press with engraved diagrams of his dark-room processes, and published *The Art of Sketching from Nature* in 1871 with chromolithographic plates by Day and Son after water-colours by early nineteenth-century artists and by himself.

The firm of Negretti and Zambra, mentioned by Phillips in his *Guide* in 1856 among the 'Fancy Manufactures' as 'Photographers to the Crystal Palace Company', sold optical equipment of all kinds; their very prosperous Court (formed by 1862 of the larger portion of the Ceramic Court near to the Concert Room and the French Court), is portrayed in an engraving of 1867. The firm took portraits, and sold those of celebrities. It also made stereoscopic photographs of every part of the building, showing many details of the interior (statues, plants and the Courts), and these were on sale as early as July 1856.[44] Negretti and Zambra published series of stereoscopic photographs, including in 1862 a hundred of Egypt taken by Francis Frith with notes by Samuel Sharpe and engravings by Joseph Bonomi.

Negretti was succeeded as official photographer to the Palace by J. Russell, and in 1914 by T.H. Everitt of Everitt and Son.

6

THE EXTERIOR

THE PARK AND WATERWORKS; THE 'GEOLOGICAL ILLUSTRATIONS' AND THE 'EXTINCT ANIMALS'

The Park

With the Park and waterworks at Sydenham Paxton set himself to 'vanquish' Chatsworth and Versailles – by now London was aware of this. He drew much of his inspiration from features of the ducal palace in Derbyshire and from his visits to historic gardens in France and Italy with the sixth Duke of Devonshire. In the same way that the people were to have a vast winter garden and sculpture gallery inspired by the amenities of the Devonshires, so the Park was to be a heightened and amplified Chatsworth for the people, with even loftier fountains, cascades and water-temples, formal features such as balustrades and a stone staircase, and an English landscape garden with inclines and swards. Paxton's wish to share with them the uplifting of the spirits to be experienced among the matchless esplanades, trees, waters and landscaped demesnes of Chatsworth seems to have been a genuine ideal and not commercially motivated.

The Park was on a colossal scale, and the complexity and daring of the waterworks were stupendous. Paxton, according to the *Illustrated London News*, had spent as much of the Company's money by the time he had finished with this obsession as went towards 'the Palace and its internal decoration and the works of art' inside it. Versailles had the most famous waterworks in the world set in a park that combined formal and informal landscape gardening; it was also, since the day in 1839 that Louis Philippe declared it so, a park for the people and a favourite resort of Parisians. Paxton was unable to fulfil his intention of having the complete hydraulic system of 11,788 jets (including all the minor mouths and spouts) ready for the opening of the Palace in June 1854, but it was surely the most ambitious scheme of its kind in history: the Italian terrace with six fountains, and below it the circular fountain, the water-temples, the cascades, and the twin *jets d'eau* that reached no less a height than 280 feet – nearly 100 feet higher than Nelson's Column.

The waterworks had two successive inaugurations,

each one attended by royalty. The first was in June 1854 and the second in 1856 when, in the first full public display, the system played with all its plumes and glitter. The Queen progressed round the Park in an open coach, conducted by Paxton riding on 'a spirited little brown charger'.[1] The date chosen for this occasion was Waterloo Day – perhaps a private joke about vanquishing the French, but the achievement was a serious one. The system at Sydenham used six times more water than Versailles. Although the unsurpassed hydraulics taught what bold new technology and capital could do, they were also the result of Paxton's creative passion, even megalomania.

The Park was for recreation, but also intended to instruct the public about the history of gardening in England and on the continent, and show what could be done. Paxton originally intended a feature to illustrate the Linnaean system in a formal Botanical Garden, as was officially announced in 1852. The Palace *Guide* summarised garden history in England from medieval times and covered the debates of the previous century associated with Sir William Chambers, William Gilpin, 'Capability' Brown, Uvedale Price and William Shenstone. More important for the 'illustrated encyclopaedia' than the gardens and waterworks were the 'Geological Illustrations' and the life-size models of the 'Extinct Animals' beneath the raised 'Plateau' at the bottom of the Park. Intellectual profit was to accrue through enjoyment of the unfamiliar. In this earnest educational programme not much *dulce* was encouraged here without the *utile* to balance it; on the other hand, the experience must have stirred imagination as well as knowledge. Samuel Phillips in the *Guide* tried to avoid overstatement when drawing a parallel between the lessons to be learnt from the Park on the one hand and the Architectural Courts inside the Palace on the other; he called the outdoor experience 'a course of investigation'.[2] The primeval world was 'reproduced' with the Antediluvian

Animals and the Geological Illustrations: the earth aeons before a palace was constructed at Nineveh. The theme park at the lower end had its agenda: to add evolution to the syllabus of the glorious history of the rise of civilisation, pointing perhaps towards the ultimate – or at any rate the newest – architectural and technological achievement: the Palace on the crown of the hill. Man's position as the artificer in nature, like Adam, was to be interpreted emblematically in the garden at Sydenham: as in the famous passage in Shakespeare's *Richard II* (Act III, scene iv) that draws an analogy between the garden and the state, man is seen as heir to an imperial authority over (and responsibility for) fallen nature. Digby Wyatt, discussing the element of formal and informal gardening exemplified at Sydenham, wrote that gardeners both 'control' and 'tend' nature;[3] possibly this was the role in the world imagined for Britannia preeminent in industry and commerce. Paxton left no written record of his work at Sydenham, but we can reconstruct some part of the meaning of his schemes from the writings of Digby Wyatt and Samuel Phillips, who must both have been familiar with his thinking.

The original park at Penge Place, viewed from the brow of the hill in an engraving published at the start of the project, shows an English country house landscape with 'clumps of ornamental timber', and 'a thick belt of plantations' along its boundaries. The park had two main *allées*, one leading to Penge church and lifting the eye up to the orchards, fields and villages beyond it – the expansive Garden of England itself. Digby Wyatt called this the 'broad champaign' and wondered how long it would remain unspoiled by building. The Gothic spire of the church appears in many pictures of the Park, and was referred to with affection.

The Park was originally of 200 acres. Paxton drove a 'Grand Centre Walk' down the centre, creating an axis from the front door of the Palace, with the terraces, waterworks and other architectural features arranged symmetrically along it. Two 'noble' cedar trees of Schuster's original pleasure-grounds marked the entrance to Paxton's English Landscape Gardens. This avenue was 96 feet wide and 2,000 feet long; the lower part was later given a new planting of a double line of plane trees – which Paxton had opposed. From a bird's eye view of the gardens at Versailles and the *Grands Eaux* published in the 1851 Crystal Palace magazine, *The Expositor*, it is apparent how Paxton took from Versailles a similar plan with a central axis, descending in a broad avenue down a hillside from the Palace with terraces and great *bassins*, and superimposed it on the South London hillside.[4] The Duke of Devonshire and Paxton also visited Le Nôtre's other masterpiece at St Cloud where there was a cascade like the one at Chatsworth, designed by Le Nôtre's pupil Grillet in the 1690s.

Paxton's assistant at Sydenham was his former apprentice and protégé from Chatsworth, Edward Milner (1819–84), who achieved fame as designer of the dramatic terraced gardens at Bodnant. Their next project, the People's Park at Halifax (1857), made use of the same axial principle, with mounds and a small lake. By 2 October 1855 Beaton reported in *The Cottage Gardener* that Paxton was now only a 'consulting oracle' in the gardens. In May 1855, 450 gardeners were said to be working there. By 1868 annual expenditure on the gardens was £6,500, with seeds, bulbs and plants costing between £400 and £500.[5]

The first point emphasised by Phillips in his account of the Park was the deliberate mathematical 'unity of parts' in the proportions of both the building and the Park: the width of the walks, the width and length of the

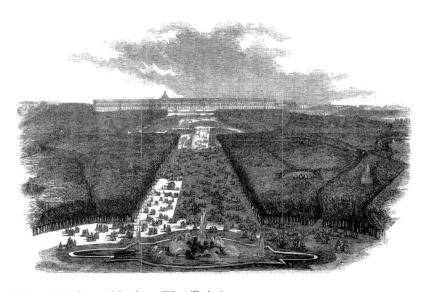

'View of the Palace and Gardens of Versailles', 1851.

Overleaf: Ordnance Survey Map, 1862. © Crown Copyright.

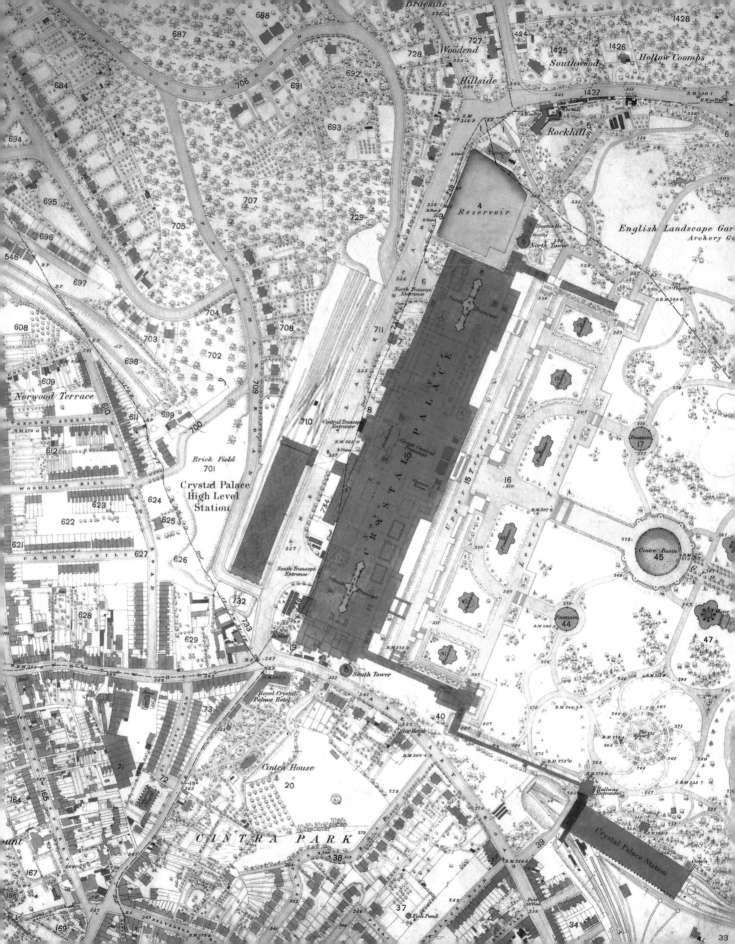

fountain basins, the length of the terraces, the breadth of the steps were all in multiples or sub-multiples of 8. By this symmetrical principle 'perfect harmony prevails, unconsciously to the onlooker, in the structure and the grounds.'[6]

Great stone Egyptian sphinxes flanked the entrance to the Park from the Central Transept. The upper terraces were Italianate viewing platforms with balustrades, statuary and fountains in basins – a feature highly fashionable at the time under the influence of Charles Barry's gardens at Trentham and Shrubland Park. A 'terraced esplanade' was an early part of the plan for the Palace, reported in the *Daily News* as early as 23 July 1852. At intervals of 24 feet were tazzas or urns on the convex corners, and on the concave corners colossal statues. Flower beds or 'panels' of colour were arranged between the paths in what Beaton called the 'promenade system', and were circular 'ring-beds', or a series of round-ended parallelograms 8 feet wide and circles. The beds were linked by colour and patterns – a technique called 'chain planting'. The Lower Terrace was to be a third of a mile long and 'adorned with one central circular basin, throwing out a *jet d'eau*, besides others of elliptical shape; as well as with statues, vases, rich-coloured flower-beds, shrubs and trees, on which the shadows of the projecting transepts will fall'. Flower beds were formed around the statues and urns. A massive central flight of steps, 96 feet wide, formed of granite slabs 12 feet long, led to the Grand Centre Walk. The walls of these terraces were planted with *berberis* trimmed into curtains and festoons. *The Cottage Gardener* stated that the gardens at Sydenham descended in three modes: nearest the Palace around the terraces was the 'artistic gardenesque'; next the 'simply gardenesque 'or 'dressed picturesque'; and at the lowest level 'rough, wild', the picturesque itself.[7]

In his account of the Park, Digby Wyatt recalled Paxton's work at Chatsworth, saying that Chatsworth itself and the 'grandeur' of the waterworks there were the most important model for Sydenham. He also observed that Paxton's principle was to combine the best features of the Italian and English garden; by 'Italian' he meant the Renaissance garden with architectural terraces, fountains, sculpture and formal beds. The continental models Wyatt mentioned were the gardens of palaces in Rome and the Campagna, the Villa d'Este at Tivoli with its balustraded terraces, Frascati where *cascatelle* flow over steps and then over an arcaded terrace as in

Paxton's own waterworks at Sydenham, and the Villa Doria Pamfili. However, the Villa Borghese in Rome was the principal model because of its perfect union of Art and Nature. Wyatt mentioned the new Italianate gardens in England by Sir Charles Barry, naming Trentham Hall (1840 onwards). Barry's magnificent garden works in the style of the Villa d'Este at Shrubland Park in Suffolk (1849–54), where Donald Beaton was the head gardener, were probably another influence. At Mentmore (1851–4) Paxton used the same Barryesque balustraded terraces. To 'avoid collision' between the formal and 'free' parts of the gardens he introduced what he called a mixed or 'transitional' style adjoining the terraces and the broad central walk. Trees planted by Paxton included rows of *Araucaria araucana* (or Chile pine), 'monkey puzzle' trees, at intervals of 50 feet – a secret enthusiasm he shared with the Duke of Devonshire.[8] Although Edward Milner had charge of the Park, it must be thought of as essentially Paxton's design. Mark Girouard, who judged that Paxton 'did not have a spark of genuine visual discrimination' with his fondness for landscapes of 'interminable lakes and walks of wriggling, early Victorian variety', considered the Crystal Place gardens his 'brassiest achievement'.[9]

'Rich-coloured beds' were mentioned in the article quoted above as part of the original scheme for the Terrace Garden. Deliberately or not, the polychromatic doctrine of primary colours massed in patterns, which had already spread between the arts of interior decoration and gardening, gained influence over the bedding, and under Milner the Palace Park was famous for patterns in strong colours. It cannot be ignored that its earliest plantings were 'geometric' and that the predominant colours were the primaries of George Field and Owen Jones. Beaton reported on his first visit in 1854 that two-thirds of the plants were of one kind only, and that the colour scheme was yellow and scarlet – formed of 'old yellow' calceolarias tied into tufts and trimmed, and scarlet geraniums massed together and trimmed to one height. There were intermediate blues and purples formed of verbenas and petunias. The following spring fourteen 'ring-beds' had been set out with tulips and hyacinths for the Imperial Visit. In June 1855 *The Observer* mentioned clumps of rhododendrons and geraniums in beds and on the parterre, and quantities of mignonette. The planting of the beds naturally changed from year to year, and by 1859 Donald Beaton thought that an admirable 'new complexity' had developed; he mentioned twenty-two new fashionable 'pincushion-beds'.[10]

This was the era when the Pre-Raphaelite painters chose prismatic colours on principle; pigments of vermilion, madder and cadmium were made and sold to Millais and Holman Hunt by the very same chromatographic George Field, colourman and theorist, and – as has been seen in chapters 1 and 3 – Owen Jones's mentor.[11] Sir John Gardner Wilkinson (1797–1873), the Egyptologist and associate of Bonomi and Jones, was another advocate of polychromy. In 1857 he was commissioned by the Crystal Palace Company to publish a book, *The Egyptians*, on daily life, subtitled *A companion to the Crystal Palace Egyptian Collections*, and in 1858 he published a more original work, *On Colour*. An important section of the latter dealt with geometrical garden design: he advocated and described the use of primaries and colour harmonies in bedding. The triumph of colour at the Crystal Palace was trumpeted by a great quantity of massed scarlet geraniums. However, Beaton was not impressed, saying that 'every available inch in all the miles is filled with scarlet Geraniums. The effect of this on the place is peculiarly monotonous and commonplace.' However, a writer in *The Cottage Gardener* praised 'the extreme unique gorgeousness' of the geraniums in the large vases along the terraces and steps:

> Considering that the Palace, with the exception of the glass, presents, as a whole, a white and blue colour, that the balustrading is dark stone, and the vases themselves a soft creamy colour, nothing could tell so powerfully as these balls of scarlet, and of one shade of colour. Much of this gorgeousness was, no doubt owing to the super-excellent cultivation the plants had received.[12]

The long glass-houses where vast amounts of geraniums and other bedding plants were prepared are to be seen on maps of the Palace gardens, adjacent to the north-east boundary road, West Hill. Beaton tells us that all the plants at the Palace were 'the work of the establishment', and described the shelves and boilers of the 'forcing house'. The Lower Terrace or Italian flower-garden was the most important site of these colour effects. The planting had a part in establishing the fashion called 'mosaiculture'; both Jones and Wyatt had published works with chromolithographic plates of historic mosaic floor patternings that had been of interest to gardeners.

Another park associated with this vogue for mosaic planting was Castle Ashby in Northamptonshire, where

Digby Wyatt was employed at the time as architect. Beaton admired Owen Jones and his lecture on colour decoration, and applied his theories to bedding patterns of blue, red and yellow with white lines to separate the primaries. Italian mosaic patterns, such as the 'wheel style' of concentric promenade borders used at Sydenham, were referred to as a 'Florentine chain', and are to be seen in early photographs of the formal gardens. As many as eleven species could be used.[13] The *pièce de résistance* of this style of carpet-bedding at the Crystal Palace was a series of flower-beds in the form of butterflies, outlined and coloured like a child's colouring-book. The harshly-coloured floral clocks, pictures, mottoes and coats of arms that were still favoured for municipal gardens in England after the Second World War were the offspring of this 'artistic' movement. The people liked colour. An undated leaflet, 'The Crystal Palace Flowers', advertised half a million flowers in 500 beds and in marble vases in reds, blue, orange, amber and yellow. It listed types of geraniums, verbena, fuchsia, petunias, lobelia and calceolaria, among others, and the plants used in festoons on the Rosery. Clearly there was delight in the bright edging and the 'ring beds'. Seen from the Terrace the beds were said to appear smooth, even and regular, with no plant overtopping its neighbour, in a 'rich and many-coloured carpet'. Trimming flowering plants for height was common at this period. There were also three circular rhododendron beds. In the course of a House of Commons debate on the Civil Service estimates and Kew Gardens in the House of Commons in 1859 Lord John Manners said that flowers attracted a hundred people for every person that was attracted by plants. Paxton in the same debate complained that Kew had been turned into 'a gaudy flower show', and was trying to compete with commercial ventures like the Crystal Palace.[14]

Edward Milner, whose role as Paxton's right-hand man at Sydenham has already been mentioned, was Principal of a successful 'School of the Art of Landscape Gardening and the Improvement of Estates' at the Palace.[15] On his death in 1884 he was succeeded in this position by his son Henry, whose *The Art and Practice of Landscape Gardening* (1890) was still Paxtonesque in its advice and its etchings of terraces, glasshouses and fountains.

When Phillips referred in his *Guide* to part of the Palace gardens as 'English' landscape, he meant the winding paths and undulating surfaces of the upper north-east section, closest to Rockhills, Paxton's house. This was taken over as it was at Penge Place and developed in the old-fashioned country house style; today, beyond the ruined masonry of the Terraces and steps, it appears the most interesting and best-preserved section of the Park to survive, nearly as Paxton intended it. The *Illustrated London News* described the pleasure of leaving 'the stately luxury of the Italian Gardens' to find 'an old English green, a coppice, or a wild dell'. On a cricket pitch lower in the Park archery was being practised in 1857; by 1860 this popular sport, 'a truly English spectacle', had been moved up to the English gardens on 'the pleasant slopes' behind the North Wing, and was managed by a fashionable Oxford Street store proprietor, Thomas Aldred, 'in attendance daily during the season'. These lawns also became the base for balloon ascents. A 'rootery', made from the uprooted Penge Place trees, and covered with wild flowers, made a 'striking and picturesque' feature.[16]

One feature that extended the architectural statements of the Palace's interior was Owen Jones' wrought-iron structure with arabesques, described in Chapter 3, and called the Rosary or Rosery; it stood on the high Mound of Roses. Originally there were to have been a pair of these 'circular enclosures of ornamental metalwork', symmetrically arranged, as is clear from the ground-plan of the Park published in the *Civil Engineer and Architect's Journal* for July 1853.[17] At this stage the plan of the Park was strictly symmetrical, and the accompanying article regretted the 'severe simplicity' of the terraces and architectural features of the gardens; though conceding that this echoed the style of the Palace, the writer wished for 'something more fanciful and tasteful'. The same article described and illustrated a grand cosmopolitan hotel designed by Wehnert and Ashdown to face the main entrance of the Palace across the Parade. However, it was never built, and the site was excavated for the Higher Level Station. The Lower Level Station appeared on the map at this date as the 'Exhibition Station'.

The Rosery was shown on the ground plan on a mound to the south with radiating paths in semi-circles; two were planned at this point: the same pattern is to be seen symmetrically on a north mound. It was described as 'a complete circle of bowers and built of light iron work', the arches plainly intended to allude to the Transept arch of the Palace. The Rosery, 31 feet high by 16 feet wide with twenty columns and twelve arches, was approached by the six winding paths, and had 'a delicious velvet of turf' around it. The curved walks were planted with verbena and heliotrope. The *Art Journal* said in an unfriendly way that it looked like Vauxhall and needed lanterns, and the horticultural press dismissed it as 'an architectural affair'. By 1872 there was a maze, formed of box hedges, on the North mound. By 1874 the Rosery was reported to be neglected and 'all ivy',[18] and a permanent circular building containing a Panorama was erected close to it and opened in 1881. The Rosery was pulled down in 1904 and the mound became the site of an extraordinary fairground and engineering contraption called the Captive Flying Machine, designed by Sir Hiram Maxim, pioneer of the machine-gun, who lived nearby; in its gondolas trippers were whirled at speed. Gone forever were the delicate stasis and geometric symmetries of Jones's arches on the Mound of Roses and all that they stood for.

The Railway Colonnade, formed of the standard iron and glass units on one side and a wall on the other, was a variation of Paxton's 'Conservative Wall' at Chatsworth (331 by 7 feet), as it was called. It was at first a bleak corridor for the weary ascent from the Lower Level Station, but within a couple of years the excellent planting served to make it a step-by-step botanical encyclopaedia, classifying and presenting every variety of creeper and climber. By the 1880s it had become dingy, with advertisements replacing the botanical encyclopaedia.

The gardens at Sydenham were on the colossal scale of so many features of the Palace, and must have been more impressive than subtle. Beaton, while admiring many technical features of the planting and design, complained of monotony: rows of identical hanging-baskets inside the Palace and rows of vases with identical planting on the terraces.[19]

Paxton's own garden at Rockhills resembled the Park in some ways; from his open verandah with a glass roof one looked over a flower-bed 20 feet wide by 114 feet long, planted with geraniums and calceolarias leading to a sloping lawn with a row of symmetrically arranged monkey-puzzle trees 40 feet apart with rhododendrons interspersed exactly in the middle of each gap, and then over a ha-ha to the English Gardens of the Palace and the grand vista. A photograph shows Paxton standing by an urn, next to a circular 'carpet' bed with concentric bands of colour and the great *Wisteria sinensis* against the verandah. Three circular beds had tall humeas in the centre with rings of scarlet geraniums, 'flower of the day' and blue lobelia. Other plants in Paxton's garden mentioned in an article by Beaton are camellia, clematis, cherry-pie, passion-flower, jasmine, ceanothus and blue hydrangea. There were two small summer-houses at each end of the terrace walk made of Crystal Palace units, and a large kitchen garden. Gorse and white broom were planted on the verge of the boundary.[20]

In July 1860 Paxton and his wife entertained 300 guests at Rockhills, including W.E. Gladstone, some nobility, and 'eminent scientific and literary men'. They gave a 'charming fête', with an improvised ball and a banquet, using the adjacent North Wing and the Terraces of the Palace. Here the fountains were lit up with coloured lights, an old and favourite effect of Paxton's; he had illuminated the waterworks at Chatsworth with different-coloured Bengal lights in 1832 for the future Queen Victoria's visit at the age of thirteen with her mother, the Duchess of Kent.[21]

On the bleak site where the fire of 1866 had destroyed

the North Transept, the North Tower Gardens were laid out in 1893–4; these included the Upper Reservoir, by then no longer used for the full system of fountains. An amusement park with water rides, built here in 1902, became a famously popular fun fair with a water chute and rapids. The cricket ground was established as early as 1857, and in 1898 Dr W.G. Grace founded the London County Cricket Club.

The Park too, like the Palace, was subject to financial strains, and already in January 1856 a scheme to lease it to a nurseryman to run, and to exhibit and sell plants in the North Wing, was reported in the press. The destruction of Paxton's 'belt' of rare trees and shrubs that made a screen along West Hill, so that the land could be sold to a speculative builder of red-brick villas was not the only loss of land for building developments: more was sold in 1871 to build Thickett Road at the bottom of the Park, and in 1883, out of the southwest corner in the shadow of the South Tower, to build Ledrington Road. Several times when the Company faced bankruptcy there were threats to divide the whole Park into building lots, and in

The Captive Flying Machine, designed by Hiram Maxim.

The North Tower Gardens, post 1893.

1898, when yet another Bill in parliament had prohibited the sale, a *Punch* cartoon by Linley Sambourne called 'To the Rescue! or the Fairy Bill, the Princess Cristalina and the Demon Toad' showed a pantomime Fairy defeating the jerry-builder.[22]

The Cottage Gardener reminded its readers that horticulture is 'one of the Fine Arts, second to none in taste and refinement'. From the writer's description of a 'shilling day' at Sydenham it seemed that at least part of the lofty aims of the promoters of the Palace was being realised in that the 'mechanic class', the 'middle and lower strata of society' to be encountered in the Park with wives and sweethearts, were really taking note of the horticulture that Paxton had elevated so high as to make him a national hero, and that the love of gardening and of the beautiful was really being aroused in 'lads' and 'lasses' – in 'Robert, Sarah, Mary and Jane'. In 1852 the official

policy for the Park had been that it was 'to raise the character of the essential recreations' of the masses,[23] giving them the refinement of the educated middle classes.

The popularisation of the Park occurred by degrees. The earliest innovations – myriad coloured lights, lanterns, fireworks and bandstands, like those at Vauxhall and Cremorne Gardens (still flourishing in 1854) – were not such as to offend seriously against the canons of good taste. However, by degrees the temptation of cockneyfied fairground elements, feared and so stoutly resisted by the founding directors and their intellectual and public-spirited friends, proved too strong, balanced against the financial losses and disgruntled shareholders. The meditative sauntering and excursions of family groups deriving instruction from the guidebooks, as are to be seen in the prints of 1854, were finally cast out in the twentieth century by the noise and tumult of the

The Crystal Palace High Level Station, 1865, showing Brunel's South Tower. Watercolour. © Dulwich College.

Railways

The short railway line built for the opening of the Palace was extended up Sydenham Hill beyond Anerley along the southern boundary of the Park, to the Lower Level Station (it is now known as the 'Crystal Palace Spur'). This line rose gently and then a magnificent theatrical effect was planned for the passengers arriving at the Palace as an expansive view of the whole scheme was revealed. The visitor looking across the Extinct Animals and the Park would have been stunned by the colossal scale of Paxton's architecture and landscape. The crowning glory was the long 'sparkling vault' of the Palace itself; below it was the series of horizontal lines about the spine of the Park forming 'the hanging gardens, stone terraces, reservoirs, fountains and conservatories'.[24]

In 1865 the London, Chatham and Dover Railway, rivals of Schuster and Laing's Brighton Railway who bought the Palace, opened a new line with a magnificent High Level Station of red brick and buff terra cotta by Edward Middleton Barry. An underground passage with pillars expanding into capitals and a vaulted ceiling, all of red and buff brickwork, took first-class passengers below Crystal Palace Parade and directly up inside the Palace. This new line and station connected by way of Nunhead with Ludgate Hill and Holborn Viaduct, and thence to King's Cross. The Low Level line had been connected to the west via Wandsworth Common in 1856, and from there in 1860 to Victoria. The 750-foot tunnel through the hill from the Lower Level Station was an extraordinary engineering feat, seeing that (in the words of a contemporary report) it was cut 'through the same treacherous material [clay], through the hill on which the Crystal Palace stands, and immediately under one of the great water towers, a superincumbent weight of 2,200 tons, which taxed in its execution all the skill and workmanship of the eminent contractors'.[25] The same line was connected to the east with Norwood Junction in 1857 and Beckenham in 1858. In 1911 the line to Victoria was electrified for the Festival of Empire. The Railway Colonnade from the Lower Level Station, with its

Football Association's Cup Final, played from 1890 till 1914 exactly where Paxton had set the southern basin for his *Grands Eaux,* now turfed over. The same fate befell the Lower Terrace for cinder-track racing.

original iron and glass Paxton units, survived till 1950 when it was damaged in a fire and demolished.

The waterworks

Visitors were reminded in the guidebooks that the Terraces, the avenues and the greenswards concealed a network of 10 miles of iron piping for the waterworks. Although the whole vast scheme was a colossal extravagance and soon failed, Paxton achieved a complex poetry of water display that was unique. Although the water tanks in his own first towers failed and Brunel was brought in as engineer for the new North and South Towers, all that he accomplished called for heroic, almost superhuman persistence and ingenuity.

Originally the waterworks had been scheduled to play at the ceremonial opening of the Palace and Park, but the schemes became ever more ambitious and the problems multiplied. The official reason given for the delays was the difficulty in procuring enough iron, partly owing to the Crimean War. Paxton reported on 2 July 1853 that the three reservoirs were in a forward state, the pipes delivered and being laid. The Upper Range of fountains was nearly complete. In the event they were not ready for the inauguration, and a water explosion meant that at the opening of the Palace – to Paxton's great dismay – none of the fountains inside the Palace worked: the pumps were still clogged and the engine and engine-house were submerged.[26]

The Upper Fountains, projecting water to a height of 90 feet, first played for the public at the Horticultural Fête in 1855, together with the lower jets of the upper series that worked by gravity from the basins above. The completion of the scheme coincided with the end of the Crimean War. The more ambitious Lower Range was said to be ready by September 1855, and was to be next year's attraction. There were many leaks from small pipes, but a serious setback occurred in October 1855 when a pipe 18 inches in diameter, close to the end of the cascade and below the masonry of the covered way, exploded under the pressure of 1,000 tons of water. It was 'like the blowing up of a mine', with stones hurled 30 feet into the air; 50 feet of solid masonry and huge masses of concrete were destroyed, and a large rhododendron bed was completely swept away.[27]

The design clearly owed much to Chatsworth and to Versailles. Paxton repeated his triumph of the Emperor Fountain at Chatsworth by sending up two central plumes of water of 280 feet, unequalled anywhere in the world at that time. At Sydenham he enlarged the dimensions of Grillet's cascade and Thomas Archer's water-temple at Chatsworth – twelve cascades from two temples extended 600 feet – and gave them more architectural embellishment, such as the tazza fountains down each side. The water fell a further 30 feet at the bottom over the stone arcade, 120 feet wide, under which one could walk. Phillips's *Guide* hardly exaggerated in claiming that this was the most 'stupendous' system in history. All that Londoners had known previously was what was referred to as the 'pigmy jets' and 'miserable squirts' of Trafalgar Square and the Temple gardens. For the full display 6,000,000 gallons were in circulation, with 120,000 gallons flowing each minute; 11,000 jets played in all. The *Illustrated London News* claimed, improbably, that this was only one sixth less in volume than Niagara Falls. To the basins as well as the central jets Paxton gave borders of delicate interlacing 'crystal tracery',[28] an effect compared at the time to the contemporary arched interlacing wire-work borders of flower-beds.

When the Crystal Palace Company first announced its prospectus in 1852, it was already sending out a challenge to the gardens and fountains of Versailles, which it expressly named. Steam power and British mechanical resources would make the fountains at Sydenham 'the finest in the world'. Fountains were 'a spectacle which has always been regarded as the most grateful and soothing that even royal munificence has been able to command'. In sheer volume Paxton easily outdid the most famous waterworks in the world, but on the other hand there was not enough money (and perhaps not enough time) to make architectural features of the fountains – it was clear that Paxton sought to express himself with the available capital (many thought, recklessly) more by water than by stone or bronze. Fountain designs for the system were commissioned but never carried out; the drawings and models were on display in the Palace's galleries for several years after the waterworks themselves were completed, as described in Chapter 2. Samuel Phillips rationalised the lack of sculpture in the basins by claiming that the display was all created by the water, but in fact the whole system of the upper fountains – together with the cascades, water-temples and the lower series of fountains – only played for an hour at a time and only perhaps four or five times a year, and to see them those without season-tickets had to pay half-a-guinea. Some

'General View of the Fountains and Grounds – designed by Sir Joseph Paxton, M.P.', June 1856.

thought that in other ways the fountains and the system did not really win the battle as implied in Paxton's joke of opening the completed works on Waterloo Day; what one shareholder referred to as the 'Paxtonian squirts' were not universally admired, particularly by anxious investors. Francis Fuller, who had resigned over Paxton's expenditure on the waterworks, wrote bitterly in 1874: 'The Cascades have not played for eleven years. In its best days all this showy water tossing had not as much beauty as a mountain streamlet.' The *Illustrated London News* reported that the waterworks cost as much as the Palace, the decorations and the works of art put together, as mentioned previously, but it has to be understood that this included the new Brunel towers.[29]

Once Penge Place had been bought, Paxton set about the question of water supply. This had also arisen at Hyde Park, where the few fountains in the Nave were served with an abundant supply from the adjacent roadway. The local water companies could have laid on a fair amount to the Park and Palace at Sydenham, but Paxton looked to his own ground and drove an artesian well at the bottom of the Park, 575 feet below the clay and chalk, with a brick shaft 8 1/2 feet in diameter reaching down

247 feet. While the Lambeth waterworks could deliver a daily supply of 40,000 gallons, Paxton said that the well would provide 100,000 gallons.[30] Phillips's *Guide* gives the details of the hydraulic system:

Three reservoirs have been formed at different levels in the grounds, the lowest one being on the same level as the largest basins placed nearly at the base of the hill; the second or intermediate reservoir is higher up, and in line with the basin in the central walk; whilst the third, or upper reservoir, stands on the top of the hill immediately adjoining the north end of the building. Next to the Artesian Well, an engine is placed which raises the water required to be permanently maintained in the reservoirs and in the basins of the fountains, and which supply, or keep up the water that is lost by waste and evaporation.

The reservoir on the summit of the hill contains the water required for use of the building, and for the fountains throughout the grounds. Close to this reservoir is an engine-house, containing the steam-engines that raise part of the water into two large tanks erected on columns at the north end of the building close to the junction of the Sydenham and Dulwich roads. The columns, twenty-four in number, are of hollowed cast iron 1 foot in diameter. The central column, which is 2 feet in diameter, supporting a portion of the superincumbent weight, and making up the number, twenty-five, is the water-pipe, by which the tank is fed, and which forms also the

'View in Park showing Cascade Temple', 1854.

conduit to the fountains in the building, and on the terraces. These two distinct actions of filling the tank and working the fountains proceed simultaneously through the same pipe. On the top of these columns are massive girders which support the plates, forming the bottom of the tank. The height from the stone curb of the reservoir to the bottom of the tank is 65 feet; the tanks are each 47 feet square by 15 feet deep and capable of containing 207,000 gallons of water. They supply also the water required in the building for the plants, and kitchens, and charge the pipes provided against casualties from fire. The vast residue of the water in the great upper reservoir, in consequence of the sloping character of the ground, does not need any help from the engines, but flows direct to the fountains on a lower level, and plays smaller jets. Through the same convenience, the waste water from the upper fountains is used a second time in the lower fountains.

The central or intermediate reservoir collects the waste water from the displays which take place on ordinary days, and which include all the fountains save the two largest and the cascades. Attached to this reservoir are also engines which pump the water back to the upper reservoir. The lowest reservoir collects similarly the waste water from the displays which take place in the two largest fountains on the days of great exhibition, and its engines return the water at once to the top level. [31]

The construction involved extraordinary earthworks and underground plumbing. Paxton's first water towers were not strong enough for the weight of the tanks, and could not sustain the vibration of the water ascending and descending. Tanks had also been placed on the top of each wing. When 500 tons of water were poured in, late in 1853, there were ominous sounds and bystanders made a hasty retreat. Glass shattered and then the rafters cracked and girders bent. This first set of towers had to be rebuilt – a further reason why the Lower Basin fountains were not ready for the opening. There were accidents, including the terrible water explosion. Paxton told the Company in August 1855 that the second system of pipes for playing the fountains, water-temples and cascades was ready, except for Monti's vases and figures.[32]

'Water Bower, at the Crystal Palace, Sydenham', June 1856.

The full waterworks, the 'Grand System', consisted of two parts. The Upper Series filled six basins with jets on the Lower Terrace just below the building, and terminated with a large circular basin below on the central walk, where the main jet reached 150 feet, and two smaller basins with jets on each side. The Lower Series was the most ambitious: it supplied the water-temples, the cascades that ended in two large waterfalls, and the two supreme jets of the vast lower basins. Two pumping engines of 30 horsepower each brought the water up to the tanks, and four 40-horsepower engines returned the water from the Intermediate Reservoir to the Upper Reservoir. A curious feature was that the lake next to the Extinct Animals was 'tidal', its water level rising and falling in relation to the movement of water from the Upper Reservoir and the high and low tanks. Mr Shields, employing six contractors, was in charge of the hydraulic engineering, and the 'architectural portions' were designed and superintended by George Stokes, architect of the Sheffield Court. *The Builder* thought that his designs, a plain arcade and 'very ordinary cornice'

were inadequate, and that the Company had missed its opportunities to provide the sort of rock-work and rustication that Inigo Jones would have added. This was compounded by poor workmanship. By 1874 the cascades and arcade, now broken, were unsafe and overgrown – a standard complaint of the shareholders against the Company. Francis Fuller described the ruin at this date: 'The enormous and ugly fountain-lakes with their miles of huge iron piping, like serpents stranded in muddy waters, are now rendered more offensive than ever by the foul-looking water having fallen low from the banks, and by the almost unaccountable ruin of the water-temple and colonnades.'[33] Thomas Hughes, in a rather feeble defence, replied that the cascades had been poorly built. In 1880 the broken stonework, including the promenade over which water had flowed, was removed and turfed over. It was said that there had never been an adequate water supply to the cascade.

Owen Jones's pair of octagonal water-temples stood at the top of the Cascade, 60 feet high. The union of architecture with sculpture was again asserted by a figure of Mercury on the top of each of them; the nude Graces in statuary inside the temples, pictured in an engraving in *The Builder,* were to be seen through the walls of water as if through plate glass. (However, they do not appear in photographs, and it would appear that they never were installed). The ironwork was polychrome, gaily coloured and gilded in accordance with the new aesthetic. Water rose through hollow iron columns similar to those used in the Palace and fell from a ring round a ball at Mercury's feet and then through cupidons' mouths to steps on the domed roof; a cistern in the cornice was perforated to make a curtain of water. Digby Wyatt says that Jones meant the Temples to convey a 'poetical idea' – of the waters falling from Mercury as an allegory of 'Abundance gushing from the feet of Fortune'.[34]

The two series forming the system and their constituent parts could be worked independently, but the full complement made their 'first gushes' at 5 o'clock in the afternoon of 18 June 1856 before the Queen and 20,000 spectators in beautiful weather. Paxton in triumph led the Queen in her pony carriage to the best vantage-points. 'The whole of the waters burst forth simultaneously for the first time, and the sun shone, and the Queen came, and the people cheered.'[35] A dry and droll report in the *Illustrated Times* described the day. The reporter arrived by train amid a great crush of fashionable people concerned to protect their clothes and their efforts at the dressing-table. Thousands of visitors were already there, and in the Park was a long, slow-moving line of bright dresses with a thousand little dots of parasols among the red geraniums. Owen Jones's Rosery still looked bare with its roses no larger than potted rose-plants; 'one or two thin, taper-looking creepers' struggled up posts but drooped their scanty leaves as if exhausted. Long plumes of smoke rose up from the chimneys of Brunel's towers beneath which the furnaces for the steam-engines had to generate 320 horsepower to force all the water into the air. Owen Jones's water-temples were painted purple and red, and gilded; Mercury at the top stood on one leg, 'so as to get out of the wet'. Very thick and already rusty pipes could be seen running like a huge serpent down the length of the long basins (it was suggested that a few groups of statuary or some sculptured decoration in the basins would help to counter the effect of this eyesore).

Suddenly the red dots on the platform turned into the band of the Coldstream Guards, which rendered selections from *Norma.* The writer had never seen so many lovely and elegant ladies, and 'a single man might lose his heart as easily as an umbrella':

> There was one Venus in a silken dress delicately green as an opening bud, and from her temples hung long flaxen ringlets, that as she nodded her head to the music, vibrated with elastic grace about her lace-covered bust. There was another in a transparent muslin, that allowed a waist, slender as a wrist, to be discovered, whilst a foot, cased in a white kid boot that would have pinched a Cinderella, peeped out from under the worked border of a petticoat. A third, in a rich robe of silver-gray silk that shone with the subdued pearly lustre, held in her hand, almost small enough for a letter-clip, a parasol of fluttering lace, which cast a transparent shade upon a countenance which must be accustomed to, at least, its ten matrimonial offers per diem.

Once away from the 'dreadful scene' and the 'lively indifference' of overheard talk, the reporter reached the Palace where attendants were watering the plants, and 'a beautiful odour of freshness filled the air. The atmosphere seemed blue with the reflection of the bright sky above the glittering glass roof, and made the white statues appear as cool as snow.' Among the ornamental water in the centre of the nave were lilies that had grown 'out of all knowledge' in one year. The reporter was disrespectful of the *Victoria regia,* its leaves grown from dessert plates to paper circus hoops. But from such big leaves the flowers were disappointing: 'It seemed a great waste of mountain strength to produce such mice of blooms.' Meanwhile, ladies in the Alhambra Court were sighing to have 'the fairy dwelling' removed to Belgrave or Eaton Square. The German band, with heavy beards, turn-down collars and spectacles were playing the Overture to *William Tell* under August Manns, its energetic conductor: 'The leader, who stood in front with his violin, had the most wonderful hair we have ever witnessed… long, black and bushy like a pony's tail.' He 'stamped his foot and waved his fiddle-stick, as if he were fencing.'

Outdoors again, and the Queen now due to arrive in a pony carriage, the band of the Royal Artillery were playing from *Il Trovatore,* while the police with some difficulty and cries of 'for Heaven's sake, ladies!' marshalled the fashionable crowd to form a 'thick hedge'. The band suddenly burst into the National Anthem and the same moment 'a sound of hissing and spitting and spirting, followed by the loud roar of rushing waters, filled the air, and the fountains sent the foaming columns high up towards the sky.' The crowd were not sure whether to look at the fountains or at the arrival of Victoria and Albert, but with no warning 'a heavy shower of spray' came down on the bonnets with 'a stormy drenching violence'. The parasols, 'scarcely larger than mushrooms', were useless but everyone laughed. In the rush away from the spray many valuable articles were dropped. Hats and handkerchiefs waved, and shrill 'huzzahs' from the ladies and gruff ones from the men greeted the royal pair. The Prince of Wales, following in a phaeton, seemed to enjoy the ducking and laughed heartily. The writer's neck ached with looking 'at the topmost spray jerking towards the clouds as though it were leaping in madness at the sky'. A heavy stream of glittering water poured from above the Temples. The company then went inside the Palace, some to eat pigeon-pie, salad and vanilla ices. Ladies who did not want their dresses crumpled had to stay for a train until nine in the evening to avoid the crush at the station. The writer ended by comparing Sydenham with Versailles:

> To compare the fountains of the Crystal Palace with those of Versailles is about as absurd as to compare English with French cookery. They are two entirely different things. The one is substantial, the feast gigantic and soon satisfying; the other is light and elegant, so that even when the entertainment is over, the appetite still remains. At Sydenham, the display of water partakes something of the baron-of-beef style of banquet: it is the intensest feast of fountains to be obtained. But the display once over, what remains? – a blank sheet of water. Now, at Versailles, whether the water is playing or not, the fountains are still interesting from the sculptures about them, which certainly help to destroy the monotony of a vast watery expanse and please the eye and excite the imagination. Both styles are essentially distinct, and both of them come as near perfection as their various characters can approach.[36]

The reporter did not mention the agreeable sound of the system, the 'continual roar and splash' and the 'delicious effect on the ear' noted by *The Times* at the third showing in July, again in a breeze. (The Company had meanwhile played the whole Grand System at a summer fête soon after the royal inauguration.[37])

When the first series of fountains on the Upper Terrace played for the first time the *Illustrated London News* had dismissed tartly the 'monotonous upright projection of the fluid', and added that it was most unlikely the Sydenham waterworks would eclipse Versailles: 'They were merely so many gigantic squirts all going together,

without the sea and river gods, the Tritons and other poetic forms that give such infinite and grotesque variety to the *Grands Eaux*.'[38] The *Observer* was also unimpressed when the inauguration of Paxton's complete *Grand Eaux* was advertised for the end of July (in the event it was postponed for a year); the critic wrote, after seeing one of the daily playings of the upper fountains during a week in June, that England was unfortunate in its fountains because the climate was not soft:

> Here at the time of midsummer, chilling breezes and cold winds transform these displays at Sydenham into shapeless clouds of surf, change the agreeable coolness of a fountain into the drenching coldness of a winter shower, while their appearance, suggesting the idea of a small army of locomotives blowing off their steam, imparts somewhat of the ridiculous to that which was intended to produce a magnificent effect... Their exposed position makes them more like geysers, jets of all heights and sizes – and their only background is the glitter of the glass of the Palace, no dark green trees and rich foliage. The visitors wait for the display and then are suddenly wetted to the skin by an east wind and a 'bounteous and widespread shower bath'.[39]

The occasion to see the fountains would have been in June 1856. Beaton also professed in *The Cottage Gardener* that for the first time the weather allowed the fountains to play to full perfection, and the effect was 'majestically grand':

> After the huge pressure had washed out the rusty water, it rose in clear silvery spouts of all shapes and sizes, to the top of its bent and bearing; and then fell down as easily and as gentle, and soft, and silvery, as if all the play was for escorting Juno herself, in one of her visits to this lower world – not an extra ripple for any other goddess.

Beaton too professed to be refreshed by the roar of the rushing waters.[40]

The fountains at Sydenham 'derived no assistance' from architecture or sculpture, said *The Observer* – by sculpture the writer meant figures or Baroque features in the basins as part of the fountains themselves, forming theatrical effects of tritons, shells and water gushing from mouths, as at Versailles. This was to become a standard criticism. By 1856 there were recumbent water gods, not in the water but at the sides of the basins: these were the oceans and rivers noted in Chapter 4. At the end of the terrace basins stood *Modesty*, *Valour*, *Prudence*, *Vigilance*, *Love*, *Friendship*, *Hope* and *Mirth*.[41]

Overleaf: 'Inauguration of the Great Fountains at the Crystal Palace', 18 June 1856

North Transept, North Tower and North Wing from gardens.

The Towers

Phillips refers to Brunel's towers – built by Fox and Henderson at a cost of £50,000[42] – as the 'Crystal Towers', but this name did not find favour. They can hardly be said to have been beautiful, forming as they did the chimneys at each end of the 'cucumber frame' (Ruskin's words) of the Palace. At least one architectural periodical said that they improved the Palace's outline.

Although Brunel carried out the engineering and deserves the credit he is given for the towers, the actual design was by Paxton. This consisted of curtain walls of Hyde Park iron and glass units fitted within twenty-four hollow cast iron columns; strictly there were twenty-four faces to each tower, 'measured from the centre of the columns, alternating 4 feet and 8 feet'. To begin with each tower was topped by a conical ornamental cap with radiating ridge and furrow glass, but this was later replaced by a plain iron cone. Girders and tie-rods accounted for a great deal of iron. Six water-columns (five vertical and one for overflow) in each tower

surrounded the central brick shaft. The tanks, to contain 1,576 tons of water, were dome-shaped at the bottom (fish were sucked up through the columns, it was said, and survived inside them). The Towers were 282 feet high and 47 feet in diameter. A spiral stair of 404 steps round the central chimney led up through ten floors, 20 feet wide, to an open corridor 550 feet above sea level and 6 feet wide. Waygood's patent water-balanced lift, which took thirty seconds to reach the top, was installed in 1894. In 1902 the admission charge for the ascent was 6d by lift and 3d by the stairs.[43] The view on a clear day extended 30 miles and included eight counties, and telescopes were provided. Settling the towers on the site to support their 800 tons, at the crest of a sloping hill and on soil desperately weak with clay, was an extraordinary feat – achieved by making deep Portland cement foundations and brick cones rising to ground level[44] (the foundations of the South Tower can still be seen). The general opinion was that the Towers and tanks were kept well painted (originally the ironwork was blue and white), but that the interiors were ignored. On 30 September 1880 a tie-rod in the square tank by Rockhills corroded and a tank burst, 80 feet above ground – a 'narrow escape' for the Company.

Without its original function the North Tower eventually became little more than a fairground attraction for the North Tower Gardens over which it presided. The circular lower floors of the South Tower were the home of the highly successful Crystal Palace School of Practical Engineering (known to the students as 'The South Tower'), founded in 1872 with Grove's encouragement, and able to teach up to 400 students. J.W. Wilson, cousin of Sir Charles Fox of Fox and Henderson, was the first Principal. John Logie Baird (1888–1946) had television studios there from 1933, when another feature of modern life started life at the Palace; the transmitting aerials can be seen in late photographs of the Tower. The towers were demolished in the summer of 1942 for fear that they would serve as landmarks for German bombers on their way to Central London; they yielded 800 tons of scrap metal. The North Tower was blown up, but the South Tower had to be dismantled because of the housing and shops so close to it.

Although at the beginning of the enterprise Samuel Laing (shortly before resigning as chairman) persistently reminded the already disgruntled shareholders that while 'the objects of fine art and their educational resources' had failed to bring in the necessary crowds, the waterworks and gardens would do so, and become the real source of prosperity. Meanwhile he had no intention of making the Palace 'a temple of Barnum'. Paxton's extravagance over the waterworks was widely thought to have ruined the Company; after their inauguration he effectively retired from the management of the Palace, and was given accommodation for life at Rockhills. He then turned to designing other public gardens and playing his new roles as a Member of Parliament and architect of Rothschild mansions. The shareholders were told decisively in August

1855 that his engagement would 'terminate entirely with the completion of the few remaining works', especially now that he had his 'other duties' to consider; he was to be 'relieved from financial and all other responsibility' and given a 'position analogous to that of Consulting Engineer' at a small salary.[45]

As it turned out, the heyday of the waterworks was short. By 1894 the great fountain basins had been filled in, and the path round the lower basin had already been made into a cycle track in 1880. The South Fountain basin in 1887 had a large model of Tower Bridge (as yet unbuilt) installed in it, 'splendidly lighted by 10,000 lamps', and constructed from the designs lent by the City of London. One of the grand basins, 784 feet long, was said to be as large as a football pitch, and in 1894 it became one. The fountains on the Lower Terrace still played, and in 1899 the two smaller ones below were converted to electricity with changing coloured lights.

On 10 June 1873, after his death, a colossal head of Paxton carved by W.F. Woodington in Carrara marble was set on the Lower Terrace facing the Park. It was placed on a slender 10-foot pedestal designed by Owen Jones and made of cement in imitation of dark red porphyry. On its Portland stone base, as if to compare Paxton and Sir Christopher Wren as architects to the people of London, Jones inscribed the lapidary imperative 'Si monumentum requiris, circumspice'.[46]

The Crystal Palace School of Practical Engineering.

The South Tower, showing Baird's transmitting aerials, post 1933.

The 'Geological Illustrations' and the 'Extinct Animals'

The group of life-size models, the 'Extinct Animals' or 'Antediluvian Creatures' as they were known, is today the only major surviving feature of the Crystal Palace as an 'illustrated encyclopaedia'. As shown in the map engraved by Delamotte as frontispiece to the official handbook, the monsters, modelled by B. Waterhouse Hawkins (1807–94), stand on islands, surrounded by a prototype 'theme park' to give them context: the lake, suitable plants and 'geological illustrations'.

The project at Sydenham was connected with the excitements of the earlier years of palaeontology and comparatively recent English and continental discoveries, theories and debates from the first half of the nineteenth century. The *Handbook to the Extinct Animals and Geological Illustrations Described*, written for the Crystal Palace Company by Richard Owen, communicates well the romantic excitement of the early discoveries and speculations: the stories of Mary Anning, who made her discoveries of fossils of the pterodactyl in the cliffs at Lyme Regis, Dorset, and of Dr Mantell who found the colossal teeth of the Iguanodon in a quarry in the Wealden (at Tilgrave Forest near Lewes, in Sussex), following the work of Cuvier and the other continental geologists and natural historians. Owen said in the handbook that it was a difficult project which some might think too bold. As might have been expected, there were objections and mockery. George Measom, for example, wrote in the Brighton Railway *Official Illustrated Guide*: 'One of the most frightful monsters of this curious assemblage is the Labyrinthodon, or gigantic frog; its yellowish green colour, huge glaring eyes and vast mouth form a disgusting ensemble, which we think would be impossible to exceed.' Nelson's *Pictorial Guide Book* referred to the 'laidly' (repulsive) antediluvian monsters, but went on to say that these are wonderful forms, 'which [the student] has vainly taxed his imagination to conceive… the spectator feels suddenly transported back over the gulf of ages to the ancient world!'[47] J. E. Gray of the British Museum, who as we have seen wrote criticising the displays and in particular the atmospheric conditions inside the Palace, and whose own zoological displays at the British Museum had been disparaged in the press by comparison with the new styles at the Palace, wrote spitefully to Sotheby of the 'crowning humbug' of the monsters 'outBarnuming Barnum himself': the directors were taking advantage of Professor Owen's name (apart from the dinner in the dinosaur mould, Owen was never at the site).[48]

When Hawkins lectured on his project to the Society of Arts on 24 May 1854 with the title 'On Visual Education as applied to Geology', he said that his aim was 'to call up from the abyss of time and from the depths of the earth those vast forms and gigantic beasts which the Almighty Creator designed with fitness to inhabit and

"THE EXTINCT ANIMALS" MODEL-ROOM, AT THE CRYSTAL PALACE, SYDENHAM.—(SEE PRECEDING PAGE.)

came on view to the public; viewing the monsters and their 'catacombs' was seen as a 'downward path through the crust of the earth'. The gigantic beasts were reconstructed (with some technical misunderstandings) from bones, teeth, scales and spines. All, Owen said, were 'selected from animals of which the entire, or nearly entire skeleton had been exhumed in a fossil state'.[49] According to the *Dictionary of National Biography* these were 'suggested and devised' by Owen. Although some onlookers suggested that the company was merely making use of his name, he did indeed supervise the original small-scale models made by Hawkins.

Owen's *Handbook for the Extinct Animals* is an attractive illustrated book; he, along with the authors of the other handbooks, presented a copy to the Queen at the inauguration ceremony. Hawkins's clay maquettes were put on display in the East Gallery of the Palace among the Precious Metals. Then a full-size model was made and 'corrected' by Owen 'by renewed comparisons with the original fossil remains'. The models can be seen with part of a mould in the *Illustrated London News* engraving of the 'Model-Room', which shows the 'large wooden house' which Victoria and Albert visited on 18 November 1853 with King Leopold I of the Belgians, crossing the mud on an improvised path of faggots; the King congratulated Her Majesty on no longer having such subjects.[50] Moulds were taken of the models, and then casts were made in more weatherproof materials. The Iguanodon was 34 feet and 9 inches long. The materials used by Hawkins for the Megalosaurus, as reported at the time, were four iron columns, 9 feet long by 7 inches in diameter, 600 bricks, 650 five-inch half-round drain tiles, 900 plain tiles, 38 casks of cement, 90 casks of broken stone, making a total of 640 bushels of artificial stone. All this

precede us in possession of this part of the earth called Great Britain'. Pestalozzi, Hawkins told his audience, had taught that children respond to *things* rather than to abstract *names*. The *Art Journal* was enthusiastic about the project: 'It will for the first time aid the scholar in distinctly realising the creatures that he has hitherto been obliged to shadow forth in his own mind after much toilsome reading.' Hawkins promised the 'true form and size' of the Extinct Animals. This was an imaginative idea, which the press were discussing a year before it

'Dinner in the Iguanadon Model', New Year's Eve, 1853.

together with 100 feet of iron hooping and 20 feet of 'cube inch' iron bars reproduced the monster's bones, sinews and muscles. It was the largest model ever made.[51] When Owen asked Hawkins about the hump he had put on the Megalosaurus, Hawkins replied that he had speculated by analogy from new fossil remnants showing 'spinous processes', which Owen admitted was feasible. The Irish Elk had real antlers, and a few heads were made of lead. Inside the lower lip of the Iguanodon the artist signed himself modestly 'B. Hawkins, Builder, 1854'. In Owen's handbook there is a passage describing the enormous eye of the Ichthyosaurus, so conspicuous in the life-size model, and explaining its extraordinary powers of vision and similarity to the eyes of fishes with its bony covering, 'a compound circle of overlapping plates'.[52]

The series of Extinct Animals was designed, like the Architectural Courts and the artificial cliff showing geological strata, to teach the series and succession of types.[53] Prominent on the Grand Plateau was the representation of the Wealden and the Iguanodons. That the

Wealden was felt by Hawkins to be his major achievement is suggested by a lithograph by Walter Ray Woods, published in 1854 with the title *The Wealden: The Restorations of the Extinct Animals at the Crystal Palace*, dedicated to Hawkins and printing the names of Mantell and Buckland as the sources for the creatures. Consistent with the Natural History tableaux inside the Palace representing actions, the herbivorous Gigantic Sloth was shown pulling down a tree to eat the leaves. Plantings to provide a primeval atmosphere included more monkey-puzzle trees and stone models of cycads. For Owen and Hawkins the Bridgewater Treatise *Geology and Mineralogy considered with reference to Natural Theology* (1837) by Buckland, Ruskin's influential and eccentric tutor, was an important source, and to design the models Hawkins also studied drawings at the Museum of the College of Surgeons, the British Museum and the Geological Society.

In 1855, when Hawkins had spent £13,729 on the project, the directors apparently got cold feet and abruptly

W. R. Woods litho.

PUBLISHED BY THE ARTIST AT 34, KIRBY ST. HATTON GARDEN, LONDON.

ICUANODONS & HYLAEOSAURUS OF THE WEALDEN.
DISCOVERED & DESCRIBED BY Dr G.A. MANTELL, F.R.S.

THE WEALDEN.

THE RESTORATIONS OF THE EXTINCT

AT THE CRYSTAL PALACE PARK, SYDENH

AS RESTORED BY B. WATERHOUSE HAWKINS, F.C.S. F.

ENT. STA. HALL.

To whom with permission, this Print is respectfully Dedic

THE MEGALOSAURUS OF THE STONEFIELD SLATE
DISCOV⁰ & DESCRI⁰ BY THE ʳEV⁰ Dʳ BUCKLAND, DEAN ᴏꜰ WESTMINSTER.

IALS

54.

Price 2/.

the Artist,
Walter Ray Woods

stopped his work and dismissed him. He had been planning a mastodon, mammoths and a *dinornis*; the mammoth frame stood 18 feet high when he had to stop work, and would have taken 50 tons of clay.[54] He then went to the United States where a brilliant project for a similar venture in New York's Central Park got as far as the making of life-size models in another wooden workshop, but was then stopped in 1868. From his letters to Sotheby and Owen's admiring description of his 'intelligence, zeal, and particular artistic skill' it seems that Hawkins had a strong and independent character. Sotheby described seeing him at work in 'mud-boots and woollens against the winter wet and blast', while others he could name sat on velvet-cushioned chairs. Like Piranesi, Sotheby said, Hawkins used both hands when sculpting.[55] The stopping of his project before it was complete caused an outcry, *The Observer* saying that it was the only original feature of the Palace, since there were rivals to be found in London for all the other departments, and plenty of shopping and horticultural displays. John Britton, among others, wrote to Sotheby in support of his attempt to have Hawkins restored. Sotheby wrote a note about a meeting of the directors Alexander Constantine Ionides and Mr Etches with a committee of shareholders to establish the expenditure he had actually incurred. He wrote to Sotheby from Paris on 9 November 1855 seeking his support for finishing his work, claiming that he himself understood the 'peculiarities and tone' of the 'public pulse for the success of all or any public exhibition, theatre or Crystal Palace'.[56] When the Crystal Palace directors stopped their workmen's pay, but not that of the superintendents and heads of department, on the National Fast Day for the Indian Mutiny (21 March 1857), Hawkins paid his men, and the directors 'were not very well pleased'. In one of his many printed pamphlets addressed to other shareholders Sotheby complained of the meanness of stopping Hawkins's work on his 'little more than journeyman's wages'.[57]

Before working at Sydenham Hawkins was already a respected modeller, and had exhibited three items at the Great Exhibition, where he worked as assistant superintendent for several sections. These were a group in bronze of the extinct European bison or aurochs 'modelled and chased for presentation to H.I.M. the Emperor of Russia from the Zoological Society of London'; a 'foxhunters' candelabra'; and a model of the anatomy of the horse.[58] He also made garden sculptures of animals and dragons for Biddulph Grange, Staffordshire, and bronze models for the Earl of Derby at Knowsley, Lancashire. Hawkins was known as a draughtsman, and illustrated natural history books by Darwin, Huxley, Owen and Buckland. As we have seen, he enjoyed Sotheby's confidence, and wrote to him praising his 'judicious sincerity' and courage in writing the pamphlet attacking Owen Jones, and expressing agreement with his strictures about the 'miscolouration' of the Courts inside the Palace.[59]

As a piece of publicity for the Extinct Animals Hawkins entertained Owen and twenty other 'eminent persons', including the scientist John Gould and the Crystal Palace officials, to 'a dinner of a recherché kind' on a table set up inside the mould of the Iguanodon on New Year's Eve, 1853. A tent was erected, ornamented with the names of Owen, Buckland, Mantell and Cuvier, in the centre of a 'vast Serbonian bog'.[60] The guests' invitation card, which Hawkins designed, showed the scene and in an inscription on a pterodactyl's wing requested their company at 'Dinner in the Iguanodon'. *Punch* congratulated those who took part in this 'scientific gastronomy' on living in their own era – otherwise 'they might perhaps have occupied the Iguanodon's inside without having any dinner there.' Professor Owen sat in the monster's brains. There was 'a full mixture of mirth and solemnity.' Toasts and eulogies were delivered, and they sang doggerel:

> *The jolly old beast*
> *Is not deceased*
> *There's life in him again.*

Never before had 'the ancient sides of the Iguanodon been shaken with philosophic mirth'.[61]

The 'Geological Illustrations' – layers of rock in an artificial cliff-face – offered 'practical lessons' on the development of the earth's surface, including coal and minerals as the sources of national prosperity. In a section of the Primary Formation one could see mountain limestone, millstone grit, bands of ironstone and seams of coal, and New Red Sandstone. Several tons of actual materials were brought in, sandstone from Bristol and limestone from Derbyshire and Yorkshire; a substantial amount came from Clay Cross, Derbyshire, Paxton's own native landscape. The credit for this project was accorded to the geologist Professor D.T. Ansted (1814–80), of Cambridge and King's College, London, with whom Paxton had discussed it early in the planning of the Palace. A 'faithfully correct model of a lead-mine at Matlock' (also in Derbyshire) close by formed another visual chapter or paragraph on Natural History and Manufactures.[62]

Hawkins returned to England from America on 26 July 1874 and, as he wrote to Francis Fuller, hastened to see his Colossal Models. He found them 'sadly depreciated', and the rocks and strata on the islands (once so carefully chosen as a geological context for the creatures, their installation 'personally superintended by Sir Joseph Paxton') all overgrown and the coal beds of the Geological Illustrations destroyed by plants the size of bushes. He was disgusted to find that the Irish Elks had been moved and ignorantly set 'on the coal measure', and offered the directors his services without a fee to supervise repairs and restore the Extinct Animals to be useful once again as teaching models. It is not known what happened next.[63]

A singular use of the primeval landscape was illustrated in *The Graphic* for 9 September 1876. With the title 'Education for Colonial Life at the Crystal Palace', men in tropical kit were shown encamped among the dinosaurs on the island, with their tents and deck chairs. The text explained that these were students from the 'colonial section' of the School of Practical Engineering, who camped out for three weeks among the extinct animals in their 'wild and overgrown' surroundings, training as 'explorers, planters and settlers in the colonies or abroad' and learned 'to use their hands' by constructing a temporary bridge.[64]

COOKING AN OMELET.

AMONG the wonderful feats of BLONDIN on the tight Rope,
what think you of his cooking an Omelet while up at that height?
BLONDIN does this, after carrying a stove, (which weighs 50lbs.)
to the middle of the Rope, lighting a fire, and, when the Omelet is done,
letting it down on a tray, for the spectators to taste! He then
straps the stove to his shoulders, and, thus laden, walks along
the Rope, smiling, to his little red house.

Dean's Moveable Book of Blondin's Astounding Exploits at the Crystal Palace & elsewhere, showing all of his most wonderful feats in large moveable pictures, 1862. © John Johnson Collection, Bodleian Library, University of Oxford.

THE PEOPLE:
EVENTS AND ENTERTAINMENTS

In the first ten years of the Palace up to June 1864, 15,266,882 visitors passed through the turnstiles. This decade in the annals of the Palace and Park was roughly the length of time in which the high tone of the enterprise prevailed, corresponding to the vision and dedication of Paxton, Laing, Fuller, Scott Russell, Owen Jones and Digby Wyatt. This was not brought about without superhuman efforts, which may well have contributed to Paxton, Jones and Digby Wyatt dying before their time.

The standard view that soon after 1854 there was a rapid decline at the Crystal Palace at Sydenham into the seedy and vulgar is incorrect. Its fortunes during the first decade were not smooth, but much was upheld, and at later stages some admirable and interesting features were incorporated. By the 1930s, under a remarkable general manager Sir Henry Buckland, the Palace, including the surviving Architectural Courts, had been well restored and was in a sound financial state, and it was by an extraordinarily unkind twist of fortune that a fire should have broken out near his office and brought the Palace to its apocalyptic end.

Cultivated visitors at the Palace

In the early years some artists and writers recorded surprisingly enthusiastic impressions of their visits to the Crystal Palace and Park. We have no reason to doubt the genuineness of the admiration expressed by George Eliot, a friend of Owen Jones, for the Palace and especially the Alhambra Court. One visit there in July 1854, combined with eating French chocolate, left her suffering from a headache the next day, but in a letter she wrote 'What a creation it is!' and that Shakespeare, the British Navy and the Crystal Palace were the three most characteristic (*eigenthümliche*) things the English had produced.[1] Jones obtained tickets for her and George Lewes to attend Garibaldi's visit to the Palace in 1864. George Grove's wide intellectual interests and circle of friends also produced eminent visitors, among them Tennyson who had a preview of the Palace in late May 1854 and

called it 'certainly a marvellous place' in spite of the confusion of its hasty preparations. 'I was much pleased', he wrote, 'with the Pompeian house and with the Iguanodons and Ichthyosaurus.' And at Hyde Park in 1851 he had been delighted with the building and in particular with the 'the great glass fountain'.[2]

Holman Hunt knew Henry Layard and Grove (partly through the Palestine Exploration Fund). He was aware of Wilkie's theory that scriptural scenes should be painted in the Holy Land, and had plenty of sketchbooks of his own of oriental backgrounds and architectural details, but in December 1856, while working on *The Finding of the Saviour in the Temple* (German Gallery, 1860; Birmingham City Art Gallery), he wrote to Edward Lear that he was staying at a hotel in Sydenham and 'painting the background from the Alhambra Court'. The back wall of the Temple in the picture was copied directly from Owen Jones's diaper patterns on the Court's exterior.[3] This of course was a notable act of homage to Jones, given Hunt's Pre-Raphaelite ideals of historical truth and prismatic colours. The columns and roof of Hunt's Temple, incidentally, look curiously like Victorian cast iron and the under side of the first galleries in the Crystal Palace.

Millais frequently attended the Saturday Concerts at the Palace, and would then dine at the Scott Russells' in the company of Grove, and take part in discussions of art, music and literature. He wrote teasingly from Scotland to W.P. Frith that he envied the latter for being able to visit the Crystal Palace Gardens 'to look at the Mastodons and Ichisosaurus (I can't spell it) in the middle of the fountains'.[4] Edward Burne-Jones at the age of twenty-one had heard too much 'fuss and nonsense' about the whole world ripening and developing to produce the Crystal Palace at Sydenham, but instead of being disgusted when at last he saw it, he admitted that 'many things pleased me, and I could pardon others.' However, he took Ruskin's view of the architecture of the building, complaining of the 'gigantic weariness' and

William Holman Hunt (1827–1910), *The Finding of the Saviour in the Temple*, 1860. Detail, showing diapers painted from Alhambra Court. Oil on canvas. © Birmingham City Art Gallery.

'cheerless monotony' of the 'iron and glass, glass and iron'. He found it 'painfully dazzling' and altogether 'a fit apartment for fragrant shrubs, trickling fountains, *muslin de laines*, *eau-de-Cologne*, Grecian statues, strawberry ices and brass bands'.[5]

When Henry James sent Isabel Archer, Ralph Touchett and the 'indestructible sight-seer' Henrietta Stackpole to the Crystal Palace at Sydenham in *Portrait of a Lady* (1881), he wrote with a sentence that typically takes back ironically more than it appears to give: 'The party went more than once to the British Museum and to

that brighter palace of art which reclaims for antique variety so large an area of a monotonous suburb.' When James spied the Palace from Green Park, on the 'sweep of the horizon of a summer's day', its 'hard modern twinkle' clearly did not gladden his eye. Emile Zola, choosing exile rather than imprisonment for his defence of Dreyfus, stayed at the Queen's Hotel in Upper Norwood for almost a year from July 1898 and took a number of striking photographs of the Palace and the neighbourhood.[6]

One sensitive boy who visited the Palace in the following decade, and whose aesthetic sense was

Camille Pissarro (1830–1903), *The Crystal Palace*, 1871, oil on canvas, 42.7 x 73.5 cm. © The Art Institute of Chicago (Gift of Mr and Mrs B.E. Bensinger).

quickened in the way that Owen Jones hoped, was Charles Ricketts (1866–1931) whose family lived in Norwood. Ricketts, who turned into a most refined and vigorous artist and designer, remembered the Palace with affection for its gardens and Courts, and for what he learnt of the culture and architecture of different civilisations: it was 'a paradise for children, and one of the most comprehensive art museums in the world (this I knew later)'. While so many features appealed to his imagination, he was stirred by the variety of sounds (an aspect rarely remarked on). He attended many concerts there later on. Frederic Harrison (1831–1923), historian, lawyer and intellectual writer on art, wrote to *The Times* when the Palace was under threat in 1913 that 'to us middle Victorians' the Crystal Palace was 'a sort of university of art, history, science, music and horticulture; and we owe it as much as we do to any public institution in the country.' He was continually there from 1854 to 1884, he said, 'studying the history of art', and learned 'as much of the history of civilisation as ever I did at the Bodleian or the British Museum'. Bishop Welldon, in turn Master of

Dulwich College and Headmaster of Harrow, wrote to the paper at the same time in praise of the work done at Sydenham for the 'physical and moral welfare' of the people, and said that 'a good many years ago [he] learnt to appreciate the beauty and value of the Palace'.[7]

These testimonials command less attention than Ruskin's astringent and trenchant loathing of the Palace. Despite all his public wit directed against it – his saying that every morning after a windy night he looked over from Herne Hill in the hope that the Palace on the next range of hills would have blown away, and that it was neither *crystal* nor a *palace* – and his rage against those who called it 'sublime' and against Charles Dickens in particular for comparing it to 'fairyland' – he was actually there often, particularly in later years for the Handel Festivals. He saw Blondin the acrobat perform, was fascinated by a troupe of Japanese jugglers, and visited the bird shows.[8] In 1854 he had written some fairly positive – or at least grudgingly optimistic – reflections in his pamphlet *The Opening of the Crystal Palace Considered in some of its Relations to the Prospects of Art*, to the effect that there were perhaps real grounds for hope of contemplation, rest, instruction and enjoyment for the masses at such a national museum for the exhibition of the monuments of art; 'dormant intellects' might be 'roused into activity within the crystal walls'. After all, the several museums and St George's Guild which he founded himself from his own pocket were directed to this end. He admired some but by no means all of the plaster casts, but was irritated at being distracted by children while taking a note on a statue. Later he developed a real phobia for the institution. His neuroses came into play: he was terrified to drop a sixpence for fear of it falling through the 'cracks in the floor'. By 1880 the building and its contents have taken on a nightmare quality: 'To enter a room in the Louvre is an education in itself; but two

'Christmas Entertainments at the Crystal Palace', 1865.

steps on the filthy floor and under the iron forks, half scaffold, half gallows, of the big Norwood glass bazaar, debase mind and eye at once below possibility of looking at anything with profit all the day afterwards.'[9]

Ruskin's most caustic tirade against the Crystal Palace was provoked by a monstrous representation of the face of the clown Grimaldi put up there at Christmas in 1866. In the course of one of his first Slade lectures at Oxford on sculpture in 1870, he created a lyrical image of the colossal mosaic image of Christ in the apse of the Duomo at Pisa, and then contrasted it to the huge head of Grimaldi set high in the Crystal Palace, the new 'Metropolitan Cathedral' of the century:

In precisely the same position with respect to the nave of the building, but of larger size, as proportioned to the three or four times greater scale of the whole, a colossal piece of sculpture was placed by English designers, at the extremity of the Crystal Palace, in preparation for their solemnities in honour of the birthday of Christ, in December 1867 or 1868. That piece of sculpture was the face of the clown in a pantomime, some

twelve feet high from brow to chin, which face being moved by the mechanism which is our pride, every half-minute opened its mouth from ear to ear, showed its teeth, and revolved its eyes, the force of these periodical seasons of expression being increased and explained by the illuminated inscription underneath, 'Here we are again'.

When it is assumed, and with too good reason, that the mind of the English populace is to be addressed, in the principal Sacred Festival of its year, by sculpture such as this, I need hardly point out to you that the hope is absolutely futile of advancing by collecting within this building (itself devoid absolutely of every kind of art, and so vilely constructed that those who traverse it are continually in danger of falling over the cross-bars that bind it together,) examples of sculpture filched indiscriminately from the past work, bad and good, of Turks, Greeks, Romans, Moors and Christians, miscoloured, misplaced and misinterpreted; here thrust into unseemly corners, and there morticed together into mere confusion of heterogeneous obstacle; pronouncing itself hourly more intolerable in weariness, until any kind of relief is sought from it in steam wheelbarrows or cheap toyshops; and most of all in beer and meat, the corks and bones being dropped through the chinks in the damp deal flooring of the English Fairy Palace.[10]

National and international, imperial and political events

Pax Firma

In 1856 George Christian Mast published a pamphlet called *Pax Firma*, or 'Proposal of a scheme to render the Crystal Palace at Sydenham the most effective instrument for the promotion of progress, civilization and a firm peace between all the Nations of the Earth'. It partly echoed the vision of Prince Albert, but with Mast's emphasis on gymnastics it perhaps came closer to proposing Olympic Games than United Nations. It suggested Universal Festivals of the Nations every four years, with music, a 'tribune' for the discussion of 'mankind', and exhibitions of arts and commerce. The 'fair hair and clear blue eyes of Germany' came into his argument; the author noted a statue of Frederick the Great in the Palace, and said that there was 'so much German spirit' to be experienced in the Palace 'that a German could give himself up for a moment to the illusion that he was in his own country'.[11] The Anglo-German Exhibition mounted in April 1913 was a sadly ironic reminder of this grand vision, and failed amid the worsening relations between the two countries. Although Mast's scheme was not adopted, it pointed to the increasing use of the Palace as a focus for political statements as well as celebrations, although these were to be chiefly imperial rather than international. In the 1930s Buckland had to reject a proposal from the British Union of Fascists for a rally in the Palace and Park.

Spurgeon's 'Humiliation Day' sermon

Something of a national event was the sermon by Charles Haddon Spurgeon (1834–92) for the national Humiliation Day decreed for the restoration of 'tranquillity' in India after the Mutiny. On 7 October 1857, with no means of amplification, Spurgeon addressed 23,654 people – considered the largest-ever audience for a sermon. The young Spurgeon, admired by 'all classes of folk' from Gladstone and the Duchess of Sutherland down, slept for three days after this event. At a rehearsal the day before, he had tried his voice inside the Palace by declaiming 'Behold the Lamb of God that taketh away the sin of the world', and a workman, thinking it was a voice from heaven, went home and repented.[12]

The welcome to Garibaldi

The Palace first acted as an arena for historic ceremonial by celebrating victory in the Crimea and welcoming the country's new ally Napoleon III. Then in April 1864 Garibaldi was welcomed twice: on his first visit he received an address and gifts of swords and flags from the Italian Committee, and spoke forcefully before over 20,000 people, and on his second he stood on the dais to be greeted by English volunteers who had fought with his army at Naples in 1860.[13]

Events of 1861–5

In February 1861, as mentioned in chapter 2, a gale blew down and ruined much of Paxton's elegant North Wing. The huge tower at the end of the wing, lacking the weight of the tanks for the fountains that had been designed to steady it, collapsed. The glass shattered into countless fragments, and in two or three minutes 110 yards of the wing collapsed, in sections of about 40 yards at a time; the cast-iron columns were 'broken up like glass' and 'the tie-rods twisted and torn into every shape'. On 1 June the same year Blondin performed for the first time on the high rope in the Centre Transept.

In June 1865 Paxton died at Rockhills. The Palace had practically recovered from debt, partly through the success of the triennial Handel Festivals begun in 1857, and the Company announced that it was at the peak of its prosperity. However, a surveyor's report pointed to decay of timber in the Centre Transept, the result of hasty construction.[14]

The High Level Station was opened in 1865, and an engineering curiosity, the underground 'Pneumatic Railway' invented by T.W. Rammell, was opened in the Park in 1864 to connect the Penge and Sydenham entrances. It had valves and a single carriage like an elongated omnibus, which was propelled 600 yards in fifty seconds by a fan-wheel enclosed in an iron case powered by a converted locomotive engine; *Building News* called it a 'costly mistake', and questioned 'the salubrity of the rarefied air'.[15] In 1865 C.T. Brock's proposal for a firework competition between manufacturers heralded a new era where fireworks took over as a new art form where Paxton's failed waterworks had left off. The Palace was thus temporarily saved from financial ruin.

Opposite: 'Garibaldi at the Crystal Palace on Saturday last', April 1864.

The fire of 1866

On the afternoon of Sunday 30 December 1866, there was a tremendous burst of white smoke and flame from the North Tower as a fierce fire broke out in the Tropical Department. Only the aviary attendant, a watchman and a policeman were on duty, and two and a half hours were allowed to pass before the Fire Brigade arrived. Scott Russell arrived on the scene and began to pull up floorboards, while another man dragged away an enormous Christmas tree. Many of the Palace's fire hoses proved to have rotted. The Alhambra, the Assyrian and Byzantine Courts and the Aboo-Simbel Colossal Figures were badly damaged. The destruction included the royal apartments, the printing offices, the library and the collection of birds, monkeys and other animals, and the great plants. If it had not been for the prudent and constant hosing of the screen from the galleries between the Tropical end and the rest of the Palace, the great wind of that evening would have set into action the 'tunnel effect'

The Colossal Figures after the fire of 30 December 1866.

of flame sweeping down the Nave that destroyed the Palace so quickly in 1936.

The dramatic destruction can be seen in photographs and was described by the *Illustrated Times*: 'The Alhambra Court is a gaudy wreck, pieces of its Moresque ornamentation lying strewn around like damp fragments of a gigantic twelfth-cake ornament'. The tropical plants were 'a scorched and tangled jungle.' Among the damaged statues 'a Greek girl carried her own head in a basket' and a stuffed hippo resembled 'a big dried sausage'. Villains tried to loot the champagne and stole the umbrellas of those helping at the scene. The insurance money was inadequate, and in spite of appeals and a concert to raise funds, the North Transept, the Colossal Figures, the Assyrian Court and the Tropical Department were never rebuilt. The North Nave and the Alhambra and Byzantine Courts were restored and re-opened in February 1868. [16]

1866–1900; royal visitors

A formula of concerts and fireworks for special occasions and important visitors became popular and eventually a tradition. In 1868 Alfred, Duke of Edinburgh, the Queen's second son who had recently escaped assassination in New South Wales, was greeted by a model of his ship H.M.S. *Galatea* illuminated in fireworks together with a 'fiery comet' descending from both towers and cascades of fire. Ismail, Khedive of Egypt (who donated £500 for repairs after the Fire) together with Ferdinand De Lesseps in July 1870 and the Prince of Wales, newly recovered from a serious illness, in 1872 all received firework tableaux. Arthur Sullivan composed and conducted a *Te Deum* for the Prince of Wales. The Shah of Persia had a particularly magnificent reception on 30 June 1873: dressed in his diamonds, he watched jugglers and trapeze artists from a pavilion under golden Alhambra arches, and told the manager that he had not spent a happier evening in all Europe. The next day the Shah came in ordinary clothes on a shilling day to mingle with the people, and watched a balloon ascent. When he was recognised the band struck up a popular tune:

> *Have you seen the Shah?*
> *Smoking his cigar?*
> *Twenty wives and two black eyes*
> *Have you seen the Shah?*

In July 1876 the Prince and Princess of Wales came with

the King and Queen of Greece to watch chariot races, when Mr Madigan drove forty horses at one time on the terraces transformed into a hippodrome. The same year in November the great clock was completed at the end of the South Nave. On 11 July 1891 Kaiser Wilhelm II and his Empress were entertained by the band playing Wagner and Sullivan, and a fantastic firework display with chains of stars descending with parachutes and men with fireworks attached to their clothes dancing the hornpipe.[17]

Several International Exhibitions were held from 1884 onwards. An Electrical Exhibition was held in 1892. Lavish and strange images in engravings show enormous glittering chandeliers, and fish among electric light bulbs hanging inside aquaria; ungainly large electroliers were installed in the Palace itself in 1891. A fascinating catalogue of exhibits and programme survives from a Royal Photographic Exhibition of 1898.[18] A convincing fantasy novel, *The Great War in England* by William Le Queux, published in 1895, included an episode of London being bombarded by the French from the Crystal Palace Parade, and all the glass in the Palace being smashed by the gunfire.

The Electrical Exhibition, 1892.

Bankruptcy

In the last quarter of the century the Company and its shareholders faced desperate difficulties. In 1874 a shilling pamphlet by A.G.E. Heine, *The Past, Present and Future of the Crystal Palace*, catalogued many depressing symptoms of decline. Heine thought that the departed Francis Fuller had been the one truly valuable supporter of the original aims of the Palace, and had fallen victim to the urgings of the other directors. In that year the shareholders called for the resignation of the entire board. A Deed of Settlement followed in 1877 when the charter was annulled and the Company reconstituted. In 1879 a Committee of Inquiry charged the board with neglect and mismanagement, and in 1887 another declared the Company insolvent. A private Bill in Parliament authorised the raising of more capital, but in 1899 a loss was made for the first time. In 1909 the Company was placed in receivership and a winding-up order followed.

Mr B.M. Jenkins' Mandoline Band of 130 performers, 'the largest in the world', 1903.

The Festival of Empire, 1911

As the fortunes of the Palace both as a resort and place of education waned, demand for it as a setting for national and imperial exhibitions and occasions increased, reaching a climax with the Festival of Empire. In the 1914–18 War the Palace was abruptly converted from an arena for celebration to direct use, and throughout those years 125,000 fighting men were trained there.

A Victoria Cross Gallery, open for three years from 1895, displayed fifty-five pictures (all for sale) by L.M. Desanges of a series of gallant actions. The Crystal Palace Jubilee of 1901 was celebrated with a Naval and Military Exhibition. An equestrian statue of Field-Marshal Earl Roberts by Harry Bates was unveiled by his wife on 24 May, the Egyptian and Roman Courts were converted to scenes in the Transvaal, and the reservoir in the North Tower gardens was used for a Battle of Trafalgar spectacle with large model ships.[19]

The Festival of Empire, coinciding with George V's Coronation, was the most ambitious event held at the Palace since its inception, and it took place in the very year, 1911, when the Palace was actually put on the market. The Festival itself made a colossal loss of £250,000, but the extraordinarily rich and public-spirited first Earl of Plymouth (1857–1923) paid the debt, and moreover bought the Palace and grounds for the nation when it looked as if it would at last fall to speculative builders who were always waiting in the wings.[20] It was placed in the hands of Trustees; public funds were raised, and

Lord Plymouth was paid back a large portion of his purchase money. In this year too, specially for the Festival, new electric trains from Victoria made the journey in a mere fifteen minutes.

The Festival had been planned for 1910 but was postponed because of the death of Edward VII, and in the event became George V's first major appearance at a public event as King. It was advertised as 'the social gathering of the British family'. The terraces became an Exhibition ground with large-scale models of parliament houses of the Empire and other imperial buildings; a 'scenic' railway, the 'All Red Route', took its passengers a mile and a half by electric train and a mechanical 'steam boat' round elaborate realistic open-air sets and buildings that appear to have been well designed to give a 'tabloid replica' of outposts of the Empire. A large area was designed as the 'Pageant Ground' to stage the history of the Empire and of London with a cast of 15,000. To begin with, the dingy Palace was reglazed and repaired, and the exterior repainted using 25 tons of paint. The great stone staircase was renewed. 'The old Palace has been thoroughly awakened from its early Victorian slumber,' the public were told, and the 'usually deserted sloping parkland with its disused fountains, moss grown stonework and antiquated decorations' had been 'rejuvenated'.[21] The Festival created much imperial sound, with military tattoos, the Coldstream Guards band playing in a new bandstand built in a sunken fountain basin, Henry Wood's Empire concerts conducted

Official tram inspection, Anerley Hill, April 1906. To the left the South Tower, and the vaults of the Palace to the right.

by himself and Sir Hubert Parry, repeated renderings of Elgar's *Pomp and Circumstance March* no. 1 ('Land of Hope and Glory'), and Charles Villiers Stanford's *Song of the Sea* and *Drake's Drum*.

The Crystal Palace had been used to stage several smaller Colonial Exhibitions and the Australasian Museum of 1873–4. At the Africa Exhibition in 1895 eighty Somalis performed in animal skins with red mud in their hair, and 200 African animals, birds and reptiles were to be seen. Emigration was a theme at these displays; at the Australasian exhibition in 1873 a conspicuous kiosk was set up for prospective settlers, and the attractions of New Zealand and the state of Victoria in Australia were prominently advertised, with 80 per cent of emigrants' passage money being advanced.[22]

Inside the Palace the statues 'and other early Victorian relics' had been removed and stored, to be replaced by an 'All-British Exhibition of Arts, Industry, Photography, Applied Chemistry and other categories'. The wood- and ironwork were repainted. In the 'city of imperial splendour' set up on the Terraces, parliament houses and palaces were recreated in one-half scale. Only in 1959 was the large Canadian parliament building, by then a ruin, pulled down.[23]

The railway in the grounds was called the 'All Red Route' as a proud reminder of Empire (in contemporary British atlases large areas of the globe which it covered were coloured red). It passed by Malay village houses built in a lake, Maori villages (inhabited by 'villagers'), an ostrich farm, a Jamaican sugar plantation, Australian log cabins and a sheep farm, and crossed trestle bridges in a Canadian mountain cutting. The 'scenic artist' was Leolyn G. Hart. A Tudor village and a reconstruction of Shakespeare's Globe Theatre were also built.

The Palace from the air, *c.* 1930.

The Festival of Empire inspired later proposals such as that of William A. Bayst 'of South Woodford', who published a twopenny pamphlet, *Empire Bridge and World Approach in lieu of War,* in 1935, proposing that Sydenham become a permanent shrine to Empire, where 'its crystal domes will shine' with 'love of country and pride of Race', as a 'lighthouse of the World'. A straight arterial road would be cut from the 'Empire Bridge' across the Thames (this had been proposed earlier but never built), making a direct link to the Strand. Annual exhibitions, involving Labour and Capital, would be 'object lessons in the meaning of Empire obligations to the world and vice versa'.[24]

The Pageant of London, 1911

Eminent people such as the architect Sir Aston Webb, Sir Edward Poynter (President of the Royal Academy) and the theatrical producer Herbert Beerbohm Tree were involved in the design and planning of the Pageant of London. Walter Crane designed some of the costumes, and the producer was Frank Lascelles. The elevated language used is evident in this stage direction for the Field of the Cloth of Gold:

> Two young knights bring in symbolic trees, artificially designed: the hawthorn for King Henry, the raspberry for King Francis. Placed close together their branches mingle as if they were but one, and upon them are hung the shields of the monarchs and those of their chief supporters. High in the air a huge salamander of fire shoots arrows across the sky from Ardres to the castle of Guisnes. Amidst renewed voices of 'Good friends, French and English, good friends all', the gorgeous cavalcades ride away and disappear.

The Pageant was opened by Prince Arthur of Connaught, who arrived in a Georgian semi-state coach and

Entrance to the 'All Red Route' railway and statue of George V, Festival of Empire, 1911.

was met by twenty armour-clad knights. He inspected a guard of honour of Australian cadets, and announced the Pageant open through a megaphone. Hundreds of picturesquely-clad early Britons trooped in to illustrate the dawn of English history. Then followed a dance 'by white-robed youths', and 'here and there are women prettily attired in flowing robes of bright tint, which harmonise exquisitely'. Merrie England and Maypoles were followed by 'a merry masque by that popular favourite, Ben Jonson, and the court is robed with all the magnificence which pertains to that period of gorgeous and elaborate costume'. The Masque Imperial at the close featured the Genius of the world summoning Britannia to her trial

> to lead the bands of weary people – the shades of the Heroes who have made great sacrifice for her sake – past the barriers made by the Damozels of Death on the steps of the Temple of Achievement. Britannia breaks their cordon through by discovering that Hope is deathless, and so proves her right to the vast Empire whose representatives now appear in vast procession to lay their riches at her feet, and with her to enter the

> Temple. As they do so, they sing 'The Earth is the Lord's', and when all have passed within, while the Genius, now well content, sinks back to rest in the Earth's heart, we hear from inside the Temple, growing softer and softer the Litany beginning 'O Lord save the King'.[25]

'Haughty with hope of endless progress and irresistible power' had been Ruskin's interpretation of the first appearance of the Palace on Sydenham Hill, and this would have remained apt long after his time.[26] The summer of the Pageant was wet and stormy, and it was reported that the turgid lines of the Pageant were inaudible, much was omitted, and it ended up being a kind of march-past – altogether 'the biggest, the most expensive and dullest ever placed before the public'. The attendance of 500,000 at the White City exhibition at Shepherd's Bush also helped to spoil its chances; only 200,000 came to Sydenham.[27]

On the other hand 'the King's Day' (22 June 1911), when 100,000 London schoolchildren were brought to the Palace from all over London by train to meet the King at his Coronation Fête for London Children, seems by all accounts and some photographs of happy cheering children (and smiling adults) to have been something genuine and moving. The Day was organised by Ernest Husey, the interim 'head' of the Palace. The girls were grouped into divisions by their large coloured hats and sashes, and the boys by their caps and badges. A Doulton Coronation mug and lunch in a paper bag provided by J. Lyons and Co. (one was inspected by the King and Queen) were given to each child. The children went on the lake in motorboats, descended the Water Chute, went for rides on the Joy Wheel, and heard part of the Pageant of London performed for them. They sang songs or whistled tunes while they were being marshalled for the King to pass; all praised how well-behaved, clean and tidy they were.

When the Palace was put on the market in 1911 immediately after the Empire Festival, a luxurious Sale Catalogue was published. It contained a good illustrated history of the Palace and its place in the national culture, with a preface expressing fervent hope that its history would continue according to the larger and world-embracing Imperial theme: 'The idea of Empire might be crystallised at the Sydenham Palace.'[28]

The sale of 1911

The sale of the Palace in 1911 became an important national issue. An appeal was made to the public for guinea subscriptions to make the Palace a national memorial to Edward VII, 'the Peace Maker'. The new King and Queen each sent £100. The proposal was that the Palace should be maintained for the recreation and amusement of the people, and plans were put forward for a School of Aviation, a permanent Empire House and large Sales Courts. At a meeting in the Mansion House on 28 November 1913, Lord Plymouth paid £230,000 for the Palace on behalf of the nation to save it from demolition and sale of the land to developers. He was later reimbursed from the Memorial Fund and from a new Mansion House Fund, which *The Times* helped to promote; the balance was said to have been made up by local authorities, but *The Times* said that Lord Plymouth ended up losing £30,000.[29] The borough of Camberwell refused to pay, and the nearby suburb of Penge paid only a quarter of its bill. The Mansion House Fund was an appeal from the Lord Mayor of London, launched on 23 October 1911, and had realised £130,000.

Thus 'What to do with the Crystal Palace' again

became an issue, and this was probably the occasion of Edwin Lutyens's quip that it should be kept under glass, like Victorian wax-flowers under a glass dome. Lord Plymouth wanted the Palace to carry on along the old lines, and he announced that the attraction of the next season would be an Anglo-German Exhibition. Under the new 1914 Act, Trustees were appointed to maintain and manage the Palace 'as a place for education and recreation and for the promotion of industry, commerce and art'. The era of shareholders was over, and national or local funds were to be used. Bernard Shaw complained that the real reason for the public subscription was to save the Palace grounds for the playing of the Football Association's Cup Final, 'consecrated in all English hearts', while nobody would subscribe towards a National Theatre. Arthur Percival Graves of the London County Council said that the dream of the previous generation ago for 'a child's palace of education' with museums, galleries, music and drama should be revived.[30]

The Anglo-German exhibition

Lord Plymouth plainly conceived his idea for an Anglo-German exhibition as a means of averting the coming war: the friendly rivalry of an Exhibition 'would go a long way to dispelling distrust, enmity, and other undesirable feelings for which there is no tangible cause'. Industry, commerce, sport and art were to be featured, but Kaiser Wilhelm II refused to open it, and it was not supported by the German Chamber of Commerce in London. British exhibits too 'were far from complete'. Gold medals were awarded, and a choir of 3,500 sang an 'Ode to Friendship' written by the Duke of Argyll and set to music by John Urich. Some hundreds of modern German paintings, toys and minor products were sent. An inauguration took place in April and the exhibition ran for six months. The Berlin Sports Club sent athletes, and a balloon race was judged a success. However, the Exhibition was inevitably an unhappy event, and after repeated quarrels its German director-general, who was found to be insulting and abusive, left in April.[31]

The naval depot; H.M.S. Victory IV

On 11 August 1914, a week after the declaration of war, the Palace was designated to become a hospital, but instead it enjoyed five years from September as host to the Royal Naval Division and as the Royal Naval Volunteer Reserve Headquarters, with the title H.M.S. *Victory IV* (the

H.M.S 'Crystal Palace': YMCA Chess Club in the Egyptian Court, 1915.

authorities tried stoutly but in vain to resist its popular name, H.M.S. *Crystal Palace*). After the War a German pilot was quoted as saying that it was obvious why the Palace had not been bombed: its two towers formed a crucial landmark for guiding bombers. The Palace was in the charge of Commodore Sir Richard Williams-Bulkeley who, *The Times* announced on 9 February 1915, had entirely closed it and the grounds to the public.

An extraordinary transformation took place: the men slept in the Palace in hammocks among the courts and in the Dominion buildings on the Terraces. The Lakes were used for training in boats, and a battleship was marked out on the Terrace, also for training. Semaphore practice took place on the grand stone stairs, and the Lower Terrace became the Quarter-Deck. The Palace was given 'port' and 'starboard' watches; men left it to go 'ashore' on alternate nights. Photographs show the recruits doing physical training and marching among the statuary in the Park. Sections of the Palace were assigned as mess-rooms, and the men are shown playing chess and billiards. The Crystal Palace band played the Boston Waltz and other pieces to the sailors for several hours

after drill: 'The men foot it with each other for half an hour before they turn in, now to a horn-pipe and now to a rag-time or two-step, enjoying themselves hugely.'

The place was hardly ideal for its new purpose: the severely leaking roof brought sickness, and the bizarre symbiosis of recruits and the Fine Arts Courts gave rise to rough British ribaldry, for which the statues were a focus: 'Venus appeared in slacks, whilst Cupid displayed a beard. It was not an easy matter to drill raw recruits in the vicinity of statues of immodest gladiators and nude women, which were poised high up on pedestals before the advancing squads.' The men 'commandeered' cats and dogs from the neighbourhood and hid them in their sweaters and their hammocks. At night the cats prowled in the building, 'making the middle hours hideous' with their calls.[32] For a further nine months after the end of the War the Palace served as a mass demobilisation centre. The Navy did not leave until 1 January 1920. On 6 June 1931 a Trophy and Bell were placed on the Lower Terrace to commemorate the four years of occupation by the Royal Naval Division and the Royal Naval Volunteer Reserve.

Buckland's glaziers repairing the roof, 1930s.

Sir Henry Buckland

The Trustees' choice of Henry Buckland (1870–1957), who for ten years had successfully managed the Spa Establishment at Harrogate, as general manager of the Palace from 1 January 1915 proved a significant move despite its closure to the public the next month. By 1923, without subsidies, he had restored the almost derelict Palace from a 'dying concern' with an overdraft of £4,072 to one with a credit balance of £18,000. Over sixteen years he was responsible for expenditure of £250,000 on reconstruction work (of this £104,000 was spent on the roof and £9,000 on the organ). He revived the Handel Festivals in 1920 and 1923, and managed to absorb losses in the region of £35,000 on each. By 1936 he had accumulated a reserve fund of £80,000. Between 1920 and 1936 the Palace received 15 million visitors.

Buckland's position involved a certain compromise with public taste and a shift from the national to the local: a programme for 1 May 1929 lists dirt-track racing, 'Television' entertainers, and the Bromley and District Dog Show. In 1927 he was involved in controversy over a proposal to introduce greyhound racing in the Park.

Motor racing was about to begin in 1936 at the time of the Fire, and from April 1938 till the War there was indeed a two-mile track, and the International Car Race was held there.[33]

At the time of the Fire *The Star* called Buckland, who had been knighted in 1931, a genius. It was said that he brought to his job many of the Victorian virtues that went to the making of the Palace; his career was a model of 'self-help'. He clung to what he referred in a pamphlet of the late 1920s as the 'original objects of the undertaking to maintain the early loyalty to art and the education of popular taste'. Unique colour photographs of the interior by the 'Dufay process' made by Arthur Talbot in August 1936 show how meticulously the Egyptian and Pompeian Courts were restored in the late 1930s – as part of a redecoration scheme that cost £300,000. The Pompeian House had been closed to the public for twenty-five years, and was opened again only in July 1935, just one year before the Fire; ten other Courts were reopened at the same time.[34]

With the old Crystal Palace destroyed, Buckland pressed for a new one to replace it for both culture and pleasure. He supervised the moving of debris and reduced his own salary by a quarter. He suggested that Halls should be built on the top site, including a permanent building to promote British industries and 200 acres for colonial and other exhibitions. It was, he said, 'still one of our principal objects to do everything in our power to encourage sport, physical training, good music and the higher arts and social activity'. Reviewing his career in his retirement speech to the Trustees at the Guildhall on 11 January 1949, he declared that he was 'waiting in hope that the government would make us an immediate grant of funds for the complete reconstruction of the Palace and restoration of the grounds as the home of the proposed Exhibition of 1951 [the Festival of Britain]'.[35] Thus he was bitterly disappointed when Herbert Morrison, Home Secretary in the Attlee government, chose the South Bank site for the 1951 Festival rather than Sydenham.

Buckland loved the building, and understood it and its history. It never had a better administrator. Even so, he had an impossible job. Christopher Hobhouse gives this description of the Palace in its last days:

> You arrived at the Crystal Palace to find it towering above you like a glass cliff – a noble building, even with the north wing truncated as it was. You entered by a dingy passage beneath the organ. On most occasions, the place was as empty as the tomb.

On your left lay the historical courts. One after another you passed through these strange tawdry reproductions of the hundred and one styles that all came alike to the Victorians. In some of them, masses of aspidistra had been introduced to give a Latin effect, and seemed positively welcome by the mere fact of being, however furtively, alive: in others, workmen were hammering away at nothing in particular, for hammer they never so loudly, the unreality, the impossibility of the place was too real to be resolved. In the centre transept stood the huge organ, in front of which, if you chose your day with skill, you might see the handsome figure of Principal Jeffreys immersing his Four-Square Gospellers in a large tank of warm water. Beside this was a little theatre, curtained off, where modest vaudeville shows were given. Beyond were innumerable sculpture courts, filled with the casts that Owen Jones brought back. A few palms and creepers gave variety to the scene. Suddenly you came upon a colony of parrots, who at the sight of a human being, would burst into raucous greetings like a group of street-walkers in the small hours. From the galleries hung a series of revolt-ing cartoons left over from some forgotten exhibition. There were refreshment rooms so long deserted as to impose upon the hungry customer the sensation that he was committing an act of awful impiety, as though he were eating food dedicated to the use of a dead Pharaoh, somewhere in King Solomon's Mines. At the end of the south nave, you would be cheered by the sight of Osler's Crystal Fountain, looking very small in a sad pool of goldfish. Downstairs you could recognize casts of Andromeda and the Greek Slave, still captive, but no longer stared at; and so you came out into the gardens, where concrete terraces, crumbled and overgrown, led down to the lawns, the lifeless fountains, to lakes whose banks were dangerous, and plaster buildings whose purpose had been long forgotten.[36]

The Victory Exhibition and the Imperial War Museum, 1920–24

After the War the Palace reverted from the practical work of training the Navy to its traditional mode of operation

Imperial War Museum, Crystal Palace, 1920–24.

Imperial War Museum, Greek Court, 1920–24.

with the highly successful and admirably staged Victory Exhibition, and the Imperial War Museum. At first this must have seemed a strange building in which to house the lumbering and menacing objects salvaged from the continental battlefields as mementoes. When in 1917 the Crystal Palace Trustees shrewdly approached the Trustees of the newly-founded War Museum, who had no home for the collections (already large before the War ended), the Museum had dismissed the Palace, which it considered among nine locations, as a rotting, leaking hulk. The surroundings were held to be 'undignified and irrelevant' by some of the Board, who associated the Palace with failure. However, Sir Alfred Mond made the decision to use the Palace rather than Olympia, White City and Alexandra Palace, partly because of its 'historic associations'.[37]

The vast and comprehensive Victory Exhibition, a 'national record' of 'remembrance and gratitude', was opened by the King on 9 June 1920 in the presence of 40,000 people. It was referred to as both the 'Victory Exhibition' and the 'Imperial War Museum'. There were tanks, howitzers, armoured cars, motor-cycles, ambulances, shells, a piece of the mole from Zeebrugge, models of ships, trophies and flags. Planes and balloons were slung from the roof. The floors were strengthened to carry the weight of ten-ton guns – 400 or 500 tons of exhibits, including the 74-foot barrel of an 18-inch naval gun, arrived in the first five weeks. Far too much was

received: some important pieces, German tanks and heavy guns, rusted and mouldered in the grounds for four years and at the end of the Museum's tenancy were almost immovable. The Women's Section contained a War Shrine and models of Land Army girls ploughing and a nurse leading blind soldiers. Dummy figures were used in the displays, and relics such as toys made by prisoners of war and a cap pierced by a bullet at Zeebrugge were exhibited. Polychromy returned with a life-size plaster maquette of Lutyens's Cenotaph, installed at the Palace on Armistice Day in 1922, with the flags painted on the sides; the architect had intended them to be rendered in coloured stone on the monument at Whitehall.

By the time the Museum closed in 1924 two and a half million visitors had passed through the turnstiles. August Bank Holiday in 1920 brought 94,179, and indeed more visitors came to the Palace in that year than in any previous year in its history. The Museum paid £25,000 a year in rent.[38]

The Exhibition also provided an impressive graphic record, with thousands of photographs and some superior paintings, including John Singer Sargent's *Gassed*, which was hung in the Greek Court. The curator was Charles ffoulkes (1868–1947), who had studied art in Paris as a young man and was brought in from the Tower of London Armoury. Where the works of art were concerned, there were fears over conservation: temperatures varied between 29 and 115 degrees Fahrenheit and the leaking roof caused rusting; a gross of waterproof sheets were bought. Security was poor, and some valuable items were stolen.[39]

Relations between ffoulkes as curator and secretary of the Museum and Buckland as manager of the Palace were difficult. ffoulkes wrote to Buckland complaining of the upper part of the roof being painted in its old blue and white – painting in different colours belonged to railway stations. He tried hard to get all the ironwork painted in a more suitable light grey, and mostly succeeded.[40] He also thought the Alhambra Court the wrong background for the exhibits, and 'dead green canvas' screens were brought in to conceal its exuberant decoration. Arthur Talbot's colour photographs of the interior of 1936 show the lower 8 feet of the columns dark grey but all the upper parts light grey. However, the small columns supporting the staircases were repainted red according to Jones's formula.

Entertainments

Concerts of classical music and fireworks were the two forms of entertainment that achieved greatness at Sydenham. The famous Handel Festivals and other choral events began in 1857 with colossal audiences and numbers of performers. In addition, the Saturday afternoon classical concerts which ran for thirty years introduced to English ears many works now in the standard concert repertoire. Concerts and fireworks were not part of the original scheme, and indeed Paxton had opposed both at an early stage. Thomas Willert Beale, later famous for his choral competitions, called on Paxton at Rockhills in 1855 to suggest the introduction of serious concerts of works by the great masters and by contemporary and British composers to be given by the New Philharmonic Society. When Beale said that the people would tire of the Palace without amusements, Paxton retorted: 'Music! Have we not Mr Schallehn's band in the Music Court?' and complained that the Palace would become a bear-garden if there were to be any more music than that provided by Mr Schallehn.[41]

Likewise the directors feared that fireworks would lower the tone of the Palace to that of Vauxhall or Cremorne Gardens, and it needed the persistence of Charles Brock in 1865 to persuade them to agree to a competitive display. The fireworks with colossal tableaux and displays raised the entertainment to a marvellous art form of animated polychromatic graphics on the night sky that could touch the people's feelings and engage their patriotism, celebrating – as the set-pieces often did – past and present national achievements. Even for a long time after the cinema came in, people said that the new medium was nothing compared to the gripping excitement of Brock's *Battle of Jutland*. Both the Handel Festivals and the fireworks undoubtedly kept at bay the recurring threat to the Company of bankruptcy and selling out to developers. In general, fireworks were for the masses and the classical concerts for the educated. At the beginning the Handel Festivals attracted the Royal Family and London 'society', and other early festivals and celebrations, dedicated to Shakespeare, Schiller and Mendelssohn, had an element of high culture about them. The Schiller and Mendelssohn Festivals of 1859 and 1860 were held in German style out of doors, with singing and torchlight processions, and torches thrown in the air. A bronze statue of Mendelssohn by Bacon was unveiled after a performance of *Elijah*, the upper fountains were lit up with blue and red lights, and sprites (in allusion to *A Midsummer Night's Dream*) ran among the crowds. Two 'serpents of light' met in a bonfire.[42]

For the tercentenary of Shakespeare's birth in 1864 a model of his house at Stratford-on-Avon, made to full size by E.T. Parris, was erected in the Centre Transept and a statue was unveiled outside. An actor, R. Phillips, impersonated the Bard in costume, 'gravely bidding welcome'. A Shakespeare Court was formed with 'Shakespeare relics', and a bust modelled from his tomb was brought in from the Renaissance Court; plaster busts of his wife and daughter and even his purported skull were displayed. The following year there was an exhibition of Shakespeare forgeries. The model house was later moved upstairs to the Gallery on the side of the concert hall, where it looks strange in engravings of the Royal Box at a Handel Festival in 1868.

Many gatherings inside the Palace included Fêtes and 'Fancy Fairs', such as the Dramatic College Festival in 1865 in which a Mrs Howard Paul was pictured in the *Illustrated London News* inside a 'whimsical and eccentric' beehive she had designed, from which she successfully sold nick-nacks for charity.[43] A Costume Contest was reviewed in *The Builder* in October 1876, some of the entries described showing a truly bizarre fantasy.[44] Dog, cat and bird shows became famous – the first cat show being in 1871, and the 1872 dog show attracting 1,200 entries. Christmas festivities in the early years were elaborate, with fantastic decorations, monster plum puddings and mince pies, twelfth-cakes with trap-door acrobats, magic shadows on huge white curtains, and balloons with floral gifts, and we catch what may have been a glimpse of Owen Jones: 'Professors of the Fine Arts relaxed their rigid rules to join in the festive scenes.'[45]

Among colourful events brought to the Park were the Foresters' Fêtes held annually in the 1860s; 90,000 attended in Lincoln green with bows and arrows to recreate Sherwood Forest. An American Fête on 17

Kennel Club Show, *c.* 1936.

September 1887 celebrated a century of the Constitution with American music, artists and amusements. Indoors the Greek Court housed an American Exhibition in July 1902. Wombwell's Menagerie in 1864 brought lions, tigers, panthers and bears 'well secured in cages'.[46]

J. W. Myers brought an Elephant Ballet in front of the concert staging in 1876. On 21 June 1879 an American crack shot, Dr William Frank Carver, hit forty-two out of fifty bottles with his rifle from a galloping horse. In 1922 an Imperial Circus and Race Track brought chariots to the terraces.

The Panorama built on the site of the Rosery was an independent commercial enterprise, for which visitors paid an admission charge. (This was a highly popular form of entertainment in Victorian England: a guide-book of 1855 listed seven that could be seen in London: Lake Thun, Kashmir, the Nile, the Lisbon earthquake of 1755, the Ascent of Mont Blanc, Constantinople, and the Crimean War. There was also Wyld's wonderful Monster Globe in Leicester Square.[47]) At Sydenham these displays were mostly the work of F. Philippoteaux, who specialised in scenes of disaster with thousands of figures, accompanied by pamphlets giving the grisly

Opposite: Arthur Talbot, South Nave: Crystal Fountain and Clock, August 1936. 'Dufay' colour photograph, © K. Talbot.

'The Aeronautical Society's Exhibition', 1868.

details of the events. Particularly ambitious were *The Siege of Tel-el-Kabir,* shown with a Diorama of the Père Lachaise cemetery (1884), *The City of Rome Defended by the Garibaldians* (1887), *The Battle of Rezonville* (1890), *The Siege of Paris* (1901), and *The Fire of London* (1905). One of Philippoteaux's panoramas covered 22,000 feet of canvas.[48]

Aeronautics

The Park was an obvious and excellent arena for some of the first aeronautics attempts. The Aeronautical Society held the First Aeronautical Exhibition with models and drawings of flying machines in the Palace in 1868. The Archery Ground became famous from 1859 for Balloon ascents, which are well recorded in engravings and

Balloon Ascent from the 'English Gardens'. Showing Rockhills, Paxton's house.

photographs. In 1862 H. T. Coxwell and James Glaisher flew their balloon in a storm from the Palace to Epping Forest. The balloon and 'car' in which Nadar had made a famous flight in 1863 with eight companions 'clinging for dear life to the cordage in the last half hour' was exhibited fully inflated in the Centre Transept and nearly filled the south end; visitors inspected the small wickerwork cottage with its wine-hamper inside the car. Nadar asked the Company for £5,000 and half the receipts. The next year Mr Coxwell's great balloon 'The Research', which had risen to a height of two miles filled with 112,000 cubic feet of gas, was half inflated in the west transept. This balloon went up in October with ten people in the car but was caught in a miniature cyclone and gyrated above the Palace before coming down in a garden in Lewisham a few miles away 'to a most hospitable and kindly welcome'.[49] The Spencer family, of the firm of C.G. Spencer & Sons which manufactured balloons and parachutes, made many ascents at Sydenham for entertainment. In 1907 the military airship *Nulli Secundus*, having circled St Paul's Cathedral, landed at the Palace. In May 1910 Claude Grahame-White flew 115 miles from the Palace to Wolverhampton.

The triumph of Cockney entertainment over lofty philanthropic and educational schemes went a stage further with the slot machines and distorting mirrors that had appeared in the Palace by August 1902.[50] Before that date Crystal Palace weekly programmes in 1884 were advertising music-hall turns such as comic Irishmen and 'burnt cork' numbers performed by Harry Liston. The grotesque Wurtemburg stuffed animal figures (which had been shown at the Great Exhibition) were still prominently advertised in the programmes of the 1890s. In the shadow of the Palace itself fairground rides were expanding: in the North Tower Gardens the 'Topsy-Turvy Railway Loop' ('the latest American sensation') and the five-minute ride 'Sea Chute and Mountain Railway' had been set up by September 1902.

Not all visitors to the Palace and Park were happy all the time. Ruskin observed the 'British lower public' at the Palace 'amusing itself in a very dismal and panic-stricken manner';[51] and both he and the poet John Davidson commented on disconsolate or apathetic faces. Davidson's poem 'The Crystal Palace,' published in *Fleet Street* in 1909, is about a dreary and mirthless bank holiday spent in the rain among a mass of people at Sydenham. The building is colossally ugly, and he deplores the fact that it could never mellow like stone or brick. The people are glum and resigned, shoving through the day somehow, fretful among the distorting mirrors indoors and on the terraces and walks and the North Terrace entertainments outside. Refuge is sought in the dining rooms:

They sit and sit, and fain would sit it out
In tedious gormandize till firework-time.

Davidson compares them to captives in a labyrinth or

'M. Blondin', 1 June 1861

herds imprisoned in a vast arena. Under the electric lights inside the Palace later in the day they look phantasmal and the Nave becomes to him 'like a beach in hell'.

Blondin

One of the more original and imaginative characteristics of the Sydenham Crystal Palace was the use of the air space above the Park as an arena for spectacular display: the fountain with its jet higher than Nelson's column; the fireworks; the balloon flights; the early aeronautics; 600 homing pigeons released into the air from the terrace in June 1871, each 'carrying a tiny souvenir of the Crystal Palace', and winging their way in a mass to Dover and thence across the Channel to Brussels, and in 1868 Miss Leona Dare in sequinned tights, holding on to a trapeze by her teeth, being raised by a balloon ascent until pulled into the basket by her manager Eduardo Spelterini at some dizzy height.[52]

Inside the Palace, Blondin* performed his astonishing and immensely popular acrobatic performances on the high rope stretched from end to end of the great Transept. The earlier American exploits of Blondin had been widely reported in England; above the Falls at Niagara he had performed in front of 10,000 people – in manacles, blindfolded in a sack, carrying a man on his back, on four-foot stilts, and lighting fireworks from a wheelbarrow. No doubt his offer to push the Prince of Wales in a wheel-barrow from the American side of the

Niagara Falls along a 1,100 foot rope for his first steps on the soil of the Crown's new territories on the Canadian side added to the crowd's eagerness to see him at the Crystal Palace, where he first appeared in the late afternoon of 1 June 1861. Even Ruskin let slip that he went to see 'the Hero of Niagara'.[53]

Blondin took his first steps on the high rope at Sydenham in a light-coloured costume covered with Red Indian beadwork from Niagara and a cap of ostrich feathers, which he took off and waved. His eyes were bandaged, and next he put on a sack over his head reaching to his knees with holes for his arms. He stood on his head at the centre of the rope, and then dropped flat on his back. His hawser, two inches thick, was strung 180

---

* Blondin was born Jean-François Gravelet at St Omer in 1824; he took his father's nickname, which described the colour of their hair. He was below middle height and the *Illustrated London News* called him 'a model of muscular compactness and symmetry', with 'the motive power of flexible steel machinery moved by clockwork'. Part of his secret was that he always fixed his eyes four feet ahead of himself.[54]

M. BLONDIN'S FIRST ASCENT AT THE CRYSTAL PALACE.—SEE PAGE 371.

feet high lengthwise from the fifth gallery, 320 feet along the entire length of the Central Transept with supporting guy lines; at 25 foot intervals there were leaden weights of 40 pounds. The 'equilibrist' carried a 28-foot 'balancing pole'. From his earliest performances he would somer-sault, sit on the rope and then stand up again; and would stop the show by making a feint of falling until the audience realised he did it only to thrill them.[55]

Blondin's most extraordinary feat at Sydenham was the cooking of an omelette on the high rope; he had already done this at Niagara, lowering the omelette on a rope from a stove fuelled with methylated spirits to the deck of a steamboat below. *The Annual Register* described his second appearance in the Centre Transept on June 6:

Belgian homing pigeons released at the Palace, June 1871.

After keeping everyone in a tremor while he walked the rope blindfolded and in a sack, pretending to miss his step and staggering and faltering in a way that seemed horrible to look at, he at last retired, and after a short absence reappeared in the costume of a *chef de cuisine*, and with a heavy and rather bulky stove on his back walked down the rope to make and cook an omelette in the centre. While walking, the stove, though large, awkward and heavy – weighing nearly 50 lbs. – seemed no manner of hindrance, but getting it off his back and securing it to the rope seemed a dreadful, perilous task. For this purpose he had to lower himself with the utmost care till seated on the rope and then make fast his balance pole. With this secured, he had then to free himself from the stove, and not only to balance himself without the pole, but to balance the stove too. For a while the audience scarcely breathed, as stove, Blondin and balance pole were all swaying more or less widely from side to side. At last, to the relief of everyone, the obdurate *cuisine* was fixed, and seating himself down coolly, without balance pole or anything but the rope between himself and the wide depth beneath, Blondin proceeded to his cooking, by first lighting his fire. He then made his omelette, breaking the eggs and casting the shells away beneath with as much *sangfroid* as if at an ordinary kitchen dresser. He stood on the rope and tossed his omelette with the dexterity of a professional, and, one being cooked, proceeded to make another. When both were ready he took from the inexhaustible stove, which seemed to contain everything, plates, dishes, and a bottle of wine, and placing them all on a tray, lowered them into the centre transept for the consumption of such visitors as chose to partake of these highly-cooked dainties. There was another short anxious interval, while Blondin got the stove on his back and resumed his pole, and then, walking quickly back along the rope, took leave of his audience amid loud cheers.[56]

On this occasion he was accompanied by the music of the 'Mohawk Minstrels'. That Blondin walked a high rope strung between Brunel's water-towers is a myth, although he did actually propose it. However, the Company directors replied that too many people would see the performance free from the Parade, on the opposite

The Palace by the light of 'the electric flash bombshell': a Brock's Benefit night, with 64,000 persons present

side of the Palace from the Park. He did actually walk a rope the whole 1,500-foot length of the Upper Terrace. During his engagement at the Palace in June 1861 1,800,000 people watched him perform.[57]

Blondin was not only an athlete of genius but possessed an extraordinary imagination. On 24 July 1861 he performed on a short rope in the Terrace Dining Room. Attired as a Siberian galley slave, he danced with his feet in panniers, his neck shackled by a chain. He performed complex antics on the rope with a four-legged chair and played the violin and military drum, favouring the March from *William Tell*. From sitting cross-legged on the rope he leaped up to erect himself on stilts. As a French peasant in *sabots* he bounded and vaulted. Five minutes later

he was seen coolly walking about the Palace 'with the air of a connoisseur who had done nothing but sit and lounge'. In 1862 he appeared in the Palace's theatre in a pantomime, *The Child of the Wreck, or the Faithful Ape*, designed to display his agility. He gave his farewell performance at the Crystal Palace at the age of seventy.[58]

Fireworks

Blondin had appeared in 1871 on the terrace of the Palace against a background of fireworks; by the 1930s he had become himself immortalised in the Palace mythology by being represented as 'Blondin', an acrobat dressed in an asbestos suit decorated with live fireworks. One programme announced 'humorous living fireworks:

BROCK'S BENEFIT CRYSTAL PALACE SEP 24. "ONE SHILLING DAY."

Blondin in his wonderful performance on the tight rope' to be followed by 'a discharge of Princess Margaret Rose bombshells'.[59] At the Crystal Palace the theme of fire runs from Blondin discharging fireworks from a wheelbarrow in the centre of the Transept to the pantomime figure of the 'Demon of Fire' in 1865 who ran on the terrace among flames during one evening performance, followed the following year by the disastrous North Transept fire. This is not to mention the apocalyptic blaze that destroyed the Palace on a winter night in 1936. The inspiration behind the fireworks extravaganzas was Charles Thomas Brock (1843–81), the brilliant pyrotechnist who came from a family who had mounted displays at Vauxhall and Ranelagh since the eighteenth century. The Crystal Palace directors, as has been mentioned, had first resisted his approaches, fearing that firework displays would degrade the Palace to the level of the popular Cremorne pleasure gardens (whose rockets above the Thames appear in Whistler's *Nocturne in Blue and Silver: Old Battersea Bridge*). However, by 1887 the *Pictorial World* could say that the fireworks 'must have had a great deal to do with saving the Palace Company from collapse'.[60]

Versailles, Paxton's model for the Park at Sydenham,

was famous not only for waterworks but, in its heyday, for fireworks too; so, at Sydenham also the tableaux were reflected in basins of water. Brock recognised the obvious suitability of the terraces and the background of the Palace at Sydenham as a theatre: here was a perfect firing ground, what became known as the 'firework terrace', with the magnificent background of the Palace at night that could be lit up with magnesium lights or changing colour effects. From 12 July 1865 until 1936 there were 1,500 displays, and a colossal number of spectators. Up until 1902 visiting potentates were given elaborate displays that were ignited by the royal personages themselves from a balcony box on the Palace with electrical devices. Two specialities the firm developed were: set pieces, or 'fire pictures', and 'living fireworks'. The set pieces began with a width of 12 feet but developed to 600 and a height of 90; they were set up on elaborate bamboo trellises. These began as tableaux, like old-fashioned line-engravings, such as an elegant pyramid, palms and sphinxes to welcome De Lesseps, the engineer of the Suez Canal, in 1870. The set pieces were later developed to convey an elaborate narrative such as a battle or disaster, a motion picture in fireworks. There were also

'A Firework Night at the Crystal Palace', October 1870.

enormous outline 'fire portraits' that were mostly patriotic, or compliments to visiting royalty or celebrities, but
included Victor Hugo and, in 1920, Douglas Fairbanks
and Mary Pickford. The 'living fireworks' were men in
asbestos suits hidden behind the two-dimensional
frameworks which they carried (some of which had moving parts, such as arms). These devices represented, for
example, boxers or 'fighting cocks'; the men and the figures moved in a stylised way and the frames were outlined in fireworks. This technique was invented in 1888
and patented by Arthur Brock.[61]

Brock developed his effects into what was virtually a
new art form. The marvellous technical vocabulary –

LIVING FIREWORKS.

'Living Fireworks', October 1891.

*rayons d'argent, the shower of pink pearls, flight of fiery
pigeons, girandoles, hexastrons, saucissons* – is mostly
forgotten now. Some effects may have been fairly crude or
sensational, such as *The Destruction of Pompeii*, with the
eruption of Vesuvius, the battles of the Nile and Trafalgar,
the set-piece battles of Dreadnoughts, and bombard-
ments of cities. Ships foundered in violent seas, and the
people on board were saved by oarsmen in lifeboats. In
The Avalanche a train ran along the base of the Alps, in
and out of tunnels, until a cascade of firework snow
destroyed a châlet and just avoided the train. Others may

have been more subtle and intricate, such as representations of palaces and architectural masterpieces – Stras-
bourg cathedral with its spire and rose window, the Arc
de Triomphe, the Escorial, the Great Mosque in Delhi,
and the Crystal Palace itself.[62] There were transformation scenes, such as the tableaux of *The Seasons*. Some
were particular Cockney favourites, reflecting the artistry
of Edwardian sentimental magazines and post-cards.
The most popular was a cartoon illustrating the popular
song *The Honeysuckle and the Bee* – the bee buzzed
around a bouquet of flowers to a line sung by the crowds

A Brock patriotic set piece or 'fire picture'.

peared. Still a glowing partial form went round and round. Enormous set pieces spluttered, smoked and burst into brilliance, displaying naval vessels shelling each other and exploding – the British winning, of course. And finally, with further splutter, hiss and smoke, the features of her most gracious majesty appeared in fire while the band played the National Anthem and everyone went home joyfully.[64]

In 1869 the Palace directors introduced a Brock's Benefit night to reward them, and this became an annual event in which the fireworks company doubled its efforts for the spectacle;[65] in 1889 the crowd numbered 6,389. The phrase 'Brock's Benefit' entered the Oxford Dictionary as a metaphor that was applied to parliamentary debates, and during the 1914–18 War it was often used to describe nocturnal artillery exchanges at the Front.

about kissing 'sweet red lips', at which point a girl emerged for the bee to kiss. A 60-foot-high portrait of Lottie Collins stood above the crowd singing 'Ta-ra-ra-boom-de-ay'; on the word 'boom' the figure kicked her leg. In 1890 one subject was *Life in the Arctic Region*, with polar seas, ice forms, sledges and a man and a bear in a fight.[63] In 1899 Walter Crane designed a gigantic set piece for Labour's May Day at the Crystal Palace which Brock carried out with great success. In his own description,

> It was a group of four figures, typifying the workers of the world, joining hands, a winged central figure with the cap of Liberty, encircled by a uniting globe, and a scroll with the words 'The Unity of Labour is the Hope for the world'. It was the first time a design of mine had been associated with pyrotechnics. I was rewarded by the hearty cheers of the vast multitude.[64]

The Fireworks were accompanied by music, usually from the Palace band, and afterwards the great organ played in the Palace. W. Macqueen-Pope in 1948 remembered from his boyhood at the turn of the century Brock's Thursday displays:

> Every pyrotechnic device came into play. Rockets ascended in droves, to long 'Oo-oo-oos' from the crowd, and burst into constellations of coloured balls; some joined up and floated in chains, others whistled like a gale. Fountains played and changed colours, silver Niagaras descended in incandescent spray, a firework gymnast turned and turned over a horizontal bar, not desisting when his legs burnt out and his head disap-

Drama

Performances by the Royal Italian Opera Company after Covent Garden Opera House was burnt out in March 1856 were given at Sydenham on twelve Fridays in May, June and July, and these were the first shows at the Palace. By 1869 what was originally known as 'the Opera Theatre', seating 15,000,[66] was opened on the north side of the Centre Transept balancing the Concert Hall, and performances of, among others, *Il Trovatore*, *Fidelio*, *Lucia di Lammermoor*, *La Somnambula* and *Don Giovanni* were given. Ninety performances of operas in English had been given by that time.

Plays were also performed in the Opera Theatre – the average 100 plays performed there annually between 1865 and 1875 was claimed as unequalled by any theatre in the world at that time.[67] At the beginning many productions would appear after a successful first run in the West End, such as Beerbohm Tree's *King John* in 1889. Henry Irving and Ellen Terry appeared in productions. Proper seasons for the theatre itself ran from the 1870s to the 1890s, with classics and old comedies under the management of Charles Wyndham, although many of these were second runs with his St James's Theatre

'Spy', Sir George Grove, *Vanity Fair*, 1891.

aux Camélias and the entire company from the Théâtre Sarah Bernhardt of Paris on 12 July 1902.[68] Wyndham also produced pantomimes to equal their competitors across the river. In the 1880s these were produced by Oscar Barrett, and the standard titles of pantomimes (with the addition of *Blue Beard* and *Robinson Crusoe*) were repeated in series into the mid-1890s. The auditorium seated 15,000. Already in 1868 the first moving pictures had being shown to a large audience, using a gas-powered Zoetrope projector; the short pieces included *The Conjurer*, *The Acrobat*, *Umbrella Man* and *Jim Crow*.[69]

The Palace was host to popular spiritualist productions – perhaps no more than Brighton Pier or Paris at that date. In 1890 in the play *Cleopatra*, suggested by a novel of H. Rider Haggard, spirit medium effects abounded:

Solid bodies, animate and inanimate, are instantly evolved from space, slowly dissolve, become transparent, and melt into thin air. Spirit hands, spirit faces, and forms appear and disappear. Living heads without bodies float about, become materialised, and finally vanish out of sight in fire which does not consume. The whole concludes with a marvellous transformation and the instantaneous appearance, in full light, of Cleopatra seated upon the throne. Whence she comes must, however, remain a mystery.

The Mystery of Proteus, in 1902, was advertised as 'America's Latest Wonder':

A statue of a Greek goddess – Proteus [sic] – is exhibited on a table in a brilliantly illuminated chamber, and after a thorough examination by the audience, slowly transforms into a living lady. She converses with the audience; a change then takes place, a pallor spreads over her face, the hair turns grey, and nothing is left but a skull (this can be handled by the audience), and in turn transforms into remarkable objects and shapes. The Lady re-appears, when finally a most sensational change is witnessed, as she is gradually transformed into a stone statue. (The Medical Faculty bewildered – Scientists dumbfounded. Must be seen to be believed).

Something of a Planetarium seems to be offered by the *Electric Panorama of Heavenly Voyages round the World* in the Greek Court, Wragge's 'Palais de l'Optique' of 1896. Early electrical entertainments sound more imaginative than modern light shows and pop videos: in 1903

Company; Wyndham's seasons were 'immensely popular', even famous. A speciality was a series of abridged Shakespeare plays; the *Much Ado* of 1874 had masque music by Arthur Sullivan. *Faust* (1874), *Oedipus at Colonus* and *Antigone* (1876) varied the repetitions of Victorian successes such as *Black-Eyed Susan* (1872), *The Waterman* (1875) and *The Corsican Brothers* (1880); Richard Temple in 1877 produced Cimarosa's *The Secret Marriage* conducted by August Manns. Visits by celebrities were common, Elinor Glyn giving a reading in 1870, Baron Kempelen with his Automatic Chess Player, Mrs Patrick Campbell in *The Second Mrs Tanqueray* in 1898; Loie Fuller with whirling Chinese dances and floating veils in 1899, Sarah Bernhardt with *La Dame* the *Wonderful Palace of Light from the Paris Exhibition* was enlivened by 'Mlle Aimée Mignon in her Mystifying Electric Dance'. A photograph of a lady on a bicycle, *La Flèche Humaine*, who descended a chute and leapt in the air, landing on to a padded track, was shown in an illustrated paper of 1904, with a background of Palace statues and palms.[70]

Arthur Sullivan's long association with the Palace and his residence in Sydenham, together with the suburban tastes of South London, made the Crystal Palace an obvious place to stage Gilbert and Sullivan's operas, and Sullivan conducted performances there himself. In 1863 he is listed as teaching ballad singing at the School of Art, Science and Literature.[71] In 1895, as a boy, P.G. Wodehouse saw *Patience* there, the first show he ever saw, and came home 'drunk with ecstasy', as he recalled in a letter written fifty-two years later.[72] By 1911 there was a third theatre, 'The Variety Theatre'. In a programme for May 11 of that year the name of Noël Coward, aged twelve at the time, appears in the cast of *The Goldfish, a Fairy Play in Three Acts* by Lila Field. Known in the profession as 'The Box',[73] in 1933 it was converted into a cinema.

Music

The Palace's long and distinguished musical career, thoroughly chronicled by Michael Musgrave in *The Musical Life of the Crystal Palace* (1995), began at the royal opening ceremony that all agreed was an improvement on the famous massed choir singing the Hallelujah Chorus at Hyde Park in 1851. Michael Costa (1810–84; knighted 1869) with the Sacred Harmonic Society* conducted 1,200 voices and nearly 500 instruments, which was more than twice the number he had marshalled at the opening ceremony at Hyde Park and an anticipation of the colossal forces involved in the later choral festivals.[75] The Hallelujah Chorus and the Old Hundredth had a powerful impact in the Central Transept and Nave, but the large effect was

'Spy', 'Crystal Palace' (August Manns), *Vanity Fair*, 1895.

not in this case the best, and the soprano Clara Novello stole the show with her famous high note at the end of her solo of 'God Save the Queen', as we heard from Lady Eastlake and Richard Redgrave in Chapter 2. Beale after his unsuccessful interview with Paxton had better luck in persuading Scott Russell and T.N. Farquhar, an influential director, to introduce concerts. George Grove, whose

---

* Costa had determined to do even better for Sydenham than Hyde Park.[74] He had conducted Handel oratorios in London with the Sacred Harmonic Society since 1845, and his choir and orchestra performed at the closing ceremony of the Great Exhibition.

THE EFFECTS OF A HEARTY DINNER AFTER VISITING THE ANTEDILUVIAN DEPARTMENT AT THE CRYSTAL PALACE.

Punch, 3 February 1855 (Nightmare from indigestion of discordant assaults on the senses).

surname of course became an institution after his creation of *Grove's Dictionary of Music*, supported him. At one point Robert Bowley, Secretary of Costa's Sacred Harmonic Society, became manager at the Crystal Palace. Sotheby in 1856 proposed an Annual Grand Musical Festival.[76] The large Crystal Palace band of fifty-three players was the finest in the country at the time, according to Lady Eastlake, and cost the Directors £7,000 annually.[77] Playing in the open air and audible almost a mile away in Sydenham, they typically played (in 1854) selections from Donizetti, Kohler, Wagner and Balfe. Some of the bandsmen appear in the corner of a *Punch* cartoon, 'Effects of a Hearty Dinner after Visiting the Antediluvian Reptiles at the Crystal Palace', ludicrously tooting at a sleeper suffering a nightmare.[78] Many bands were German in those days (and up till 1914) because they were cheaper and more sober. Henry Schallehn, the director, was from the Prussian army and had been recommended for the post by 'a member of the

royal family'. His bandsmen were of several nationalities besides German: Italians, French, Hungarians and even Englishmen played under him. The first we hear of him in the press is a subscription among the band to present him with an elegant silver baton.[79] However, serious trouble broke out: there were 'disagreements about principles of art', and the men wrote to complain that Schallehn conducted badly, had a 'general rude and insulting manner', had got the police to eject them and ordered them to leave their instruments and uniforms and go home without their coats and trousers. Forty-nine men resigned, and one English bandsman threatened to throw him into the fountain.[80] In the first year Schallehn disgraced himself by selling a Quadrille written by August Manns to a publisher for £50, a medley of national airs celebrating the war alliance: English, French and Turkish. Manns at the time was the first clarinettist and sub-director of the band, and when he complained, Schallehn said that his own name would sell the piece better, offered him a pound, and when Manns refused dismissed him. Manns' letter of 9 November 1854 describing his treatment was published in *The Musical Times*. By next April the band was in revolt again and raucously hooted the director in public. Schallehn was dismissed and Manns (1825–1907), who had previously conducted military bands in Germany, was appointed in his place – supposedly due to Grove's influence – on 20 October 1855.[81]

August Manns was to devote his whole career to the musical life of the Palace and had an important influence in educating his audiences with new works, from both continental and contemporary English repertoires. In short, he became a national figure, and was knighted in 1903. At Sydenham he started with no orchestra, no concert room and no musical audience. Of the situation in 1855 he said, 'I had to battle with strongly-rooted prejudices against the so-called instrumental music.' He wrote of his own 'patience, prudence, perseverance and pluck' in holding out for high-class music.[82] Costa, the conductor of the Handel Festivals, fell ill in 1883 and at short notice Manns took over the conducting of the rehearsals. The choir did not at first respond to him and many expected that the Festivals would die out. However, by sheer energy and force of character he made the Festival in that year one of the most successful. At the Festival in 1890 he was sixty-five, but conducted again in 1896 and 1900. He was conspicuous from the start: his hair was so long that he was sent curling papers through the post.[83] Immediately he set himself to improving the quality of works for the band. As we have seen, he was also a composer, and published a *Prince Albert Gavotte* with a Crystal Palace design on the cover. In 1859 he was the conductor of a performance of *Fidelio* at the palace. He continued to conduct the Band and a small daily orchestra, including the music for Blondin's performance on the high rope.

The band continued to perform daily at the Palace until 1900. From 1861 onwards massed brass band festivals and contests were a regular feature, the groups travelling from collieries, works like Morris Motors, and railway cities, or as representatives of towns and Temperance Societies. The National Band Contests were associated from 1900 to 1936 with J. Henry Iles, their director and founder.[84] Military bands frequently attended for functions, particularly in the early days. By March 1856 Saturday Classical Concerts conducted by

Manns were performed under the painting of Prince Albert, Paxton and the 1851 Commissioners before 1,500 people, and were a 'triumphant success'.[85]

The main impetus for the development of music at the Palace behind the scenes came from George Grove (1820–1900), the original Secretary of the Company, a considerable intellect and a polymath with many friends among artists, writers, travellers, scientists and musicians. Grove's contribution to the musical scene in London as first Director of the Royal College of Music from 1883 (when he was knighted), and to the great international musical world with the *Dictionary* (1879–89), is well acknowledged and the subject of several books.[86] His analytical notes in Crystal Palace concert programmes – he invented the genre – are said to be the origin of the *Dictionary*; Beethoven's Eroica Symphony received a thirty-page commentary. At the same time he wrote major articles for William Smith's *Dictionary of the Bible* and was active in the Palestine Exploration Fund. He had begun his career as an engineer working with Brunel and Stephenson on the Clifton Suspension Bridge, but at the Society of Arts, where he was Secretary, he became involved with the Great Exhibition – for one thing he was responsible for issuing season tickets. From a trip to Vienna with Sullivan he returned with the discovery of Schubert's *Rosamunde*, and he had much to do with the first-ever performance at the Palace of Schubert's Great C Major Symphony in 1856, which the two of them had discovered, and with the introduction of Brahms to English audiences. His contacts must have been invaluable to the Company in every way; it is disappointing that his suggestion to Tennyson to write an Ode for Berlioz to set did not materialise. Grove's son told an anecdote illustrating his father's 'prompt mind'. One day at the top of one of Brunel's Towers he met a wild-looking stranger who said that he had been waiting for an hour for someone to see if he would get to the ground if he jumped off the side of the tower. Grove thereupon took his keys out of his pocket and threw them down to prove their gravity, and said, "Now I'll tell you what would be more clever still. Let's go to the bottom and try to jump up again." To which the man agreed and Grove thereafter had the top of the Tower fenced off.[87]

The first Saturday concerts, vocal and instrumental rather than orchestral, were an immediate success, and Grove was congratulated in the *Crystal Palace Herald*. However, by July 1855 the press were saying that 'the building is totally unfit for vocal concert'. Madame Albani sang that month for the season ticket-holders. This French-Canadian singer, a particular favourite with Palace audiences over many years, made a speciality of Rossini, and in 1860 'her *fioriture* was more than usually brilliant, and the low short notes were brought out with a strength and clearness that was perfectly astonishing'.[88]

Michael Costa's Italian concerts in 'the German and Italian Music Court' in 1856 provoked several calls for English songs and glees, in the same spirit that led to calls for a maypole after the 'German' Christmas tree.[89] Costa was said to send his fellow-countryman Rossini a Stilton cheese every year.[90]

The Handel Festivals

The acoustics of the Palace presented problems for the Handel Festivals. Despite the staging introduced for the large choir at the Inauguration, concerts had no place in the thought of the planners and hence no accommodation in the layout. Seen in a Delamotte photograph is the erection of the 'monster Orchestra' in the Great Transept for the Handel Festival to seat 3-4,000 performers with an audience of 14-15,000, as proposed by Sotheby in 1856.[91] Concerts took place first in the Court of Musical Instruments, then in December 1855 in the North Transept, and then in the Lecture Room outside the Queen's apartments at the north end of the palace, before being moved to an enclosure on the garden side of the central transept. A New Music Room, 96 feet square and able to accommodate sixty performers and an audience of 3,000, was built in November 1856 on one side of the Transept for vocal, chamber and classical music. Translucent *toile métallique* was stretched overhead. Although in 1866 it was not only enlarged but glazed, noises from other parts of the Palace remained a problem.[92]

A special Collard grand piano on a platform in front of the dais, designed for the immense dimensions of the Palace, was used early on. But an organ was the quintessential Crystal Palace musical instrument: there was one at each end of the Nave at Hyde Park, one by Gray and Davison, and its companion by Willis. When the latter was played its 'magnificent tones' brought all circulation to a halt. A small organ at Sydenham, mentioned as early as 1855, played during the Horticultural Society show. The great organ for Sydenham was discussed early: in December 1853 a committee consisting of the Rev. Sir F.A.G. Ouseley, Bart, Professor the Rev. Robert Willis of

Cambridge and Professor John Donaldson of Edinburgh. The figure of £25,000 was mentioned – completion was expected within three years and the result would be 'one of the wonders of the world'. In April 1854 it was reported by the *Gentleman's Magazine* that 'the idea of a monster organ is relinquished,'[93] but in August 1854 John Donaldson left for North Germany with the Edinburgh organ-builder David Hamilton. The famous organ by Gray and Davison, with four manuals, seventy-four stops, 4,568 pipes and weighing 20 tons, and at the time the largest in Britain, was installed in 1857. In 1920–3 Buckland spent £9,000 on 'discus' fan-blowers for it, and the pitch was lowered and 'an entirely new system of tubular pneumatic action' installed. While the Fire was raging in 1936 the hot air got into the organ pipes and there were reports of eldritch sounds like a Titan in agony.[94]

The 'Orchestra' for the first Crystal Palace Handel Festival in 1857 was designed by Fergusson who gave much thought to the difficult acoustic problems involved. This was 42 feet high, 150 feet wide and 50–60 feet deep and was later expanded to 216 feet wide and 100 feet depth, giving a choral space double that of St Paul's. It was also a shrine to Handel – cartouches were made containing the names of his oratorios inscribed in gold; the decoration of the organ and this upper part of the Orchestra was by Thomas Hayes, superintendent of the Fine Art Department. But a problem remained: the Handel choruses were 'sublime', George Eliot wrote to a friend, but the solos 'total futility'.[95] Fergusson wrote in his *History of the Modern Styles of Architecture*:

> 15–20,000 in the audience have heard the choruses of Handel in a very perfect manner, and one-half that number have heard the solos with very enjoyable distinctness; yet the Crystal Palace is about the worst possible building, except in so far as size is concerned, for the purpose. The floor is perfectly flat; the galleries accommodate very few, but are thrust most obtrusively into the area, so as to hinder those under and behind them from hearing; all the arrangements of the building are of the most temporary and accidental character, and the external sounds very imperfectly shut off; yet the perfection with which the earlier opera concerts and the later oratorios have been heard in the building has surprised and delighted every one.

Over the roof of the Orchestra an oiled calico fabric was suspended – a *velarium*, another Hyde Park term – and later an acoustic shell of a metallic fabric was added to form a sounding board.[96]

The Builder wrote in 1857 that brick and stone were

'A Sketch at the Handel Festival in the Crystal Palace', July 1865, showing Sims Reeves and Distin's Monster Bass Drum.

better acoustically than iron and glass, and that in the unlimited length of the nave the sounds became dispersed and there were numerous echoes. With 2,500 performers the Handel Festival beginning on 15 June was the grandest musical congress ever held in the country. The solos 'lost much of their beauty,' the piano notes were inaudible, the florid passages lost their effects, as did the low notes of the basses and contraltos. High and sustained notes, such as Clara Novello's in 'Let the Bright Seraphim' and Sims Reeves, in 'Sound the Alarm', told with great effect. The chief honours went 'by general consent' to Mr Sims Reeves, who entered so completely into the spirit of performances that he was said to have sobbed with emotion in the gardens afterwards.[97] Clara Novello and he were undoubtedly the favourites of the audiences. After the 1865 Festival, when the number of voices was increased to 3,600 and the orchestra was expanded, 'a man must shout and a woman must scream'. The nightly attendance was 16,000, and *Israel in Egypt* was 'absolutely stupendous'.[98]

Great Handel performances with large forces probably date from 1791 when 1,068 musicians took part in a
commemoration in Westminster Abbey. The first
Handel Festival at the Palace, conducted by Michael
Costa with the Sacred Philharmonic Society, with 1,000
metropolitan amateurs, 200 professional singers and 850
choristers, was held in 1857; Victoria and Albert
attended on the second day. The organ, then on trial, was
heard a mile away in Sydenham, and the Hallelujah
Chorus half a mile away. Although the Transept was
again thought 'little better for musical purposes than an
open field' for hearing the solos, *Israel in Egypt* with its
double choir had 'unparalleled grandeur', even allowing
for 'the skipping frogs from the puerilities of Handel's
age'. Apart from the Handel Festival and the Manchester
Art Treasures exhibition, 1857 was thought by the *Illustrated London News* to have been generally a dull year.
The Festival was repeated in 1858 and in 1859, the centenary of Handel's death, and then became triennial. In
1883 with a choir of 4,000 and 4,441 instrumentalists it
reached its most colossal, and 22,000 attended daily.
When the High Level Station was first opened in 1865,
trains arriving could deliver 7–8,000 people in an hour,
but by the 1880s that number had risen to 12,000.[99] A set
formula developed of *Messiah* being given on the first
day, minor works on the second and *Israel in Egypt* on
the third. The *Dettingen Te Deum* was popular.

People wrote that the spectacle of so many performers and of London 'society' in the audience made the
concerts as much a pleasure for the eyes as for the ears.
The size of the forces were epitomised in Distin's Monster Bass Drum made of buffalo-hide and almost seven
feet in diameter; Costa, who once altered a Beethoven
score where he did not like it, added notes for this drum,
notably in the Hallelujah Chorus. Ruskin was a frequent
attender at these concerts, complaining in *Ethics of the
Dust* of the 'thundering things with a million of bad
voices in them and a headache the following morning'.
Yet in 1879 and 1880 he was at many concerts and admitted to enjoying them. In 1888 Gladstone's unpopularity
became apparent as the immense audience 'showed their
displeasure in an unpleasant manner'.[100]

The Festivals had become 'symbols of national pride,
social cohesion, and sheer size and power.' The receipts
for the 1859 Festival were £30,000, with net profit to the
Company of £10,000. As an innovation, a Haydn Festival
was held in 1861.[101]

The Saturday Concerts

The Saturday Concerts began on 20 October 1855, and
continued until 1901, and before Henry Wood's Promenade Concerts began in 1895 they were virtually the only
orchestral concerts in London. Bernard Shaw began his
reviews of them in 1885. They waned in popularity at the
end through the prosperity of the Queen's Hall, and the
general decline of the Palace. Under Buckland there was
a revival, with 4,000 voices and 216 choirs at the English
Church Music Festival in 1933 and his two Handel
Festivals.

Camille Saint-Saëns, Clara Schumann and the violin-
ist Anton Rubinstein performed at the Palace. In 1877
Liszt was present when Manns conducted his work and
continually leaped up to shake his hand. The roll-call of
first performances of works now standard in the concert
repertoire and in educated people's consciousness is
remarkable. It includes Mozart's *Eine kleine Nachtmusik*
(1880); Richard Strauss's *Till Eulenspiegel* (1896) and
Also Sprach Zarathustra (1897); Brahms's First Piano
Concerto (1870), Second Piano Concerto (1882),
Second Symphony (1878), Violin Concerto (1879, performed by Joachim), and St Antoni Variations (1873); the
Prelude from Wagner's *Parsifal* (1882); Berlioz's *Grande
Messe des Morts* (1883); Tchaikovsky's *Romeo and Juliet*
(1876), *Capriccio Italien* (1885) and First Piano Concerto (1876); and Schubert's Symphonies – the First
(1881), Second (1877), Third (1881), Fourth (1854), Fifth
(1873), Sixth (1868), Seventh (1883), Eighth (1867), and
Ninth (1856). From his early years at the Palace Manns
conducted works by Wagner and Berlioz, and the English
taste for Brahms and Berlioz was largely due to his cultivation. After Manns' memorial concert for Wagner in
1883 the young Edward Elgar wrote that he would never
forget his first hearing the *Liebestod* in *Tristan und
Isolde*.[102] Manns was also deeply interested in contemporary English music, and gave first performances of works
by Parry, Stanford, Elgar and many others. When he
retired in 1900 and the Saturday Orchestra was dis-
banded, music became more local than national, and the
organist Walter Hedgecock became musical director in
1904. Several Saturday series followed, however, with
visiting orchestras conducted by Manns, Sir Henry
Wood, Landon Ronald and Hedgecock. Altogether the
Saturday orchestral concerts lasted for 45 years.

Though many jeered at the Handel Festivals and
other colossal performances at the Palace, their part in

From winter to green, leafy summer he bounds,

And stands with the crowd in the beautiful grounds

Where thousands are watching, with keen, straining eyes,

The balloon that is sailing away to the skies.

education is exemplified by the impressions of the young Lance Sieveking recalling 1911:

> As one came through the little doorway at the top of the long sloping passage one saw the limitless glass-covered spaces, floors wider than the widest streets, and galleries stretching away into vast and incredible perspectives. There were plaster copies of classical and other statues in niches up the sloping passage, and all over the place inside the Palace. The assembled thousands were far more startlingly breathtaking than any huge crowd. I thought: this is what Judgment Day will look like. The central auditorium was not divided on each side, and therefore the acoustics had a perfection which has never since been attained. To hear a great orchestra from the other end of those vast glass-canopied empty paces was an unforgettable foretaste (one might imagine) of heavenly music. [103]

About sport

Recreation for Londoners in the form of 'manly sports' was part of the original proposal of the Crystal Palace Company for use of the Park: cricket, archery, tennis, 'raquet' and golf, swimming and skating were specified in a statement to the press of July 1852.[104] Cricket and archery, as has been seen, were early features of the Park, and might be regarded as picturesque English activities. Then came German gymnasts. By 1895 sports were assigned 17 acres. In 1899 W.G. Grace was hired by the Company to be manager and secretary of first-class cricket; on Saturday he was always to be seen ensuring that his groundsmen were paid. The bicycling mania of the turn of the century was given its track around the fountains, and – as seen in chapter 5 – the Football Association Cup Finals were played from 1894 to 1914 on the site of the large basin of one of Paxton's fountains.[105] Sir Gerald Barry designed the Sports Centre next to its famous running-track. Some innovations took place, such as Bicycle Polo, invented here in 1897. The 'ornamental swimming of Miss Florence Boyce, the celebrated lady swimmer' was advertised at the Diving Pavilion in 1893.[106]

With the strident restless triumph of football and dirt-track motor-racing in the Park it might appear that the directors of the Crystal Palace and the architects of the Fine Arts Courts had failed in their quixotic programme to refine the people by teaching them the history of civilisations and natural history and introducing them to the culture of architecture, music and sculpture. Television, the prefabrication of buildings, shopping malls, theme parks, mass entertainments and pop concerts all could be said to have taken hold and grown to maturity on this arena of sloping English parkland once set among Kent orchards.

Although the vast scale of the Crystal Palace bred some colossal and over-blown features more characteristic of the world a century and a half later, the vitality of its imagination, originality and use of colour and the humour and affection it aroused in such a great mass of Londoners prove its underlying success. Many were well able to learn from its displays and to think of their own times in relation to the past and to the natural world around them: their eyes and ears were educated as they walked among the 'pages' of the strange and wonderful illustrated encyclopaedia. This was what Owen Jones had envisaged in his address at the Society of Arts in 1852, in response to the question of what was to be done with the vast quantities of iron and glass units to be disposed of from the Crystal Palace in Hyde Park.

Jane Bown, Crystal Palace Statue, 1952. © Jane Bown

8

THE FIRE AND AFTER

Sir Henry Buckland among the ruins, 1 December 1936.

The Crystal Palace was destroyed by fire during the night of 30 November 1936. True to the Palace itself, the blaze was colossal, and the sky was blood-red. Against such a conflagration eighty-nine fire-engines and 438 firemen proved powerless. Police arrived swiftly – 749 of them – to protect the half-million spectators and the surrounding houses and premises on the hill – even so, the crowds held up the fire-engines for an hour.

The loss of this monument to Victorian enterprise caused 'a wave of emotion for Londoners'. *The Times* wrote that as the years passed it had become 'steadily more historic and symbolic'. Sir Henry Buckland, who wept openly, said: 'I am afraid it is the Crystal Palace's last and biggest firework show of all.' There were many spectacular photographs and accounts in the press the following day: for the *Manchester Guardian* 'Brock's Last Benefit' was the obvious headline; the *Daily Express* said that the scene looked 'as if an immense iceberg was on fire'. It was well recorded in the newsreels. The fire had soon run its course: after an hour almost the entire Palace lay a tangled mass of red-hot iron and molten glass.

The Crystal Palace at Hyde Park suffered only one small fire, and it was immediately put out. Inside the building no smoking was allowed, and only cold food was served; soup and beverages were warmed by

Previous page: The Fire. *Daily Sketch*, 1 December 1936.

steam power from the smaller of the two boiler houses. The fire precautions were excellently organised, with twelve large fire-engines in the building and 200 sappers on hand to man a stand-pipe in Hyde Park. In the absence of electricity gas was used – only for lighting the offices and work-shops. By the time of the 1866 fire at Sydenham, as has been men-tioned, the hoses had been allowed to perish, and in that year fire-fighting difficulties had been increased by an early hard frost which reduced the water supply. In 1920 there was a serious fire in the Theatre that destroyed part of the Palace roof.

One might have thought that the iron and glass at Sydenham would hardly have been com-bustible, but the floor-boards were dry from the heating pipes which they covered, and dust had accu-mulated through the half-inch gaps between them. The Orches-tra was largely made of wood, and 20,000 wooden chairs were stored under it for use in the gardens in summer. The iron buckled and the glass melted. The flames leaped higher into the air than Paxton's fountains, some sources said 300 feet, others 500. A high wind from

Gallery above Medieval Court, facing towards South Tower, 1 December 1936.

the north-west swept through the building, as if through a giant flue, swiftly causing a 'funnel effect'. Beneath the Palace a deep air passage ran under the wooden stands and timber galleries. Seen by a *Daily Mail* reporter from a plane, the Palace was 'like the blazing crater of a vol-cano'. At 8.30, according to Buckland's secretary Syd-ney Legg, the Nave blazed as if petrol had been flooded on the floor; the most terrifying moment, he said, came twenty or thirty minutes into the fire when the whole of the great central transept 384 feet long collapsed, 'sink-ing slowly with a long, continuous rumble'.[1] Although the Transept fell, the arched ironwork of the roof stood,

and a considerable section of the North Nave was to sur-vive the fire. A spiral staircase inside made an incandes-cent pillar. An army of rats scuttled from below the Palace past the statues and fountain basins. Molten glass flowed among the fire hoses, but the tale that it ran down the steep road at Anerley Hill is fictitious. The great glow in the sky was seen on the horizon in Brighton and from an aeroplane above Margate far away in the east of Kent. Hampstead Hill was crowded with spectators by 9 p.m., and M.P.s left a debate in the House of Commons to watch from the terraces and committee rooms.[2]

Several theories have been advanced as to how and

The South Nave ablaze.

where the fire started. Buckland 'seemed convinced that an electric spark near a gas canister caused the blaze'. A cigarette stubbed through the grating in the North Nave is another possibility; it was said that the Palace firemen 'regularly put out small fires started in this way'. The fire was also said to have started in an office staff lavatory. A fused electrical circuit and sparks from poorly insulated wires were possibilities suggested by reports from those who visited behind the scenes.

Buckland when interviewed that same evening revealed that the destruction of the statuary was one of the first things on his mind. He understood the calamity of the loss of the Palace as a 'cherished and venerated historical document' – the phrase he used about it to *The Times*. All his restoration work, the rearrangement of the statuary and the immense amount of general reconditioning, together costing £300,000, had gone for nothing.[3] The Pompeian Court, so recently restored, had relived its Last Days before final destruction. In the photographs taken the next day much of the actual brick structure and some of the plaster walls of the Fine Arts Courts to the north are seen to be still standing. Curiously, the feature of the Palace to suffer the least damage was Jones's Alhambra Court at the northern end of the Nave, and one photograph taken after the Fire showed Buckland's daughter Chrystal removing some of the Moresque tiling. Souvenirs of the Fire, such as pieces of congealed molten glass from Osler's Crystal Fountain and from the building itself, are now in the collections of several museums in the neighbourhood, and in the gardens of nearby houses some were used to make edging for flower-beds.

Re-enacting the calamitous fall of some of their originals, the Fine Arts Courts and the statuary were consumed once again as if they had been smitten, in the style of the Old Testament, by some vengeance from the skies:

> The ruins in this section, where strips of steel and glass swing dangerously in the breeze, had an exotic and melancholy appearance, due to the interior architecture and exhibits. Venus and a fawn in plaster, still intact on the edge of chaos, gazed across at the equally intact fountain with the bronze nymphs and the blackened (but still swimming) gold-fish. Effigies of the Kings of England on their tombs were surrounded by debris, and a small chapel, with a sagging floor and one end destroyed, irresistibly recalled Madrid [in the Civil War then raging]. Towards the centre and southern sections the confusion was less romantic, more like an aftermath of war in its formlessness.[4]

December 1936.

The next morning about 200 of the Palace's 700 employees were given notice. The Baird studios announced that their premises in the South Tower were not sufficiently damaged to stop television transmission; their receiving sets production department had escaped the full force of the fire-storm.[5] Buckland had to organise the removal of the debris, which was carried out by Messrs T.H. Ward of Sheffield and went on well into 1938. One of the Trustees remarked that it was tragic the Coronation celebrations would not take place there;* Gracie Fields had been booked to sing.

Once again there was discussion, some of it familiar, about what should become of the best building site in London. J.B.S. Comper wrote to *The Times* that rebuilding the Palace would cost less than a battleship. G.M.

Young, the historian, wrote suggesting that a permanent exhibition of domestic architecture, decoration and equipment be set up on the site. Others suggested halls for exhibitions, a hospital, a university, a convalescent home and a monument of Empire. Alexander Korda said it should be anything but another film studio.[6] In 1938 Buckland managed to stage the seventh South London Exhibition in single-span pavilions straddling the pavement roads of the Lower Terrace; he was not keen to break into the £120,000 insurance money. After war started in 1939, anti-aircraft guns were installed and military equipment was stored. Brunel's Towers were demolished as likely to serve as a landmark for the German bombers. Rubble from the bombed buildings of London, estimated by Buckland at 385,000 tons, filled

* The planned Coronation was still that of Edward VIII, who abdicated on December 10, less than a fortnight after the Fire.

up the site of the building; a level surface was made for a new floor. It appears that some of the iron scrap was sold to the German armaments giant Krupp, and thus some part of the Palace may have returned to Britain in the form of bombs.[7]

Buckland continued to lobby for a proper use of the site, bearing in mind the terms of the 1854 Charter and the needs of modern London: 'One of the principal objects is to do everything in our power to encourage sport, physical training, good music and the higher arts and social activities.' In 1946, with the encouragement of Lord Keynes, an architectural competition was launched, but Keynes died before it could be judged or presented to the Cabinet. In January 1948 Buckland was advocating a half-mile-long Imperial Shop Window for the Great Exhibition of 1951, to promote the 'miracle of the British nature and character'. Loyal to the last, he spoke in his retirement speech to the Trustees of 'the project which had formed in my mind and my ambition, that of a new Crystal

Destruction of Brunel's North Tower by dynamite, 1942.

Palace set upon Sydenham Hill, more splendid than its predecessor and in every way more suited to modern requirements and to the modern spirit'.[8]

In 1950 fire destroyed the School of Art and the last remaining original Crystal Palace units still in the south wing. Winston Churchill visited the site and said to the press it was 'the end of an era'.[9] The Trustees were abolished in 1951 under the Crystal Palace Act that gave the Park to the London County Council from 1 January 1952; the Act stipulated again that any redevelopment of the top site must be 'for education and recreation for the promotion of industry, commerce and art'. The Trustees paid out £75,600 to the nine local councils that had advanced funds in 1914.[10] A decision of the Home Secretary, Herbert Morrison, determined that the 1951 Festival

of Britain would be held on the South Bank of the Thames near Waterloo and not in Sydenham, but after the Festival closed it was proposed at a meeting of the London County Council that the Dome of Discovery, the Skylon and the Land of Britain Pavilion be moved to the Crystal Palace grounds.[11] On the other hand, Lord Ammon expressed the hope in a speech at a Guildhall lunch that Sydenham would not become 'a dumping ground for white elephants from the South Bank exhibition'. It was noted that all that happened in 1951 on the Palace site was the opening of a new caravan park.

The scheme for a National Youth and Sports Centre of 1955 designed by Leslie Martin, Chief Architect to the L.C.C., was only part of the original £10 million scheme, which was to provide 705,000 square feet of exhibition

January 1952.

space, with a huge covered amphitheatre, for boxing, horse riding, circuses and band concerts. There would have been a multi-storey garage on the site of the former High Level Station for 5,000 cars, and another on the site of the North Tower reservoir for 2,000 cars. Sir Gerald Barry, director-general of the Festival, said that Britain should have exhibition buildings at least as good as those in Germany and elsewhere.[12] The National Recreation Centre – 'recreation' being limited to sport – was not opened until mid-1964.

In the late 1950s the B.B.C. erected a great aerial on the site of the North Transept, to be answered by the Independent Television aerial further away from the site on South Norwood hill. The railway branch line to Nunhead was closed in 1954 and the splendid High Level Station demolished soon after. In 1961 a Concert Bowl was built, and the pop group 'Santana' played there to 15,000 fans in 1977. The International Construction Equipment Exhibition of 1961, with a forest of enormous cranes on the top site, created strange images.[13] In 1979 the Crystal Palace Foundation was formed to promote an interest in the Palace's history, following the exhibition of May 1962 and others by the Norwood Society. In 1986 the Crystal Palace Museum Trust, a new registered charity and limited company, was formed which looks after an excellent small collection in the museum on Sydenham Hill.

In a further transfer of ownership in 1986 the Palace site and Park passed to the Borough Council of Bromley, a few miles away. A ruling of 1990 insisted that any building on the site should reflect the original style. In October 1995 *The Independent*, under the heading 'The Crystal Palace may rise from Ashes', reported that among plans submitted for a Millennium building was one to rebuild the Palace in its original form at a cost of £50 million.[14] The government's controversial decision to build a Millennium Dome beside the Thames near Greenwich ensured that, for the foreseeable future and perhaps for ever, the Crystal Palace would live on only as a potent dream.

REFERENCES

For abbreviations of books and periodicals, see Bibliography, p. 223.

CHAPTER 1

1. T, II, pp. 239–42.
2. B, XIX, 21 Dec 1861, p. 869.
3. E, I, 8, 21 Dec 1850, p. 125.
4. Auerbach, p. 139.
5. E, II, 52, 25 Oct 1851, p. 418.
6. ER, XCIV, 192, Oct 1851, p. 559.
7. Whewell. L, I, p. 4.
8. Albert, pp. 111–14; T, I, 13, p. 186.
9. Q, January 1862, p. 180.
10. AJIC, p. ix.
11. 1851, I, p. 1.
12. E, II, 28, 10 May 1851, p. 27.
13. Auerbach, p. 106.
14. T, II, p. 43.
15. L, II, p. 197.
16. *Ibid.*, p. 202; cf. John Wilson: 'Teaching the Laws of Nature as well as the Literature of Man and that the Literature of the Present be admitted to equal claims with the lore of the mythic Past.' L, II, p. 40.
17. P. vii.
18. T, II, p. 97.
19. L, I, p. 34.
20. *Ibid.*, p. 12.
21. I, p. iii.
22. See H. Hobhouse, passim.
23. L, I, p. 16.
24. E, I, 15, 8 Feb 1851, p. 227.
25. T, I, pp. 57–8.
26. L, I, p. 131.
27. 'The Preservation of the Crystal Palace', RC, II.
28. SCPE, p. iii.
29. 2 November 1850. *Punch* took credit for this name; Bonython and Burton, p. 139, say it is found earlier in the *ILN*.
30. P. 56. In 1844 Victoria gave Albert for his birthday Daniel Maclise's painting *Undine*.
31. E, I, 4, 23 November 1850, p. 62.
32. T, I, p. 8.
33. AJIC, p. xvii.
34. T, I, p. 19.
35. AJIC, p. xiv.
36. Downes and Cowper, p. 1.
37. Paxton, speech to Society of Arts, 9 Nov 1850. E, I, 4, 23 Nov 1850, p. 60.
38. 9 June 1865.
39. 1873, pp. 554–6.
40. Berlyn and Fowler, p. 90.
41. Cowper and Downes, p. ii; *Archt. Quarterly Review*, 1851, p. 26.
42. P, XX, 1851, p. 171.
43. T, III, p. 100.
44. 'The Paxton Architecture', E, I, 2, 9 Nov 1850, p. 18.
45. T, III, p. 100.
46. Ruskin, XII, p. 419.
47. P. 26. ILN, XXVI, 28 April 1855, p. 652, refers to the iron and glass used in the Oxford Museum as 'railway materials'.
48. Ruskin, XVI, p. 349; cf. *The Stones of Venice*, 2nd edn, 1858, pp. 379–81: the Palace was clever, but lacked humanity and was therefore not architecture.
49. XII, 1851, p. 269.
50. Downes and Cowper, p. 2.
51. Watkin, 1974, p. 173.
52. T, III, p. 97.
53. Undated press cutting. RC, I.
54. Cowper and Downes, p. ii.
55. B, XXIII, 24 June 1865, p. 443.
56. AJ, 1 Sept 1853, p. 209 (n.).
57. L, I, pp. 151–2.
58. 1873, p. 556.
59. Bird, p. 87; ILN, 7 Dec 1850, p. 432.
60. E, II, 42, 16 August 1851, pp. 254–5.
61. B, IX, 415, 18 Jan 1851, p. 39.
62. E.M. Barry, p. 84.
63. J. Gage (ed.), *Collected Correspondence of J.M.W. Turner*, Oxford: Clarendon Press, 1980, p. 227.
64. *Archt. Quarterly Review*, 1851, p. 26.
65. E.M. Barry, p. 82.
66. *Ibid.*, p. 96.
67. See n. 66.
68. *Trans. R.I.B.A.*, 1859–60, p. 14. The press of the day seemed to accept this version of events; see untitled cutting, n.d., RC II (in sequence *c.* July 23 1852).
69. AJIC, p. xix; 1851, I, p. 67.
70. *Illus. Exhibitor*, p. 97.
71. P. xvii.
72. External view with dome, B, XVIII, 11 Feb 1860, p. 89; internal view, 'Volunteer's Ball', ILN, XXXVI, 17 Mar 1860, p. 257. E.M. Barry used an iron and glass barrel-vault design again in 1853 in his (rejected) design for the University Museum at Oxford; illus., H. Colvin, *Unbuilt Oxford*, 1983, p. 127.
73. Lees-Milne, p. 113.
74. 'A Peep Roundabout', CEJ, n.s., 517, 26 Nov 1854, unpag.
75. E, I, 2, 22 March 1851, p. 330.
76. Illus. of interior, Chadwick, p. 136.
77. ILN, XXV, 22 July 1854, p. 98; John E. Findling, 'America at the Great Exhibition' in Bosbach and Davis, pp. 202–4.
78. Illus., *The Victorian*, 7, July 2001, p. 7.
79. V & A, Print Room, E 10 1937.
80. 1873, p. 558.
81. Jones proposed simply a Crystal Palace vault, a vast semi-cylindrical cloche or hanger. See Carol Flores, *Elvehjem Museum of Art Bulletin*, 1999–2001, pp. 17–26; for Muswell Hill, ibid., pp. 22–4.
82. E, II, 35, 4 Jan 1851, p. 151.
83. I suspect that this was on Platform One. *Survey of London,* XXXVIII, p. 77.
84. E, I, 4, 23 Nov 1850, p. 62.
85. At Rothschild insistence. Watkin, 1986, p. 408.
86. Barker and Hyde, pp. 138–9.
87. *Proc. R.I.B.A.*, 1864–5, p. 2.
88. For the building, see Chadwick, pp. 104–36.
89. *Daily Express*, 2 December 1936.
90. LXXXI, January 1937, pp. 65–72.
91. Richards, p. 58.
92. Hitchcock, p. 12.
93. T, I, p. 101.
94. See n. 90; AJIC, p. xxiii.
95. See n. 63.
96. G.F. Chadwick, *Architectural History*, 84, 1961, p. 90.
97. T, II, p. 44.
98. 'The vegetable world as contributing to the Great Exhibition', AJIC, pp. ii–vi
99. E, II, 32, 7 June 1851, p. 99; 1851, II, p. 851.
100. T, II, p. 192.
101. T, I, p. 44.
102. T, III, p. 22.
103. 1851, IV, p. 735.
104. T, I, p. 44.
105. I, p. 114.
106. T, II, pp. 158–9.
107. 1851, I, p. 15.
108. 1851, II, p. 836.
109. T, I, p. 202; III, pp. 77–9.
110. Berlyn and Fowler, p. 91; 1851, I, p. 52.
111. L, II, pp. 271–4 (Jones on Field; a diagram of colours layered on cornice mouldings). See also O. Jones, 'On the Decorations

Proposed…', pp. 11–13, *Lectures.*

112. *Ibid.*, p. 14.

113. I, 14, 1 Feb 1851, p. 211.

114. E, I, 7, 14 Dec 1850, p. 111.

115. V & A, Print Room. 546, 1897.

116. 'On the Decorations Proposed…', *Lectures,* p. 6. See Brino, pp. 81–130.

117. Berlyn and Fowler, pp. 83–6. Field said that blue corresponded to middle C.

118. 'On the Decorations Proposed…', *Lectures,* p. 14.

119. *Ibid.*, p. 3.

120. 'An Attempt to Define the Principles…', *Lectures*, p. 37; *Annual Register,* Chronicle, 1851, p. 488.

121. ER, CXCII, Oct 1851, p. 578.

122. 27 April 1874.

123. RIBA Ms. SP/10/38, p. 16; *Lectures*, 1863, p. 14.

124. IX, 414, 11 Jan 1851, p. 18.

125. I, 12, 18 Jan 1851, p. 184.

126. I, 13, 25 Jan 1851, p. 195.

127. *Ibid.*, I, 21, 22 March 1851, p. 323.

128. *Ibid.*, I, 14, 1 Feb 1851, p. 211.

129. *Ibid.*, I, 16, 15 Feb 1851, p. 243.

130. 'History of the Great Exhibition', AJIC, p. xv.

131. E, I 18, 1 March 1851, p. 282.

132. E, I, 27, 10 May 1851, p. 30.

133. XXI, 1851, p. 161.

134. *Designs for Mosaic Pavements*, 1842; *Plans, Elevations, Sections and Details of the Alhambra*, 2 vols, 1842–5.

135. 1851, IV, *Reports of the Juries*, pp. 688, 696.

136. E, II, 28, 10 May 1851, p. 35.

137. E, II, 33, 14 June 1851, p. 114.

138. *Illus. Exhib*, 1, 7 June 1851, p. 12.

139. 'On the Decorations Proposed…', *Lectures*, p. 5.

140. 'An Attempt to Define…', *Lectures*, p. 24.

141. I, 13, 25 Jan 1851, p. 184.

142. AJIC, p. xxiv.

143. T, III, p. 54.

144. Bird, p. 82; E, I, 19, 8 March 1851, p. 303.

145. 'Pugin in his home', *Architectural History*, 31, 1988, p. 187.

146. T, I, p. 227.

147. AJIC, p. 317.

148. P. 191.

149. L, II, p. 291.

150. See L, II, p. 392.

151. L, II, p. 243.

152. 'An Essay on Ornamental Art as displayed in the Industrial Exhibition in Hyde Park', AJIC, p. v.

153. An (unnamed) 'acute and learned contemporary', *ibid.*, p. vi.

154. 1851, IV, pp. 716–19.

155. AJIC, p. ii.

156. Jerrold, p. 25.

157. Quoted, L, II, pp. 247–8.

158. L, II, p. 233.

159. 1851, IV, pp. 709–10.

160. T, I, p. 139.

161. 1851, IV, pp. 721–3.

162. T, III, p. 53.

163. Letter to Hardman, 1851. P. Stanton, 'Welby Pugin and the Gothic Revival', Ph.D. thesis, University of London, 1950, pp. 464–5.

164. R. Hill, *The Victorian*, March 2002, p. 9.

165. E.g. T, I, p. 101.

166. AJIC, p. 157.

167. T, I, p. 115.

168. *Expo*, I, 5, 30 Nov 1850, pp. 66–7.

169. AJIC, p. 51.

170. T, III, p. 52.

171. *Ibid.*, II, p. 46.

172. E, II, 51, 18 Oct 1851, p. 403.

173. *Ibid.*, I, 2, 9 Nov 1850, p. 28.

174. T, I, p. 196.

175. E, I, 7, 14 Dec 1850, p. 103.

176. T, I, p. 107.

177. AJIC, p. v.

178. *Ibid.*, p. 7.

179. 'On the Leading Principles…', p. 22; *Lectures; Grammar of Ornament*, 1856, p. 77.

180. L, I, p. 508.

181. T, III, p. 63.

182. L, I, p. 160; *cf.* II, p. 142.

183. Tallis, I, p. 185.

184. AJIC, p. iii.

185. *Ibid.*, p. 118.

186. *Ibid.*, p. 85.

187. *Ibid.*, p. 189.

188. *Ibid.*, pp. 129, 298; T, I, p. 81.

189. AJIC, p. 27.

190. *Ibid.*, p. 80; T, I, p. 87.

191. AJIC, p. 193.

192. *Ibid.*, p. 29.

193. T, II, p. 205.

194. AJIC, p. 20.

195. *Ibid.*, p. 28.

196. L, II, pp. 229–30.

197. T, II, p. 202.

198. AJIC, p. vi.

199. 1851, IV, pp. 708–16; see 'British Contributions', C. Hobhouse, pp. 70–116.

200. AJIC, pp. xi–xxi.

201. *Ibid.*, p. 227.

202. E, II, 29, 17 May 1851, p. 54.

203. AJIC, p. ii.

204. T, II, p. 85.

205. T, I, p. 134; L, I, p. 375.

206. T, II, p. 73.

207. *Ibid.*, p. 79.

208. L, I, p. 294.

209. T, I, p. 108; L, I, p. 569.

210. AJIC, p. 5.

211. E, II, 32, 7 June 1851, p. 99.

212. U. Haltern, 'Die Welt als Schaustellung', *Vierteljahrschrift für Sozial- und Wirtschafts-geschichte*, 60, 1973, p. 281.

213. *Illus. Exhib.*, p. 13.

214. T, II, pp. 62, 147; III, pp. 40, pp. 75–6.

215. Quoted L. Kriegel, in Purbrick, p. 167.

216. ER, XCIV, Oct 1851, p. 192.

217. P, XX, 1851, p. 171.

218. T, I, pp. 122, 125.

219. T, I, p. 87.

220. 1 Sept 1853, p. 210.

221. AJIC, p. 325.

222. *Illus. Exhib.*, 2, 14 June 1851, p. 33.

223. T, II, p. 32.

224. AJIC, p. 37.

225. Quoted E, II, 41, 9 Aug 1851, p. 237.

226. *Op. cit.*, I, p. 39.

227. E, II, 28, 10 May 1851, p. 35.

228. 'United States', *Dickinson's Comprehensive Pictures of the Great Exhibition of* 1851, 1854, n.p.

229. Millais, I, p. 126.

230. T, I, p. 126.

231. XX, 1851, 'America in Crystal', p. 209; *ibid.*, p. 231.

232. L, II, pp. 127–9.

233. L. Kriegel in Purbrick, pp. 154, 174 (n. 26).

234. Boase, p. 267.

235. T, III, p. 8.

236. P, XX, 1851, p. 252; T, I, pp. 101–2.

237. T, I, 255–6.

238. E, II, 50, 11 Oct 1851, p. 386.

239. *Ibid.*, II, 36, 5 July 1851, p. 163.

240. *Ibid.*, I, 1, 21 Nov 1850, p. 8.

241. See n. 239.

242. *Ibid.*, II, 45, 6 Sept 1851, p. 311; P. Gurney in Purbrick, pp. 119–20.

243. T, III, p. 55.

244. T, III, p. 90.

245. E, II, 52, 25 Oct 1851, p. 425.

246. L, II, p. 300.

CHAPTER 2

1. CPH, IX, 12, August 1854, p. 30.

2. E, I, 21, 22 March 1851, p. 330.

3. Quoted, E, II, 39, 26 July 1851, p. 211.

4. T, 17 April 1852.

5. Paxton, p. 8.

6. RC, I.

7. J.C. Sparkes, *Schools of Art*, 1884, p. 61.

8. SLS, II, 'Birmingham Court', p. 13.

9. Paxton, pp. 4-14; E, II, 43, 23 Aug 1851, p. 277.

10. B, X, 1 May 1852, pp. 280-1.

11. *Observer*, 4 April 1852.

12. Desmond, p. 193.

13. *Observer*, 4 April 1852.

14. (Chromolithograph). Guildhall Library, La Pr B; PAR.

15. H. Hobhouse, p. 78.

16. Ts, I, p. 6.

17. 1851 Royal Commission Archives, VII, 28.

18. Haden, p. vii.

19. E, II, 40, 22 August 1851, p. 226.

20. RC, I, 'The Crystal Palace. Report of a meeting at Mr Oliviera's' (29 March 1852), p. 11; see report of further meeting with Paxton in chair.

21. RC, I, n.d., *c*. March 1852.

22. Royal Archive, Windsor, F 225.

23. Bird, p. 121.

24. Royal Archive, Windsor, F. 25/89, p. 3.

25. Letter to T, 15 July 1851.

26. RC, I, report of meeting.

27. Chadwick, p. 144.

28. RC, I, 'The Crystal Palace', n.d., p. 2.

29. Ts, III, p. 100.

30. 18 April 1854.

31. SLS, II, Meeting of 28 Feb 1854, p. 16.

32. *Survey of London*, XXXVIII, p. 50.

33. Small, pp. 3, 4, 9.

34. *ILN*, XXIV, 4 March 1854, p. 193; DNB.

35. 'The Crystal Palace in Adversity', 1876, p. 4.

36. CPH, I, 2, Dec 1852, p. 17.

37. CPH, III, 8, Aug 1856, p. 172.

38. Phillips, p. 2.

39. RC, I.

40. Bird, p. 125.

41. T, 23 June 1852.

42. CPE, p. 6.

43. CPH, I, 2, Nov 1853, p. 19.

44. ICPG, 10, June 9 1854, p. 113.

45. 14 May 1852.

46. RC, I.

47. *Annual Register*, 1854, (Chronicle), p. 97.

48. *ILN*, XX, 5 June 1852, p. 440.

49. CPH, I, 2, Nov 1853, p. 1; T, 8 May 1854: 'only one small ivy-covered corner remains'; transformation of Park 'startling'.

50. CPH, II, 4, April 1855, p. 42.

51. SLS, I, C.P.Co. Report, March 17 1853.

52. CEJ, XX, 516, 19 Nov 1853, Pl. p. 343-4.

53. C.P.Co. report, 8 Feb 1855. C.P.Co. Bill in Parlt., III, 1, Jan 1856, p. 112, SLS, II.

Pamphlet by SLS, p. 5: 'Unless C.P.Co. lays out £33,000 in buildings by Lady Day 1858, Mr W. will pocket £15,000 due to him from the Co., SLS II.'

54. *Observer*, 3 June 1855.

55. Lees-Milne, p. 204.

56. CPH, III, 1, January 1856, p. 114.

57. T, 7 Dec 1855; T, 15 Jan 1856.

58. Lees-Milne, p. 206.

59. CPH, II, 13, Nov 1854, p. 76

60. CPH, III, 5, May 1855, pp. 40, 51.

61. Sale handbill and map, Bromley. Samuel Laing died at Rockhills. Crystal Palace Club members could stay there in 1900.

62. ICPG, I, 3, Dec 1853, p. 27; CPH, I, 2, Dec 1852, p. 15.

63. 1 Dec 1835. *Lectures*, pp. 6, 15.

64. SLS, II.

65. XX, 516, 19 Nov 1853, p. 321.

66. Ts, I, p. 256.

67. C.P.Co. Report, 17 Mar 1853, p. 9. SLS, I.

68. RC, I. Meeting, Paxton in chair.

69. CEJ, XX, 516, 19 Nov 1853, p. 323.

70. *Views*, p. 18.

71. 8 May 1854.

72. CPH, I, 8, June 1854, p. 6.

73. *Annual Register*, 1851 (Chronicle), p. 497.

74. *Annual Register*, 1851 (Chronicle), p. 449.

75. *Athenaeum*, 1289, 10 July 1852, p. 751.

76. Ts, III, p. 105.

77. CPH, I, 8, June 1854, p. 6; I, 4, Feb 1854, p. 33.

78. *ILN*, XXXIII, 6 Nov 1858, p. 440. Desachy made the bas-relief and angels in the auditorium at Covent Garden Theatre, 1857-8.

79. Phillips, p. 12.

80. Grove, p. 17.

81. Colquhoun, p. 203.

82. XXIII, 24 January 1865, p. 444.

83. XXVII, 19 July 1874, p. 57.

84. *The Record*, 19 August 1853.

85. 1289, 10 July 1852, p. 751. *A Glossary of Architecture*, London: Tilt, 1838, p. 41: 'Dome' in Italian architecture may refer to a 'lofty semi-circular roof', but in French and English is restricted to a synonym for 'cupola'.

86. Alfred Barry, p. 285; (illus., p. 284). Barry died from a paralytic fit after an afternoon at the Palace and Park, *ILN*, XXXVI, 2 June, 1860, p. 516.

87. 1873, p. 556-7.

88. T, 21 Nov 1874.

89. *ILN*, XXI, 6 Nov 1852, p. 368.

90. RC II, Prospectus; letter to *Times*, n.d., SLS, II; *Athenaeum*, 1290, 17 July 1852, p. 775.

91. XXIV, 15 April 1854, p. 346.

92. Phillips, p. 12.

93. ICPG, I, 3, Dec 1853, p. 27.

94. ICPG, I, 2, Nov 1853, p. 19.

95. T, 8 May 1854.

96. P. 15.

97. Digby Wyatt, 1851, I, p. 52.

98. Bird, p. 128.

99. P. 12.

100. George L. Purchase, *Letter to the Shareholders*, 7 Dec 1855, SLS I.

101. XIX, 21 Dec 1861, p. 387.

102. Bird, p. 128.

103. *Observer*, 15 July 1855.

104. XXXV, p. 47.

105. Illus., *ILN*, XXXVIII, 2 Mar 1861, p. 194.

106. XI, 15 Jan 1853, p. 33.

107. E, I, 4, 23 Nov 1850, pp. 59, 77.

108. Charles Welch, *History of the Tower Bridge*, London: Smith, Elder, 1894, p. 216.

109. Robert Thorne, 'The Removal of the Crystal Palace to Sydenham', unpub. lecture, Iron and Glass Conference, I.C.E., London, 17 Oct 2001.

110. RC, II, Report pamphlet, 2 July 1853.

111. B, XI, 555, 20 Aug 1853, p. 603.

112. *ILN*, XXIII, 20 Aug 1853, p. 138; 30 Aug 1853, p. 143.

113. CPH, Oct 1853, p. 57.

114. B, XXIII, 24 June 1865, p. 444. Grove wrote to Sotheby that two injured men were employed in the Refreshment Department.

115. *ILN*, XXIV, 15 April 1854, p. 346.

116. Report to the Co., 2 July 1853. SLS I.

117. CPH, I, 1, Nov 1853, p. 2; CEJ, XX, 516, 19 Nov 1853, p. 322.

118. CPH, I, 5, March 1854, pp. 41-2.

119. *Guide to the Ten Chief Courts*, p. 230.

120. *The Crystal Palace*, Nelson, *c*. 1862, p.21.

121. ICPG, I, 6, March 1854, p. 68. £1 in 1854 is equivalent to £42.67 in August 2003.

122. Fuller, 1874, p. 12.

123. Phillips, p. 8.

124. Digby Wyatt, 1851, I, p.87.

125. ICPG, I, 3, Dec 1853, p. 30.

126. CEJ, XX, 516, 19 Nov 1853, p. 322; ICPG, I, 5, Feb 1854, p. 50.

127. CPH, I, 2, Dec 1853, p. 19.

128. CEJ, XX, 517, 26 Nov 1853, p. 344.

129. ICPG, I, 4, Jan 1854, p. 40.

130. ICPG, I, 1, Oct 1853, p. 3.

131. *Crystal Palace District*, p. 2

132. CPH, II, 11, Nov 1855, p. 100.

133. *The Panmure Papers*, I, pp. 428 and *passim*.

134. P. 134.

135. *Ibid.*, p. 155.

136. *Ibid.*, p. vii.
137. XX, 516, 19 November 1853, p. 322.
138. La VI/NOR cry.
139. CPH, I, 6, April 1854, p. 50.
140. CPH, II, 4, April 1854, p. 38.
141. *Observer*, 15 July 1855.
142. XX, 516, 19 Nov 1853, p. 324.
143. p. 2.
144. *Letter*, 1855, p. 20.
145. SLS to Rawlinson, a.l.s. of 4 Feb 1856, SLS II.
146. ICPG, I, 2, 17 June, p. 135.
147. Phillips, P. 136.
148. Cole diary, 23 January 1854, NAL.
149. *Observer*, 12 Aug 1855.
150. Report of 8 Feb 1855, p. 3.
151. A.l.s. of 2 Dec 1854, p. 3, SLS II.
152. *Letter*, p. 29 (n).
153. C.P.Co. Report, Dec 1859; marked on map in Hollingshead, 1867.
154. B, XVII, 12, Feb 1859, p. 114.
155. 'On the Decorations…', p. 14, *Lectures*.
156. 'An Attempt to define…', p. 18, *Lectures*.
157. Quoted ICPG, I, 2, Nov 1853, p. 19; CEJ, XX, 516, 19 Nov 1853, p. 322.
158. XII, 592, 10 June 1854, p. 297.
159. CPH, I, 14, Oct 1854, p. 57.
160. *Annual Register*, (Chronicle), 1854, p. 97.
161. I, 9, 27 May 1854, p. 109.
162. T, 8 May 1854.
163. CPH, I, 11, July 1854, p. 20.
164. *Observer*, 31 Dec 1854.
165. 'Cant in Crystal', XXVIII, 1855, p. 7.
166. T, 8 June 1853.
167. *ILN*, XXIII, 5 Nov 1853, p. 383.
168. 2 Nov 1853.
169. *Letters*, VII, p. 360.
170. Martin, II, p. 366.
171. CPH, II, 9, July 1854, pp. 16, 23.
172. Redgrave, p. 111.
173. *ILN*, XXIV, 17 June 1854, p. 581.
174. Cole Diary, 10 June 1854; 2 June 1854. NAL.
175. CPH, II, 9, July 1854, p. 18.
176. 11 June 1854.
177. *Letters*, VII, p. 453.
178. S. Laing at Inauguration, ICPG, I, 11, 17 June 1854, p. 132.
179. CPE, p. 3; T, 8 May 1854; CEJ, XX, 516, 19 Nov 1853; AJ, n.s., V, 1 March, 1853.
180. Cutting, SLS II, n.d.
181. ICPG, I, 9, 27 May 1854, p. 110.
182. CPE, p. 2.
183. XII, 10 June 1854, p. 297.
184. Phillips, p. 12.
185. *Spectator*, 1854. Rossetti, p. 52.
186. *Guide to the Ten Chief Courts*, p. 208.

187. XII, p. 418.
188. VI, 1 August 1854, p. 233.
189. 'The Crystal Palace', for private circulation, n.d., p. 2, RC, I.
190. VI, 1 Oct 1854, p. 314.
191. *ILN*, XXIV, 24 June 1854, p. 600.
192. 25 July 1908.
193. P, XXVIII, (Almanack, 1855), n.p.
194. II, 10, August 1854, p. 33.
195. CPH, II, 2, March 1855, p. 27.
196. T, 25 Dec 1855.
197. T, 1 Sept 1855.
198. See n. 195.
199. C.P.Co. programme, 24 August 1881.
200. C.P.Co. programme, 24 March 1881.
201. T, 11 July 1902; 18 Sept 1902.
202. CPE, pp. 3-4.
203. C.P.Co. leaflet, 17 March 1853, SLS I.
204. 'Exhibitors' Department', SLS ms., Nov 1855, SLS I.
205. *Observer*, 13 May 1855.
206. *Notes and Queries*, 2nd series, 17, 26 April 1856, n.p.
207. *Observer*, 15 July 1855.
208. *Letter*, p. 1.
209. C.P.Co., Report, Dec 1862, p. 5.
210. CPH, I, 8, June 1854, p. 1.
211. Pp. 3, 13-15.
212. ICPG, I, 14, August 1854, pp. 182, 186.
213. Guildhall Library, B VI Nor/Cro 7 1858.
214. *Morning Herald*, 19 August 1855; leaflet, 1853, p. 13, SLS I.
215. SLS, II.
216. E.g. 'The Gin Palace and the Crystal Palace on a Sunday', P, XXIII, 3 July 1852, p. 11.
217. Guildhall Library.
218. 18 August 1852.
219. 11 Feb 1856.
220. 'Lord Stanley's Speech…', pamphlet, RC, I.
221. Nov 1853, SLS, I.
222. N.d., RC, I.
223. 18 April 1854, SLS, I.
224. T, 21 and 22 Feb 1856.
225. P. Gurney, in Purbrick (ed.), p. 124.
226. P. 17.
227. CPH, II, 4, April 1855, pp. 42-4.
228. I, 13, 25 March 1854, p. 238.
229. XXVIII, (Almanack) 1855, n.p.
230. SLS, *Letter*, 1855, p. 9.
231. CPH, II, 11, Sept 1854, p. 40.
232. CPH, II, 9, July 1854, p. 20; for daily consumption, see ICPG, II, 1, Sep 1854, p. 197.
233. ICPG, II, 12, 24 June 1854, p. 147.
234. T, 1 Sept 1855.
235. CPH, II, 2, Feb 1855, p. 14.

236. VI, 1 Sept 1854, p. 281.
237. *A Few Words…*, 1855, pp. 8-9.
238. Sotheby, 1856, p. 11.
239. Sotheby, 1855, p. 8.
240. *Daily Telegraph*, 29 April 1910.
241. *Memories of Dulwich College*, London: Dulwich College, 1919, p. 48.
242. CPH, II, 2, Feb 1855, p. 14.
243. 3 June 1855.
244. T, 11 Sept 1856.
245. XXVI, 9 June 1855, p. 548.
246. SLS, II.
247. Phillips, p. 9.
248. CPH, II, 5, May 1855, pp. 50-52.
249. Martin, III, pp. 252-3.
250. *ILN*, XXIV, 22 April 1854, p. 375.
251. CG, 14, 1 May 1855, p. 66.
252. CPH, II, 10, August 1854, p. 28.
253. Meeting of 28 Feb 1854, p. 15, leaflet, SLS, I.
254. ICPG, I, 14, August 1854, p. 183.
255. *ILN*, XXV, 30 Dec 1854, p. 650.
256. CPH, II, 11, Sept 1855, p. 81; T, 25 Dec 1855; *Observer*, 13 May 1855.
257. III, 1 Sept 1857, pp. 293-4.
258. XIV, 17 May 1856; T, 10 May 1856.
259. 9 May 1856. Quoted on mount of watercolour of the occasion by John Tenniel, Royal Library, Windsor, RL 16788.
260. T, 10 May 1856.
261. CPH, III, 6, June 1856, p. 154.
262. C.P.Co., 3rd Ordinary Meeting, 9 August 1855, SLS, I.
263. S. Laing at meeting of 8 Feb 1855. *Morning Post*, 9 Feb 1855.
264. *Crystal Palace District*, p. 4
265. Ts, III, p. 102.
266. C.P.Co. to shareholders, 15 March 1853, p. 15, SL. I.
267. 9 Feb 1855, SLS, I.
268. Gibbs, p. 11.
269. *ILN*, XXI, 23 Aug 1852, p. 147.
270. 1856, p. 8.
271. III, 4, April 1856, p. 135.
272. T, 21 Nov 1874.
273. Shareholders' pamphlet, 4 July 1854, SLS; draft letter to Paxton against 'profuse expenditure', *c.* May 1855, SLS, II.
274. ICPG, I, 14, 1854, p. 183.
275. CPH, II, 11, Sept 1855, p. 85.
276. T, 21 Nov 1874; for a list of shareholders see *Crystal Palace Company: Deed of Settlement…*, 1856.
277. 'Francis Fuller's Plan…', SLS, I; CPH, II, 5, May 1855, p. 50.
278. T, 8 Jan 1856.

279. 'The Shorthand Writer', p. 25.
280. T, 21 Nov 1874.
281. XIV, Nov 1856, p. 130.
282. 15 Dec 1855; I Feb 1856; T, 27 Dec 1855.
283. Report of Directors to Shareholders, 23 June 1856, p. 1, ALS, II.
284. C.P.Co. Report, 1858, p. 3.
285. *Daily Telegraph*, 29 April 1910.
286. T, 21 Nov 1874.
287. Fuller, 1876, p. 33.
288. Fuller, 1875, p. 13.
289. T, 21 Nov 1874.
290. CPH, III, 1, Jan 1856, p. 115; P.G. Wodehouse, *The Swoop*, London: Alston Rivers, 1909, p. 29.
291. *Observer*, 15 July 1855.
292. Peter Cunningham to SLS, a.l.s, 4 Jan 1855, SLS, I; 'A Few Observations to the Shareholders, made by proxy on the part of SLS', p.5, SLS, I.
293. A.l.s. to SLS, signature illeg., 28 Jan 1855, SLS I.
294. C.P. Co., Report, SLS, I.
295. Shareholders' Meeting, 20 July 1854, CPH, II, 10, August 1854, p. 26; ICPG, 14, August 1854, p. 184.
296. C.P.Co. pamphlet, 1 Feb 1856, SLS, II.
297. Redgrave, p. 148.
298. Handbill, signed George Grove, 20 Sept 1856, SLS II.
299. *Annual Register*, December 1856, p. 760.
300. 6 and 8 January 1855. NAL. Redgrave, p. 120.
301. CPH, II, 11, November 1855, p. 97
302. CPH, II, 2, Feb 1855, p. 14.
303. CPH, II, 3, p. 129.
304. Leading article, n.d. (c. Feb 1856), SLS, II.
305. *ILN*, XXIX, 5 July 1856, p. 11; CPH, III, 7, July 1856, p. 160; DNB.
306. *ILN*, XXXIV, 12 Feb 1859, pp. 148, 168; XXXVI, 17 March 1860, p. 257; XXXVI, 31 March 1860, pp. 304-5.
307. Fuller, 1874, p. 14.
308. Fuller, 1875, p. 6; *Crystal Palace: Evidence before the Court of Enquiry*, p. 8; T, 12 Nov 1874; T, 3 Nov 1879.

CHAPTER 3
1. 'Les Beaux Arts en Angleterre', *Revue des Deux Mondes*, 15 Oct 1857, p. 874.
2. *Routledge's Guide*, p. 50.
3. 'Living reproductions', n.d., SLS, II; 'restoration of Palace Courts of Nineveh', C.P. Co., August 1853, SLS, I.
4. CPE, p. 143.
5. III, 1 March 1857, p. 95.
6. XXIV, 1855, prelims, n.p.
7. Phillips, p. viii.
8. *Letters*, VI, p. 252 and n.
9. *Letters*, VII, p. 370.
10. *ILN*, XXV, 21 Oct 1854, p. 391.
11. Waring, p. 212.
12. *ILN*, XXIV, 4 March 1854, p. 207. Wilkinson's 'companion' to 'the Egyptian Collections', *The Egyptians*, a study of 'everyday life', was published by the Crystal Palace Company in 1857.
13. P. 7.
14. *The Alhambra Court*, p. 15.
15. Ts, III, p. 80.
16. *Views*, pp. 8-11.
17. *Description of the Egyptian Court*, pp. 14-15.
18. B, XII, 15 April, p. 194.
19. Rossetti, p. 53.
20. 'On the Influence of Religion', 1835, p. 7, *Lectures*.
21. P. 39.
22. Phillips, p. 52.
23. *Routledge's Guide*, p. 94.
24. CPE, p. 106.
25. *Ibid.*, p. 34; Rossetti, p. 77; *Routledge's Guide*, p. 94.
26. *Private Correspondence*, London: Colburn, 1824, I, p. 193.
27. CPE, p. 6.
28. 'On the Decorations Proposed…', p. 4, *Lectures*.
29. *Guide to the Ten Chief Courts*, p. 25.
30. *Ibid.*, p. 185.
31. 'On the Decorations Proposed…', p. 5, *Lectures*.
32. 4 April 1857, p. 442.
33. III, 1 May 1857, p. 159.
34. *British Art*, p. 187-8.
35. *A Few Words…*, pp. 25, 30.
36. 'On the Decorations Proposed…', p. 5, *Lectures*.
37. VI, 1 August 1854, p. 233.
38. *ILN*, XXIV, 22 April 1854, p. 379.
39. *Guide to the Ten Courts*, p. 116.
40. *ILN*, XVIII, 3 May 1851, p. 364.
41. O.E.D.
42. 'The New Crystal Palace', RC, I; *Athenaeum*, 1289, 10 July 1852, p. 751; London Journal, n.d., RC, II.
43. C.P. Co., 19 Feb 1856, SLS, II.
44. 1496, 28 June 1856, pp. 814-5.
45. CPH, II, 11, Nov 1855, p. 100.
46. *ILN*, XXVI, 12 May 1855, p. 540.
47. *Athenaeum*, 1289, 10 July 1852, p. 751.
48. *Gentleman's Magazine*, XXXVIII, Oct 1852, p. 384; Darby, 1974, p. 337.
49. Phillips, p. 5; B, XI, 15 April 1854, pp. 193-4.
50. Vaughan, p. 21.
51. Devonshire Mss., Chatsworth, Paxton GP.853.
52. CPE, p. 3.
53. *Alhambra Court*, p. 7; Wornum, p. xx; see account of historical development in Palgrave, 1862, pp. 76-81.
54. Wyatt, *The Byzantine Court*, p. 8; CPE, p. 78; B, XII, 8 July 1854, p. 353.
55. CPE, p. 82.
56. XCVI, cxcii, March 1855, p. 340.
57. *Ibid.*, pp. 317, 307, 304.
58. Quoted by Dresser, 'The Writings of Owen Jones, I', *The Architect*, XI, 25 Apr 1874, p. 241.
59. Q, XCVI, cxcii, March 1855, p. 333.
60. Eastlake, I, p. 318-21.
61. *Ibid.*, pp. 324-5.
62. Pp., 153-5.
63. McCarthy, p. 121.
64. Poole, p. 64.
65. B, XII, 23 Sept 1854, p. 498.
66. 'Letter to the Shareholders', 1855, p. 6, SLS, I.
67. 'The Crystal Palace', 1854, SLS, I.
68. B, XXXII, 9 May 1874, pp. 383-4.
69. 'On the Influence of Religion upon Art', p. 4, *Lectures*.
70. See n. 68.
71. See n. 68; Ferry, pp. 176-7.
72. *Alhambra Court*, p. 63.
73. T, 27 April 1874.
74. *Guide to the Ten Chief Courts*, p. 18.
75. *The Leader*, 19 Aug 1854, RC, II.
76. 'On the Influence of Religion upon Art', pp. 18-19, *Lectures* (L, I, p. 538); *Alhambra Court*, p. 14.
77. B, XXXII, 9 May 1874, p. 383; obit., T, 21 April 1874; 'An attempt to define…', p. 16, *Lectures*.
78. B, XI, 20 June 1874, p. 345; 'An attempt to define…', p. 39, *Lectures*.
79. B, XXXII, 9 May 1874, p. 384.
80. III, 2, Aug 1845, p. 367.
81. 'The Necessity of an Art Education', p. 47, *Lectures*.
82. *Journal of Design*, June 1851, p. xx.
83. *Athenaeum*, 25 April 1874, p. 569. B, XXXII, 9 May 1874, pp. 384-5.
84. XXVI, 24 April 1874, p. 440.
85. 'An Attempt to Define…', p. 4, *Lectures*.
86. *Ibid.*, p. 18; 'On the Decorations Proposed…', p. ii, *Lectures*.
87. Poole, et al., p. 84.
88. *Guide to the Egyptian Court*, p. 72.
89. B, XXXII, 16 May 1874, p. 422.
90. 'On the Decorations Proposed…', ms. At

RIBA, p. 10; cf. *ibid.*, p. 9, *Lectures*. 'An Attempt to Define…', p. 15, *Lectures*.

91. *ILN*, XXXIII, 6 Nov 1858, pp. 440, 442; XXXII, 10 April 1858, p. 369.

92. *Guide to the Ten Chief Courts*, pp. 25, 18.

93. ICPG, I, 10, p. 114; CPE, p. 22, *Guide to Egyptian Court*, p. 4.

94. *Weekly News*, 21 May 1853, John Johnson coll.

95. *Letter*, 1855, p. 19 (n); a.l.s. (name illegible) 27 Dec 1854, to SLS, SLS, I.

96. CPE, pp. 14,18.

97. AJ, VI, 1 Sept 1854, p. 258; Q, XCVI, cxcii, March 1855, pp. 311-2; Jones, *Apology*, p. 54.

98. Patrick Conner, 'Wedding Archaeology to Art': Poynter's *Israel in Egypt*, in Macready, Sarah, and F.H. Thompson, *Influences in Victorian Art and Architecture*, London: Society of Antiquaries, 1985, pp. 118-9.

99. *Letter*, 1855, p. 21 (n.); CPE, p. 23.

100. Wyatt, *Views*, p. 19; *ILN*, XXV, 22 July 1854, p. 70; Darby, 1974, p. 339.

101. AJ, VI, 1 Sept 1854, p. 258; Rossetti, p. 58; Q, XCVI, cxcii, March 1855, p. 314.

102. *Letter*, pp. 24 (n) 20, 13.

103. Q, XCVI, cxcii, March 1855, p. 311.

104. A.l.s., SLS, II.

105. CPH, II, 5, May 1855, p. 51; II, 6, June 1855, p. 57.

106. *Alhambra Court*, p. 45; B, XII, 8 July 1854, p. 353.

107. R. Ashton, *George Eliot: A Life*, London: Penguin, 1996, p. 289.

108. *Letter*, p. 25; *Guide to the Ten Chief Courts*, p. 93.

109. *Limbo and other Essays*, London: Grant Richards, 1897, p. 23.

110. III, 1 August 1857, p. 245; Phillips, p. 23; Hollingshead, p. 58.

111. Phillips, p. 38; AJ, 1 March, 1854, p. 80; *Alhambra Court*, p. 83.

112. *Routledge's Guide*, p. 212; *Alhambra Court*, p. 83; CPH, IX, 11, July 1854, p. 1.

113. 'On the influence exercised on Ceramic Manufactures by the late H. Minton', 26 May 1858, London: for private distribution, p. 20; Blashfield, p. 28.

114. *Observer*, 29 July 1855, SLS, Inventory, II, 501, LMA; CG, 19, 2 March 1858, p. 335.

115. 21 April 1874.

116. Rossetti, p. 76.

117. V & A, 323-26. 1880; Darby, 1983, p. 48; see A. Enriqueta Harris, 'La Alhambra en el Museo Victoria & Albert…' *Separata de Cuadernos de Arte e Iconografia*, I, I, Madrid, 1988.

118. *Guide to the Ten Chief Courts*, p. 99.

119. IX, p. 469 (*Stones of Venice*, I, Appendix 22, 2nd edn. 1858, p. 396).

120. Rossetti, p. 188.

121. *Alhambra Court*, pp.18, 36-39, 60-1.

122. B, XII, 26 Sept 1874, p. 159.

123. Rossetti, pp. 77-8; *Alhambra Court*, p. 87.

124. John Cornforth, 'Arabian Nights in the Mall', *Country Life*, 18 May 1989, pp. 246-8.

125. XXIV, 1 Dec 1866, p. 833; XXXII, 9 May 1874, p. 385.

126. A.l.s. to SLS from Henry (surname illeg.), 6 Dec 1855, SLS, I.

127. XII, 24 June 1854.

128. *ILN*, XLIV, 10 June 1854, p. 548.

129. *London: What to see…*, p. 135; see I. Bristow, 'British Museum, Entrance Hall. Report on the colours used in the polychromatic scheme of 1847', 2001, unpub.

130. Scharf, *Greek Court*, p. 93.

131. 2 Nov 1853; T, 27 April 1874.

132. Darby, 1974, p. 64; CPH, I, 8, Jun 1854, p. 3; *ILN*, XXIII, 5 Nov 1853, p. 383; *ILN*, XLIV, 19 June 1854, p. 548; *Blackwoods*, LXXVI, cccclxvii, Sept 1854, p. 334; B, XII, June 24, 1854, p. 331.

133. *Morning Post*, RC, II; Q, XCVI, cxcii, March 1855, p. 313; AJ, 1 Dec 1853, p. 312.

134. Wilkinson, 1858, p. 193; Layard, II, p. 208.

135. Rossetti, pp. 59, 66; AJ, 1 Sept 1854, pp. 318, 323, 326, 329.

136. LXXXVI, Sept 1854, pp. 318, 323, 326, 329.

137. VI, p. 69 (n).

138. *Apology*, pp., ii, 5-7, 11, 31.

139. XII, 24 June 1854, p. 332; *Apology*, p. 22.

140. *Apology*, pp. 55-6.

141. Royal Collection, RL 19991.

142. *Apology*, pp. 19, 33.

143. *Routledge's Guide*, p. 54; CPH, II, 16, Dec 1854, p. 76.

144. I, 15 May 1865, p. 124.

145. *Ivories*, London: Chapman and Hall, 1876, p. 17.

146. Palgrave, 1862, p. 144; B, XXXII, 18 July 1874, p. 600. Jones's drawing in Print Room, V & A, E 1711.

147. Maskell, 1876, p. v.

148. E.g., *Furniture Gazette*, XIII, 3 Jan 1880, p. 8; Dresser, 1873, p. 5.

149. *The Architect*, XI, 25 April 1874, p. 241; *Journal of Society of Arts*, XIX, 10 Feb 1871, p. 217.

150. P. 157.

151. [1853], Redgrave, 1876, pp. 166-7; Ruskin, XVI, p. 264.

152. See Redgrave, 1853; Durant, p. 26.

153. Gottfried Semper, 'Specimens of Metal Work, Catalogue of Ornamental art at Marlborough House', 1853, p. 37 (NAL).

CHAPTER 4

1. T, 24 May 1877; B, XXXV, 2 June 1877, p. 545.

2. Wyatt, *Memoirs*, p. 31; ICPG, I, 13, 1 July 1854, p. 169.

3. Pp. 47-8.

4. L, II, p. 229.

5. XXXV, 2 June 1877, p. 545.

6. P. 12.

7. *Fine Art*, pp. 20, 32-3, 47 (n); 120, 322; L, II, pp. 238, 233.

8. *Letter*, p. 29.

9. *Guide to the Ten Chief Courts*, p. 139; Measom, p. 27.

10. Wyatt, *Views*, p. 14; CPH, I, 3, January 1854, p. 26; RIBA Session Papers, 1853.

11. CPE, p. 98; *Letter*, p. 25; ICPG, I, 6, March 1854, p. 68.

12. I, pp.142-78.

13. I, 31-44; II, 221 seq.

14. ICPG, I, 6, March 1854, p. 66; E, I, 1, 21 Nov 1850, p. 10.

15. (Deysbrook: unlocated). E. Morris, 'Alfred Stevens', *Connoisseur*, 190, 763, Sept 1975, p. 10.

16. Scharf, *Pompeian Court*, p. 72.

17. B, XII, 7 Jan 1854, p. 1.

18. *Guide to the Ten Chief Courts*, p. 42.

19. B, XII, 7 Oct 1854, p, 523; Scharf, *Pompeian Court*, pp.31-2; *The Crystal Palace*, Nelson, p. 26; CPH, V, ii, May 1855, p. 51.

20. *Grammar of Ornament*, pp. 39-40; Jones, *Designs for Mosaic Pavements*, p. 6.

21. *Journal of Society of Arts*, XIX, 951, 10 Feb 1871, p. 220.

22. *Guide to the Ten Chief Courts*, p. 40.

23. B, XII, 7 Jan 1854, p. 1.

24. Pp. 46-7.

25. *CP News*, II, 24 June 1860, p. 202.

26. Scharf, *Pompeian Court*, p. iv; Lytton, III, pp. 309-12.

27. Frankfurt, Deutsches Architektur-Museum, 347-001-001. Semper built a theatre elaborated from this design inside the *Glaspalast* in Munich for King Ludwig in 1864. This drawing (and others for the Munich Theatre) belonged to Wagner 'for several years', and were used in discussions of the Festspielhaus at Bayreuth. Mallgrave, p. 254.

28. 'On the Study of Polychromy and its Revival', *Museum of Classical Antiquities*, III, July 1851, p. 230.

29. ER, CXCIV, 192, Oct 1851, p. 575; Herrmann, p. 209; Mallgrave, p. 192.

30. Wyatt, *Byzantine Court*, p. 5.

31. Print Room, V & A, V.1, Box 85; Pevsner, p. 7.

32. Wyatt, *Byzantine Court*, pp. 73, 46, 6.

33. *Ibid.*, p. 59; Grove to Sotheby, a.l.s., 3 December 1852, SLS, II.

34. CPE, 187-198.

35. Wyatt, *Byzantine Court*, p. 67.

36. XX, 29 March 1862, p. 224.

37. Wyatt, *Byzantine Court*, p. 38.

38. Rossetti, pp. 81-2.

39. Wyatt, *Byzantine Court*, p. 28; *Guide to the Ten Chief Courts*, p. 150.

40. B, XII, 8 July 1854, p. 354.

41. T, 2 Nov 1853; B, XXXV, 2 June 1877, p. 547.

42. *Views*, p. 30; *Guide to the Ten Chief Courts*, p. 178.

43. XII, 29 July 1854.

44. *Routledge's Guide*, p. 103; Wyatt, *Medieval Court*, pp. 110, 118.

45. III, 1 August 1857, p. 246.

46. Wyatt, *Medieval Court*, p. 5.

47. *Routledge's Guide*, p. 94; SLS, *Letter*, p. 20.

48. Wyatt, *Medieval Court*, p. 29.

49. *ILN*, XLIV, 10 June 1854, p. 548.

50. Wyatt, *Views*, p. 30; ICPG, I, 7, Apr 1854, p. 77.

51. B, XII, 29 July, p. 397-8; Rossetti, p. 83; B, XII, 16 Sept 1854, p. 482; Q, XCVI, cxcii, March 1855, p. 314.

52. Wyatt, *Medieval Court*, p. 58; Ruskin, XXIII, p. 243.

53. Wyatt, *Medieval Court*, p. 109.

54. *Views*, p. 31.

55. Wyatt, *Renaissance Court*, p. 15; Measom, p. 23.

56. Q, XCVI, cxcii, March 1855, p. 318; ICPG, I, 14, p. 185; Wyatt's screen for a 'Renaissance' morning-room at Ashridge Park, executed by Desachy, resembles the arcade of the Garden Gallery in the Court. B, XVIII, 18 Feb 1860, p. 105.

57. *Renaissance Court*, p. 9.

58. CPE, p. 70.

59. *Renaissance Court*, p. 41.

60. *Ibid.*, p. 28.

61. Rossetti, p. 90; Q, XCVI, cxcii, March 1855, p. 320.

62. Wyatt, *Italian Court*, pp. 17, 29.

63. Q, see note 61.

64. *Italian Court*, p. 75; Charles Ricketts, *A Self-Portrait*, London: Peter Davies, 1939, p. 45; Beattie, pl. 35, p. 32.

65. *The Ten Chief Courts*, p. 119.

66. Fergusson, 1851, p. 6

67. Fergusson, 1855, p. x.

68. RIBA *Transactions*, 1851; Fergusson, 1851, pp. 124, 267, 305 (n).

69. Layard, 1853, Plate 67.

70. Layard, 1854, pp. 47, 52. Fergusson, 1851, p. 89.

71. *Routledge's Guide*, p. 69; B, XII, 10 June 1854, p. 298.

72. Fergusson, 1849, pp. 251-2, 8, 110, 293-5.

73. IX, p. 441; X, 364.

74. *Official Catalogue of the Fine Arts Department*, 1862, p. 82.

75. DNB; T, 11 Jan 1886.

76. Layard, 1854, p. 38; *ILN*, XXIV, 15 April 1854, p. 346.

77. CPE, p. 6.

78. II, p. 263.

79. VI, 1 Oct 1854, p. 314; Layard, 1853, II, pp. 294-7; Jones, 1865, nos. 4, 12, 13, 14.

80. Rossetti, p. 74; T, III, p. 104; Layard, 1854, p. 45 (n); *The Ten Chief Courts*, p. 124.

81. Layard, 1854, p. 53; 1850 (1848), II, pp. 265 (n), I, 257, II, 263-5.

82. Q, XCVI, cxcii, March 1855, p. 314; *Athenaeum*, 1436, 5 May 1855, pp. 526-7.

83. Rossetti, pp. 75-6; Fergusson, 1849, p. 289.

84. Layard, 1850, II, pp. 319, 262; Wyatt, 1870, p. 122.

85. LMA, CP Trustees, 15; Bromley Public Library.

86. *Annual Register* (Chronicle), 1854, p. 98.

87. Leading article, n.d., SLS, I.

88. X, p. 114, 416; XXIX, p. 50; XI, p. 19.

89. Devonshire, pp. 183-9.

90. Jameson, pp. 85-91; 'The New Crystal Palace', RC, I; *Athenaeum*, 1289, 10 July 1852, p. 751; B, XI, 15 April 1854, p. 194.

91. P. 5.

92. 12 August 1855, SLS, I.

93. Phillips, pp. 6-7.

94. CPH, III, 1, Jan 1856, p. 114; Jameson, p. 13.

95. XXIV, 10 June 1854, pp. 546-7.

96. *Daily Chronicle*, 16 Feb 1928; *Household Words*, 193, 3 Dec 1853, p. 315; ICPG, I, 12, 24 June 1854, p. 146; 'The New Crystal Palace', n.d. (1853), SLS, I; Ruskin, XXIX, p. 569.

97. Read, p. 97; Hollingshead, p. 44.

98. 1851, III, pp. 847-54.

99. *ILN*, XXIV, 15 April 1854, p. 346; *Letter*, p. 3.

100. Scott, p. 20.

101. VI, 1 Sept 1854, p. 280; Ruskin, XIX, p. 218; *ILN*, XXIV, 22 April 1854, p. 373.

102. H. D Molesworth, *Sculpture in England: Renaissance to Early Nineteenth Century*, London: British Council, 1951, p. 18.

103. Jameson, p. 5.

104. Hollingshead, p. 52; (Rimmel) *ibid.*, pp. 64, 65; Ruskin, XVII, p. 243.

105. CPE, p. 86; *Routledge's Guide*, p. 122.

106. Jameson, pp. 13, 11, 48, 74.

107. Pp. 135-7.

108. 1878, p. 5; Burton, p. 122.

109. B, XXXII, 16 May 1874, p. 421.

110. 'The Statue Doctor', *Westminster Gazette*, 4 Feb 1925.

111. *Crystal Palace Magazine*, n.d., Croydon Library.

112. ICPG, I, 14, August 1854, p. 187.

113. Jameson, p. 56; Paxton, Report to C.P. Co., 23 January 1855, CPH, II, 2, Feb 1855, p. 24.

114. *Greek Court*, p. 60.

115. Jameson, pp. 6, 55.

116. *Ibid.*, p. 12-13.

117. Wyatt, 1867, pp. 338, 342, 352.

118. Jameson, p. 61.

119. Read, p. 313.

120. Palgrave, p. 252 (n).

121. *Ibid.*, pp. 82, 86, 122, 201; Ruskin, XII, p. 155; Phillips, p. 157.

122. *ILN*, XLIV, 10 June 1854, p. 548. Phillips, *Portrait Gallery*, pp. 187, 102.

123. ICPG, I, 2, Oct 1853, p. 4; B, XI, 3 Sept 1853, p. 566; Read, p. 26.

124. ICPG, I, 14, August 1854, p. 187; *Pacific* now at Dacres Road, Sydenham, and *Thames* at Lechlade, Gloucestershire.

125. *Daily News*, 24 March 1928.

126. V & A Archive, MA/1/C3432.

CHAPTER 5

1. Phillips, p. 16; Colquhoun, p. 106.

2. ICPG, I, 6, March 1854, p. 60; CG, 16, 24 June 1856, p. 217.

3. CPH, II, 4, April 1855, p. 38; illus. in *ILN*, XXV, 5 August 1854, p. 113.

4. Phillips, p. 127.

5. CG, 21, 18 Jan 1859, p. 243; ICPG, 14, August 1854, p. 186; CPH, II, 5, May 1855, p. 50; ICPG, I, 2, Nov 1853, p. 24; ICPG, I, 10, 9 June 1854, pp. 114, 116; ICPG, I, 1, Oct 1853, p. 5; *ILN*, XLIV, 10 June 1854, p. 548; CG, 12, 22 June 1854, p. 212; CG, 14, 1 May 1855, p. 69.

6. CG, XIX, 2 March 1858, p. 334; ICPG, I, 4, Jan 1854, p. 45; Phillips, p. 134; CPH, II, 8, Aug 1855, p. 74; *Observer*, 29 July 1855; T, 7 Jan 1954.

7. Leading article, n.d., SLS, II; *Letter*, p. 15; Heine, p. 11; *Crystal Palace: Evidence*, p. 12.

8. VI, Sept 1854, p. 281; Hollingshead, p. 55; CG, 19, 16 March 1858, p. 365.

9. 25 Oct 1853. *Letters*, VII, p. 171; C.P. Co. programme, n.d., before 1866, Mander and Mitchenson colln.

10. Phillips, p. 21; ICPG, I, 14, August 1854, p. 186; C.P. Co. programme, 1893, Theatre Museum.

11. Measom, p. 12; Phillips, p. 81.

12. Latham, p. 92; Grove, p. 21; Phillips, p. 91; T, 8 May 1854.

13. L. Kriegel, in Purbrick, p. 164; Latham, p. 6.

14. Phillips, p. 8; Latham, p. 13, 66, 16, 91.

15. Phillips, p. 95.

16. Pp. 13-17.

17. RC, I.

18. Latham, pp. 93-100; ICPG, I, 10, 9 June 1855, p. 114; Latham, p. 54.

19. Phillips, p. 8; CPH, I, 4, Feb 1854, p. 35. Warwick papers, Minet Library, IV/80/VIII/35/87, p. 8; *Daily News*, 26 Sept 1855.

20. Wroth, Museum of London, I, p. 269; R. Routledge, *Discoveries and Inventions of the Nineteenth Century*, London: Routledge, 1903, pp. 677-82; C.P. Co. programme, 24 March 1881.

21. Phillips, p. 76; *ILN*, XXV, 8 July 1854, p. 53; Hollingshead, p. 60; ICPG, I, 8, June 1854, p. 6; CPE, p. 147; C.P. Co. chairman's report, p. 11, RC, II; Hollingshead, pp. 56-7.

22. Albert, p. 145.

23. C.P. Co leaflet, meeting of 28 Feb, 1854, p. 5, SLS, I; B, XII, 7, Oct 1854, p. 43; ICPG, I, 4, Jan 1854, p. 43; Cole, 23 January 1854, Diary, NAL.

24. *Athenaeum*, 1501, 2 Aug 1856, p. 965; B, XII, 7 Oct 1854, p. 523.

25. ICPG, I, 8, May 1854, p. 86; Herrmann, pp. 75, 215.

26. *Athenaeum*, see n. 24; Phillips, pp. 82-3; CPE, pp. 222 (fuller description of colours), 220.

27. ICPG, I, 7, April 1854, p. 82; Phillips, p. 84.

28. ?1857. (Loose pages) SLS, II; CPE, p. 169; Phillips, p. 85; CPE, p. 168-9.

29. B, XII, 7 Oct 1854, p. 522; Phillips, p. 85; ICPG, I, 7, April 1854, p. 86; *Athenaeum*, 1501, 2 Aug 1856, p. 965.

30. ICPG, 24 June 1854, p. 149; AJ, see n. 28; C.P. Co., 30 June 1855, SLS, II; Phillips, p. 179.

31. Phillips, p. 143; ICPG, I, 15, Sept 1854, p. 197; CPE, pp. 243, 147; *Observer*, 15 July 1855, SLS II.

32. CPH, I, 14, August 1854, p. 186. AJ, VI, 1 July 1854, p. 215; ibid., 1 Sept 1854,

p. 281; AJ, III (n.s.)., Jan 1857, p.34; CPH, II, 8, August 1855, p. 75.

33. *Crystal Palace Magazine*, n.d., Croydon Library; *Crystal Palace News*, II, 24, June 1860, p. 202; CPE, p. 206; AJ, III (n.s.), Mar 1857, p. 96; James Fergusson, a.l.s. to SLS, SLS, II; C.P. Co., 17 July 1856, SLS II; CPH, III, 9, Sept 1856, p. 178; CPE, pp. 187-205.

34. Phillips, p. 83; Hollingshead, p. 71; CPH, December 1854, p. 74; *ILN*, XXIV, 22 April 1854, p. 374; ICPG, I, 2, 17 June 1854, p. 134; CPH, II, 9, Nov 1855, p. 98.

35. CPE, p. 239; ICPG, I, 12, 24 June 1854, p. 146.

36. Q, XCVI, cxcii, March 1855, p. 340; 'Picture Gallery at the C.P.', n.d., SLS, II; Hollingshead, p. 56; Phillips, p. 10.

37. *ILN* review (1856), n.d., SLS, II; B, XIV, 22 Nov 1856, p. 636; AJ, VI, 1 Oct 1854, p. 314; CPH, III, 9, Sept 1856, p. 176. 'Picture Gallery at the C.P.' n.d., SLS, II.

38. *c.* 1856, SLS, II; *ILN*, XXIX, 30 August 1856; *ILN*, XLIV, 11 June 1864, p. 575; AJ, VI, 1 Oct 1857, p. 325.

39. Phillips, p. 140; C.P. Programme, 24 Mar 1881; *The Crystal Palace*, 1911, p. 31; chapter in J.M. Tough and C.A. O'Flaherty, *Passenger Conveyors*, London: Allan, 1971.

40. CPE, p. 234; ICPG, I, 13, July 1854, p. 186; ICPG, I, 5, Feb 1854, p. 51.

41. SLS, II; Delamotte, London: Cundall, 1853, p.151.

42. CPH, II, 2, March 1855, p. 27; ICPG, I, 7, April 1854, p. 81; *ILN*, XXVI, 28 April 1854, p. 430.

43. ICPG, I, 9, 27 May 1854, p. 110; ICPG, I, 14, August 1854, p. 186; T, 10 May 1856; *ILN*, XXVI, 9 June 1855, p. 551.

44. Phillips, p. 8; *The Crystal Palace* (Nelson), 1862, p. 9; Hollingshead, p. 67; *Crystal Palace News*, II, 24 June 1860, p. 204; *ILN*, XXIX, 26 July 1856, p. 108.

CHAPTER 6

1. XXIX, 5 July 1856, p. 22; CG, 16, 24 June 1856, p. 217.

2. Grove, p. 27; Phillips, p. 163.

3. Wyatt, *Views*, p. 35.

4. *ILN*, XX, 5 June 1852, p. 440; Wyatt, *Views*, p. 36; E, 42, 16 August 1851, p. 260.

5. CG, 15, 2 Oct 1855, p. 18; CG, 14, I May 1855, p. 68; Walton, p. 9.

6. Phillips, p. 150.

7. Elliott, p. 111; CG, 15, 2 Oct 1855, p. 18; *ILN*, XXIII, 31 Dec 1853, p. 599; CG, 12, 22 June

1854, p. 212; Elliott, p. 122; CG, 16, 30 Sept 1856, p. 467.

8. *Views*, pp. 37, 34; Phillips, p. 34, 152, 156; CG, 17, 14 Oct 1856, p. 21.

9. *Country Life*, 138, 3588, 9 Dec 1956, p. 1607.

10. *ILN*, XXIII, 31 Dec 1853, p. 599.CG, 12, 22 August 1854 p. 402; *ibid.*, 12, 29 August 1854, p. 422; *ibid.*, 14, 1 May 1855, p. 67; *Observer*, 24 June 1855, SLS, I; CG, 23, 24 Oct 1859, p. 2.

11. Holman Hunt, p. 455.

12. CG, 18, 18 August 1857, p. 311.

13. CG, 16, 30 Sept 1856, p. 468; *ibid.*, 19, 2 March 1858, p. 333; Phillips, pp. 157-8; Elliott, p. 127; Elliott, 'Mosaiculture', Garden History, 9, 1, 1981, p. 89.

14. University of Reading, Crystal Palace colln.; Desmond, p. 181; T, 25 Nov 1859.

15. C.P. Co. programme, 21 Aug 1884. Mander and Mitchenson collection; Elliott, p. 156.

16. Phillips, p. 35; *ILN*, XXIII, 31 Dec 1853, p. 599; *ILN*, XXXV, 6 Aug 1859, p. 135; Phillips, p. 168.

17. XVI, 232, July 1853, p. 241, Plate 22.

18. CPH, I, 8, June 1855, p. 7; T, III, p.107; CG, 12, 22 Aug 1854, p. 401; *ibid.*, 15, 16 Oct 1855, p. 35; AJ, VI, 1 Sept 1854, p. 281; Heine, p. 12.

19. CG, 15, 2 Oct 1855, p. 18; Heine, p. 14; CG, 13, 17 Oct 1854, p. 40.

20. Sale map, n.d., Bromley Library; photo *c.* 1860, Devonshire Collection, Colquhoun, p. 213; Elliott, p. 110; CG, 4 September 1860, p. 337.

21. *ILN*, XXXVII, 4 Aug 1860, p. 114; Lees-Milne, p. 105.

22. CPH, III, 1, Jan 1856, p. 118; P, CXIV, 14 May 1898, p. 218; drawing in Guildhall Library.

23. CG, 16, 23 Sept 1856, p. 450; Grove, p. 7.

24. T, 17 May 1853; Measom, pp. 8-9.

25. *ILN*, XXIX, 1 Nov 1856, p. 441.

26. *ILN*, XLIV, 30 April 1864, p. 410; C.P. Co. leaflet, 4 July 1853, SLS, I; ICPG, I, 12, 24 June 1854, p. 148.

27. CPH, II, 10, October 1855, p. 90.

28. Phillips, p. 174; *Athenaeum*, 1289, 10 July 1852, p. 752; *ILN*, XXIII, 31 Dec 1853, p. 599, 'a volume of water only one-sixth less than that of the cataracts of Niagara'; Phillips, p. 175.

29. C.P. Co, 1852, SLS, I; CPH, III, 9, Sept 1856, p. 178; CG, 16, 24 June, 1856, p. 217; CPH, III, 7, July 1856, p. 163; *Morning Post*, 9 Feb 1855, SLS, I; Fuller, 1874, p. 13; *ILN*, see n. 1 above.

30. CPH, II, 10, August 1854, p. 28.

31. Phillips, pp. 173-4.

32. *ILN*, XXIX, 5 July 1856, p. 22. C.P.Co., 28 Feb 1854, SLS, I; Paxton's report, C.P.Co., 9 August 1855, SLS, I.

33. B, XIV, 21 June 1856, p. 337; CPH, III, 7, July 1856, pp. 161-2; B, XII, 15 April 1854, p. 194; Fuller, 1874, pp. 412-3.

34. CPH, I, 8, June 1854, p. 7; Phillips, p. 17; CPH, II, 1, Feb 1854, p. 7; CPH, II, 1, Feb 1854, p. 7; CPH, III, 7, July 1856, p. 162; *Views*, p. 36

35. CPH, III, 7, July 1856, p. 163.

36. *Illustrated Times*, 28 June 1856 p. 466.

37. T, 28 July 1856; C.P. Co., 1856 season hand-bill, Guildhall Library.

38. *ILN*, XXVI, 9 June 1855, p. 582.

39. *Observer*, 24 June 1855, SLS, I.

40. CG, 16, 24 June 1856, p. 217.

41. *Observer*, 28 June 1855.

42. Ruskin, XXXV, p. 47; B, XIV, 21 June 1856, p. 337; CPH, III, 3, March 1856, p. 129.

43. CPH, III, 3, Mar 1856, p. 129; *ibid.*, III, 7, July 1856, p. 162; Phillips, p. 171; C.P. programme, 12 July, 1902.

44. *The Times* printed a photographic view and key, 1929. Guildhall, La/PR/V9/P5; B, XIV, 21 June 1856, p. 337.

45. *Morning Post*, 9 Feb 1955, SLS I; C.P. Co., 3rd ordinary general meeting, 9 August 1855, SLS, I.

46. C.P. Co. programme, 22 Aug 1887; Owen Jones design at V & A, D 1478-1898; B, XXXI, 14 June 1873, p. 472.

47. Owen, pp. 7, 31, 41.

48. A.l.s., 20 December 1854, SLS I.

49. Pamphlet, reprinted from *Journal of Society of Arts*, p. 1; AJ, V, 1 Oct 1853, p. 266; Atlas, 26 May 1853, Owen, p. 5.

50. *ILN*, XXIII, 31 Dec 1853, p. 600; CPH, I, 1, Nov 1853, p. 2; *ILN*, XXIII, 5 Nov 1853; B, XII, 10 June 1854, p. 297.

51. *The Ten Chief Courts*, p. 217.

52. Owen, p. 28.

53. Owen, p. 7.

54. P. Doyle and E. Robinson, 'The Victorian Geological illustrations at Crystal Palace Park', *Proc. Geol. Assoc*, 1998, 104, pp. 181-94; CPH, II, 10, Oct 1855, p. 91.

55. SLS, II; Owen, p. 7; Sotheby, *Letter*, pp. 32-3.

56. *Observer*, 2 Sept 1855; Britton, a.l.s., SLS, II, 5 Dec 1855; SLS, memo. of meeting of 3 Nov 1855; Hawkins, a.l.s., SLS, I.

57. Hawkins to Sotheby, ms. Note by SLS, SLS, II; *Letter*, p. 14-15.

58. 1851, II, p. 829.

59. Hawkins to Sotheby, 18 Dec 1854, a.l.s., SLS, I; see *ILN*, XXIX, 20 Sept 1856, p. 303, for drawing of a Gambian mud-fish at the Palace drawn by Hawkins.

60. AJ, VI, 1 April 1854, p. 117; *Observer*, 31 Dec 1854.

61. 'Fun in a Fossil', P, XXVI, Jan 1855, p. 24. ICPG, I, 5, Feb 1854, p. 53; *ILN*, XXIV, 7 Jan 1854, p. 22.

62. Phillips, p. 164; T, III, p. 10.

63. *Crystal Palace: Evidence…*, pp. 27-9, ICE Library.

64. *Graphic*, 9 September 1876, p. 261.

CHAPTER 7

1. *Letters*, II, p. 165.

2. Tennyson, I, pp. 376, 340.

3. Warwick, p. 179; Holman Hunt, II, p. 3; WHH, letter of 31 Dec 1854, John Rylands Library, Manchester.

4. Millais, II, pp. 421, 322.

5. Burne-Jones, I, p. 101.

6. *Portrait of a Lady*, London: Macmillan 1883, I, xv, p. 160; *Essays in London*, London: Osgood, 1893, p. 21; *Emile Zola, Photographer*.

7. J.G.P. Delaney, *Charles Ricketts*, Oxford University Press, 1990, pp. 10-11; T, 1 Aug 1913.

8. XXVIII, p. 338; X, p. 110; XVII, p. 340; XXXVII, p. 10.

9. XII, p. 418; XXIV, p. 249.

10. XX, p. 235.

11. Mast, pp. 14, 4.

12. *ILN*, XXXI, 17 Oct 1857, p. 400; *Evening Standard*, 12 Dec 1936; Bacon, p. 57.

13. *ILN*, XXIV, 23 April 1864, p. 401; *ILN*, XXIV, 30 April 1864, p. 407 (illus. p. 408).

14. C.P. Manager, quoted *ILN*, XXXVIII, 2 March 1861, p. 194; C.P.Co., report Dec 1862, p. 9.

15. *ILN*, XLV, 10 Sept 1864, pp. 275-6; *Building News*, 9 Sept 1864, p. 163.

16. Muddock, p. 57; Robert K. Bowley, general manager, 'Fire at the Palace', Leaflet, 30 Dec 1866; *Illustrated Times*, 5 Jan 1866, p. 175; C.P. Co. Report, 1868, p. 6.

17. *Evening Standard*, 11 Dec 1936; Grand Fête programme, 11, July, 1891, p. 4. Guildhall Library.

18. St. Bride's Printing Library.

19. Catalogue at NAL; T, 17 May 1901.

20. Buckland, retirement speech, Guildhall, 1 Jan 1949, p, 2, LMA; T, 8 March 1923.

21. *Pageant Notes*, no. 11, 1 March 1911, pp. 6, 12. Museum of London; *Evening Standard*, 18 Dec 1936.

22. *Evening Standard*, 14 Dec 1936, 4 Oct 1873.

23. Official Commemorative booklet, p. 1; *Sphere*, 11 May 1911, with photos; *The Crystal Palace Story: an Exhibition organised by the Norwood Society*, May 1962, p. 8.

24. Bayst, pp. 2-10, 12.

25. Pageant of London programme, Part II, May-October 1911, pp. x, 9, Museum of London.

26. XII, p. 417.

27. Warwick Wroth Album, I, p. 208. Museum of London.

28. Husey, p. 3 and passim.

29. Muddock, p. 79; T, 3 May 1911.

30. Hobhouse, 1950, p. xix; Act of Parlt., 1914, Museum of London; T, 15 July 1913.

31. *Daily News*, 8 March 1913; T, 12 June 1913, 6 October, 1913, 12 April 1913; *Evening News*, 14 June 1913; clipping in Brock Archive, Crystal Palace Museum.

32. *Evening Standard*, 21 Dec 1936; Griff [A.S. Griffiths], *Surrendered*, Twickenham: privately published, n.d., p. 20; *With the R.N.D., on board H.M.S. "Crystal Palace"*, London: W.H. Smith, 1915, p. 71, 23 and passim.

33. *Star*, 1 Dec 1936; Buckland, p. 5; programme, Museum of London; Buckland, retirement speech, 11 Jan 1949, p. 5, LMA CPT 10.

34. *Daily Mail*, 1 Dec 1936; Buckland, p. 5

35. 1 March 1937, LMA CPT 10; T, 31 Dec 1951; obit., T, 17 Dec 1957.

36. Hobhouse, 1950, pp. 162-3.

37. Miller, p. 29; IWM, C/F A1/2; ffoulkes, p. 131.

38. Opening programme, p. 2, IWM; ffoulkes, pp. 137, 133; IWM Archive.

39. Miller, p. 58; ffoulkes, p. 131.

40. 31 Oct 1919. IWM Archive; A.M. Hind, to ffoulkes, 11 Sept 1919; 8 Sept 1919, IWM Archive.

41. Beale, II, pp. 188-91.

42. *ILN*, XXXV, 19 Nov 1859, p. 483; *ILN* XXXVI, 12 May 1860, p. 459.

43. *ILN*, XLV, 30 July 1864, p. 112; C.P.Co. programme, 16 July 1864, Guildhall; Hollingshead, p. 74; *ILN* XLIV, 30 April 1864, p. 423; *ILN*, LXII, 20 June 1868, p. 613.

44. XXXIV, 14 Oct 1876, p. 998.

45. *ILN*, XXXIV, 8 Jan 1859, p. 42.

46. Handbill, Peter Jackson collection; handbill of 16 July 1864, Guildhall.

47. *London: What to See*, pp. 151, 153, 157.

48. *The Crystal Palace, Sydenham, to be sold*, p. 25.

49. *ILN*, XLIII, 12 Dec 1863, p.585; *ILN*, XLIII, 14 Oct 1863, p. 407; *ILN*, XLIV, 25 June 1864, p. 627; *ILN*, XLVII, 21 Oct 1865, p. 389.

50. C P Co. programme, 8 Aug 1902.

51. XIX, p. 217.

52. *Graphic*, 8 July 1871, p. 46; Warwick, p. 195.

53. *Annual Register* (Chronicle), Aug 1859, pp. 132-3. Ruskin, XVII, p. 340.

54. *ILN*, XXXVIII, 8 June 1861, p. 537.

55. *Ibid.*; Warwick papers IV/80/1A/14/24, Minet Library.

56. *Annual Register* (Chronicle), 1861, pp. 73-4.

57. *ILN*, XLIII, 24 Oct 1863, p. 407; London, Brighton and South Coast Railway handbill, John Johnson Collection, 22/6/59-26/12/89, no. 24.

58. 'Performance on the tight-rope', C.P.Co. circular, John Johnson, 22/6/59 –26/12/89, no. 2; *ILN*, XL, 11 Jan 1862, p. 56; Blondin on the High Rope', Crystal Palace Press, n.d.,(1893), Univ. Of Reading, C.P. collection.

59. 1930s Brock's programme, Theatre Museum.

60. Competition, T, 20 July 1865; *Pictorial World*, 4 Aug 1887.

61. Brock, pp. 221-6, passim; *Strand*, II, 4, Oct 1891, pp. 468-74.

62. *Graphic*, II, 22 Oct 1870, p. 404; VI, 26 Oct 1862, p. 379; *Country Life*, 5 Nov 1987, p. 88.

63. *Evening Standard*, 19 Dec 1936; programmes, 'Fireworks 1' folder, John Johnson Collection.

64. Crane, p. 467.

65. Macqueen-Pope, p. 360; Brock, pp. 133-6.

66. C.P. Co. to shareholders, June 1869, p. 26; *ILN*, LXII, 4 Jan 1873, p. 17.

67. *The Crystal Palace, Sydenham, to be sold at auction*, p. 19.

68. T, 30 June 1913; 1874 programme, Upper Norwood Library; leaflets, programmes at Guildhall Library, Mander and Mitchenson Collection.

69. Reeves, p. 33.

70. Mander and Mitchenson Collection, *Proteus*, 27 Sept 1902; *Illustrated Mail*, 9 January 1904.

71. C.P. programme, Mander and Mitchenson Collection.

72. E. McIlvaine, *P.G. Wodehouse*, New York: James H. Heinemann, 1990, p. 411. Wodehouse added lines to Cole Porter's 'You're the Top', for the London production of *Anything Goes*, 1935, recalling his schooldays below the Palace: 'You're the run of a film by Arliss/ You're the sun – on the Crystal Parliss' (information from Tony Ring).

73. Programme, Mander and Mitchenson Collection; *Evening Standard*, 14 Dec 1936.

74. Musgrave, p. 59.

75. Programme, SLS, I.

76. Beale, II, p. 191; Sotheby, 1856, p. 19, SLS, II.

77. Q, XCVI, cxcii, March 1855, p. 307; Eastlake, I, p. 325.

78. ICPG, I, 9, 27 May 1854, p. 99; P, XXVIII, 1855, p. 50.

79. Wroth Album, I, p. 70; Saxe Wyndham, p. 21 (n); *ILN*, XXV, 7 Oct 1854, p. 342.

80. CPH, II, 5, May 1855, p. 54; SLS, I.

81. CPH, I, 10, Nov 1854, p. 75; CPH, II, 4, April 1855, p. 38; CPH, II, 11, Nov 1855, p. 97; *Evening Standard*, 17 December 1936.

82. Saxe Wyndham, p. 35.

83. *Evening Standard*, 17 Dec 1936; *Star*, 1 Dec 1936.

84. 30th. Anniversary Band Concert programme, Sept 1930, Theatre Museum.

85. CPH, III, 3, March 1856, p. 129.

86. M. Musgrave, ed., *George Grove, Music and Victorian Culture*, London: Palgrave, 2003.

87. Graves, pp. 45-7; *Evening Standard*, 17 Dec 1936.

88. SLS II, c. Feb 1856; CPH, III, 3, March 1856, p. 130; CPH, II, 7, July 1855, p. 65; *C.P. News*, II, 24, p. 198.

89. CPH, III, 4, April 1856, pp. 135-6; *ibid.*, III, 6, June 1856, p. 154.

90. Sims Reeves, I, p. 79.

91. SLS, II; CPH, III, 3, March 1856, p. 142.

92. Musgrave, pp. 69-72; Phillips, p. 11; C.P.Co. report, Dec 1866, p. 222.

93. *Dickinson's Comprehensive Pictures…*, vol I; SLS, I; ICPG, I, 3, Dec 1853, p. 26; *Gentleman's Magazine*, XLI, April 1854, p. 390; ICPG, I, 14, August 1854, p. 187.

94. Musgrave, p. 35; Buckland, p. 5; Warwick, p. 241.

95. B, XVII, 2 July 1859, p. 438; Eliot, V, 2 August 1871, p. 173.

96. Fergusson, 1873, p. 543.

97. B, XV, 20 June 1857, p. 353; XVII, 25 June 1859, p. 423; *Evening Standard*, 15 Dec 1936; *ILN*, XLVII, 8 July 1865, p. 18.

98. *ILN*, XXX, 13 June 1857, p. 572; *ILN*, XXX, 27 June 1857, p. 640; *ILN*, XXXII, 2 Jan 1858, p. 2.

99. *ILN*, XLVII, 30 Sept 1865, p. 306.

100. *ILN*, XXX, 27 June 1857, p. 627; Ruskin: XVIII, p. 243; XIX, p. xxxiv; XXXVII, p. 321; Muddock, p. 70.

101. Michael Musgrave, 'The Musical Legacy of the Great Exhibition,' *Die Weltausstellung von 1851 und ihre Folgen*, Prinz-Albert-Studien 20, Munich, 2002, p. 62; B, XVII, 2 July 1859, p. 438; B, XI, 4 May 1861, p. 302.

102. Musgrave, p. 111, passim.

103. *The Eye of the Beholder*, London: Hulton, 1957, pp. 44-5.

104. *Athenaeum*, 1289, 10 July 1852, p. 752.

105. See Bevan *et al*.

106. C.P. programme, Theatre Museum.

CHAPTER 8

1. *Illustrated*, 30 Jan 1954.

2. Bound volume of fire newspapers, Anerley Library, Bromley.

3. Cutting, n.d., Guildhall, BV Nov; *Illustrated*, 1 Jan 1954; T, 2 Dec 1936; T, 12 Dec 1951; *Daily Telegraph*, 1 Dec 1936; T, 1 Dec 1936.

4. T, 2 Dec 1936.

5. *Evening Standard*, 1 Dec 1936.

6. T, 4 Dec 1936; T, 7 Dec 1936; *ILN*, 15 Dec 1936, pp. 26-30.

7. *The Crystal Palace is on Fire*, p., 42.

8. Buckland Speeches, LMA, CPT 10;

9. *The News*, 10 Nov 1972.

10. T, 31 Dec 1951.

11. 21 July 1951.

12. T, 1 Jan 1952; *Evening Standard*, 15 Dec 1955.

13. *Evening Standard*, 21 Nov 1977; B, CC, 5 May 1961, p. 862.

14. 18 Oct 1995.

BIBLIOGRAPHY

MANUSCRIPTS AND ALBUMS

Abbreviations

IWM   Imperial War Museum Archives

LMA   London Metropolitan Archives

NAL   National Art Library, Victoria and Albert Museum

RC   Scrap Albums (I: 'Preservation of the Crystal Palace'; II: 'The Crystal Palace and Park in 1853'), Archives of the Royal Commission for the Exhibition of 1851, 2 vols (quoted with kind permission of the Royal Commission)

RIBA   Royal Institute of British Architects, London

SLS   Samuel Leigh Sotheby Scrap Album, 2 vols, 'Papers and Memoranda of the Crystal Palace Company', 1852–6. Bromley Local Studies Library

V&A   Victoria and Albert Museum

Archives of the Royal Commission for the Great Exhibition of 1851, Imperial College, London

Bromley Local Studies Library, London Borough of Bromley

Chatsworth, Devonshire Mss. (Joseph Paxton papers)

Imperial War Museum Archives, London

John Johnson Collection, Bodleian Library, University of Oxford

London Metropolitan Archive (Crystal Palace Trustees papers)

Mander and Mitchenson Theatre Collection, Greenwich, London

Minet Library, London borough of Southwark (Alan Warwick papers)

Museum of London (Warwick Wroth album, 'Pleasure Gardens of South London')

National Art Library, Victoria and Albert Museum, London

Royal Institute of British Architects, Library, London

Theatre Museum, Covent Garden, London

University of Reading, Crystal Palace Collection

Upper Norwood Library, London Borough of Croydon

Victoria and Albert Museum Archive (Crystal Palace Trustees Correspondence)

NEWSPAPERS AND PERIODICALS

Abbreviations

AJ   *The Art Journal*

B   *The Builder*

CEJ   *Chambers's Edinburgh Journal*

CG   *The Cottage Gardener*

CPE   *The Crystal Palace Expositor*

CPH   *The Crystal Palace Herald*

E   *The Expositor*

ER   *The Edinburgh Review*

ICPG   *Illustrated Crystal Palace Gazette*

ILN   *Illustrated London News*

P   *Punch*

Q   *The Quarterly Review*

SCPE   *Sydenham Crystal Palace Expositor*

T   *The Times*

The Annual Register

The Architect

The Art Journal

Architectural History

The Architectural Quarterly Review

The Architectural Review

The Athenaeum

The Atlas

The Builder

Building News

Cassell's Illustrated Family Paper

Chambers's Edinburgh Journal

The Civil Engineer and Architect's Journal

The Crystal Palace Herald

The Crystal Palace Magazine

Crystal Palace News

The Connoisseur

The Cottage Gardener

Country Life

Daily Chronicle

Daily Express

Daily Mail

Daily News

Daily Telegraph

The Ecclesiologist

The Edinburgh Review

The Evening News

The Evening Standard

The Expositor

The Fortnightly Review

The Furniture Gazette

Garden History

The Gentleman's Magazine

The Graphic

Household Words

Illustrated

The Illustrated Exhibitor

The Illustrated London News

The Illustrated Mail

The Illustrated Times

The Independent
The Journal of Design
The Journal of the Society of Arts
The Leader
The Morning Herald
The Morning Post
The Museum of Classical Antiquities
Notes and Queries
The Observer
Punch
The Quarterly Review
The Record
Revue des Deux Mondes
R.I.B.A., Session Papers; Transactions
The Sphere
The Star
Strand Magazine
The Sydenham Crystal Palace Expositor
The Times
The Victorian
The Weekly News
The Westminster Gazette

BOOKS

Abbreviations

1851   *Exhibition of the Works of Industry of All Nations. Official Descriptive and Illustrated Catalogue*, 1851
AJIC   *Art Journal Illustrated Catalogue*, 1851
L   *Lectures on the Results of the Great Exhibition*
T   *Tallis's History and Description of the Crystal Palace.*

Albert, *The Principal Speeches and Addresses of H.R.H. The Prince Consort* [1857], London: John Murray, 1862.

Allen, Leslie Lewis, *The World's Show: Crystal Palace Medals and Tokens, 1851–1936*, London: Coincraft, 2000.

Art Journal Illustrated Catalogue: *The Industry of All Nations*, 1851, London: Virtue, 1851.

Auerbach, Jeffrey A., *The Great Exhibition of 1851: a Nation on Display*, London and New Haven: Yale University Press, 1999.

Bacon, Ernest W., *Spurgeon: Heir of the Puritans*, London: Geo. Allen & Unwin, 1967.

Barker, Felix and Ralph Hyde, *London as it Might Have Been*, London: John Murray, 1982.

Barry, Rev. Alfred, *The Life and Works of Sir Charles Barry*, London: John Murray, 1867.

Barry, E.M., *Lectures on Architecture, Delivered at the Royal Academy*, London: John Murray, 1881.

Bayst, William A., *Empire Bridge and World Approach: in Lieu of War*, London: Forsaith, 1935.

Beale, Thomas Willert, *The Light of Other Days*, 2 vols, London: Bentley, 1890.

Beattie, Susan, *Alfred Stevens*, London: Victoria and Albert Museum, 1975.

Beaver, Patrick, *The Crystal Palace*, London: Evelyn, 1970.

Berlyn, Peter and Charles Fowler, *The Crystal Palace: its Architectural History and Constructive Marvels*, London: Gilbert, 1851.

Bevan, Ian, S. Hibberd and M. Gilbert, *To the Palace for the Cup*, Beckenham: Replay, 1999.

Bird, Antony, *Paxton's Palace*, London: Cassell, 1976.

Blashfield, John Marriott, *An Account of the History and Manufacture of Ancient and Modern Terra Cotta*, London: Weale, 1855.

Bonython, Elizabeth and Anthony Burton, *The Great Exhibitor: the Life and Work of Sir Henry Cole*, London: Victoria and Albert Museum, 2003.

Bosbach, Franz, and John R. Davis, *Die Weltausstellung von 1851 und ihre Folgen*, Prinz-Albert-Studien, 20, Munich: Saur, 2002.

Bouchier, Rev. Burton, *The Poor Man's Palace and the Poor Man's Day*, London: Shaw, 1854.

Brino, Giovanni, *Crystal Palace. Cronaca di un'avventura progettuale*, Genoa: Sagep, 1995.

Bristow, Maurice, *The Postal History of the Crystal Palace*, London: Postal History Group, 1983.

British Art, Art Journal Royal Jubilee Number, London: Virtue, June 1887.

Brock, Alan St. H., *A History of Fireworks*, London: Harrap, 1949.

Buckland, Sir Henry, *The Crystal Palace*, London: Crystal Palace Company, n.d., *c*. 1925.

Buckland, Rev. William, *Geology and Mineralogy considered with Reference to Natural Theology*, Bridgewater Treatise VI, London: Pickering, 1837.

Burne-Jones, G. (ed.), *Memorials of Edward Burne-Jones*, 2 vols, London: Macmillan, 1904.

Burton, Anthony, *Vision and Accident*, London: Victoria and Albert Museum, 1999.

Cavendish, Deborah, Duchess of Devonshire, *The House*, London: Macmillan, 1982.

Chadwick, George F., *The Works of Sir Joseph Paxton*, London: Architectural Press, 1961.

Cole, Henry, *Fifty Years of Public Work*, 2 vols, London: Bell, 1884.

—— ['Denarius'], *Shall we keep the Crystal Palace, and Have Riding and Walking in all Weathers among Flowers, Fountains and Sculptures?*, London: John Murray, 1851.

Colquhoun, Kate, *A Thing in Disguise: the Visionary Life of Joseph Paxton*, London: Fourth Estate, 2003.

Crane, Walter, *An Artist's Reminiscences*, London: Methuen, [1907].

Cruikshank, George, *The Glass and the New Crystal Palace*, London: Cassell, 1853.

The Crystal Palace District, Past and Present, London: Platt's Pennyworth, 1888.

Crystal Palace: Evidence given before the Court of Inquiry, February 24, 1875, London: Boot, 1875.

The Crystal Palace, Sydenham, to be sold by auction, London: Knight, Frank and Rutley, 1911.

The Crystal Palace, with 24 Illustrations (Nelson's Picture Guidebooks for Travellers), London: Nelson, n.d. (1862 *seq.*)

Crystal Palace Company: Deed of Settlement, Royal Charters, List of Shareholders, London: Bohn, 1856.

The Crystal Palace is on Fire, London: Crystal Palace Foundation, 1986.

Darby, Michael, 'Owen Jones and the Eastern Ideal', Ph.D. thesis, University of Reading, 1974.

——, *The Islamic Perspective*, Catalogue of an Exhibition held at Leighton House, London 1983.

Delamotte, Philip H., *Photographic Views of the Crystal Palace Sydenham, taken during the Progress of the Works*, 2 vols, London: Photographic Institution, 1854.

Desmond, Ray, *Kew*, London: Harvill, 1995.

Dickens, Charles, *The Letters of Charles Dickens*, ed. Graham Storey *et al.*, vols VI, VII, Oxford: Clarendon Press, 1988, 1993.

Dickinson's Comprehensive Pictures of the Great Exhibition from the Originals Painted for Prince Albert, London: Dickinson, 1854.

Downes, Charles, and Charles Cowper, *The Building Erected in Hyde Park for the Great Exhibition of the Works of Industry of all Nations, 1851… from the working drawings of the contractors, Messrs. Fox and Henderson and Co.*, London: Weale, 1851.

Doyle, Richard, *An Overland Journey to the Great Exhibition showing a few Extra Articles and Visitors*, London: Chapman and Hall, (1852).

Dresser, Christopher, *Art of Decorative Design*, London: Day, 1862.

——, *Principles of Decorative Design*, London: Cassell, 1873.

Durant, Stuart, *Christopher Dresser*, London: Academy, 1993.

Dyce, William, *The Drawing Book of the Government School of Design*. London: Chapman and Hall, 1842–3.

Eastlake, Elizabeth (Lady), *Letters and Journals* (ed. C.E. Smith), London: John Murray, 1895.

Elliott, Brent, *Victorian Gardens*, London: Batsford, 1986.

Eliot, George, *The George Eliot Letters* (ed. G.S. Haight), vols II, IV, V, Oxford University Press, 1954 *seq.*

Emile Zola, Photographer, in Norwood, 1898–9, London: Norwood Society, 1997.

The Exhibition of the Works of Industry of All Nations, *Reports by the Juries*, London: Spicer, 1852.

——, *Official Descriptive and Illustrated Catalogue*, 3 vols, London: Spicer, 1851.

Fergusson, James, *An Historical Enquiry into the True Principles of Beauty in Art, more especially with reference to Architecture*, London: Longman, 1849.

——, *The Palaces of Nineveh and Persepolis Restored*, London: John Murray, 1851.

——, *Illustrated Handbook of Architecture*, London: John Murray, 1855.

——, *History of Modern Styles of Architecture*, 2nd edn, London: John Murray, 1873.

Ferry, Kathryn, 'Printing the Alhambra: Owen Jones and Chromolithography', *Architectural History*, 46, 2003, pp. 175–88

ffoulkes, C.J., *Arms and the Tower*, London: John Murray, 1939.

Fuller, Francis, *Shall We Spend £100,000 on a Winter Garden for London: or in Endowing Schools of Design…?* London: Ollivier, 1851.

——, *A Letter to the Shareholders of the Crystal Palace Company*, London: Boot, [1874].

——, *Letter to the Court of Inquiry on the Restoration of Prosperity and Utility to the Crystal Palace*, London: Boot, [Feb. 1875].

——, *The Crystal Palace in Adversity*, London: Boot, 1876.

Gell, Sir William, *Pompeiana: the Topography, Edifices and Ornaments of Pompeii*, 2 vols, 2nd series. London: Jennings and Chaplin, 1832.

Gibbs, William, *The Misfortunes of the Crystal Palace and How to Retrieve them*, London: 1876.

Gibbs-Smith, C.H., *The Great Exhibition of 1851*, London: HMSO, 1951.

Guide to the Ten Chief Courts of the Sydenham Palace (from *The Athenaeum*), London: Routledge, 1854.

Graves, C. L., *The Life of Sir Charles Grove*, London: Macmillan, 1903.

[Grove, George], *The Crystal Palace and Park in 1853: What has been Done, What will be Done*. London: Crystal Palace Company, 1852.

Haden, Francis Seymour, *A Medical Man's Plea for a Winter Garden in the Crystal Palace*, London: Van Voorst, 1851.

Heine, A.G.E., *The Past, Present and Future of the Crystal Palace*, London, 1874.

Herrmann, Wolfgang, *Gottfried Semper: in search of Architecture*, Cambridge, MA. MIT Press, 1989.

Hitchcock, H.-R., *Modern Architecture in England*, New York: Museum of Modern Art, 1937.

Hobhouse, Christopher, *1851 and the Crystal Palace*, 2nd edn, London: John Murray, 1950

Hobhouse, Hermione, *The Crystal Palace and the Great Exhibition*, London: Athlone Press, 2002.

Hollingshead, John, *Official Illustrated Guide to the Crystal Palace and Park*, London: Burt, 1867.

Holman Hunt, W., *Pre-Raphaelitism and the Pre-Raphaelite Brotherhood*, 2 vols, London: Macmillan, 1905.

Husey, E.I., *The King's Day with the Children*, London: Simpkin Marshall, 1911.

The Industrial Directory of the Crystal Palace, London: Crystal Palace Library, Bradbury and Evans, 1854.

International Exhibition 1862, *Official Catalogue of the Fine Art Department*, London: Truscott, 1862.

Jameson, Anna, *Handbook to the Courts of Modern Sculpture*, London: Crystal Palace Library, Bradbury and Evans, 1854.

Jerrold, William Blanchard, *How to See the Exhibition: In Four Visits*, London: Bradbury and Evans, 1851.

Jones, Owen, *An Apology for the Colouring of the Greek Court in the Crystal Palace*, London: Crystal Palace Library, Bradbury and Evans, 1854.

——, *Designs for Mosaic and Tessellated Pavements*, London: Weale, 1842.

——, *Plans, Elevations, Sections and Details of the Alhambra*, 2 vols, London: the author, 1842–5.

——, *The Alhambra Court in the Crystal Palace Erected and Described by Owen Jones*, London: Crystal Palace Library, Bradbury and Evans, 1854.

——, *Lectures on Architecture and the Decorative Arts*, London: for private circulation, 1863

—— and Joseph Bonomi, *Description of The Egyptian Court Erected in the Crystal Palace*, London: Crystal Palace Library, Bradbury and Evans, 1854.

——, *Grammar of Ornament*, [1856] 2nd. edn., London: Day, 1865.

Latham, R.G., and E. Forbes, *The Natural History Department in the Crystal Palace Described*, London: Crystal Palace Library, Bradbury and Evans, 1854.

Layard, A. Henry, *The Assyrian Court in the Crystal Palace Erected by James Fergusson*, London: Crystal Palace Library, Bradbury and Evans, 1854.

——, *Autobiography and Letters*, ed. W.N. Bruce, 2 vols, London: John Murray, 1903.

——, *Nineveh and its Remains*, London: John Murray, 1848.

——, *The Monuments of Nineveh*, 2 vols, London: John Murray, 1853.

Lees-Milne, James, *The Bachelor Duke*, London: John Murray, 1991.

Lectures on the Results of the Great Exhibition of 1851, delivered before the Society of Arts, Manufactures and Commerce, 2 vols, London: Bogue, 1852–3.

Lindley, John, *The Symmetry of Vegetation*, London: Chapman and Hall, 1854.

London: What to See and How to See it, London: Clarke, 1855.

Lytton, Bulwer, *Last Days of Pompeii*, 2 vols, London: Bentley.

MacCarthy, Fiona, *William Morris: a Life for our Time*, London: Faber, 1994.

Macqueen-Pope, W., *Twenty Shillings in the Pound*, London: Hutchinson, 1948.

Mallgrave, Harry Francis, *Gottfried Semper: Architect of the Nineteenth Century*, New Haven and London: Yale University Press, 1989.

Markham, Violet, *Paxton and the Bachelor Duke*, London: Hodder and Stoughton, 1935.

Marlborough House, *Catalogues of Museum of Ornamental Art*, London: HMSO, 1852–3.

Marsh, Catherine M.], *English Hearts and English Hands, or the Railway and the Trenches*, London: 1858.

Martin, Sir Theodore, *Life of H.R.H. the Prince Consort*, London: Smith, Elder, 1880.

Maskell, William, *The Industrial Arts*, London: Chapman and Hall, 1876.

Mast, George Christian, *Pax Firma: or a proposal of a scheme to render the Crystal Palace, at Sydenham, the most effective instrument of progress, civilization, and a firm peace between all the Nations of the Earth*, London, 1856

Measom, George, *Official Illustrated Guide to the Brighton and South Coast Railways, including a Descriptive Guide to the Crystal Palace at Sydenham*, London: Collins, n.d. [1854].

Millais, J.G., ed., *Life and Letters of Sir J.E. Millais*, 2 vols, London: Methuen, 1899.

Miller, Robert, *Four Victorians and a Museum: an Unofficial Account*, London, 1999.

Milner, H., *Art and Practice of Landscape Gardening*, London: the author, 1890.

Muddock, J. E. Preston, *The Romance and History of the Crystal Palace*, London: Upcott Gill, 1911.

Musgrave, Michael, *The Musical Life of the Crystal Palace*, Cambridge University Press, 1995.

——, *George Grove: Music and Victorian Culture*, London: Palgrave, 2003.

Owen, Richard, *The Extinct Animals and the Geological Illustrations Described*, London: Crystal Palace Library, Bradbury and Evans, 1854.

Palgrave, Francis Turner, *Essays on Art*, London: Macmillan, 1866.

——, *International Exhibition, 1862, Fine Art Department*, London:Truscott and Simmons, pp. 76–81.

The Panmure Papers, ed. Sir George Douglas, Bt, and Sir George Dalhousie Ramsay, 2 vols, London: Hodder and Stoughton, 1908.

Paxton, Joseph, *What is to Become of the Crystal Palace?* London: Bradbury and Evans, 1851.

Pevsner, Nikolaus, *Matthew Digby Wyatt*, Cambridge University Press, 1950.

Phillips, Samuel, *Guide to the Crystal Palace and its Park, Sydenham*, London: Crystal Palace Library, Bradbury and Evans, [1854] 2nd edn revised by F.K.J. Shenton, 1857.

——, *The Portrait Gallery of the Crystal Palace*, Crystal Palace Library, London: Bradbury and Evans, 1854.

Poole, Reginald Stuart, William Morris *et al.*, *Lectures on Art*, London Macmillan, 1882.

The Preservation of the Crystal Palace: a Meeting held on 29 March, 1852, London: James Ridgway, 1852.

Pugin, Augustus Welby, *Floriated Ornament*, London: Bohn, 1849.

Purbrick, Louise, ed., *The Great Exhibition of 1851*, Manchester University Press, 2001.

Read, Benedict, *Victorian Sculpture*, London and New Haven, Yale University Press, 1982.

Redgrave, Richard, *Elementary Manual of Colour*, London: Chapman and Hall, 1853.

——, *Manual of Design*, London: Chapman and Hall, 1876.

Reeves, Graham, *Palace of the People*, London: Bromley Library, 1986.

Redgrave, Richard, RA, Memoir, ed. F.M. Redgrave, London: Cassell, 1891.

Richards, J. M., *An Introduction to Modern Architecture*, London: Penguin, 1940.

Rossetti, William Michael, 'The Epochs of Art as Represented in the Crystal Palace' (from *The Spectator*, 1854) in *Fine Art, Chiefly Contemporary: Notices Re-printed with Revisions*, London: Macmillan, 1867.

Routledge's Guide to the Crystal Palace and Park at Sydenham, London: Routledge, 1854.

Ruskin, John, *The Works of John Ruskin*, ed. E.T. Cook and Alexander Wedderburn, 39 vols, London: Geo. Allen, 1903–12.

Saxe Wyndham, Henry, *August Manns and the Saturday Concerts*, London: Walter Scott, 1909.

Scharf, George, Jun., *The Greek Court Erected in the Crystal Palace, by Owen Jones*, London: Crystal Palace Library, Bradbury and Evans, 1854.

——, *The Pompeian Court in the Crystal Palace*, London: Crystal Palace Library, Bradbury and Evans, 1854.

——, *The Roman Court Erected in the Crystal Palace by Owen Jones*, London: Crystal Palace Library, Bradbury and Evans, 1854.

Scott, William Bell, *The British School of Sculpture*, London, 1872.

Semper, Gottfried, *The Four Elements of Architecture and other Writings*, Cambridge University Press, 1989.

Sims Reeves, his Life and Recollections, 2 vols, London: Simpkin Marshall, 1888.

Small, John, *Caution!! To the Brighton Shareholders and the Public at large against the Crystal Palace Removal to Sydenham*, London, 1852.

Sotheby, Samuel Leigh, *A Few Words by way of a Letter Addressed to the Directors of the Crystal Palace Company*, London: John Russell Smith, 1855.

——, *A Few Words by way of a Letter addressed to the Shareholders of the Crystal Palace Company*, London: John Russell Smith, 1855.

——, *Suggestion to Remedy Deficit*, London: John Russell Smith, 1856.

Steegman, John, *Consort of Taste, 1830–70*, Sidgwick and Jackson, 1950.

Survey of London: XXXVIII: *Museums Area of South Kensington*, London: GLC/ Athlone Press, 1975.

Tallis, John, *Tallis's History and Description of the Crystal Palace, and the Exhibition of the World's Industry in 1851*, 3 vols, London: Tallis, 1852.

Tennyson, Hallam (Lord), ed., *Alfred, Lord Tennyson: a Memoir*, 2 vols. London: Macmillan, 1897.

'The Shorthand Writer' [T.S.W.], *The Crystal Palace in Adversity*, London: 1876.

Vaughan, Charles John, *A Few Words on the Crystal Palace Question*, London: John Murray, 1854.

Walton, H.M., *To the Shareholders of the Crystal Palace Company, Facts and Figures*, London: 1868.

Waring, J.B., *A Record of my Artistic Life*, London: 1873.

Warwick, Alan R., *Phoenix Suburb: a South London Social History*, London: Blue Boar [1972], 2nd. edn, 1982.

Watkin, David, *Life and Work of C. R. Cockerell*, London: Zwemmer, 1974.

——, *A History of Western Architecture*, London: Barrie and Jenkins, 1986.

Wilkinson, Sir John Gardner, *On Colour, and on the Necessity for a General Diffusion of Taste among all Classes*, London: John Murray, 1858.

——, *The Egyptians*, London: Crystal Palace Company, Bradbury and Evans, 1857.

Wornum, Ralph Nicolson, 'The Exhibition as a Lesson in Taste' in *The Art Journal Illustrated Catalogue*, London: Virtue, 1851.

Wyatt, Matthew Digby, *Specimens of the Geometrical Mosaic of the Middle Ages*, London: Day, 1848.

——, *Views of the Crystal Palace and Park, Sydenham*, London: Day, 1854.

—— and J.B Waring, *The Byzantine and Romanesque Court in the Crystal Palace*, London: Crystal Palace Library, Bradbury and Evans, 1854.

—— and J.B. Waring, *The Italian Court in the Crystal Palace*, London: Crystal Palace Library, Bradbury and Evans, 1854.

——, and J.B. Waring, *The Mediæval Court in the Crystal Palace*, London: Crystal Palace Library, Bradbury and Evans, 1854.

—— and J.B. Waring, *The Renaissance Court in the Crystal Palace*, London: Crystal Palace Library, Bradbury and Evans, 1854.

——, *On the Influence Exercised on Ceramic Manufactures by the late Mr. Herbert Minton*, Society of Arts, London: for private distribution, 1858.

——, *Fine Art*, London: Macmillan, 1870.

Wyatt, Memoirs of Thomas Henry, and Sir Matthew Digby Wyatt, Architects, reprinted from *The Builder*, London: 1888.

INDEX

For buildings, see under city. The main Courts at Sydenham are grouped under 'Fine Arts Courts' and 'Industrial Courts'.

Abbate, Giuseppe, 67, 94, 98, 100
Aboo-Simbel, colossal figures, 68, 80, 86–7, 98, 123, 126, 172
accidents, 45
admission charges, 57–8
Aeronautical Exhibition, 186
aeronautics, 186–7
Africa Exhibition, 175
Albani, Mme, 200
Albert, Prince, 1–4, 10–11, 13–14, 28–9, 33–35, 50, 52–3, 60, 64, 99, 129, 160, 170, 202
'Albertopolis', 4, 34
alcohol, 35, 37, 57–9
Alhambra, the (Granada) 67, 78, 83, 90–1
'All-Red Route', 175
Alma-Tadema, Lawrence, 102
Anderson, Arthur, 64, 103, 134
Anglo-German Exhibition, 178
Ansted, Prof. David Thomas, 164
Aquarium, 128
archery, 144, 186, 203
Architectural Courts, *see* Fine Arts Courts
architectural models, 94
Architectural Society, 80
Arnold, Matthew, 61
'art-manufactures', 2, 103
artesian well, 43, 149
Arundel Society prints, 107
Assyria, 109–10

Baird, John Logie, 157; studios, 210
balloon ascents, 147, 186–7
bands: brass, 199; Crystal Palace, 179, 183, 195, 198–9
bankruptcy, 173
Barrett, Oscar, 196
Barry, Sir Charles, 5–6, 8, 12, 14, 17, 40, 42, 61, 129, 142
Barry, Edward Middleton, 8–9, 147
Barry, Sir Gerald, 203, 212
Barry, John Wolfe, 45
Bartlett, A.D., 127–8
Baxter, George, 98
Bayst, William A., 176
Beale, Thomas Willert, 183, 198
Beaton, Donald, 123, 125, 139, 142, 144, 153

Bell, Jacob, 26, 46
Bell, John, 50, 116, 119–21
Belshaw, Mr, 29, 128
Belzoni, Giovanni, 86–7, 105
Bernhardt, Sarah, 196
Betjeman, John, 10, 133
bicycle polo, 203
birds: 48, 126, 168, 181, 183
Blashfield, John M.; 91, 99, 106
Blondin, 168, 170, 188–91, 199
Boase, T.S.R., 28
Bonomi, Joseph, 56, 74, 76, 80, 84–5, 87, 115, 119, 136
botany (1851), 11; (1854) 32, 35, 48, 50, 95, 123–5
Boutell, Rev. Charles, 68, 76, 91, 102, 104
British Museum, 33, 56, 61, 87, 92, 109, 121, 126–7, 158, 161
Britton, John, 81, 163
Brock, Charles Thomas, 170, 192
Bromley, London Borough of, 212
Browning, E.B., 27
Brunel, Isambard Kingdom, 5–6, 8, 35, 62, 134, 148, 152, 156, 199
Buckland, Sir Henry, 65, 121, 166, 180–2, 190, 202, 206–7, 210
Buckland, William, 161, 164
Burdett-Coutts, Angela, 28, 126
Burne-Jones, Edward, 166
Burton, Charles, 32

Cambridge, Addenbrooks Hospital, 97
Campbell, Mrs Patrick, 196
casts, plaster: 24, 41, 46, 57, 67, 76–7, 92–4, 103–5, 113, 117–8, 179, 181; Fontevrault effigies, 103, 121
catering, 59–60
Chance, Messrs, 43
Chatsworth, 6–9, 11, 31–2, 43, 101, 114–15, 123, 138, 142, 144–5, 148
Cheek, Joseph, 118
Chinese Court, 77
chromolithography, 15–17, 74, 76, 80–81, 83–4, 91, 95, 98, 103, 109–10, 131, 133
Churchill, Sir Winston, 211
'Cleopatra's needle', 48
Cobden, Richard, 28
Cockerell, Charles Robert, 5, 7, 93, 98, 129
Cole, Sir Henry, 3, 22, 33–5, 53, 61, 64, 101, 114, 129
Collmann, Leonard William, 111

colonial exhibitions, 175
colour 17, 22–3, 50–52, 68, 75–6, 79, 81, 83, 86–7, 90–94, 98–9, 100, 103–4, 110–12; 131, 143; *see also* polychromy
commerce, 56–7, 76, 100; *see also* Industrial Courts
Commissioners, Great Exhibition, 5, 15
'conventionalising', 20–1, 81, 98
Corbusier, Le, 10
Costa, Sir Michael, 197, 199, 200, 202
Coward, Noël, 197
Cowper, William, 75
Coxwell, H.T., and J. Glaisher, 187
Crace, J.G., 15, 17, 61, 129
Crane, Walter, 176, 195
cricket, 203
Crimean War, 47–8, 61, 123, 148, 170
Cruikshank, George, 4, 41, 59
Crystal Palace (1854): construction, 39–84; costs, 46–7; decorative scheme, 50–1, 182–3; trustees, 182
Crystal Palace Company, 2, 11, 31, 34, 36–7, 53, 59–60, 62–5, 114, 132, 148, 173
Crystal Palace Museum, 212
Crystal Palace Press, 68
Crystal Palace School of Art, Music, Science and Literature, 56, 211
Crystal Palace School of Practical Engineering, 157, 164
Crystal Palaces: Dublin, 9, 116; New York, 9, 31, 126; continental, 9
Cubitt, William, 5, 33, 35

Dare, Leona, 188
Darwin, Charles, 123
Davidson, John, 187–8
Day and Co., 133, 136
Day, Lewis, 76
De Lesseps, Ferdinand, 192
Delamotte, Philip Henry, 39, 46–7, 85, 87, 104–5, 125, 128, 134–6, 158, 200
Derby, Lord, 59
Desachy, M., 41, 87, 106
design: 20–1, 23, 29, 31, 34, 74, 86, 106; *see also* conventionalising, ornament
Devonshire, 6th Duke of, 8–9, 26, 34, 37–9, 103, 114, 118–9, 123, 125, 139
Dickens, Charles, 53, 68, 126, 168
dog shows, 183
Donaldson, Thomas, 5, 98

Doulton, Sir Henry; ceramics, 24
Doyle, Richard, 22, 27
drama, 195–7
Dresser, Christopher, 21, 32, 74, 92, 95, 100; *Art of Decorative Design*, 95
Dyce, William, 95

Eastlake, Sir Charles, 61, 94
Eastlake, Lady (Elizabeth Rigby), 3, 78, 86–7, 93, 105–7, 112, 198
Edward VII, *see* Wales, Prince of
'education of the eye', 29; *see also* Pestalozzi
Egyptian Hall, Piccadilly, 11, 24
Egyptian tomb, proposed 'reproduction', 77
Electrical Exhibition, 173
elephant ballet, 184
Elgin Marbles, 79, 93
Eliot, George, 90, 94, 166, 200
Elkington, Messrs, 99
ethnographic models, 11–12, 59–60, 79, 117, 125, 126–8
Everitt, T.H. and Son, 136
Extinct Animals (Antediluvian Animals), 5, 50, 52, 57, 68, 79, 138, 158–164, 166
Eyles, George, 60, 123

Fairbanks, Douglas, Sr, 192
Faraday, Michael, 94
Farquhar, T.N., 35, 62, 189
Fenton, Roger, 61
Fergusson, James, 6–7, 10, 42, 48, 52, 61, 64, 77–8, 86, 98, 103, 109–12, 119, 200
Festival of Britain (1951), 180, 211
Festival of Empire (1911), 112, 174–8
ffoulkes, Charles, 182–3
Field, George, 13, 81, 95, 142–3
Fine Arts Courts: (1851) 12–13, 48, 76; (1854) 13, 23, 46–8, 56–7, 65, chs. 3 and 4 *passim*, 76, 179–81, 209; Alhambra, 15, 48, 60–1, 68, 77, 79, 81, 87–92, 95, 98, 123, 166, 172, 182, 209; Assyrian (Nineveh) 50, 52, 58, 64, 67, 75–7, 95, 109–12, 123, 172; Byzantine, 48, 98, 102–4, 125; Egyptian, 58, 74–7, 80, 101, 174; Elizabethan, 98; Greek, 52, 56, 92–5, 101, 184; Italian 78, 98; Medieval, 48, 98, 104–5; Pompeian, 48, 56, 58, 60–1, 67, 75–7, 79, 83, 85, 97–102, 166, 180, 209; Renaissance, 78–9,